PENGUIN 🐧 CLASSICS

THE KORAN

ADVISORY EDITOR: BETTY RADICE

Born in Baghdad, N. J. Dawood came to England as an Iraq State Scholar in 1945 and graduated from London University. He is a director of Contemporary Translations Ltd. In 1959 he founded The Arabic Advertising & Publishing Co. Ltd, London, which is now one of the major producers of Arabic typesetting outside the Middle East. His translation of *Tales from the Thousand and One Nights* was first published as Penguin No. 1001 in 1954 and has since been printed in fourteen various editions. He has retold for children a comprehensive selection of tales from *The Arabian Nights* (first published, with illustrations, in 1978). He has edited and abridged *The Muqaddimah of Ibn Khaldoun* (Princeton University Press), translated numerous technical works into Arabic, written and spoken radio and film commentaries, and contributed to specialized English–Arabic dictionaries. An illustrated hardback edition of *The Koran* (Allen Lane) was first published in 1978.

THE
KORAN

*

TRANSLATED WITH NOTES BY
N. J. DAWOOD

PENGUIN BOOKS

Penguin Books Ltd, Harmondsworth, Middlesex, England
Viking Penguin Inc., 40 West 23rd Street, New York, New York 10010, U.S.A.
Penguin Books Australia Ltd, Ringwood, Victoria, Australia
Penguin Books Canada Limited, 2801 John Street, Markham, Ontario, Canada L3R 1B4
Penguin Books (N.Z.) Ltd, 182–190 Wairau Road, Auckland 10, New Zealand

—

This translation first published 1956
First revised edition 1959
Reprinted 1961, 1964
Second revised edition 1966
Reprinted 1967
Third revised edition 1968
Reprinted 1970, 1971, 1972, 1973
Fourth revised edition 1974
Reprinted 1974, 1975, 1976, 1977 (twice), 1978, 1979 (twice),
1980, 1981 (twice), 1983 (twice), 1985 (twice), 1986

—

—

Made and printed in Great Britain
by Richard Clay (The Chaucer Press) Ltd,
Bungay, Suffolk
Set in Monotype Garamond

CONTENTS

CONTENTS

6

CONTENTS

CONTENTS

An index of the chapters (suras) with their Arabic titles and in their traditional sequence appears at the end of the book, on page 445.

INTRODUCTION

THE Koran[1] is the earliest and by far the finest work of Classical
Arabic prose. For Muslims it is the infallible word of God, a
transcript of a tablet preserved in heaven, revealed to the Prophet
Mohammed by the Angel Gabriel. Except in the opening verses
and some few passages in which the Prophet or the Angel speaks
in the first person, the speaker throughout is God.[2]

The posthumous son of Abdullah bin Abdul-Muttalib, of the
tribe of Quraysh, Mohammed was born in Mecca about the year
A.D. 570. His mother Aminah died when he was still a child, and
he was brought up by his grandfather and then by his uncle Abu
Talib. As a youth he travelled with the trading caravans from
Mecca to Syria, and at the age of twenty-five married Khadija,
daughter of Khuwailid, a rich widow fifteen years his senior.
Meanwhile he had acquired a reputation for honesty and wisdom,
and had come under the influence of Jewish and Christian teach-
ings.

Long before Mohammed's call, Arabian paganism was showing signs of decay. At the Ka'ba the Meccans worshipped not
only Allah, the supreme Semitic God, but also a number of
female deities whom they regarded as the daughters of Allah.
Among these were Al-Lat, Al-Uzzah, and Al-Manat, who repre-
sented the Sun, Venus, and Fortune respectively. Impressed by
Jewish and Christian monotheism, a number of men known as
hanifs had already rejected idolatry for an ascetic religion of their
own. Mohammed appears to have been influenced by them. It
was his habit to retire to a cave in the mountains in order to give
himself up to solitary prayer and meditation. According to
Muslim tradition, one night in Ramadhan about the year 610, as
he was asleep or in a trance, the Angel Gabriel came to him and
said· 'Recite!' He replied: 'What shall I recite?' The order was
repeated three times, until the angel himself said:

'Recite in the name of your Lord who created, created man
from clots of blood.

1. The Arabic name means *The Recital*.
2. God speaks in the first person plural, which often changes to the
first person singular or the third person singular in the course of the
same sentence.

9

'Recite! Your Lord is the Most Bountiful One, who by the pen taught man what he did not know.'

When he awoke, these words, we are told, seemed to be 'inscribed upon his heart'.

Mohammed, who disclaimed power to perform miracles, firmly believed that he was the messenger of God, sent forth to confirm previous scriptures. God had revealed His will to the Jews and the Christians through chosen apostles, but they disobeyed God's commandments and divided themselves into schismatic sects. The Koran accuses the Jews of corrupting the Scriptures and the Christians of worshipping Jesus as the son of God, although He had expressly commanded them to worship none but Him. Having thus gone astray, they must be brought back to the right path, to the true religion preached by Abraham. This was Islam – absolute submission or resignation to the will of Allah.

The Koran preaches the oneness of God and emphasizes divine mercy and forgiveness. God is almighty and all-knowing, and though compassionate towards His creatures He is stern in retribution. He enjoins justice and fair dealing, kindness to orphans and widows, and charity to the poor. The most important duties of the Muslim are faith in Allah and His apostle, prayer, almsgiving, fasting, and (if possible) pilgrimage to the Sacred House at Mecca, built by Abraham for the worship of the One God.

The Koranic revelations followed each other at brief intervals and were at first committed to memory by professional remembrancers. During Mohammed's life-time verses were written on palm-leaves, stones, and any material that came to hand. Their collection was completed during the caliphate of Omar, the second Caliph, and an authorized version was established during the caliphate of Othman, his successor (644–56). To this day this version remains as the authoritative word of God. But, owing to the fact that the kufic script in which the Koran was originally written contained no indication of vowels or diacritical points, variant readings are recognized by Muslims as of equal authority.

It is unfortunate that in preparing the contents of the Koran for book-form its editor or editors followed no chronological sequence. Its chapters were arranged generally in order of length, the longest coming first and the shortest last. Attempts have been made by Noldeke, Grimme, Rodwell, and Bell to arrange the chapters in chronological order, but scholars are agreed that a strictly chronological arrangement is impossible without dissecting some of the chapters into scattered verses, owing to the inclusion of revelations spoken in Medina in chapters begun several years earlier in Mecca.

In preparing this new translation it has been my aim to present the modern reader with an intelligible version of the Koran in contemporary English. It is my belief that the Koran is not only one of the greatest books of prophetic literature but also a literary masterpiece of surpassing excellence. In adhering to a rigidly literal rendering of Arabic idioms, previous translations have, in my opinion, practically failed to convey both the meaning and the rhetorical grandeur of the original. It ought to be borne in mind that the Koran contains many statements which, if not recognized as altogether obscure, lend themselves to more than one interpretation. I have taken great pains to reproduce these ambiguities wherever they occur, and have provided explanatory footnotes in order to avoid turning the text into an interpretation rather than a translation. Throughout this rendering the standard commentaries of Az-Zamakhshari, Al-Beidhawi, and Al-Jalalein have been closely followed.

I have already described the mechanical plan according to which the chapters of the Koran were arranged after the Prophet's death. In this edition the traditional arrangement has been abandoned. The present sequence, while not following a strictly chronological order, begins with the more Biblical and poetic revelations and ends with the much longer, and often more topical, chapters. In short, the new arrangement is primarily intended for the uninitiated reader who, understandably, is often put off by such mundane chapters as 'The Cow' or 'The Table', which are traditionally placed at the beginning of the book. For purposes of reference the traditional number of each chapter will be found in the list of contents at the beginning of the book. The spelling of all Arabic words has been simplified.

Here a word should also be said about the cryptic Arabic letters which head certain chapters of the Koran. Various theories have been put forward by Muslim and Western scholars to explain their meaning, but none of them is satisfactory. The fact is that no one knows what they stand for. Traditional commentators dismiss them by saying· 'Allah alone knows what He means by these letters.'

Finally I should point out that in the foregoing paragraphs I have endeavoured to confine myself to a bare outline of the facts regarding the genesis of the Koran and its subsequent preservation, without touching on such controversial issues as the nature of Mohammed's prophethood or his theological sources. It is the work itself that matters; and the intelligent reader, if allowed to approach it with a free and unprejudiced mind, should be able to form his own opinions.

London, July 1968   N. J. D.

NOTE ON THE FOURTH REVISED EDITION

In this twelfth reprint, which is also the fourth revised edition, the major change I have made is to insert chapter and verse numbers at the head, middle, and foot of each page for easier reference to the Arabic.

London, 1973   N.J.D.

CHRONOLOGICAL TABLE OF THE
MAIN EVENTS IN THE LIFE
OF MOHAMMED

c. 570   Birth of Mohammed (his father having died a few months earlier)

576   Death of his mother Aminah

595   Marriage to Khadija

c. 610   Beginning of Call

615   Flight of his followers to Ethiopia

619   Death of Khadija

620   Mohammed's reputed 'Night Journey' from Mecca to Jerusalem, and thence to the Seventh Heaven

622   The *Hijra* (Flight or Migration) of Mohammed and his followers to Medina, and beginning of the Muslim Era

624   Battle of Badr: the Quraysh defeated by the Muslims

625   Battle of Uhud: the Muslims defeated

626   The Jewish tribe of al-Nadhir crushed and expelled

627   'The War of the Ditch' – the Meccans' expedition against the Muslims in Medina. Attackers driven off

627   The Jewish tribe of Qurayza raided by Mohammed; some 800 men beheaded (only one Jew

13

	abjuring his religion to save his life) and all the women and children sold as slaves
628	The Treaty of Hudaybiyya: truce with the Quraysh, who recognize Mohammed's right to proselytize without hindrance
629	The Jews of Khaybar put to the sword
629	Mohammed sends letters and messengers to the Kings of Persia, Yemen, and Ethiopia and the Emperor Heraclius, inviting them to accept Islam
630	Truce broken by the Quraysh. Mecca taken by Mohammed – the entire population converted, and the Ka'ba established as the religious centre of Islam
631	'The Year of Embassies' – Islam accepted by the Arabian tribes
632	Mohammed's Farewell Pilgrimage to Mecca
632, 8 June	Death of Mohammed, three months after his return to Medina

THE EXORDIUM

IN THE NAME OF ALLAH
THE COMPASSIONATE
THE MERCIFUL

Praise be to Allah, Lord of the Creation,
The Compassionate, the Merciful,
King of Judgement-day!
You alone we worship, and to You alone
we pray for help.
Guide us to the straight path
The path of those whom You have favoured,
Not of those who have incurred Your wrath,
Nor of those who have gone astray.

*

THE EARTHQUAKE

99:1 WHEN Earth is rocked in her last convulsion; when Earth shakes off her burdens and man asks 'What may this mean?' – on that day she will proclaim her tidings, for your Lord will have inspired her.

On that day mankind will come in broken bands to be shown their labours. Whoever has done an atom's weight **99:8** of good shall see it, and whoever has done an atom's weight of evil shall see it also.

THE CATACLYSM

In the Name of Allah, the Compassionate, the Merciful

82:1 WHEN the sky is rent asunder; when the stars scatter and the oceans roll together; when the graves are hurled about; each soul shall know what it has done and what it has failed to do.

O man! What evil has enticed you from your gracious Lord who created you, gave you an upright form, and well-proportioned you? In whatever shape He could have surely moulded you according to His will.

Yes, you deny the Last Judgement. Yet there are guardians watching over you, noble recorders who know of all your actions.

The righteous shall surely dwell in bliss. But the wicked shall burn in Hell-fire upon the Judgement-day: they shall not escape.

Would that you knew what the Day of Judgement is! Oh, **82:19** would that you knew what the Day of Judgement is! It is the day when every soul will stand alone and Allah will reign supreme.

THE CESSATION

In the Name of Allah, the Compassionate, the Merciful

WHEN the sun ceases to shine; when the stars fall 81:1 down and the mountains are blown away; when camels big with young are left untended and the wild beasts are brought together; when the seas are set alight and men's souls are reunited; when the infant girl,[1] buried alive, is asked for what crime she was slain; when the records of men's deeds are laid open and the heaven is stripped bare; when Hell burns fiercely and Paradise is brought near: then each soul shall know what it has done.

I swear by the turning planets and by the stars that rise and set; by the fall of night and the first breath of morning: this is the word of a gracious and mighty messenger, held in honour by the Lord of the Throne, obeyed in heaven, faithful to his trust.

No, your compatriot[2] is not mad. He saw him[3] on the clear horizon. He does not grudge the secrets of the unseen; nor is this the utterance of an accursed devil.

Whither then are you going?

This is an admonition to all men: to those among you that have the will to be upright. Yet you cannot will, except 81:29 by the will of Allah, Lord of the Creation.

MAN

In the Name of Allah, the Compassionate, the Merciful

DOES there not pass over a man a space of time when 76:1 his life is a blank?[4] We have created man from the union of the two sexes so that We may put him to the proof. We have endowed him with sight and hearing and, be he thankful or 76:2

---

1. An allusion to the pre-Islamic custom of burying unwanted newborn girls.
  2. Mohammed.   3. Gabriel.   4. In the womb.

76:3 oblivious of Our favours, We have shown him the right path.

For the unbelievers We have prepared fetters and chains, and a blazing Fire. But the righteous shall drink of a cup tempered at the Camphor Fountain, a gushing spring at which the servants of Allah will refresh themselves: they who keep their vows and dread the far-spread terrors of Judgement-day; who, though they hold it dear, give sustenance to the poor man, the orphan, and the captive, saying: 'We feed you for Allah's sake only; we seek of you neither recompense nor thanks: for we fear from Him a day of anguish and of woe.'

Allah will deliver them from the evil of that day and make their faces shine with joy. He will reward them for their steadfastness with robes of silk and the delights of Paradise. Reclining there upon soft couches, they shall feel neither the scorching heat nor the biting cold. Trees will spread their shade around them, and fruits will hang in clusters over them.

76:15 They shall be served with silver dishes, and beakers as large as goblets; silver goblets which they themselves shall measure: and cups brim-full with ginger-flavoured water from the Fount of Selsabil. They shall be attended by boys graced with eternal youth, who to the beholder's eyes will seem like sprinkled pearls. When you gaze upon that scene you will behold a kingdom blissful and glorious.

They shall be arrayed in garments of fine green silk and rich brocade, and adorned with bracelets of silver. Their Lord will give them pure beverage to drink.

Thus you shall be rewarded; your high endeavours are gratifying to Allah.

We have made known to you the Koran by gradual revelation; therefore await with patience the judgement of your Lord and do not yield to the wicked and the unbelieving. Remember the name of your Lord morning and evening; in the night-time worship Him: praise Him all night long.

The unbelievers love this fleeting life too well, and thus *76:28* prepare for themselves a heavy day of doom. *We* created them, and endowed their limbs and joints with strength; but if We please We can replace them by other men.

This is indeed an admonition. Let him that will, take the *76:29* right path to his Lord. Yet you cannot will, except by the will of Allah. Allah is wise and all-knowing.

He is merciful to whom He will: but for the wrongdoers *76:31* He has prepared a grievous punishment.

THE MERCIFUL[1]

In the Name of Allah, the Compassionate, the Merciful

IT is the Merciful who has taught the Koran. *55:1*
He created man and taught him articulate speech. The sun and the moon pursue their ordered course. The plants and the trees bow down in adoration.

He raised the heaven on high and set the balance of all things, that you might not transgress it. Give just weight and full measure.

He laid the earth for His creatures, with all its fruits and blossom-bearing palm, chaff-covered grain and scented herbs. Which of your Lord's blessings would you[2] deny?

He created man from potter's clay and the jinn from smokeless fire. Which of your Lord's blessings would you deny?

The Lord of the two easts[3] is He, and the Lord of the two *55:17* wests. Which of your Lord's blessings would you deny?

He has let loose the two oceans:[4] they meet one another. Yet between them stands a barrier which they cannot overrun. Which of your Lord's blessings would you deny?

Pearls and corals come from both. Which of your Lord's blessings would you deny?

His are the ships that sail like banners[5] upon the ocean. Which of your Lord's blessings would you deny? *55:25*

1. Compare this chapter with Psalm 136 of the Old Testament.
2. The pronoun is in the dual number, the words being addressed to mankind and the jinn. This refrain is repeated no less than 31 times.
3. The points at which the sun rises in summer and winter.
4. Salt water and fresh water.   5. Or *mountains.*

55:26   All who live on earth are doomed to die. But the face of your Lord will abide for ever, in all its majesty and glory. Which of your Lord's blessings would you deny?

All who dwell in heaven and earth beseech Him. Each day some new task employs Him. Which of your Lord's blessings would you deny?

Mankind and jinn, We shall surely find the time to judge you! Which of your Lord's blessings would you deny?

Mankind and jinn, if you have power to penetrate the confines of heaven and earth, then penetrate them! But this you shall not do except with Our own authority. Which of your Lord's blessings would you deny?

Flames of fire shall be lashed at you, and molten brass. There shall be none to help you. Which of your Lord's blessings would you deny?

When the sky splits asunder and reddens like a rose or stainéd leather (which of your Lord's blessings would you deny?), on that day neither man nor jinnee shall be asked about his sins. Which of your Lord's blessings would you deny?

55:41   The wrongdoers shall be known by their looks; they shall be seized by their forelocks and their feet. Which of your Lord's blessings would you deny?

That is the Hell which the sinners deny. They shall wander between fire and water fiercely seething. Which of your Lord's blessings would you deny?

But for those that fear the majesty of their Lord there are two gardens (which of your Lord's blessings would you deny?) planted with shady trees. Which of your Lord's blessings would you deny?

Each is watered by a flowing spring. Which of your Lord's blessings would you deny?

Each bears every kind of fruit in pairs. Which of your Lord's blessings would you deny?

They shall recline on couches lined with thick brocade, and within their reach will hang the fruits of both gardens. Which of your Lord's blessings would you deny?

55:56   They shall dwell with bashful virgins whom neither man

nor jinnee will have touched before. Which of your Lord's *55:57*
blessings would you deny?

Virgins as fair as corals and rubies. Which of your Lord's
blessings would you deny?

Shall the reward of goodness be anything but good?
Which of your Lord's blessings would you deny?

And beside these there shall be two other gardens
(which of your Lord's blessings would you deny?) of darkest green. Which of your Lord's blessings would you deny?

A gushing fountain shall flow in each. Which of your
Lord's blessings would you deny?

Each planted with fruit-trees, the palm and the pome-
granate. Which of your Lord's blessings would you deny?

In each there shall be virgins chaste and fair. Which of
your Lord's blessings would you deny?

Dark-eyed virgins sheltered in their tents (which of your
Lord's blessings would you deny?) whom neither man nor
jinnee will have touched before. Which of your Lord's
blessings would you deny?

They shall recline on green cushions and rich carpets.
Which of your Lord's blessings would you deny?

Blessed be the name of your Lord, the Lord of majesty *55:78*
and glory!

NOAH

In the Name of Allah, the Compassionate, the Merciful

WE sent forth Noah to his people, saying: 'Give *71:1*
warning to your people before a woeful scourge
overtakes them.'

He said: 'My people, I come to warn you plainly. Serve
Allah and fear Him, and obey me. He will forgive you
your sins and respite you till an appointed time. When
Allah's time arrives, none shall put it back. Would that you
understood this!'

'Lord,' said Noah, 'day and night I have pleaded with my
people, but my pleas have only added to their aversion.
Each time I call on them to seek Your pardon, they thrust *71:7*

their fingers in their ears and draw their cloaks over their heads, persisting in sin and bearing themselves with in-71:8 solent pride. I called out loud to them, and appealed to them in public and in private. "Seek forgiveness of your Lord," I said. "He is ever ready to forgive you. He sends down for you abundant water from the sky and bestows upon you wealth and children. He has provided you with gardens and with flowing rivers. Why do you deny the greatness of Allah when He has made you in gradual stages? Can you not see how He created the seven heavens one above the other, placing in them the moon for a light and the sun for a lantern? Allah has brought you forth from the earth like a plant, and to the earth He will restore you. Then He will bring you back afresh. He has made the earth a vast expanse for you, so that you may traverse its spacious paths.'"

71:21 And Noah said: 'Lord, my people disobey me and follow those whose wealth and offspring will only hasten their perdition. They have devised an outrageous plot, and said to each other: "Do not renounce your gods. Do not forsake Wad or Sowa or Yaghuth or Ya'uq or Nasr."[1] They have led numerous men astray. You surely drive the wrongdoers to further error.'

And because of their sins they were overwhelmed by the Flood and cast into the Fire. They found none to help them besides Allah.

And Noah said: 'Lord, do not leave a single unbeliever in the land. If you spare them they will mislead Your ser-71:28 vants and beget none but sinners and unbelievers. Forgive me, Lord, and forgive my parents and every true believer who seeks refuge in my house. Forgive all the faithful, men and women, and hasten the destruction of the wrong-doers.'

1. Names of idols.

THE WAR STEEDS

In the Name of Allah, the Compassionate, the Merciful

B Y the snorting war steeds, which strike fire with their 100:1
hoofs as they gallop to the raid at dawn and with a
trail of dust split the foe in two; man is ungrateful
to his Lord! To this he himself shall bear witness. 100:7
    He loves riches with all his heart. But is he not aware that
when the dead are thrown out from their graves and men's
hidden thoughts are laid open their Lord will on that day 100:11
know all that they have done?

DAYBREAK

In the Name of Allah, the Compassionate, the Merciful

S AY: 'I seek refuge in the Lord of Daybreak from the 113:1
mischief of His creation; from the mischief of the
night when she spreads her darkness; from the mischief of conjuring witches; from the mischief of the
envier, when he envies.' 113:5

MEN

In the Name of Allah, the Compassionate, the Merciful

S AY: 'I seek refuge in the Lord of men, the King of 114:1
men, the God of men, from the mischief of the slinking
prompter who whispers in the hearts of men; from jinn
and men.' 114:6

THE FIG

In the Name of Allah, the Compassionate, the Merciful

B Y the Fig, and by the Olive! 95:1
    By Mount Sinai, and this inviolate land![1]
    We moulded man into a most noble image and in
the end We shall reduce him to the lowest of the low: 95:5

1. Mecca.

23

95:6 except the believers who do good works, for theirs shall be a boundless recompense.

What, then, can after this make you deny the Last Judgement?

95:8 Is Allah not the best of judges?

DAYLIGHT

In the Name of Allah, the Compassionate, the Merciful

93:1 BY the light of day, and by the fall of night, your Lord has not forsaken you,[1] nor does He abhor you.

The life to come holds a richer prize for you than this present life. You shall be gratified with what your Lord will give you.

Did He not find you an orphan and give you shelter?

Did He not find you in error and guide you?

Did He not find you poor and enrich you?

Therefore do not wrong the orphan, nor chide away the *93:11* beggar. But proclaim the goodness of your Lord.

NIGHT

In the Name of Allah, the Compassionate, the Merciful

92:1 BY the night, when she lets fall her darkness, and by the radiant day! By Him that created the male and the female, your endeavours have different ends!

For him that gives in charity and guards himself against evil and believes in goodness, We shall smooth the path of salvation; but for him that neither gives nor takes and disbelieves in goodness, We shall smooth the path of affliction. When he breathes his last, his riches will not avail him.

It is for Us to give guidance. Ours is the life of this world, Ours the life to come. I warn you, then, of the blazing fire, in which none shall burn save the hardened sinner, who denies the truth and gives no heed. But the *92:18* good man who purifies himself by almsgiving shall keep

1. Mohammed.

away from it: and so shall he that does good works for the sake of the Most High only, not in recompense for a *92:21* favour. Such men shall be content.

THE DAWN

In the Name of Allah, the Compassionate, the Merciful

B Y the Dawn and the Ten Nights;[1] by that which is *89:1* dual, and that which is single; by the night, when it comes!

(Is there not in this a mighty oath for a man of sense?)

Have you not heard how Allah dealt with Aad?[2] The people of the many-columned city of Iram, whose like has never been built in the whole land?

And with Thamoud,[2] who hewed out their dwellings among the rocks of the valley?

And with Pharaoh, who impaled his victims upon the stake?

They had all led sinful lives and made the land teem with wickedness. Therefore your Lord let loose on them the scourge of His punishment; for from His eminence He observes all.

As for man, when his Lord tests him by exalting him and *89:15* bestowing favours on him, he says: 'My Lord is bountiful to me.' But when He tests him by grudging him His favours, he says: 'My Lord despises me.'

No! But you show no kindness to the orphan, nor do you vie with each other in feeding the poor. Greedily you lay your hands on the inheritance of the weak, and you love riches with all your hearts.

No! But when the earth is crushed to fine dust, and your Lord comes down with the angels, in their ranks, and Hell is brought near – on that day man will remember his deeds. But what will memory avail him?

He will say: 'Would that I had been charitable in my life- *89:24*

1. The first ten nights of the sacred month of Dhul-hajja.
2. Tradition has it that the tribes of Aad and Thamoud were destroyed on account of their sins.

89:25 time!' But on that day none will punish as He will punish, nor will any bind with chains like His.

89:30 O serene soul! Return to your Lord, joyful, and pleasing in His sight. Join My servants and enter My Paradise.

COMFORT

In the Name of Allah, the Compassionate, the Merciful

94:1 HAVE We not lifted up your heart and relieved you[1] of the burden which weighed down your back? Have We not given you high renown?

Every hardship is followed by ease. Every hardship is followed by ease.

94:8 When your task is ended resume your toil, and seek your Lord with all fervour.

THE BLOOD CLOTS

In the Name of Allah, the Compassionate, the Merciful

96:1 RECITE in the name of your Lord who created, created man from clots of blood! Recite! Your Lord is the Most Bountiful One, who by the pen taught man what he did not know.

Indeed, man transgresses in thinking himself his own master: for to your Lord all things return.

Observe the man who rebukes Our servant when he prays. Think: does he not follow the right guidance or enjoin true piety?

Think: if he denies the truth and gives no heed, does he not know that Allah observes all things?

Let him desist, or We will drag him by the forelock, his lying, sinful forelock.

96:18 Then let him call his helpmates. We, in Our turn, will call the guards of Hell.

1. Mohammed.

No, never obey him! Prostrate yourself and come *96:19* nearer.

QADR

In the Name of Allah, the Compassionate, the Merciful

WE revealed the Koran on the Night of Qadr.[1] *97:1*
Would that you knew what the Night of Qadr is
like!

Better is the Night of Qadr than a thousand months.

On that night the angels and the Spirit by their Lord's leave come down with His decrees.

That night is peace, till break of dawn. *97:5*

WORLDLY GAIN

In the Name of Allah, the Compassionate, the Merciful

YOUR hearts are taken up with worldly gain from the *102:1*
cradle to the grave.

But you shall know. You shall before long come to know.

Indeed, if you knew the truth with certainty, you would see the fire of Hell: you would see it with your very eyes.

Then, on that day, you shall be questioned about your *102:8* joys.

THE DECLINING DAY

In the Name of Allah, the Compassionate, the Merciful

I SWEAR by the declining day that perdition shall be the *103:1*
lot of man, except for those who have faith and do good *103:3*
works and exhort each other to justice and fortitude.

1. Lit., *glory*.

THE SLANDERER

In the Name of Allah, the Compassionate, the Merciful

104:1 WOE to all back-biting slanderers who amass riches and sedulously hoard them, thinking their treasures will render them immortal!

By no means! They shall be flung to the Destroying Flame.

Would that you knew what the Destroying Flame is like!

It is Allah's own kindled fire, which will rise up to the hearts of men. It will close upon them from every side, in 104:9 towering columns.

ALMS

In the Name of Allah, the Compassionate, the Merciful

107:1 HAVE you thought of him that denies the Last Judgement? It is he who turns away the orphan and does not urge others to feed the poor.

Woe to those who pray but are heedless in their prayer; 107:7 who make a show of piety and give no alms to the destitute.

ABUNDANCE

In the Name of Allah, the Compassionate, the Merciful

108:1
108:3 WE have given you[1] abundance. Pray to your Lord and sacrifice to Him. He that hates you shall remain childless.

1. Mohammed.

THE DISASTER

In the Name of Allah, the Compassionate, the Merciful

THE Disaster! What is the Disaster?
Would that you knew what the Disaster is!
On that day men shall become like scattered moths
and the mountains like tufts of carded wool.

Then he whose scales are heavy shall dwell in bliss; but he whose scales are light, the Abyss shall be his home.

Would that you knew what this is like!

It is a scorching fire.

THE PROOF

In the Name of Allah, the Compassionate, the Merciful

THE unbelievers among the People of the Book[1] and the pagans did not desist from unbelief until the Proof was given them: an apostle from Allah reading sanctified pages from eternal scriptures.

Nor did the People of the Book disagree among themselves until the Proof was given them. Yet they were enjoined to serve Allah and to worship none but Him, to attend to their prayers and to pay the alms-tax. That, surely, is the true faith.

The unbelievers among the People of the Book and the pagans shall burn for ever in the fire of Hell. They are the vilest of all creatures.

But of all creatures those that embrace the Faith and do good works are the noblest. Allah will reward them with the gardens of Eden, gardens watered by running streams, where they shall dwell for ever.

Allah is well pleased with them and they with Him. Thus shall the God-fearing be rewarded.

1. Jews and Christians.

THE SUN

91:1 BY the sun and his midday brightness; by the moon, which rises after him; by the day, which reveals his splendour; by the night, which veils him!

91:5 By the heaven and Him that built it; by the earth and Him that spread it; by the soul and Him that moulded it and inspired it with knowledge of sin and piety: blessed shall be the man who has kept it pure, and ruined he that has corrupted it!

In their pride the people of Thamoud denied their apostle when their arch-sinner rose against him. The Lord's apostle said: 'This is Allah's own she-camel. Let her drink.'

They disbelieved him, and slaughtered her. And for that crime their Lord let loose His scourge upon them and razed
91:15 their city to the ground. He did not fear what might follow.

THE OVERWHELMING EVENT

88:1 HAVE you heard of the Event which will overwhelm mankind?

On that day there shall be downcast faces, of men broken and worn out, burnt by a scorching fire, drinking from a seething fountain. Their only food shall be bitter thorns, which will neither sustain them nor satisfy their hunger.

On that day there shall be radiant faces, of men well-pleased with their labours, in a lofty garden. There they shall hear no idle talk. A gushing fountain shall be there, and raised soft couches with goblets placed before them; silken cushions ranged in order and carpets richly spread.

Let them reflect on the camels, and how they were
88:19 created; the heaven, how it was raised on high; the moun-

tains, how they were set down; the earth, how it was *88:20* levelled flat.

Therefore give warning. Your duty is only to warn them: you are not their keeper. As for those that turn their backs and disbelieve, Allah will inflict on them the supreme chastisement. To Us they shall return, and We will bring *88:26* them to account.

THE CITY

In the Name of Allah, the Compassionate, the Merciful

I SWEAR by this city (and you[1] yourself are a resident of *90:1* this city), by the begetter[2] and all whom he begot: We created man to try him with afflictions.

Does he think that none has power over him? 'I have wasted vast riches!' he boasts. Does he think that none observes him?

Have We not given him two eyes, a tongue, and two lips, and shown him the two paths?[3] Yet he would not scale the Height.

Would that you knew what the Height is! It is the freeing of a bondsman; the feeding, in the day of famine, of an orphaned relation or a needy man in distress; to have faith and to enjoin fortitude and mercy.

Those that do this shall stand on the right hand; but those that deny Our revelations shall stand on the left, with Hell-fire close above them. *90:20*

THE MOST HIGH

In the Name of Allah, the Compassionate, the Merciful

PRAISE the Name of your Lord, the Most High, who *87:1* has created all things and well proportioned them; who has ordained their destinies and guided them; who brings forth the green pasture, then turns it to withered grass.

We shall make you recite Our revelations, so that you *87:6*

1. Mohammed.   2. Adam.   3. Of right and wrong.

87:7 shall not forget any of them except what Allah pleases. He has knowledge of all that is manifest, and all that is hidden.

We shall guide you to the smoothest path. Therefore give warning, if warning will avail them.[1] He that fears Allah 87:11 will heed it, but the wicked sinner will flout it. He shall be cast into the raging Fire; he shall neither live nor die. Happy shall be the man who purifies himself, who remembers the name of his Lord and prays to Him.

Yet you[2] prefer this life, although the life to come is better and more lasting.

87:19 All this is written in earlier scriptures; the scriptures of Abraham and Moses.

MARY

In the Name of Allah, the Compassionate, the Merciful

19:1 KAF *ha ya ain sad.* An account of your Lord's goodness to his servant Zacharias:

He invoked Him in secret, saying: 'My bones are enfeebled, and my head glows silver with age. Yet never, Lord, have I prayed to You in vain. I now fear my kinsmen who will succeed me, for my wife is barren. Grant me a son who will be my heir and an heir to the house of Jacob, and who will find grace in Your sight.'

'Rejoice, Zacharias,' came the answer. 'You shall be given a son, and he shall be called John; a name no man has borne before him.'

19:8 'How shall I have a son, Lord,' asked Zacharias, 'when my wife is barren, and I am well advanced in years?'

He replied: 'Such is the will of your Lord. It shall be no difficult task for Me, for I brought you into being when you were nothing before.'

'Lord,' said Zacharias, 'what sign will you give me concerning this event?'

'For three days and three nights,' He replied, 'you shall be bereft of speech, though otherwise sound in body.'

19:11 Then Zacharias came out from the Shrine and exhorted

1. The unbelievers of Mecca.   2. The unbelievers of Mecca.

his people to give glory to their Lord morning and evening.

To John We said: 'Observe the Scriptures with a firm re- *19:12* solve.' We bestowed on him wisdom, grace, and purity while yet a child, and he grew up a righteous man; honouring his father and mother, and neither arrogant nor rebellious. Blessed was he on the day he was born and the day of his death; and may peace be on him when he is raised to life.

And you shall recount in the Book the story of Mary: how she left her people and betook herself to a solitary place to the east.

We sent to her Our spirit in the semblance of a full-grown man. And when she saw him she said: 'May the Merciful defend me from you! If you fear the Lord, leave me and go your way.'

'I am the messenger of your Lord,' he replied, 'and have come to give you a holy son.'

'How shall I bear a child,' she answered, 'when I am a virgin, untouched by man?'

'Such is the will of your Lord,' he replied. 'That is no difficult thing for Him. "He shall be a sign to mankind," says the Lord, "and a blessing from Ourself. This is Our decree."'

Thereupon she conceived him, and retired to a far-off *19:22* place. And when she felt the throes of childbirth she lay down by the trunk of a palm-tree, crying: 'Oh, would that I had died and passed into oblivion!'

But a voice from below cried out to her: 'Do not despair. Your Lord has provided a brook that runs at your feet, and if you shake the trunk of this palm-tree it will drop fresh ripe dates in your lap. Therefore rejoice. Eat and drink, and should you meet any mortal say to him: "I have vowed a fast to the Merciful and will not speak with any man today."'

Carrying the child, she came to her people, who said to her: 'This is indeed a strange thing! Sister of Aaron,[1] your *19:28*

---

1. i.e., virtuous woman – Aaron being held in the Koran as a 'prophet' and a saintly man. Such idiomatic expressions are common in Arabic. Muslim commentators deny the charge, often made by

father was never a whore-monger, nor was your mother a harlot.'

19:29 She made a sign to them, pointing to the child. But they replied: 'How can we speak with a babe in the cradle?'

Whereupon he spoke and said: 'I am the servant of Allah. He has given me the Gospel and ordained me a prophet. His blessing is upon me wherever I go, and He has commanded me to be steadfast in prayer and to give alms to the poor as long as I shall live. He has exhorted me to honour my mother and has purged me of vanity and wickedness. I was blessed on the day I was born, and blessed I shall be on the day of my death; and may peace be upon me on the day when I shall be raised to life.'

Such was Jesus, the son of Mary. That is the whole truth, which they are unwilling to accept. Allah forbid that He Himself should beget a son! When He decrees a thing He need only say: 'Be,' and it is.

Allah is my Lord and your Lord: therefore serve Him. That is the right path.

Yet the Sects are divided concerning Jesus. But when the fateful day arrives, woe to the unbelievers! Their sight and hearing shall be sharpened on the day when they appear before Us. Truly, the unbelievers are in the grossest error.

19:39 Forewarn them of that woeful day, when Our decrees shall be fulfilled whilst they heedlessly persist in unbelief. For We shall inherit the earth and all who dwell upon it. To Us they shall return.

You shall also recount in the Book the story of Abraham:

He was a prophet and a saintly man. He said to his father: 'How can you serve a worthless idol, a thing that can neither see nor hear?

19:43 'Father, the truth has been revealed to me about many mysteries: therefore follow me, that I may guide you along an even path.

Western scholars and based solely on this text, that Mohammed confused Miriam, Aaron's sister, with Maryam (Mary), mother of Jesus.

'Father, do not worship Satan; for he has rebelled against 19:44
the Lord of Mercy.

'Father, I fear that Allah's scourge will fall upon you and
you will become one of Satan's minions.'

His father replied: 'Do you dare renounce my gods,
Abraham? Desist from this folly or you shall be stoned to
death. Begone from my house this instant!'

'Peace be with you,' said Abraham. 'I shall implore my
Lord to forgive you: for to me He has been gracious. But I
will not live with you or with your idols. I will call on my
Lord, and trust that my prayers will not be ignored.'

And when Abraham had cast off his people and the idols
which they worshipped, We gave him Isaac and Jacob.
Each of them We made a prophet, and We bestowed on
them gracious gifts and high renown.

Tell also of Moses, who was an apostle, a prophet, and a
chosen man.

We called out to him from the right side of the Mountain,
and when he came near We communed with him in secret.
We gave him, of Our mercy, his brother Aaron, himself a 19:53
prophet.

Then you shall tell of Ishmael: he, too, was an apostle, a
seer, and a man of his word.

He enjoined prayer and almsgiving on his people, and his
Lord was pleased with him.

And of Idris[1]: he, too, was a saint and a prophet, whom
We honoured and exalted.

These are the men to whom Allah has been gracious: the
prophets from among the descendants of Adam and of
those whom We carried in the Ark with Noah; the descendants of Abraham, of Israel, and of those whom We
have guided and chosen. For when the revelations of the
Merciful were recited to them they fell down on their
knees in tears and adoration.

But the generations who succeeded them neglected their
prayers and succumbed to temptation. These shall assuredly
be lost. But those that repent and embrace the Faith and do 19:60

1. Enoch.

what is right shall be admitted to Paradise and shall not be

19:61 wronged. They shall enter the gardens of Eden, which the Merciful has promised His servants in reward for their faith. His promise shall be fulfilled.

There they shall hear no idle talk, but only the voice of peace. And their sustenance shall be given them morning and evening. Such is the Paradise which the righteous shall inherit.

We do not descend from Heaven save at the bidding of your Lord.[1] To Him belongs what is before us and behind us, and all that lies between.

Your Lord does not forget. He is the Lord of the heavens and the earth and all that is between them. Worship Him, then, and be loyal in His service; for is there any other god like Him?

'What!' says man, 'When I am once dead, shall I be raised to life?'

19:67 Does man forget that We created him out of the void? By the Lord, We will call them to account in company with all the devils and set them on their knees around the fire of Hell: from every sect We will carry off its stoutest rebels and cast them down. We alone know who deserves most to be burnt therein.

There is not one of you who shall not pass through the confines of Hell: such is the absolute decree of your Lord. We will deliver those who fear Us, but the wrongdoers shall be left to endure its torments on their knees.

When Our clear revelations are recited to them the unbelievers say to the faithful: 'Will that in any way add to your wealth or place you in better company than ours?'

How many generations have We destroyed before them, far greater in riches and in splendour!

19:75 Say: 'The Merciful will bear long with the unbelievers, until they witness the fulfilment of His threats: be it a worldly scourge or the Hour of Doom. Then shall they

1. Commentators say that these are the words of the Angel Gabriel, in reply to Mohammed's complaint of long intervals elapsing between periods of revelation.

know whose is the worse plight and whose the smaller following.'

Allah will increasingly guide those that have followed the 19:76 right path. Deeds of lasting merit shall earn you a better reward in His sight and a more auspicious end.

Mark the words of the unbeliever: 'I shall surely be given wealth and children!' he boasts.

Has the future been revealed to him? Or has the Merciful made him such a promise?

By no means! We will record his words and make his punishment long and terrible. All he speaks of he shall leave behind and come before us all alone.

The unbelievers have chosen other gods to help them. But in the end they will renounce their worship and turn against them.

Know that we send down to the unbelievers devils who incite them to evil. Therefore have patience: their days are numbered. The day will surely come when We will gather the righteous in multitudes before the Lord of Mercy, and drive the sinful in great hordes into Hell-fire. None has power to intercede for them save him who has received the sanction of the Merciful.

Those who say: 'The Lord of Mercy has begotten a son,' 19:88 preach a monstrous falsehood, at which the very heavens might crack, the earth break asunder, and the mountains crumble to dust. That they should ascribe a son to the Merciful, when it does not become Him to beget one!

There is none in the heavens or on earth but shall return to Him in utter submission. He has kept strict count of all His creatures, and one by one they shall approach Him on the Day of Resurrection. He will cherish those who accepted the true faith and were charitable in their life-time.

We have revealed to you the Koran in your own tongue that you may thereby proclaim good tidings to the upright and give warning to a contentious nation.

How many generations have We destroyed before them! 19:98 Can you find one of them still alive, or hear so much as a whisper from them?

THE NIGHTLY VISITANT

In the Name of Allah, the Compassionate, the Merciful

86:1 By the heaven, and by the nightly visitant! Would that you knew what the nightly visitant is! It is the star of piercing brightness.

For every soul there is a guardian watching over it. Let man reflect from what he is created. He is created from an ejected fluid that issues from between the loins and the ribs.

Allah has power to bring him back to life, on the day when men's consciences are searched. Helpless he shall be, with none to succour him.

By the heaven with its recurring cycles, and by the earth, ever bursting with new growth; this[1] is a discerning utterance, no flippant jest.

They scheme against you: but I, too, have My schemes. 86:17 Therefore bear with the unbelievers, and let them be awhile.

JOSEPH

In the Name of Allah, the Compassionate, the Merciful

12:1 Alif *lam ra*. These are the verses of the Glorious Book. We have revealed the Koran in the Arabic tongue so that you may understand it.

In revealing this Koran We will recount to you the best of histories, though before We revealed it you were heedless of Our signs.

Joseph said to his father: 'Father, I dreamt that eleven stars and the sun and the moon were prostrating themselves before me.'

'My son,' he replied, 'say nothing of this dream to your brothers, lest they should plot evil against you: Satan is the 12:6 sworn enemy of man. You shall be chosen by your Lord. He will teach you to interpret visions and will perfect His favour to you and to the house of Jacob, as He perfected it

1. The Koran.

to your forefathers Abraham and Isaac before you. Your Lord is all-knowing and wise.'

Surely in the tale of Joseph and his brothers there are 12:7 signs for doubting men.

They said to each other: 'Joseph and his brother are dearer to our father than ourselves, though we are many. Truly, our father is much mistaken. Let us kill Joseph, or cast him away in some far-off land, so that we may have no rivals in our father's love, and after that be honourable men.'

One of them said: 'Do not kill Joseph. If you must get rid of him, cast him into a dark pit. Some caravan will take him up.'

They said to their father: 'Why do you not trust us with Joseph? Surely we are his friends. Send him with us to-morrow, that he may play and enjoy himself. We will take good care of him.'

He replied: 'It would much grieve me to let him go with you; for I fear lest the wolf should eat him when you are off your guard.'

They said: 'If the wolf could eat him despite our num- 12:14 bers, then we should surely be lost!'

And when they took Joseph with them, they decided to cast him into a dark pit. We addressed him, saying: 'You shall tell them of all this when they will not know you.'

At nightfall they returned weeping to their father. They said: 'We went racing and left Joseph with our goods. The wolf devoured him. But you will not believe us, though we speak the truth.' And they showed him their brother's shirt, stained with false blood.

'No!' he cried. 'Your souls have tempted you to evil. But I will be patient: Allah alone can help me to bear the misfortune of which you speak.'

And a caravan passed by, who sent their waterman to the pit. And when he had let down his pail, he cried: 'Rejoice! A boy!'

They took Joseph and concealed him among their goods. But Allah knew what they did. They sold him for a trifling 12:20

price, for a few pieces of silver. They cared nothing for him.

12:21   The Egyptian who bought him said to his wife: 'Use him kindly. He may prove useful to us, or we may adopt him as our son.'

Thus We found in that land a home for Joseph, and taught him to interpret mysteries. Allah has power over all things, though most men may not know it. And when he reached maturity We bestowed on him wisdom and knowledge. Thus We reward the righteous.

His master's wife sought to seduce him. She bolted the doors and said: 'Come!'

'Allah forbid!' he replied. 'My lord has treated me with kindness. Wrongdoers never prosper.'

She made for him, and he himself would have yielded to her had he not been shown a veritable sign by his Lord. Thus We warded off from him indecency and evil, for he was one of Our faithful servants.

12:25   He raced her to the door, but as she clung to him she tore his shirt from behind. And at the door they met her husband.

She cried: 'Shall not the man who sought to violate your wife be thrown into prison or sternly punished?'

Joseph said: 'It was she who sought to seduce me.'

'If his shirt is torn from the front,' said one of the people, 'she is speaking the truth and he is lying. If it is torn from behind, then he is speaking the truth, and she is lying.'

And when her husband saw Joseph's shirt rent from behind, he said to her: 'This is one of your tricks. Your cunning is great indeed! Joseph, say no more about this. Woman, ask pardon for your sin. You have done wrong.'

In the city women were saying: 'The Prince's wife has sought to seduce her servant. She has conceived a passion for him. It is clear that she has gone astray.'

12:31   When she heard of their intrigues, she invited them to a banquet at her house. To each she gave a knife, and ordered Joseph to present himself before them. When they saw him, they were amazed at him and cut their hands, exclaiming: 'Allah preserve us! This is no mortal, but a gracious angel.'

'This is the man,' she said, 'on whose account you re- *12:32* proached me. I sought to seduce him, but he was unyielding. If he declines to do my bidding, he shall be thrown into prison and held in scorn.'

'Lord,' said Joseph, 'sooner would I go to prison than give in to their advances. Shield me from their cunning, or I shall yield to them and lapse into folly.'

His Lord heard his prayer and warded off their wiles from him. He hears all and knows all.

Yet despite the evidence they had seen, the Egyptians thought it right to jail him for a time.

Two young men went to prison with him. One of them said: 'I dreamt that I was pressing grapes.' And the other said: 'I dreamt that I was carrying a loaf upon my head, and that the birds came and ate of it. Tell us the meaning of these dreams, for we can see you are a man of learning.'

Joseph replied: 'I can interpret them long before they are *12:37* fulfilled. This knowledge my Lord has given me, for I have left the faith of those that disbelieve in Allah and deny the life to come. I follow the faith of my forefathers, Abraham, Isaac, and Jacob. We must never serve idols besides Allah. Such is the gift which Allah has bestowed upon us and all mankind. Yet most men do not give thanks.

'Fellow-prisoners! Are numerous gods better than Allah, the One, the Almighty? Those whom you serve besides Him are names which you and your fathers have invented and for which Allah has revealed no sanction. Judgement rests with Allah only. He has commanded you to worship none but Him. That is the true faith: yet most men do not know it.

'Fellow-prisoners, one of you will serve his king with wine. The other will be crucified, and the birds will peck at his head. That is the meaning of your dreams.'

And Joseph said to the prisoner who he knew would be *12:42* freed: 'Remember me in the presence of your king.'

But Satan made him forget to mention Joseph to his king, so that he stayed in prison for several years.

12:43   Now it so chanced that one day the king said: 'I saw seven fatted cows which seven lean ones devoured; also seven green ears of corn and seven others dry. Tell me the meaning of this vision, my nobles, if you can interpret visions.'

They replied: 'It is but an idle dream; nor can we interpret dreams.'

Thereupon the man who had been freed remembered Joseph after all those years. He said: 'I shall tell you what it means. Give me leave to go.'

He said to Joseph: 'Tell us, man of truth, of the seven fatted cows which seven lean ones devoured; also of the seven green ears of corn and the other seven which were dry: for I would inform my masters.'

12:47   Joseph replied: 'You shall sow for seven consecutive years. Leave in the ear the corn you reap, except a little which you may eat. Then there shall follow seven hungry years which will consume all but little of that which you have stored for them. Then there will come a year of abundant rain, in which the people will press the grape.'

The king said: 'Bring this man before me.'

But when the king's envoy came to him, Joseph said: 'Go back to your master and ask him about the women who cut their hands. My master knows their cunning.'

The king questioned the women, saying: 'Why did you seek to entice Joseph?'

'Allah forbid!' they replied. 'We know no evil of him.'

'Now the truth must come to light,' said the Prince's wife. 'It was I who sought to seduce him. He has told the truth.'

'From this,' said Joseph, 'my lord will know that I did not betray him in his absence, and that Allah does not 12:53 guide the work of the treacherous. Not that I am free from sin: man's soul is prone to evil, except his to whom Allah has shown mercy. My Lord is forgiving and merciful.'

The king said: 'Bring him before me. I will make him my *12:54* personal servant.'

And when he had spoken with him, the king said: 'You shall henceforth dwell with us, honoured and trusted.'

Joseph said: 'Give me charge of the granaries of the realm. I shall husband them wisely.'

Thus We gave power to Joseph, and he dwelt at his ease in that land. We bestow Our mercy on whom We will, and never deny the righteous their reward. Better is the reward of the life to come for those who believe in Allah and keep from evil.

Joseph's brothers came and presented themselves before him. He recognized them, but they knew him not. And when he had given them their provisions, he said: 'Bring me your other brother from your father. Do you not see that I give just measure and am the best of hosts? If you do *12:60* not bring him, you shall have no corn, nor shall you come near me again.'

They replied: 'We will request his father to let him come with us. This we will surely do.'

Joseph said to his servants: 'Put their money into their packs, so that they may find it when they return to their people. Perchance they will come back.'

When they returned to their father, they said: 'Father, corn is henceforth denied us. Send our brother with us and we shall have our measure. We will take good care of him.'

He replied: 'Am I to trust you with him as I once trusted you with his brother? But Allah is the best of guardians: of all those that show mercy He is the most merciful.'

When they opened their packs, they found that their money had been returned to them. 'Father,' they said, 'what more can we desire? Here is our money untouched. We will buy provisions for our people and take good care of our brother. We shall receive an extra camel-load; that should not be hard to get.'

He replied: 'I shall not let him go with you until you *12:66* swear in Allah's name to bring him back to me, unless you are prevented.'

And when they had given him their pledge, he said:
12:67 'Allah is the witness of your oath. My sons, enter the town by different gates. If you do wrong, I cannot ward off from you the wrath of Allah; judgement is His alone. In Him I have put my trust. In Him alone let the faithful put their trust.'

And when they entered as their father had advised them, his counsel availed them nothing against the decree of Allah. It was but a wish in Jacob's soul which he had thus fulfilled. He was possessed of knowledge which We had given him, though most men were unaware of it.

When they presented themselves before him, Joseph embraced his brother, and said: 'I am your brother. Do not grieve at what they did.'

12:70 And when he had given them their provisions, he hid a drinking-cup in his brother's pack.

Then a crier called out after them: 'Travellers, you are thieves!'

They turned back and asked: 'What have you lost?'

'The king's drinking-cup,' he replied. 'He that restores it shall have a camel-load of corn. I pledge my word for it.'

'By Allah,' they cried, 'you know we did not come to do evil in this land. We are no thieves.'

The Egyptians said: 'What penalty shall we inflict on him that stole it, if you prove to be lying?'

They replied: 'He in whose pack the cup is found shall be your bondsman. Thus we punish the wrongdoers.'

Joseph searched their bags before his brother's, and then took out the cup from his brother's bag.

Thus We directed Joseph. By the king's law he had no right to seize his brother: but Allah willed otherwise. We exalt in knowledge whom We will: but above those that have knowledge there is One more knowing.

12:77 They said: 'If he has stolen – know then that a brother of his has committed a theft before him.'[1]

But Joseph kept his secret and did not reveal it to them.

1. Commentators say that Joseph had stolen an idol of his maternal grandfather's and broken it, so that he might not worship it.

44

He thought: 'Your crime was worse. Allah well knows that you are lying.'

They said: 'Noble prince, this boy has an aged father. *12:78* Take one of us, instead of him. We can see you are a generous man.'

He replied: 'Allah forbid that we should seize any but the man with whom our property was found: for then we should be unjust.'

When they despaired of him, they went aside to confer together. The eldest said: 'Have you forgotten that you gave your father a solemn pledge, and that you broke your faith before this concerning Joseph? I shall not stir from this land until my father gives me leave or Allah makes known to me His judgement: He is the best of judges. Return to your father and say to him: "Your son has committed a theft. We testify only to what we know. How could we guard against the unforeseen? Ask the townsfolk *12:82* with whom we stayed and the caravan in which we travelled. We speak the truth."'

'No!' cried their father. 'Your souls have tempted you to evil. But I will be patient. Allah may bring them all to me. He alone is wise and all-knowing.' And he turned away from them, crying: 'Alas for Joseph!' His eyes went white with grief and he was oppressed with silent sorrow.

His sons exclaimed: 'By Allah, will you not cease to think of Joseph until you ruin your health and die?'

He replied: 'I complain to Allah of my sorrow and sadness. He has made known to me things beyond your knowledge. Go, my sons, and seek news of Joseph and his brother. Do not despair of Allah's spirit; none but unbelievers despair of Allah's spirit.'

And when they presented themselves before Joseph, they said: 'Noble prince, we and our people are scourged with famine. We have brought but little money. Give us some corn, and be charitable to us: Allah rewards the charitable.'

'Do you know,' he replied, 'what you did to Joseph and *12:89* his brother in your ignorance?'

12:90 They cried: 'Can you indeed be Joseph?'

'I am Joseph,' he answered, 'and this is my brother. Allah has been gracious to us. Those that keep from evil and endure with fortitude, Allah will not deny them their reward.'

'By the Lord,' they said, 'Allah has exalted you above us all. We have indeed been guilty.'

He replied: 'None shall reproach you this day. May Allah forgive you: He is most merciful. Take this shirt of mine and throw it over my father's face: he will recover his sight. Then return to me with all your people.'

When the caravan departed their father said: 'I feel the breath of Joseph, though you will not believe me.'

'By Allah,' said those who heard him, 'this is but your old illusion.'

And when the bearer of good news arrived, he threw Joseph's shirt over the old man's face, and his sight came back to him. He said: 'Did I not tell you that Allah has made known to me things beyond your knowledge?'

12:97 His sons said: 'Father, implore forgiveness for our sins. We have indeed been sinners.'

He replied: 'I shall implore my Lord to forgive you. He is forgiving and merciful.'

And when they presented himselves before Joseph he embraced his parents and said: 'Welcome to Egypt, safe, if Allah wills!'

He helped his parents to a couch, and they all fell on their knees and prostrated themselves before him.

'This,' said Joseph to his father, 'is the meaning of my old vision: my Lord has fulfilled it. He has been gracious to me. He has released me from prison and brought you out of the desert after Satan had stirred up strife between me and my brothers. My lord is gracious to whom He will. He alone is wise and all-knowing.

12:101 'Lord, You have given me power and taught me to interpret mysteries. You are the Creator of the heavens and the earth, my Guardian in this world and in the next. Let me die in submission and join the righteous.'

That which We have now revealed to you[1] is secret *12:102* history. You were not present when Joseph's brothers conceived their plans and schemed against him. Yet strive as you may, most men will not believe.

You shall demand of them no recompense for this. It[2] is an admonition to all mankind.

Many are the marvels of the heavens and the earth; yet they pass them by and pay no heed to them. The greater part of them believe in Allah only if they can worship other gods besides Him.

Are they confident that Allah's scourge will not fall upon them, or that the Hour of Doom will not overtake them unawares, without warning?

Say: 'This is my path. With sure knowledge I call on you *12:108* to have faith in Allah, I and all my followers. Glory be to Him! I am no idolater.'

Nor were the apostles whom We sent before you other than mortals inspired by Our will and chosen from among their people.

Have they not travelled in the land and seen what was the end of those who disbelieved before them? Better is the world to come for those that keep from evil. Can you not understand?

And when at length Our apostles despaired and thought that none would believe in them, Our help came down to them, delivering whom We pleased. The evil-doers did not escape Our scourge. Their history is a lesson to men of *12:111* understanding.

This[3] is no invented tale, but a confirmation of previous scriptures, an explanation of all things, a guide and a blessing to true believers.

1. Mohammed.   2. The Koran.   3 The Koran.

47

THE CONSTELLATIONS

In the Name of Allah, the Compassionate, the Merciful

85:1 BY the heaven with its constellations! By the Promised Day! By the Witness, and that which is witnessed!

Cursed be the diggers of the trench, who lighted the consuming fire and sat around it to watch the faithful being put to the torture! Nor did they torture them for any reason save that they believed in Allah, the Mighty, the Praised One; the Sovereign of the heavens and the earth, the Witness of all things.

Those that persecute believers, men or women, and never repent shall be rewarded with the scourge of Hell, 85:11 the scourge of the Conflagration. But those that have faith and do good works shall be rewarded with gardens watered by running streams. That is the supreme triumph.

Stern indeed is the vengeance of your Lord. His is the creation and His the re-creation. Forgiving and benignant, He is the Lord of the Glorious Throne, the Executor of His own will.

Have you not heard the story of the warriors, of Pharaoh and of Thamoud? Yet the unbelievers still deny it.

Allah surrounds them all. Surely this is a glorious Koran, 85:22 inscribed on a preserved tablet.

THE RENDING

In the Name of Allah, the Compassionate, the Merciful

84:1 WHEN the sky is rent apart, obeying her Lord in true submission; when the earth expands and casts out all that is within her and becomes empty, obeying her Lord in true submission; then, O man, who labour constantly to meet your Lord, shall you meet Him.

He that is given his book in his right hand shall have a lenient reckoning and go back rejoicing to his people. 84:11 But he that is given his book behind his back shall call down

destruction on himself and burn in the fire of Hell; for he 84:12
lived without a care among his people and thought he
would never return to Allah. But his Lord was ever watching over him.

I swear by the glow of sunset; by the night, and all that it
brings together; by the moon, in her full perfection: that
you shall march onwards from state to state.

Why then do they[1] not have faith, or kneel in prayer
when the Koran is read to them?

The unbelievers deny it; but Allah knows best the falsehoods they believe in.

Therefore proclaim to all a woeful doom, save those who 84:25
embrace the true faith and do good works; for theirs is an
unfailing recompense.

THE UNJUST

In the Name of Allah, the Compassionate, the Merciful

WOE to the unjust who, when others measure for 83:1
them, exact in full, but when they measure or
weigh for others, defraud them!

Do such men think that they will not be raised to life
upon a fateful day, the day when all mankind will stand
before the Lord of the Creation?

Truly, the record of the sinners is in Sidjeen. Would that
you knew what Sidjeen is! It is a sealed book.

Woe on that day to the disbelievers who deny the Last
Judgement! None denies it except the transgressors, the
evil-doers who, when Our revelations are recited to them,
cry: 'Fables of the ancients!'

No! Their own deeds have cast a veil over their hearts.

No! On that day a barrier shall be set between them and
their Lord. They shall burn in Hell, and a voice will say to
them: 'This is the scourge that you denied!'

But the record of the righteous shall be in Illiyun.[2] 83:18

1. The unbelievers of Mecca.
2. This word has puzzled Muslim commentators. But it is probably
related to *El Elion* (the Most High God), in the Old Testament.

83:19 Would that you knew what Illiyun is! It is a sealed book, seen only by those who are closest to Allah.

The righteous shall surely dwell in bliss. Reclining upon soft couches they will gaze around them: and in their faces you shall mark the glow of joy. They shall drink of a pure wine, securely sealed, whose very dregs are musk (for this let all men emulously strive); a wine tempered with the waters of Tasnim, a spring at which the favoured will refresh themselves.

The evil-doers scoff at the faithful and wink at one another as they pass by them. When they meet their own folk they speak of them with jests and when they see them they say: 'These are erring men!' Yet they were not sent to be their guardians.

But on that day the faithful will mock the unbelievers as they recline upon their couches and gaze around them.

83:36 Shall not the unbelievers be rewarded according to their deeds?

HE FROWNED

In the Name of Allah, the Compassionate, the Merciful

80:1 HE[1] frowned and turned his back when the blind man came towards him.

How could you[1] tell? He might have sought to purify himself. He might have been forewarned, and might have profited from Our warning.

But to the wealthy man you were all attention: although the fault would not be yours if he remained uncleansed. Yet you gave no heed to him that came to you with zeal and awe.

This is an admonition; let him who will, bear it in mind. It is set down on honoured pages, purified and exalted, by the hands of devout and gracious scribes.

Confound man! How ungrateful he is!

From what did Allah create him? From a little germ He *80:20* created him and proportioned him. He makes his path

1. Mohammed.

smooth for him, then causes him to die and stows him in a *80:21*
grave. He will surely bring him back to life when He
pleases. Yet he declines to do His bidding.

Let man reflect on the food he eats: how We pour down
the rain in torrents and cleave the earth asunder; how We
bring forth the corn, the grapes, and the fresh vegetation;
the olive and the palm, the thickets, the fruit-trees and
the green pasture, for you and for your cattle to delight
in.

But when the dread blast is sounded, on that day each
man will forsake his brother, his mother and his father, his
wife and his children: for each one of them will on that day
have enough sorrow of his own.

On that day there shall be beaming faces, smiling and
joyful. On that day there shall be faces veiled with darkness,
covered with dust. These shall be the faces of the wicked *80:42*
and the unbelieving.

THE SOUL-SNATCHERS

In the Name of Allah, the Compassionate, the Merciful

B Y those who violently snatch away men's souls, and *79:1*
those who gently release them; by those who float at
will and those who speed headlong; by those who
govern the affairs of this world! On the day when the
Trumpet sounds its first and second blast, all hearts shall be
filled with terror, and all eyes shall stare with awe.

They say: 'When we are turned to hollow bones, shall we
be restored to life? A fruitless transformation!' But with
one blast they shall return to the earth's surface.

Have you heard the story of Moses?

His Lord called out to him in the sacred valley of Towa,
saying: 'Go to Pharaoh: he has transgressed all bounds;
and say: "Will you reform yourself? I will guide you to
your Lord, so that you may have fear of Him."'

He showed Pharaoh the mightiest miracle, but he denied
it and rebelled. He quickly went away and, summoning all *79:23*

79:24 his men, made to them a proclamation. 'I am your supreme Lord,' he said.

Allah smote him with the scourge of this life and of the life to come. Surely in this there is a lesson for the God-fearing.

Are you harder to create than the heaven which He has built? He raised it high and fashioned it, giving darkness to its night and brightness to its day.

After that He spread the earth, and, drawing water from *79:32* its depth, brought forth its pastures. He set down the mountains, for you and for your cattle to delight in.

But when the supreme day arrives – the day when man will call to mind his labours – when the Fire is brought in sight of all – those that transgressed and chose this present life will find themselves in Hell; but those that feared to stand before their Lord and curbed their souls' desires shall dwell in Paradise.

They question you about the Hour of Doom. 'When will it come?' they ask. But how are you to know? Your Lord alone knows when it will come. Your duty is but to warn those that fear it.

79:46 On the day when they behold that hour, they will think they stayed away one evening, or one morning.

THE TIDINGS

In the Name of Allah, the Compassionate, the Merciful

78:1 ABOUT what are they asking? About the fateful tidings – the theme of their disputes.

But they shall know the truth; before long they shall know it.

Did We not spread the earth like a bed and raise the mountains like pillars?

We created you in pairs and gave you rest in sleep. We made the night a mantle, and ordained the day for work. *78:12* We built above you seven mighty heavens and placed in

them a shining lamp. We sent down abundant water from 78:13
the clouds, bringing forth grain and varied plants, and
gardens thick with foliage.

Fixed is the Day of Judgement. On that day the Trumpet
shall be sounded and you shall come in multitudes. The
gates of heaven shall swing open and the mountains shall
pass away and become like vapour.

Hell will lie in ambush, a home for the transgressors.
There they shall abide long ages; there they shall taste
neither refreshment nor any drink, save boiling water and
decaying filth: a fitting recompense.

They disbelieved in Our reckoning and roundly denied
Our revelations. But We counted all their doings and 78:29
wrote them down. We shall say: 'Taste this: you shall have
nothing but mounting torment!'

As for the righteous, they shall surely triumph. Theirs
shall be gardens and vineyards, and high-bosomed maidens
for companions: a truly overflowing cup.

There they shall hear no idle talk nor any falsehood. Such
is the recompense of your Lord – a gift that will suffice
them: the Lord of the heavens and the earth and all that lies
between them; the Merciful, with whom no one can speak.

On the day when the Spirit and the angels stand up in
their ranks, they shall not speak; except him who shall receive the sanction of the Merciful and declare what is right.

That day is sure to come. Let him who will, seek a way
back to his Lord. We have forewarned you of an imminent 78:40
scourge: the day when man will look upon his works and
the unbeliever cry: 'Would that I were dust!'

THOSE THAT ARE SENT FORTH

In the Name of Allah, the Compassionate, the Merciful

By the gales, sent forth in swift succession; by the 77:1
raging tempests and the rain-spreading winds; by
your Lord's revelations, discerning good from evil
and admonishing by plea and warning: that which you have 77:7
been promised shall be fulfilled!

77:8   When the stars are blotted out; when the sky is rent asunder and the mountains crumble into dust; when Allah's apostles are brought together on the appointed day – when will all this be? Upon the Day of Judgement!

Would that you knew the import of that day! Woe on that day to the disbelievers! Did We not destroy the men of old and cause others to follow them? Thus shall We deal with the guilty.

Woe on that day to the disbelievers! Did We not create you from an unworthy fluid, which We kept in a safe receptacle[1] for an appointed time? All this We did; how excellent is Our work!

Woe on that day to the disbelievers! Have We not made the earth a home for the living and for the dead? Have We not placed high mountains upon it and given you fresh water for your drink?

77:28   Woe on that day to the disbelievers! Begone to that Hell which you deny! Depart into the shadow that will rise high in three columns, giving neither shade nor shelter from the flames and throwing up sparks as huge as towers, as bright as yellow camels!

Woe on that day to the disbelievers! On that day they shall not speak, nor shall their pleas be accepted.

Woe on that day to the disbelievers! Such is the Day of Judgement. We will assemble you all, together with past generations. If then you are cunning, try your spite against Me!

Woe on that day to the disbelievers! The righteous shall dwell amidst cool shades and fountains and feed on such fruits as they desire. We shall say to them: 'Eat and drink, and may every joy attend you! This is the guerdon of your labours.' Thus shall the righteous be rewarded.

Woe on that day to the disbelievers! Eat and enjoy yourselves awhile. You are wicked men.

77:48   Woe on that day to the disbelievers! When they are bidden to kneel down, they do not kneel.

1. The womb.

54

Woe on that day to the disbelievers! In what revelation, 77:50
after this, will they believe?

THE RESURRECTION

In the Name of Allah, the Compassionate, the Merciful

I SWEAR by the Day of Resurrection, and by the self- 75:1
reproaching soul!
Does man think We shall never put his bones together again? Indeed, We can remould his very fingers!

Yet man would ever deny what is to come. 'When will
this be,' he asks, 'this day of Resurrection?'

But when the sight of mortals is confounded and the
moon eclipsed; when sun and moon are brought together –
on that day man will ask: 'Whither shall I flee?'

No, there shall be no escape. For on that day all shall
return to your Lord.

On that day man shall be informed of all that he has
done and all that he has failed to do. He shall become his
own witness; his pleas shall go unheeded.

(You[1] need not move your tongue too fast to learn this 75:16
revelation. We Ourself shall see to its collection and recital.
When We read it, follow its words attentively; We shall
Ourself explain its meaning.)

Yet you[2] love this fleeting life and are heedless of the life
to come.

On that day there shall be joyous faces, looking towards
their Lord. On that day there shall be mournful faces, dreading some great affliction.

But when a man's soul is about to leave him and those
around him cry: Will no one save him? When he knows it is
the final parting and the pangs of death assail him – on that
day to your Lord he shall be driven. For in this life he
neither believed nor prayed; he denied the truth and, turning his back, went to his kinsfolk elated with pride.

Well have you deserved this doom; well have you deserved 75:34

1. Mohammed.   2. The Meccans.

75:35 it. Well have you deserved this doom: too well have you deserved it!

Does man think that he lives in vain? Was he not a drop of ejected semen? He became a clot of blood; then Allah formed and moulded him and gave him male and female
75:40 parts. Is He then not able to raise the dead to life?

THE CLOAKED ONE

In the Name of Allah, the Compassionate, the Merciful

74:1 YOU[1] that are wrapped up in your vestment, arise and give warning.

Magnify your Lord, cleanse your garments, and keep away from all pollution.

Bestow no favours where you expect in return more than you have given. Be patient, for your Lord's sake.

The day when the Trumpet sounds shall be a day of woe and anguish for the unbelievers. Leave to Me the man whom I created and endowed with vast riches and thriving children. I have made his progress smooth and easy: yet he hopes for more. But because he has stubbornly denied Our revelations, I will lay on him a mounting torment.

74:19 He pondered, and he schemed. Confound him, how he schemed! Confound him, how he schemed!

He looked around him, frowning and leering; then he turned away in scornful pride and said: 'This is no more than borrowed magic, the words of a mere mortal!'

I will surely cast him into the fire of Hell. Would that you knew what the fire of Hell is like! It leaves nothing, it spares no one; it burns the skins of men. It is guarded by nineteen keepers.

74:31 We have appointed none but angels to guard the Fire, and made their number a subject for dispute among the unbelievers, so that those to whom the Scriptures were given may be convinced and the true believers strengthened in their faith; that those to whom the Scriptures were given,

1. Mohammed.

and the true believers, may have no doubts; and that the infidels and hypocrites may say: 'What could Allah mean by this?' Thus Allah misleads whom He will and guides whom He pleases. None knows the warriors of your Lord but Himself. This is no more than an admonition to mankind.

No, by the moon! By the departing night and the com- *74:32* ing dawn, it is a dire scourge, a warning to all men; alike to those of you that would march on and those that would remain behind.

Each soul is the hostage of its own deeds. Those on the right hand will in their gardens ask the sinners: 'What has brought you into Hell?' They will reply: 'We never prayed or fed the hungry. We engaged in vain disputes and denied the Day of Reckoning till death at last overtook us.'

No intercessor's plea shall save them. Why then do they turn away from this reminder, like frightened asses fleeing from a lion?

Indeed, each one of them demands a scripture of his own to be unrolled before him. No, they have no fear of the hereafter.

This is an admonition. Let him who will, take heed. But none takes heed except by the will of Allah. He is the spring *74:56* of goodness and forgiveness.

THE LADDERS

In the Name of Allah, the Compassionate, the Merciful

A SCEPTIC[1] once demanded that punishment be *70:1* visited forthwith upon the unbelievers.

No power can hinder Allah from punishing them. He is the Lord of the Ladders, by which the angels and the Spirit will ascend to Him in one day: a day whose space is fifty thousand years.

Therefore conduct yourself with becoming patience. They think the Day of Judgement is far off: but We see it *70:7* near at hand.

1. Lit., a questioner.

70:8   On that day the heavens shall become like molten brass, and the mountains like tufts of wool scattered in the wind. Friends will meet, but shall not speak to one another. To redeem himself from the torment of that day the sinner will gladly sacrifice his children, his wife, his brother, the kinsfolk who gave him shelter, and all the people of the earth, if then this might deliver him.

But the fire of Hell shall drag him down by the scalp, shall claim him who had turned his back on the true faith and amassed riches and covetously hoarded them.

Indeed, man was created impatient. When evil befalls him he is despondent; but blessed with good fortune he grows niggardly.

70:22   Not so the worshippers who are steadfast in prayer; who set aside a due portion of their goods for the needy and the dispossessed; who truly believe in the Day of Reckoning and dread the punishment of their Lord (for none is secure from the punishment of their Lord); who restrain their carnal desire (save with their wives and slave-girls, for these are lawful to them: he that lusts after other than these is a transgressor); who keep their trusts and promises and bear true witness; and who attend to their prayers with promptitude. These shall be laden with honours and shall dwell in fair gardens.

But what has befallen the unbelievers, that they scramble before you in multitudes from left and right?

70:38   Are they seeking to enter a garden of delight?

Let them remember of what We created them!

I swear by the Lord of the East and the West that We have the power to destroy them and replace them by others better than them: nothing can hinder us from so doing. So leave them to amuse themselves and blunder about in their folly until they face the day with which they are threatened; the day when they shall rush from their graves, like men *70:44* rallying to a standard, with downcast eyes and countenances distorted with shame.

Such is the day with which they are threatened.

THE MANTLED ONE

In the Name of Allah, the Compassionate, the Merciful

YOU[1] that are wrapped up in your mantle, keep vigil 73:1
all night, save for a few hours; half the night, or
even less: or a little more – and with measured tone
recite the Koran, for We are about to address to you words
of surpassing gravity. It is in the watches of the night that
impressions are strongest and words most eloquent; in the
day-time you are hard-pressed with work.

Remember the name of your Lord and dedicate yourself
to Him utterly. He is the Lord of the East and the West:
there is no god but Him. Accept Him for your Protector.

Bear patiently with what they[2] say and leave their company without recrimination. Leave to Me those that deny
the truth, those that enjoy the comforts of this life; bear
with them yet a little while. We have in store for them
heavy fetters and a blazing fire, choking food and a harrowing torment. This shall be their lot on the day when the 73:14
earth shakes with all its mountains, and the mountains
crumble into heaps of shifting sand.

We have sent forth to you an apostle to testify against
you, just as We sent one to Pharaoh before you. Pharaoh
disobeyed Our messenger, so that We smote him with a
dreadful scourge.

If you persist in unbelief, how will you escape the day
that will make your children grey-haired, the day on which
the heaven will split apart? Allah's promise shall be fulfilled.

This is but an admonition. Let him who will, take the
right path to his Lord.

Your Lord knows that you[3] sometimes keep vigil nearly 73:20
two-thirds of the night and sometimes half or one-third of
it, as do others among your followers. Allah measures the

1. Mohammed.　　2. The unbelievers.　　3. Mohammed.

night and the day. He knows that you[1] cannot with precision count the hours, and turns to you mercifully. Recite from the Koran as many verses as you are able; He knows that among you there are sick men and others travelling the road in quest of Allah's bounty; and yet others fighting for His cause. Recite from it, then, as many verses as you are able. Attend to your prayers, pay the alms-tax, and give Allah a generous loan. Whatever good you do you shall surely find it with Allah, ennobled and richly rewarded by Him. Implore Allah to forgive you; He is forgiving and merciful.

THE INEVITABLE

In the Name of Allah, the Compassionate, the Merciful

69:1 THE Inevitable: and what is the Inevitable? Would that you knew!

Thamoud and Aad denied the Last Judgement. By a deafening shout was Thamoud destroyed, and Aad by a howling, violent gale which He let loose on them for seven nights and eight long days: you might have seen them lying dead as though they had been hollow trunks of palm-trees. Can you see any of them still alive?

Pharaoh, and those before him, and the inhabitants of the Ruined Cities, also committed sin and disobeyed their Lord's apostle. With a terrible scourge He smote them.

When the Flood rose high We carried you[2] in the floating Ark, making the event a warning, so that all attentive ears might heed it.

When the Trumpet sounds a single blast; when earth with all its mountains is raised high and with one mighty crash is shattered into dust – on that day the Dread Event will come to pass.

Frail and tottering, the sky will be rent asunder on that 69:17 day, and the angels will stand on all its sides with eight of them carrying the throne of your Lord above their heads.

1. The believers.   2. i.e. Your forefathers.

On that day you shall be displayed before Him, and all 69:18
your secrets shall be brought to light.

He who is given his book in his right hand will say to his
companions: 'Take this, and read it! I knew that I should
come to my account.' His shall be a blissful state in a lofty
garden, with clusters of fruit within his reach. We shall say
to him: 'Eat and drink to your heart's content. Here is
your reward for what you did in days gone by.'

But he who is given his book in his left hand will say:
'Would that my book were not given me! Would that I
knew nothing of my account! Would that my death had 69:28
ended all! My wealth has availed me nothing and I am
bereft of all my power.'

We shall say: 'Lay hold of him and bind him. Burn him in
the fire of Hell, then fasten him with a chain seventy cubits
long. For he did not believe in Allah, the Most High, nor
did he care to feed the poor. Today he shall be friendless
here; filth shall be his food, the filth which sinners eat.'

I swear by all that you can see, and all that is hidden from
your view, that this is the utterance of a noble messenger.
It is no poet's speech: scant is your faith! It is no soothsayer's divination: how little you reflect! It is a revelation
from the Lord of all creatures.

Had he invented lies concerning Us, We would have
seized him by the right hand and cut off his heart's vein: not
one of you could have protected him!

It[1] is but an admonition to righteous men. We know that
there are some among you who will deny it.

It is the despair of the unbelievers. It is the indubitable
truth. Praise, then, the name of your Lord, the Almighty. 69:52

THE PEN

In the Name of Allah, the Compassionate, the Merciful

B Y the Pen, and what they[2] write, you[3] are not mad: 68:1
thanks to the favour of your Lord! A lasting recompense awaits you, for yours is a sublime nature. You 68:4

1. The Koran.   2. The angels.   3. Mohammed.

68:5 shall before long see – as they will see – which of you is mad.

Your Lord knows best those who stray from His path, and those who are rightly guided. Give no heed to the disbelievers: they desire you to overlook their doings that they may overlook yours. Nor yield to the wretch of many oaths, the mischief-making slanderer, the opponent of good, the wicked transgressor, the bully who is of doubtful birth to boot. Though such a man be blessed with wealth and children, when Our revelations are recited to him, he says: 'They are but fables of the ancients.' On the nose We will brand him!

We have afflicted them[1] as We afflicted the owners of the orchard who had declared that they would pluck its fruit next morning, without adding any reservation.[2] A visitant from Allah came down upon it while they slept and in the morning it was as black as midnight.

68:21 At daybreak they called out to one another, saying: 'Hurry to your orchard, if you would pick its fruit.' And off they went, whispering to one another: 'No beggar shall set foot today in our orchard.'

Thus they went out, fixed in their resolve. But when they saw it they cried: 'We have been wrong. We are utterly ruined.'

The most upright among them said: 'Did I not bid you praise Allah?'

'Glory to our Lord,' they answered. 'We have assuredly done wrong.' And they began to blame one another.

'Woe to us!' they cried. 'We have been great transgressors. We beseech our Lord to give us a better orchard in its place.'

Such was their punishment. But the punishment of the life to come is more terrible, if they but knew it.

With gardens of delight the righteous shall be rewarded by their Lord. Are We to deal with the true believers as We *68:36* deal with the wrongdoers? What has come over you[3] that you should judge so ill?

1. The Meccans.
2. Without saying: 'If Allah wills.'   3 The unbelievers.

Have you a scripture that promises you whatever you *68:37*
choose? Or have We sworn a covenant with you – a
covenant binding till the Day of Resurrection – that you
shall have what you yourselves ordain? Ask if any of them[1]
will vouch for that!

Or have they other gods besides Allah? Let them produce these gods, if what they say be true!

On the day when the dread event takes place and they
are bidden to prostrate themselves, they will not be able.
Utterly humbled, they shall stand with eyes downcast; for
they were already bidden to prostrate themselves when they
were safe.

Therefore leave to Me those that deny this revelation. We
will lead them step by step to their ruin, in ways beyond
their knowledge. I shall bear long with them: My stratagem *68:45*
is sure.

Are you demanding pay of them so that they are burdened with debt?

Or have they knowledge of what is hidden? Can they
write it down?

Wait, then, the judgement of your Lord and do not act
like him[2] who was swallowed by the whale when he called
out to Allah in despair. Had his Lord not bestowed on him
His grace, he would have been abandoned in the open to
be blamed by all. But his Lord chose him and made of him
a righteous man.

When they hear Our revelations, the unbelievers almost
devour you with their eyes. 'He is surely possessed,' they
say.

Yet it is a warning to all men.   *68:52*

1. The unbelievers.   2. Jonah.

JONAH

In the Name of Allah, the Compassionate, the Merciful

10:1 ALIF *lam ra*. These are the verses of the Wise Book:
Does it seem strange to mankind that We should
have revealed Our will to a mortal from among
themselves, saying: 'Give warning to mankind, and tell
the faithful their endeavours shall be rewarded by their
Lord?'

The unbelievers say: 'This man[1] is a skilled enchanter.'
Yet your Lord is Allah, who in six days created the heavens
and the earth and then ascended His throne, ordaining all
things. None has power to intercede for you to save him
who has received His sanction. Such is Allah, your Lord:
therefore serve Him. Will you not take heed?

To Him you shall all return: Allah's promise shall be fulfilled. He gives being to all His creatures, and in the end He
will bring them back to life, so that He may justly reward
those who have believed in Him and done good works. As
for the unbelievers, they shall drink boiling water and be
sternly punished for their unbelief.

10:5 It was He that gave the sun his brightness and the moon
her light, ordaining her phases that you may learn to compute the seasons and the years. He created them only to
manifest the truth. He makes plain His revelations to men
of understanding.

In the alternation of night and day, and in all that Allah
has created in the heavens and the earth, there are signs for
righteous men.

Those who deny that they will ever come before Us, delighting in the life of this world and contenting themselves
with it, and those who give no heed to Our revelations,
shall be cast into Hell and be punished for their misdeeds.

10:9 As for those that believe and do good works, Allah will
guide them through their faith. Rivers will run at their feet

1. Mohammed.

in the Gardens of Delight. Their prayer will be: 'Glory to *10:10* You, Lord!' and their greeting: 'Peace!' 'Praise be to Allah, Lord of the Creation,' will be the burden of their hymn.

Had Allah hastened the punishment of men as they would hasten their reward, their fate would have long been sealed. Therefore We let those who deny the Last Judgement blunder about in sin.

When misfortune befalls man, he prays to Us standing, sitting, and lying down. But as soon as We relieve his affliction he pursues his former ways, as though he never prayed for Our help. Thus their foul deeds seem fair to the transgressors.

We destroyed many generations before you when they did wrong and denied the veritable signs which their apostles had given them. Thus shall the guilty be rewarded. Then We made you their successors in the land, so that We might see how you would conduct yourselves.

When Our clear revelations are recited to them, those *10:15* that deny the Last Judgement say to you: 'Give us a different Koran, or make some changes in it.'

Say: 'It is not for me to change it. I follow only what is revealed to me. I cannot disobey my Lord, for I fear the punishment of a fateful day.'

Say: 'Had Allah pleased, I would never have recited it to you, nor would He have given you any knowledge of it. A whole life-time I dwelt amongst you before it was revealed. Will you not understand?'

Who is more wicked than the man who invents a falsehood about Allah or denies His revelations? Truly, the evil-doers shall not triumph.

They worship idols that can neither harm nor help them, and say: 'These will intercede for us with Allah.'

Say: 'Do you presume to tell Allah of what He knows to be neither in the heavens nor in the earth? Glory to Him! Exalted be He above their idols!'

There was a time when men followed but one religion. *10:19* Then they disagreed among themselves: and had Allah not deferred their punishment, their differences would have long been settled.

10:20 The unbelievers ask: 'Why has no sign been given him by his Lord?'

Say: 'Allah alone has knowledge of what is hidden. Wait if you will: I too am waiting!'

No sooner do We show mercy to a people after some misfortune has afflicted them than they begin to scheme against Our revelations. Say: 'More swift is Allah's scheming. Our angels are recording your intrigues.'

It is He who guides you by land and sea. You embark: and as you set sail, rejoicing in a favouring wind, a raging tempest overtakes you. Billows surge upon you from every side and you fear that you are encompassed by death. You pray to Allah with all fervour, saying: 'Deliver us from this peril and we will be truly thankful.'

Yet when He has delivered you, you commit evil in the land and act unjustly.

Men, it is your own souls that you are corrupting. Take your enjoyment in this life: to Us you shall in the end return, and We will declare to you all that you have done.

10:24 This present life is like the golden robe with which the earth bedecks itself when watered by the rain. Crops, sustaining man and beast, grow luxuriantly: but as its hopeful tenants prepare themselves for the rich harvest, down comes Our scourge upon it, by night or in broad day, laying it waste, even though it blossomed but yesterday. Thus We make plain Our revelations to thoughtful men.

Allah invites you to the Home of Peace. He guides whom He will to a straight path. Those that do good works shall be rewarded with abundant blessings. Neither blackness nor misery shall cover their faces. They are the heirs of Paradise: in it they shall abide for ever.

10:27 As for those that have earned evil, evil shall be rewarded with like evil. Misery will cover them (they shall have none to defend them from Allah), as though their faces were veiled with the night's black darkness. They are the heirs of Hell: in it they shall abide for ever.

On the day when We assemble them all together, We 10:28
shall say to the idolaters: 'Keep to your places, you and your
idols!' We will separate them one from another, and then
their idols will say to them: 'It was not us that you worshipped. Allah is our all-sufficient witness: we were unaware of your worship.'

Thereupon each soul will know what it has done. They
shall be sent back to Allah, their true Lord, and the idols
they invented will forsake them.

Say: 'Who provides for you from heaven and earth? Who
has endowed you with sight and hearing? Who brings
forth the living from the dead, and the dead from the living? Who ordains all things?'

They will reply: 'Allah.'

Say: 'Will you not take heed, then? Such is Allah, your
true Lord. That which is not true must needs be false. How
then can you turn away from Him?'

Thus the word of your Lord is made good. The evil-
doers have no faith.

Say: 'Can any of your idols conceive Creation, then 10:34
renew it? Allah conceives Creation, then renews it. How is
it that you are so misled?'

Say: 'Can any of your idols guide you to the truth? Allah
can guide you to the truth. Who is more worthy to be followed: He that can guide to the truth or he that cannot and
is himself in need of guidance? What has come over you
that you cannot judge?'

Most of them follow nothing but mere conjecture. But
conjecture is no substitute for Truth. Allah is cognizant of
all their actions.

This Koran could not have been composed by any but
Allah. It confirms what was revealed before it and fully
explains the Scriptures. It is beyond doubt from the Lord
of the Creation.

If they say: 'It is your own invention,' say: 'Compose
one chapter like it. Call on your false gods to help you, if
what you say be true!'

Indeed, they disbelieve what they cannot grasp, for 10:39

events have not yet justified it. Those who passed before them acted in the same way. But see what was the end of the wrong-doers.

10:40   Some believe in it, while others do not. But your Lord best knows the evil-doers.

If they disbelieve you, say: 'My deeds are mine and your deeds are yours. You are not accountable for my actions, nor am I for yours.'

Some of them listen to you. But can you make the deaf hear you, incapable as they are of understanding?

Some of them look upon you. But can you show the way to the blind, bereft as they are of sight?

Indeed, Allah does not in any way wrong mankind, but they wrong themselves.

The day will come when He will gather them again, as though they had stayed away but an hour. They will recognize one another. Lost are those that disbelieve in meeting their Lord and do not follow the right path.

10:46   Whether We let you witness the scourge with which We threaten them, or cause you to die before it falls upon them, to Us they shall return. Allah is watching over all their actions.

An apostle is sent to every nation. When their apostle comes, justice is done among them; they are not wronged.

They ask: 'When will this promise be fulfilled, if what you say be true?'

Say: 'I have not the power to acquire benefits or to avert evil from myself, except by the will of Allah. A space of time is fixed for every nation; when their hour is come, not for one moment shall they delay: nor can they go before it.'

Say: 'Tell me. Should His scourge fall upon you by night or by day, what punishment would the guilty hasten? Will you believe in it when it overtakes you? You will surely believe in it then! Yet you challenge its fulfilment.'

10:52   On that day it shall be said to the wrongdoers: 'Feel the everlasting torment! Shall you not be rewarded according to your deeds?'

They ask if it is true. Say to them: 'It is, by the Lord! 10:53 You shall not escape.'

To redeem himself on that day, each sinner would gladly give all that the earth contains if he possessed it. When they face their punishment they will avow repentance. But judgement shall be fairly passed upon them; they shall not be wronged.

To Allah belongs all that the heavens and the earth contain. The promise of Allah is true, though most of them may not know it. It is He who ordains life and death, and to Him you shall all return.

Men, an admonition has come to you from your Lord, a healing ointment for your souls, a guide and a blessing to true believers.

Say: 'Let them rejoice in Allah's grace and mercy, for these are better than the worldly riches they amass.'

Say: 'Tell me. Which of the things that Allah has given you have you pronounced unlawful and which of them do you regard as lawful? Has Allah given you His leave, or do you invent falsehoods in His name?'

What will those who invent falsehoods about Allah think 10:60 on the Day of Resurrection? Allah is bountiful to men: yet most of them do not give thanks.

We are the witnesses of all your thoughts and all your prayers and all your actions. Not an atom's weight in earth or heaven escapes your Lord, nor is there any object smaller or greater, but is recorded in a glorious book.

The servants of Allah have nothing to fear or to regret. Those that have faith and keep from evil shall rejoice both in this world and in the next: the word of Allah cannot be changed. That is the supreme triumph.

Let their words not grieve you. All glory belongs to Allah. He alone hears all and knows all.

To Allah belong all who dwell on earth and in heaven. Those that worship false gods follow nothing but idle fancies and preach nothing but falsehoods.

He it is who has ordained the night for your rest and 10:67

given the day its light. Surely in this there are signs for prudent men.

10:68 They say: 'Allah has begotten a son.' Allah forbid! Self-sufficient is He. His is all that the heavens and the earth contain. Surely for this you have no sanction. Would you say of Allah what you do not know?

Say: 'Those that invent falsehoods about Allah shall not triumph. They may take their ease in this life, but to Us they shall in the end return, and We will sternly punish them for their unbelief.'

Recount to them the tale of Noah. He said to his people: 'If it offends you that I should dwell in your midst and preach to you Allah's revelations (for in Him I have put my trust), muster all your idols and decide your course of action. Do not intrigue in secret. Execute your judgement and give me no respite. Do not turn away from me; I demand of you no recompense. Allah will reward me. I am commanded to surrender myself to Him.'

10:73 But they disbelieved him. Therefore We saved Noah and those who were with him in the Ark, so that they survived the Flood, and drowned the others who denied Our revelations. Consider the fate of those who were given warning.

After that we sent apostles to their descendants. They showed them veritable signs, but they persisted in their unbelief. Thus We seal up the hearts of the transgressors.

Then We sent forth Moses and Aaron with Our signs to Pharaoh and his nobles. But they rejected them with scorn, for they were wicked men. When Our truth was shown to them they said: 'This is plain magic.'

Moses replied: 'Do you call the truth magic? Magicians never prosper.'

They said: 'Have you come to turn us away from the faith of our fathers, so that you two may become rulers in the land? We will never believe in you.'

Then Pharaoh said: 'Bring every skilled magician to my presence.'

When the magicians came Moses said to them: 'Cast *10:81* down your staffs.' And when they had thrown down their staffs he said: 'Allah will surely confound your sorcery. He does not bless the work of the evil-doers. By His words He vindicates the truth, much as the guilty may dislike it.' *10:82*

Few of his[1] people believed in Moses, for they feared the persecution of Pharaoh and his nobles. Pharaoh was a tyrant in the land, an evil-doer.

Moses said: 'If you believe in Allah, my people, and have surrendered yourselves to Him, in Him alone put your trust.'

They replied: 'In Allah we have put our trust. Lord, do not let us suffer at the hands of wicked men. Deliver us, through Your mercy, from the unbelievers.'

We revealed Our will to Moses and his brother, saying: 'Build houses in Egypt for your people and make your homes places of worship. Conduct prayers and give good news to the faithful.'

'Lord,' said Moses. 'You have bestowed on Pharaoh and his princes splendour and riches in this life, so that they may stray from Your path. Lord, destroy their riches and harden their hearts, so that they shall persist in unbelief until they face their woeful punishment.'

Allah replied: 'Your prayer is heard. Follow the right *10:89* path and do not walk in the footsteps of ignorant men.'

We led the Israelites across the sea, and Pharaoh and his legions pursued them with wickedness and hate. But as he was drowning, Pharaoh cried: 'Now I believe that there is no god save the God in whom the Israelites believe. To Him I give up myself.'

'Now you believe!' Allah replied. 'But before this you were a rebel and a wrongdoer. We shall save your body this day, so that you may become a sign to all posterity: for most men give no heed to Our signs.'

We settled the Israelites in a blessed land and provided them with good things. Nor did they disagree among themselves until knowledge was given them. Your Lord will judge their differences on the Day of Resurrection.

If you doubt what We have revealed to you, ask those *10:94*

1. Pharaoh's.

who have read the Scriptures before you. The truth has come to you from your Lord: therefore do not doubt it. *10:95* Nor shall you deny the revelations of Allah, for then you shall be lost.

Those concerning whom the word of your Lord will be fulfilled will not have faith, even if they witness every sign, until they face their woeful punishment. Had this been otherwise, every nation, had it believed, would have profited from its faith. But it was so only with Jonah's people. When they believed, We spared them the penalty of disgrace in this life and gave them comfort for a while. Had your Lord pleased, all the people of the earth would have believed in Him. Would you then force faith upon men?

None can have faith except by the will of Allah. He will visit His scourge upon the senseless.

Say: 'Behold what the heavens and the earth contain!' But neither signs nor warnings will avail the unbelievers.

What can they wait for but the fate of those who have gone before them? Say: 'Wait if you will; I too am waiting.'

10:103 We shall save Our apostles and the true believers. It is but just that We should save the faithful.

Say: 'Men! If you are in doubt concerning my religion, know that I worship none of your idols. I serve Allah, to whom you shall all return: for I am commanded to be one of the faithful. I was bidden: "Dedicate yourself to the Faith in all uprightness and serve none beside Allah. Do not pray to idols which can neither help nor harm you, for if you do you will become a wrongdoer. If Allah afflicts you with a misfortune none can remove it but He; and if He bestows on you a favour, none can withhold His bounty. He is bountiful to whom He will. He is the Forgiving One, the Merciful."'

Say: 'Men! The truth has come to you from your Lord. He that follows the right path follows it to his own advantage, and he that goes astray does so at his own peril. I am not your keeper.'

10:109 Observe what is revealed to you, and have patience till Allah makes known his judgement. He is the best of judges.

SOVEREIGNTY

In the Name of Allah, the Compassionate, the Merciful

BLESSED be He to whom all sovereignty belongs: He 67:1
has power over all things.

He created life and death that He might put you to the proof and find out which of you acquitted himself best. He is the Mighty, the Forgiving One.

He created seven heavens, one above the other. His work is faultless. Turn up your eyes: can you detect a single flaw?

Then look once more and yet again: your eyes will in the end grow dim and weary.

We have adorned the lowest heaven with lamps, missiles for pelting devils. We have prepared a scourge of flames for these, and the scourge of Hell for unbelievers: an evil fate!

When they are flung into its fire they shall hear it roaring 67:7 and seething as though bursting with rage. And every time a multitude is thrown therein, its keepers will say to them: 'Did no one come to warn you?' 'Yes,' they will reply, 'but we rejected him and said: "Allah has revealed nothing: you are in grave error."' And they will say: 'If only we listened and understood, we should not now be among the tenants of Hell.'

Thus they shall confess their sin. Far from Allah's mercy are the heirs of Hell.

But those that fear their Lord although they cannot see Him shall be forgiven and richly rewarded.

Whether you speak in secret or aloud, He knows your inmost thoughts. Shall He who has created all things not know them all? He is wise and all-knowing.

It is He who has subdued the earth to you. Walk about its regions and eat of His provisions. To Him all shall return at the Resurrection.

Are you confident that He who is in heaven will not 67:16 cause the earth to cave in beneath you, so that it will shake to pieces and overwhelm you?

67:17   Are you confident that He who is in heaven will not let loose on you a sandy whirlwind? You shall before long know the truth of My warning.

Those who have gone before you also denied their apostles: but how terrible was My vengeance!

Do they not see the birds above their heads, spreading their wings and closing them? None save the Merciful sustains them. He observes all things.

Who is it that will defend you like an entire army, if not the Merciful? Truly, the unbelievers are in error.

Who will provide for you if *He* withholds His sustenance? Yet they persist in arrogance and in rebellion.

Who is more rightly guided, he that goes grovelling on his face, or he that walks upright upon a straight path?

Say: 'It is He who has created you and given you ears and eyes and hearts. Yet you are seldom thankful.'

67:24   Say: 'It was He who placed you on the earth, and before Him you shall all be assembled.'

They ask: 'When will this promise be fulfilled, if what you say be true?'

Say: 'Allah alone has knowledge of that. My mission is but to warn you plainly.'

But when they see it drawing near, the faces of the unbelievers will turn black with gloom and a voice will say: 'This is the doom which you have challenged.'

Say: 'Think: whether Allah destroys me and all my followers or has mercy upon us, who will protect the unbelievers from the woeful scourge?'

Say: 'He is the Lord of Mercy: in Him we believe and in Him we put our trust. You shall soon know who is in grave error.'

67:30   Say: 'Think: if all the water that you have were to sink down into the earth, who would give you running water in its place?'

THE STORY

In the Name of Allah, the Compassionate, the Merciful

T̲A *sin mim*. These are the revelations of the Glorious 28:1
Book. In all truth We shall recount to you some of
the history of Moses and Pharaoh for the instruction
of the faithful.

Now Pharaoh made himself a tyrant in the land. He
divided his people into castes, one group of which he
persecuted, putting their sons to death and sparing their
daughters. Truly, he was an evil-doer.

But it was Our will to favour those who were oppressed
and to make them leaders of mankind, to bestow on them
a noble heritage and to give them power in the land; and
to inflict on Pharaoh, Haman, and their army, the very
scourge dreaded by their victims.

We revealed Our will to Moses' mother, saying: 'Give
him suck, but if you are concerned about his safety put him
down the river. Have no fears, nor be dismayed; for We
shall restore him to you and make him one of the apostles.'

But it was decreed that Pharaoh's household should take 28:8
him up, so that he might become their adversary and their
scourge. For Pharaoh, Haman, and their warriors were
sinners all.

His wife said to Pharaoh: 'This child may bring us joy.
Do not slay him. He may show promise and we may adopt
him as our son.' But they little knew what they were doing.

His mother's heart was sorely troubled. She would have
revealed who he was, had We not given her strength so that
she might become a true believer. She said to Moses' sister:
'Go, and follow him.'

She watched him from a distance, unseen by others. Now
We had caused him to refuse the breasts of his nurses. His
sister said to them: 'Shall I direct you to a family who will
bring him up for you and take good care of him?'

Thus We restored him to his mother, so that she might 28:13

75

rejoice in him and grieve no more, and that she might know that Allah's promise was true. Yet most men are not aware of this.

28:14 And when he had reached maturity and grown to manhood We bestowed on him wisdom and knowledge. Thus We reward the righteous.

One day he entered the town unnoticed by the people and found two men fighting, the one of his own race, the other an enemy. The Israelite appealed for Moses' help against his enemy, so that Moses struck him with his fist and killed him. 'This is the work of Satan,' said Moses. 'He is the sworn enemy of man and seeks to lead him astray. Forgive me, Lord, for I have sinned against my soul.'

And Allah forgave him; for He is the Forgiving One, the Merciful. He said: 'By the favour You have shown me, Lord, I vow that I will never lend a helping hand to a wrong-doer.'

Next morning, as he was walking in the town in fear and caution, the man he had helped the day before cried out to him again for help. 'Clearly,' said Moses, 'you are a quarrelsome man.'

28:19 And when Moses was about to lay his hands on their enemy, the Egyptian said: 'Moses, would you kill me as you killed that wretch yesterday? You are surely seeking to be a tyrant in this land, not an upright man.'

But someone came running from the other end of the city. 'Moses,' he cried, 'the elders are plotting to kill you. Fly for your life, if you will heed my counsel!'

He went away in fear and vigilance, saying: 'Lord, deliver me from these evil men.' And as he made his way towards Midian, he said: 'May the Lord guide me to the even path.'

28:23 When he came to the well of Midian he found around it a band of men watering their flocks, and beside them two women who were keeping back their sheep. 'What is your trouble?' he asked.

They replied: 'We cannot water them until the shepherds have driven away their flocks. Our father is an aged man.'

Moses watered for them their sheep and then retired to *28:24*
the shade, saying: 'Lord, I stand in need of the blessing
which you have sent me.'

One of the girls came bashfully towards him and said:
'My father calls you. He wishes to reward you for watering
our flock.'

And when Moses went and recounted to him his story,
the old man said: 'Fear nothing. You are now safe from
those wicked men.'

One of the girls said: 'Father, take this man into your
service. Men who are strong and honest are the best that
one can hire.'

The old man said: 'I will give you one of my daughters in
marriage if you stay for eight years in my service; but if you
wish it you may stay ten. I shall not deal harshly with you;
Allah willing, you shall find me an upright man.'

'So be it,' said Moses. 'Whichever term I fulfil, I trust
that I shall not be wronged. Allah is the witness of what we
say.'

And when he had fulfilled his term and was journeying *28:29*
with his folk, Moses descried a fire on the mountain-side.
He said to his people: 'Stay here, for I can see a fire. Perhaps I can bring you news, or a lighted torch with which
you may warm yourselves.'

When he came near, a voice called out to him from a
bush in a blessed spot on the right side of the valley, saying: 'Moses, I am Allah, Lord of the Creation. Throw down
your staff.'

And when he saw his staff writhing like a serpent, he
turned his back and fled, running on and on.

'Moses,' said the voice, 'approach and have no fears.
You are safe. Put your hand in your pocket: it will come
out white, although unharmed. Now draw back your hand,
and do not stretch it out in consternation. These are two
signs from your Lord for Pharaoh and his people. Truly,
they are evil-doers.'

'Lord,' said Moses, 'I have killed one of their men and fear
that they will slay me. Aaron my brother is more fluent in *28:34*

77

speech than I; send him with me that he may help me and confirm my words, for I fear that they will deny me.'

28:35 He replied: 'We will give you your brother to help you, and bestow such power on you both, that none shall harm you. Set forth, with Our signs. You, and those who follow you, shall surely triumph.'

And when Moses came to them with Our undoubted signs, they said: 'This is nothing but deceitful magic; nor have we heard of the like among our forefathers.'

Moses replied: 'My Lord knows best the man who brings guidance from His presence and gains the reward of Paradise. The wrongdoers shall never prosper.'

'Nobles,' said Pharaoh, 'you have no other god that I know of except myself. Make me, Haman, bricks of clay, and build for me a tower that I may climb to the god of Moses. I am convinced that he is lying.'

28:39 Pharaoh and his warriors conducted themselves with pride and injustice, and thought they would never be recalled to Us. But Our vengeance overtook them and We cast them into the sea. Consider the fate of the evil-doers.

We made them leaders of unbelief. They called men to Hell-fire, but on the Day of Resurrection none shall help them. In this world We laid Our curse on them, and on the Day of Resurrection We shall dishonour them.

And after We had destroyed the previous generations We gave Moses the Scriptures as a clear testimony, a guide and a blessing for men, so that they might give thought.

You[1] were not present on the western side of the Mountain when We charged Moses with his commission, nor did you witness the event. We raised many generations after him whose lives We prolonged. You did not dwell among the people of Midian, nor did you recite to them Our revelations; for We sent forth to them other apostles.

28:46 You were not present on the Mountain-side when We called out to Moses. Yet We have sent you forth as a blessing from your Lord to forewarn a nation to whom no apostle has been sent before, so that they may take heed and

1. Mohammed.

may not say, when evil befalls them on account of their 28:47
misdeeds: 'Lord, had You sent us an apostle, we should
have obeyed Your revelations and believed in them.'

And now that they have received from Us the truth they
ask: 'Why is he not given the like of what was given to
Moses?' But do they not deny what was given to Moses?
They say: 'Two works¹ of magic supporting one another!' And they declare: 'We will believe in neither of
them.'

Say: 'Bring down from Allah a scripture that is a better
guide than these and I will follow it, if what you say be
true!'

If they make no answer, know that they are the slaves of
their caprices. And who is in greater error than the man who
is led by his caprice without guidance from Allah? Allah
does not guide the evil-doers.

We have sent Our Word to them so that they may give
thought. Those to whom the Scriptures were given before 28:52
this believe in it. When it is recited to them they say: 'We
believe in it because it is the truth from Our Lord. We
surrendered ourselves to Him long before it came.'

Twice shall their reward be given them, because they
have endured with fortitude, requiting evil with good and
giving in alms a part of that which We bestowed on them;
and because they pay no heed to those that slander them,
but rather wish them peace, saying: 'We have our actions
and you have yours. We do not seek the company of
ignorant men.'

You cannot guide whom you please: it is Allah who
guides whom He will. He best knows those who yield to
guidance.

They say: 'If we accept your guidance, we shall be
driven from our land.' But have We not given them a
sanctuary of safety to which fruits of every kind are brought
as a provision from Ourself? Indeed, most of them are
ignorant men.

How many nations have We destroyed who once 28:58

1. The Torah and the Koran.

79

flourished in wanton ease! Their dwellings are but rarely inhabited; We were their only heirs.

28:59 Nor did your Lord destroy them until He had sent apostles to their capital cities proclaiming to them Our revelations. We destroyed them only because they sinned.

The things you have been given are but the provision and the gaudy show of this present life. Better is Allah's reward and more lasting. Have you no sense to reason with?

Can he who has received Our gracious promise, and will see it fulfilled, be compared with him to whom We have given the comforts of this life and who will be summoned on the Day of Resurrection?

On that day Allah will call to them, saying: 'Where are the gods whom you alleged to be My partners?'

Those who have justly earned Our doom will say: 'Lord, these are the men whom we misled. We led them astray as we ourselves were led astray. We plead innocent before You; it was not us that they worshipped.'

28:64 Then a voice will say to them: 'Call on your idols!' And they will call on them, but they shall get no answer. They shall see Our punishment and wish that they were rightly guided.

On that day Allah will call to them, saying: 'What answer did you give Our apostles?' And on that day such will their confusion be that they will ask no questions. But those that repent and embrace the faith and do what is right may hope for salvation.

Your Lord creates what He will and chooses freely, but their idols have no power to choose. Glorified and exalted be He above their false gods!

Your Lord knows what their bosoms hide and what they reveal. He is Allah: there is no god but Him. Praise is His in this world and in the next. His is the power supreme. To Him you shall be recalled.

Say: 'Think! If Allah should enshroud you in perpetual night till the Day of Resurrection, what other god could give you light? Have you no ears to hear with?'

28:72 Say: 'Think! If Allah should give you perpetual day until the Resurrection, what other god could bring you the night to sleep in? Have you no eyes to see with?'

In His mercy He has given you the night that you may   *28:73* rest in it, and the day that you may seek His bounty and render thanks.

On that day He will call out to them, saying: 'Where are the gods whom you alleged to be My partners?' From every nation We will bring a witness, and We shall say to them: 'Show Us your proof.' Then they shall know that the truth is Allah's, and the gods of their own invention will forsake them.

Korah was one of Moses' people. But he treated them with insolence, for We had given him such treasures that their very keys would have weighed down a band of sturdy men. His people said to him: 'Do not exult in your riches; Allah does not love the exultant. But seek, by means of that which Allah has given you, to attain the Paradise to come. Do not forget your share in this world. Be good to others as Allah has been good to you, and do not strive for evil in the land, for Allah does not love the evil-doers.'

But he replied: 'These riches were given me on account   *28:78* of the knowledge I possess.'

Did he not know that Allah had destroyed before him men who were mightier and more opulent than he? The wrongdoers shall not be questioned about their sins.

And when he went out in all his finery among his people, those who loved this life said: 'Would that we had the like of Korah's fortune! He is indeed a lucky man.'

But those to whom knowledge had been given said: 'Alas for you! Better is the reward of Allah for him that has faith and does good works; but none shall attain it save those who have endured with fortitude.'

We caused the earth to swallow him, together with his dwelling, so that he found none to protect him from Allah; nor was he delivered from Our scourge. And those who on   *28:82* the day before had coveted his lot began to say: 'Behold! Allah gives abundantly to whom He will and sparingly to whom He pleases. Had He not shown us favour, He could have caused the earth to swallow us. Behold! The ungrateful shall never prosper.'

28:83   As for the Paradise to come, it shall be theirs who seek neither glory in this world nor evil. The righteous shall have a blessed end.

He that does good shall be rewarded with what is better. But he that does evil shall be requited with evil.

He who has committed the Koran to your keeping will surely bring you home[1] again. Say: 'My Lord best knows him who brings guidance and him who is in gross error.'

You never hoped that this Book would be revealed to you. Yet through your Lord's mercy you have received it. Therefore give no help to the unbelievers. Let no one turn you away from Allah's revelations, now that they have been revealed to you. Call men to your Lord, and serve none besides Him.

28:88   Invoke no other god with Allah. There is no god but Him. All things shall perish except Himself. His is the judgement, and to Him you shall return.

THE ANT

In the Name of Allah, the Compassionate, the Merciful

27:1   TA *sin*. These are the revelations of the Koran, the Glorious Book; a guide and joyful news to true believers, who attend to their prayers and pay the alms-tax and firmly believe in the life to come.

As for those that deny the life to come, We make their foul deeds seem fair to them, so that they blunder about in their folly. They shall be sternly punished and in the hereafter have much to lose.

You have received the Koran from Him who is wise and all-knowing. Tell of Moses, who said to his people: 'I can descry a fire. I will go and bring you news and a lighted torch with which you may warm yourselves.'

27:8   And when he came near, a voice called out to him:

1. To Mecca.

'Blessed be He who is in this fire and all around it! Glory to Allah, Lord of the Creation! Moses, I am Allah, the Mighty, 27:9 the Wise One. Throw down your staff.'

And when he saw his staff writhing like a serpent, he turned his back and fled, running on and on.

'Moses, do not be alarmed,' said He. 'My apostles are never afraid in My presence. As for those who sin and then do good instead of evil, I am forgiving and merciful to them.

'Put your hand into your pocket. It will come out white, although unharmed. This is but one of the nine signs which shall be shown to Pharaoh and his people; for, truly, they are wicked men.'

But when Our undoubted signs were shown to them, they said: 'This is plain witchcraft.' Their souls knew them to be true, yet they denied them in their wickedness and their pride. Consider the fate of the evil-doers.

We bestowed knowledge on David and Solomon. They said: 'Praise be to Allah who has exalted us above many of His believing servants.'

Solomon succeeded David. He said: 'Know, my people, 27:16 we have been taught the tongue of birds and endowed with all good things. Surely this is a signal favour.'

Solomon marshalled his forces of jinn and men and birds, and set them in battle array. When they came to the Valley of the Ants, an ant said to her sisters: 'Go into your dwellings, ants, lest Solomon and his warriors should unwittingly crush you.'

Solomon smiled at her words, and said: 'Inspire me, Lord, to render thanks for the favours You have bestowed on me and on my parents, and to do good works that will please You. Admit me, through Your mercy, among Your righteous servants.'

He inspected his birds and said: 'Where is the lapwing? I cannot see him here. If he does not give me a good excuse, I shall sternly punish him or even slay him.'

The bird, who was not long in coming, said: 'I have just 27:22 seen what you know nothing of. With truthful news I come

27:23 to you from Sheba, where I found a woman reigning over the people. She is possessed of every virtue and has a splendid throne. But she and her subjects worship the sun instead of Allah. Satan has seduced them and debarred them from the right path, so that they might not be guided to the worship of Allah, who brings to light all that is concealed in heaven and earth and knows what you hide and what you reveal. Allah; there is no god but Him, the Lord of the Glorious Throne.'

Solomon replied: 'We shall soon see if what you say is true or false. Go and deliver to them this message of mine. Then turn aside and wait their answer.'

The Queen of Sheba said: 'Know, my nobles, that I have received a gracious message. It is from Solomon and reads as follows: "In the Name of Allah, the Compassionate, the Merciful. Do not exalt yourselves above me, but come to me in all submission." Nobles, let me hear your counsel, for I make no decision without your consent.'

27:33 They replied: 'We are a valiant and mighty nation. It is for you to command, and we shall wait your pleasure.'

She said: 'When a king invades a city he ruins it and enslaves its chieftains. These men will do the same. But I shall send them a present and see with what reply my envoys will return.'

And when her envoy came to him, Solomon said: 'Is it gold that you would give me? That which Allah has bestowed on me is better than all the riches He has given you. Yet you glory in your gift. Go back to your people: we will march against them with forces they cannot oppose, and drive them from their land humbled and contemned.'

And to his nobles he said: 'Which of you will bring to me her throne, before they sue for peace?'

A demon from among the jinn replied: 'I will bring it to you before you rise from your seat. I am strong enough and faithful.'

27:40 But he who was deeply versed in the Scriptures[1], said: 'I will bring it to you in a twinkling.'

1. Assaf ben Berachia, according to the commentators.

And when he saw it set before him, Solomon said: 'This is a favour from Allah with which He would test my gratitude. He that gives thanks has much to gain; but he who is ungrateful ... Allah is all-sufficient and bountiful!'

Then he said: 'Let her throne be altered, so that we may *27:41* see whether or not she will recognize it.'

And when she came to Solomon, she was asked: 'Is your throne like this?' And she replied: 'It resembles it.'

Solomon said: 'Before her we were given knowledge, and before her we surrendered to Allah. Her false gods have led her astray, for she comes from an unbelieving nation.'

She was bidden to enter the palace; and when she saw it she thought it was a pool of water and bared her legs. But Solomon said: 'It is a palace paved with glass.'

'Lord,' she said, 'I have sinned against my own soul. Now I submit with Solomon to Allah, Lord of the Creation.'

To Thamoud We sent their compatriot Saleh. He said: *27:45* 'Serve none but Allah.' But they divided themselves into two warring factions.

'My people,' he said, 'why do you wish to hasten evil rather than good? If you seek forgiveness of Allah, you may yet receive His mercy.'

They said: 'We presage evil from you and from your followers.'

He replied: 'The evil you presage can come only from Allah; you are being put to the proof.'

In the town there was a band of nine men, who did evil in the land and nothing that was good. They said: 'Let us swear by Allah to kill him in the night, together with all his household. We will say to his next of kin: "We were not even present when they were killed. It is the truth we are telling."'

Thus they plotted: but We too plotted, without their knowledge. And behold the consequences of their plots! We destroyed them utterly, together with all their people. Because they sinned, their dwellings are desolate ruins. *27:52*

27:53 Surely in this there is a sign for prudent men. But We delivered the true believers and those who kept from evil.

And tell of Lot. He said to his people: 'Are you blind that you should commit indecency, lustfully seeking men instead of women? Surely you are an ignorant people.'

Yet this was their reply: 'Banish the house of Lot from your city. They are men who would keep chaste.'

So We delivered him and all his tribe, except his wife, whom We caused to stay behind, pelting the others with rain; and evil was the rain which fell on those who had been warned.

Say: 'Praise be to Allah and peace upon His servants whom He has chosen! Who is more worthy, Allah or the idols they serve besides Him? Surely worthier is He who made the heavens and the earth. He sends down water from the sky, bringing forth gardens of delight. Try as you may, you cannot cause such trees to grow.' Another god besides Allah? Yet they set up equals with Him.

27:61 Surely worthier is He who has established the earth and watered it with running rivers; who has set mountains upon it and placed a barrier between the Two Seas. Another god besides Allah? Indeed, most of them are ignorant men.

Surely worthier is He who answers the oppressed when they cry out to Him and relieves their affliction. It is He who has given you the earth to inherit. Another god besides Allah? How little you reflect!

Surely worthier is He who guides you in the darkness of land and sea and sends the winds as harbingers of His mercy. Another god besides Allah? Exalted be He above their idols!

Surely worthier is He who has made His creatures and who will hereafter bring them back to life; who gives you sustenance from earth and sky. Another god besides Allah? Say: 'Show us your proof, if what you say be true!'

27:65 Say: 'No one in the heavens or the earth has knowledge of what is hidden except Allah. Nor shall men ever know when they will be raised to life.'

Have they attained a knowledge of the life to come? *27:66*
By no means! They are in doubt about it and their eyes are
sealed.

The unbelievers say: 'When we and our fathers are turned
to dust, shall we be raised to life? We were promised this
once before, and so were our fathers. It is but a fable of the
ancients.'

Say: 'Roam the world and see what was the end of the
guilty.' Do not grieve for them, nor be distressed at their
intrigues.

And they ask: 'When will this promise be fulfilled, if
what you say be true?'

Say: 'A part of what you challenge may well be near at
hand.'

Your Lord is bountiful to men: yet most of them do not *27:73*
give thanks.

Your Lord has knowledge of what they hide in their
bosoms and what they say aloud. There is no secret in
heaven or earth but is recorded in His glorious book.

This Koran declares to the Israelites most of that concerning which they disagree. It is a guide and a blessing to
true believers. Your Lord will rightly judge them. He is the
Mighty One, the All-knowing. Therefore put your trust in
Allah, for the undoubted truth is on your side.

The dead cannot hear you, nor can you make the deaf
hear your call when they turn their backs and pay no heed.
It is not for you to guide the blind out of their error. None
shall hear you except those who believe in Our revelations
and surrender themselves to Us.

On the day when Our judgement overtakes them, We
will bring out from the earth a monster that shall speak to
them. Truly, men have no faith in Our revelations.

On that day there shall be gathered from every nation a
multitude of those who disbelieved Our revelations. They
shall be led in separate bands before Allah, who will say to
them: 'You denied My revelations although you knew nothing of them. What was it you were doing?' Our doom *27:85*

will smite them for their sins, and they shall be dumb-founded.

27:86 Do they not see how We have made the night for them to rest in and the day to give them light? Surely there are signs in this for true believers.

On that day the Trumpet shall be sounded and all who dwell in heaven and earth be seized with fear, except those whom Allah will be pleased to save. All shall come to Him in utter humility.

The mountains, for all their firmness, will pass away like clouds. Such is the might of Allah, who has rightly disposed all things. He has knowledge of all your actions.

Those that have done good shall be rewarded with what is better, and shall be secure from the terrors of that day.

27:90 But those that have done evil shall be hurled headlong into the Fire. Shall you not be rewarded according to your deeds?

Say: 'I am bidden to serve the Lord of this City, which He has made sacred. All things are His.

'I am commanded to surrender to Him, and to proclaim the Koran. He that takes the right path shall himself have much to gain.'

To him who goes astray, say: 'I have warned you.'

27:93 Then say: 'Praise be to Allah! He will show you His signs and you will recognize them. Your Lord is watching over all your actions.'

CHEATING

In the Name of Allah, the Compassionate, the Merciful

64:1 ALL that is in heaven and earth gives glory to Allah. His is the sovereignty, and His the glory. He has power over all things.

It was He that created you: yet some of you are un-believers, while others have faith. He is cognizant of all your actions.

He created the heavens and the earth to manifest the truth *64:3* and fashioned you into a comely shape. To Him you shall all return.

He knows what the heavens and the earth contain. He knows all that you hide and all that you reveal. He knows your inmost thoughts.

Have you not heard of those who disbelieved before you? They tasted the fruit of their unbelief, and a grievous punishment is yet in store for them. That is because, when their apostles brought them veritable signs, they said: 'Shall mortals be our guides?' They denied the truth and gave no heed. But Allah was in no need of them: He is self-sufficient and glorious.

The unbelievers deny the Resurrection. Say: 'By the Lord, you shall assuredly be raised to life! Then you shall be told of all that you have done. That is easy enough for Allah.'

Believe then in Allah and His apostle and in the light which We have revealed. Allah has knowledge of all your actions.

The day on which He will assemble you, the day on *64:9* which you shall all be gathered – that shall be a day of cheating.[1] Those that believe in Allah and do what is right shall be forgiven their sins and admitted to gardens watered by running streams, where they shall dwell for ever. That is the supreme triumph. But those that disbelieve Our revelations and deny them shall be the heirs of Hell and shall abide therein for ever. Evil shall be their fate.

No misfortune befalls except by Allah's will. He guides the hearts of those who believe in Him. Allah has knowledge of all things.

Obey Allah and obey the Apostle. If you give no heed to *64:12* him, know that Our apostle's duty is no more than to make plain his message.

1. i.e. when the blessed will 'cheat' the damned of their places in Paradise which would have been theirs had they been true believers. (Al-Beidhawi)

89

64:13   Allah – there is no god but Him. In Allah let the faithful put their trust.

Believers, you have an enemy in your wives and children: beware of them. But if you overlook their offences and forgive and pardon them, then know that Allah is forgiving and merciful.

Your wealth and children are but a temptation. Allah's reward is great. Therefore fear Him with all your hearts, and be attentive, obedient, and charitable. That will be best for you.

Those that preserve themselves from their own greed will surely prosper. If you give a generous loan to Allah He will pay you back twofold and will forgive you. Rewarding is He, and benignant.

64:18   He has knowledge of the visible and the unseen. He is the Mighty, the Wise One.

THE HYPOCRITES

In the Name of Allah, the Compassionate, the Merciful

63:1 WHEN the hypocrites come to you they say: 'We bear witness that you are Allah's apostle.' Allah knows that you are indeed His apostle, and bears witness that the hypocrites are lying!

They use their faith as a disguise and debar others from the path of Allah. Evil is what they do.

They believed and then renounced their faith: their hearts are sealed, so that they are devoid of understanding.

When you see them their good looks please you, and when they speak you listen to what they say. Yet they are like propped-up beams of timber. Every shout they hear they take to be against them. *They* are the enemy. Guard yourself against them. Allah confound them! How perverse they are!

63:5   When it is said to them: 'Come, Allah's apostle will beg forgiveness for you,' they turn their backs and you see them go away in scorn.

It is alike whether or not you ask forgiveness for them: 63:6 Allah will not forgive them. He does not guide the evil-doers.

It is they who say: 'Give nothing to those that follow Allah's apostle until they have deserted him.' Allah's are the treasures of heaven and earth: but this the hypocrites cannot understand.

They say: 'If we return to Medina,[1] the strong will soon drive out the weak.' But strength belongs to Allah and His apostle and the faithful: yet the hypocrites do not know it.

Believers, let neither your riches nor your children beguile you of Allah's remembrance. Those that forget Him shall have much to lose.

Give, then, of that with which We have provided you before death befalls you and you say: 'Reprieve me, Lord, awhile, that I may give in charity and be among the righteous.'

But Allah reprieves no soul when its term expires. Allah 63:11 has knowledge of all your actions.

THE CAVE

In the Name of Allah, the Compassionate, the Merciful

PRAISE be to Allah who has revealed the Book to His 18:1 servant shorn of falsehood and unswerving from the truth, so that he may give warning of a dire scourge from Him, proclaim to the faithful who do good works that a rich and everlasting reward awaits them, and admonish those who say that Allah has begotten a son. Surely of this they could have no knowledge, neither they nor their fathers: a monstrous blasphemy is that which they utter. They preach nothing but falsehoods.

Yet, if they deny this revelation, you may destroy yourself with grief, sorrowing over them.

We have decked the earth with all manner of ornaments 18:7 to test mankind and to see who would acquit himself

1. To which the Prophet and his followers had fled from Mecca.

18:8 best. But We will surely reduce all that is on it to barren dust.

Did you think the Sleepers of the Cave[1] and Al-Raquim[2] were a wonder among Our signs?

When the youths sought refuge in the Cave, they said: 'Lord, have mercy on us and guide us out of our ordeal.'

We made them sleep in the cave for many years, and then awakened them to find out who could best tell the length of their stay.

We shall recount to you their story in all truth. They were young men who had faith in their Lord, and on whom We had bestowed Our guidance. We put courage in their hearts when they stood up and said: 'Our Lord is the Lord of the heavens and the earth. We call on no other god besides Him: for if we did we should be blaspheming. Our people serve other gods besides Him, though they have no convincing proof of their divinity. Who is more wicked than the man who invents a falsehood against Allah?

18:16 'When you depart from them and from their idols, go to the Cave for shelter. Allah will extend to you His mercy and prepare for you a means of safety.'

You might have seen the rising sun decline to the right of their cavern and, as it set, go past them on the left, while they stayed within. That was one of Allah's signs. He whom Allah guides is rightly guided; but he whom He misleads shall find no friend to guide him.

You might have thought them awake, though they were sleeping. We turned them about to right and left, while their dog lay at the cave's entrance with legs outstretched. Had you looked upon them, you would have surely turned your back and fled in terror.

18:19 We roused them that they might question one another. 'How long have you been here?' asked one of them. 'A

1. The allusion is to the story of the Seven Sleepers. Compare Gibbon's account in his *Decline and Fall of the Roman Empire*.

2. This may either be the name of their dog, the tablet on which their names were inscribed, or the mountain in which the cave was situated.

day, or but a few hours,' replied some; and others: 'Your Lord knows best how long we have stayed here. Let one of you go to the city with this silver coin and bring you back some wholesome food. Let him conduct himself with caution and not disclose your whereabouts to anyone. For *18:20* if they find you out they will stone you to death or force you back into their faith. Then you shall surely be ruined.'

Thus We revealed their secret, so that men might know that Allah's promise was true and that the Hour of Doom was sure to come.

The people argued among themselves concerning them. Some said: 'Build a monument over their remains. Their Lord alone knows who they were.' Those who were to win said: 'Let us build a chapel over them.'

Some will say: 'The sleepers were three: their dog was the fourth.' Others, guessing at the unknown, will say: 'They were five: their dog was the sixth.' And yet others: 'Seven: their dog was the eighth.'

Say: 'My Lord alone knows their number. Few know them.'

Therefore, when you dispute about them, adhere only to that which is revealed and do not ask any Christian concerning them.

Do not say of anything: 'I will do it tomorrow,' without *18:23* adding: 'If Allah wills.' When you forget, remember your Lord and say: 'May Allah guide me and bring me nearer to the truth.'

Some say they stayed in the cave three hundred years and nine. Say: 'None but Allah knows how long they stayed in it. His are the secrets of the heavens and the earth. Clear is His sight, and keen His hearing. Man has no other guardian besides Him. He allows none to share His sovereignty.'

Proclaim what is revealed to you in the Book of your Lord. None can change His words. You shall find no refuge besides Him.

Restrain yourself, together with those who pray to their *18:28* Lord morning and evening, seeking His pleasure. Do not turn your eyes away from them in quest of the good things of this life, nor obey him whose heart We have made heedless of Our remembrance; who follows his appetite and gives a loose rein to his desires.

18:29   Say: 'This is the truth from your Lord. Let him who will, believe in it, and him who will, deny it.'

For the wrongdoers We have prepared a fire which will encompass them like the walls of a pavilion. When they cry out for drink they shall be showered with water as hot as molten brass, which will scald their faces. Evil shall be their drink, dismal their resting-place.

But those that have faith and do good works shall not lose their reward. They shall dwell in the gardens of Eden, with rivers rolling at their feet. Reclining there upon soft couches, they shall be decked with bracelets of gold and arrayed in garments of fine green silk and rich brocade: blissful their reward and happy their resting-place!

Give them this parable. Once there were two men, to one of whom We gave two vineyards set about with palm-trees and watered by a running stream, with a cornfield lying in between. Each of the vineyards yielded an abundant crop, and when their owner had gathered in the harvest, he said to his companion while conversing with him: 'I am richer than you, and my clan is mightier than yours.'

18:35   And when, having thus wronged his soul, he entered his vineyard, he said: 'Surely this will never perish! Nor do I believe that the Hour of Doom will ever come. Even if I returned to my Lord, I should surely find a better place than this.'

His companion replied: 'Have you no faith in Him who created you from dust, from a little germ, and fashioned you into a man? As for myself, Allah is my Lord. I will associate none with Him. When you entered your garden, why did you not say: "That which Allah has ordained must surely come to pass: there is no strength save in Allah"? Though you see me poorer than yourself and

18:40   blessed with fewer children, yet my Lord may give me a garden better than yours, and send down thunderbolts from heaven upon your vineyard, turning it into a barren

waste, or drain its water deep into the earth so that you can   18:41
find it no more.'

His vineyards were destroyed, and he began to wring his
hands with grief at all that he had spent on them: for the
vines had tumbled down upon their trellises. 'Would that I
had served no other gods besides my Lord!' he cried. He
had none to help him besides Allah, nor was he able to defend himself.

In such ordeals protection comes only from Allah, the
true God. No reward is better than His reward, and no
recompense more generous than His.

Coin for them a simile about this life. It is like the green
herbs that flourish when watered by the rain, soon turning
into stubble which the wind scatters abroad. Allah has
power over all things.

Wealth and children are the ornament of this life. But
deeds of lasting merit are better rewarded by your Lord
and hold for you a greater hope of salvation.

Tell of the day when We shall blot out the mountains
and make the earth a barren waste; when We shall gather
all mankind together, leaving not a soul behind.

They shall be ranged before your Lord, who will say to   18:48
them: 'You have returned to Us as We created you at first.
Yet you thought Our promise was not to be fulfilled.'

Their book will be set down before them, and you shall
see the sinners dismayed at that which is inscribed in it.
They shall say: 'Woe to us! What can this book mean? It
omits nothing small or great: all are noted down!' and they
shall find their deeds recorded there. Your Lord will wrong
none.

When We said to the angels: 'Prostrate yourselves before
Adam,' all prostrated themselves except Satan, who was a
jinnee disobedient to his Lord. Would you then serve him
and his offspring as your Masters rather than Myself, despite their enmity towards you? A sad substitute the wrongdoers have chosen!

I did not call them to witness at the creation of the   18:51
heavens and the earth, nor at their own creation; nor

was I to seek the aid of those who were to lead mankind astray.

18:52 On that day Allah will say to them: 'Call on the idols which you supposed divine.' They will invoke them, but receive no answer; for We shall place a deadly gulf between them. And when the sinners behold the fire of Hell they will know it is there they shall be flung. They shall find no escape from it.

In this Koran We have set forth for men all manner of parables. But man is exceedingly contentious.

Nothing can prevent men from having faith and seeking forgiveness of their Lord, now that guidance has been revealed to them: unless they are waiting for the fate of the ancients to overtake them or to see Our scourge with their own eyes.

We send Our apostles only to proclaim good news and to give warning. But with false arguments the unbelievers seek to confute the truth, scoffing at My revelations and My warnings.

18:57 Who is more wicked than the man who, when reminded of his Lord's revelations, turns away from them and forgets what his hands have done? We have cast veils over their hearts, lest they should understand Our words, and made them hard of hearing. Call them as you may to the right path, they shall never be guided.

Your Lord is forgiving and merciful. Had it been His will to scourge them for their sins, He would have hastened their punishment; but He has set for them an appointed hour, which they shall never escape.

And all those nations! We destroyed them when they did wrong; yet of their imminent destruction We gave them warning.

Moses said to his servant: 'I will journey on until I reach the land where the two seas meet, though I may march for ages.'

18:61 But when at last they came to the land where the two seas met, they forgot their fish, which made its way into the water, swimming at will.

And when they had journeyed farther on, Moses said to *18:62* his servant: 'Bring us some food; we are worn out with travelling.'

'Know,' replied the other, 'that I forgot the fish when we were resting on the rock. Thanks to Satan, I forgot to mention this. The fish made its way into the sea in a miraculous fashion.'

'This is what we have been seeking,' said Moses. They went back the way they came and found one of Our servants to whom We had vouchsafed Our mercy and whom We had endowed with knowledge of Our own. Moses said to him: 'May I follow you so that you may guide me by that which you have been taught?'

'You will not bear with me,' replied the other. 'For how can you bear with that which is beyond your knowledge?'

Moses said: 'If Allah wills, you shall find me patient: I shall not in anything disobey you.'

He said: 'If you are bent on following me, you must ask no question about anything till I myself speak to you concerning it.'

The two set forth, but as soon as they embarked, *18:71* Moses' companion bored a hole in the bottom of the ship.

'A strange thing you have done!' exclaimed Moses. 'Is it to drown her passengers that you have bored a hole in her?'

'Did I not tell you,' he replied, 'that you would not bear with me?'

'Pardon my forgetfulness,' said Moses. 'Do not be angry with me on account of this.'

They journeyed on until they fell in with a certain youth. Moses' companion slew him, and Moses said: 'You have killed an innocent man who has done no harm. Surely you have committed a wicked crime.'

'Did I not tell you,' he replied, 'that you would not bear with me?'

Moses said: 'If ever I question you again, abandon me; for then I should deserve it.'

They travelled on until they came to a certain city. They *18:77* asked the people for some food, but they declined to receive them as their guests. There they found a wall on the point of falling down. His companion restored it, and Moses said: 'Had you wished, you could have demanded payment for your labours.'

18:78   'Now has the time arrived when we must part,' said the other. 'But first I will explain to you those acts of mine which you could not bear to watch with patience.

'Know that the ship belonged to some poor fishermen. I damaged it because in their rear there was a king who was taking every ship by force.

'As for the youth, his parents both are true believers, and we feared lest he should plague them with his wickedness and unbelief. It was our wish that their Lord should grant them another in his place, a son more righteous and more filial.

'As for the wall, it belonged to two orphan boys in the city whose father was an honest man. Beneath it their treasure is buried. Your Lord decreed in His mercy that they should dig out their treasure when they grew to manhood. What I did was not done by my will.

'That is the meaning of what you could not bear to watch with patience.'

18:83   They will ask you about Dhul-Qarnain.[1] Say: 'I will give you an account of him.

'We made him mighty in the land and gave him means to achieve all things. He journeyed on a certain road until he reached the West and saw the sun setting in a pool of black mud. Hard by he found a certain people.

'"Dhul-Qarnain," We said, "you must either punish them or show them kindness."

'He replied: "The wicked We shall surely punish. Then they shall return to their Lord and be sternly punished by Him. As for those that have faith and do good works, we shall bestow on them a rich reward and deal indulgently with them."

18:90   'He then journeyed along another road until he reached the East and saw the sun rising upon a people whom We

1. Alexander the Great.

had utterly exposed to its flaming rays. So he did; and We   *18:91*
had full knowledge of all the forces at his command.

'Then he followed yet another route until he came between the Two Mountains and found a people who could
barely understand a word. "Dhul-Qarnain," they said,
"Gog and Magog are ravaging this land. Build us a rampart against them and we will pay you tribute."

'He replied: "The power which my Lord has given me is
better than any tribute. Lend me a force of labourers, and I
will raise a rampart between you and them. Come, bring
me blocks of iron."

'He dammed up the valley between the Two Mountains,
and said: "Ply your bellows." And when the iron blocks
were red with heat, he said: "Bring me molten brass to pour
on them."

'Gog and Magog could not scale it, nor could they dig
their way through it. He said: "This is a blessing from my
Lord. But when my Lord's promise has been fulfilled, He
will level it to dust. The promise of my Lord is true."'

On that day We will let them come in tumultuous   *18:99*
throngs. The Trumpet shall be sounded and We will gather
them all together.

On that day Hell shall be laid bare before the unbelievers,
who have turned a blind eye to My admonition and a deaf
ear to My warning.

Do the unbelievers think that they can make My servants
patrons besides Me? We have prepared Hell to be their
dwelling-place.

Say: 'Shall we tell you who will lose most through their
labours? Those whose endeavours in this world are misguided and who yet think that what they do is right; who
disbelieve the revelations of their Lord and deny that they
will ever meet Him.' Vain are the works of these. On the
Day of Resurrection We shall not honour them.

Hell is their reward: because they had no faith and scoffed
at My apostles and My revelations. As for those that have
faith and do good works, they shall for ever dwell in the
gardens of Paradise, desiring no change to befall them.   *18:108*

Say: 'If the waters of the sea were ink with which to write the words of my Lord, the sea would surely be consumed before His words were finished, though we brought another sea to replenish it.'

18:110 Say: 'I am but a mortal like yourselves. It is revealed to me that your Lord is one God. Let him that hopes to meet his Lord do what is right and worship none besides Him.'

ABRAHAM

In the Name of Allah, the Compassionate, the Merciful

14:1 ALIF *lam ra*. We have revealed to you this Book so that, by the will of their Lord, you may lead men from darkness to the light; to the path of the Mighty, the Glorious One: the path of Allah, to whom belongs all that the heavens and the earth contain.

Woe to the unbelievers, for they shall be sternly punished! Woe to those who love this life more than the life to come; who debar others from the path of Allah and seek to make it crooked. They have strayed far from Allah's path.

Each apostle We have sent has spoken only in the language of his own people, so that he might make plain to them his message. But Allah leaves in error whom He will and guides whom He pleases. He is the Mighty, the Wise One.

14:5 We sent forth Moses with Our signs, saying: 'Lead your people out of the darkness into the light, and remind them of Allah's favours.' Surely in this there are signs for every steadfast, thankful man.

Moses said to his people: 'Remember Allah's goodness to you when He delivered you from Pharaoh's people, who had oppressed you cruelly, putting your sons to death and sparing your daughters. Surely that was a great trial from your Lord. For He had said: "If you give thanks, I will bestow abundance upon you: but if you deny My favours, know that My punishment is terrible indeed."'

14:8 And Moses said: 'If you and all mankind prove thankless, He does not need your thanks, though He deserves your praise.'

Have you not heard what befell the nations that have *14:9* gone before you? The people of Noah, Aad, and Thamoud, and those who came after? Allah alone knows their number. Their apostles came to them with veritable signs, but they shut their mouths with their hands and said: 'We will not believe in your message. Indeed, we strongly doubt the faith to which you call us.'

Their apostles answered: 'Is there any doubt about Allah, the Creator of the heavens and the earth? He calls you to Him that He may forgive you your sins and respite you till your appointed hour.'

They said: 'You are but mortals like ourselves. You wish to turn us away from the gods of our fathers. Give us some palpable proof.'

Their apostles replied: 'We are indeed mortals like you. But Allah bestows His grace on those of His servants whom He chooses. We cannot give you proof, except by Allah's will. In Him let true believers put their trust. And *14:12* why should we not trust in Allah, when He has already guided us to our paths? We will endure your persecution patiently. In Allah let all the faithful put their trust.'

'Return to our fold,' said the unbelievers, 'or we will banish you from our land.'

But Allah said to His apostles: 'We shall destroy the wrongdoers and let you dwell in the land after them. Let him take heed who dreads My eminence and fears My threats.'

And when they called for help, every hardened sinner was destroyed.

Hell lies before them. They shall drink stinking water: they will sip, but scarcely swallow. Death will assail them from every side, yet they shall not die. A dreadful torment awaits them.

The works of the unbelievers are like ashes which the *14:18* wind scatters on a stormy day: they shall gain nothing from what they do. Their heresy is extreme.

14:19   Do you not see that Allah has created the heavens and the earth with truth? He can destroy you if He wills and bring into being a new creation: that is no difficult thing for Him.

All shall appear before Allah. The humble will say to those who supposed themselves mighty: 'We were your followers. Can you protect us from Allah's vengeance?'

They will reply: 'Had Allah given us guidance, we would have guided you. Neither panic nor patience will help us now. We shall never escape.'

And when Our judgement has been passed, Satan will say to them: 'True was the promise which Allah made you. I too made you a promise, but did not keep it. Yet I had no power over you. I called you, and you answered me. Do not now blame me, but blame yourselves. I cannot help you, nor can you help me. I never shared your belief that I was Allah's equal.'

The wrongdoers shall be sternly punished. As for those that have faith and do good works, they shall be admitted to gardens watered by running streams, in which, by their Lord's leave, they shall abide for ever. Their greeting shall be: 'Peace!'

14:24   Do you not see how Allah compares a good word to a good tree? Its root is firm and its branches are in the sky; it yields its fruit in every season by Allah's leave. Allah gives parables to men so that they may take heed. But an evil word is like an evil tree torn out of the earth and shorn of all its roots.

Allah will strengthen the faithful with His steadfast Word, both in this life and the hereafter. He leads the wrongdoers astray. Allah accomplishes what He pleases.

Have you not seen those who repay the grace of Allah with unbelief and drive their people into the House of Perdition? They shall burn in Hell; evil shall be their fate.

They set up false gods as Allah's equals to lead others astray. Say to them: 'Take your pleasure in this life: you are surely destined for Hell.'

14:31   Tell My servants, those who are true believers, to be steadfast in prayer and to give alms in private and in public, before that day arrives when all trading shall cease and friendships be no more.

It was Allah who made the heavens and the earth. He 14:32 sends down water from the sky with which He brings forth fruits for your sustenance. He drives the ships which by His leave sail the ocean in your service. He has created rivers for your benefit, and the sun and the moon, which steadfastly pursue their courses. And He has subdued to you the night and the day. He grants you all that you ask Him. If you reckoned up Allah's favours you could not count them. Truly, man is wicked and thankless.

Abraham said: 'Lord, make this[1] a land of safety. Preserve me and my descendants from serving idols. Lord, they have led many men astray. He that follows me shall become my brother, but if any one turns against me, You are surely forgiving and merciful.

'Lord, I have settled some of my offspring in a barren valley near Your Sacred House, so that they may observe true worship. Put in the hearts of men kindness towards them, and provide them with the earth's fruits, so that they may give thanks.

'Lord, You have knowledge of all that we hide and all 14:38 that we reveal: nothing in heaven or earth is hidden from Allah.

'Praise be to Allah who has given me Ishmael and Isaac in my old age! All prayers are heard by Him.

'Lord, make me and my descendants steadfast in prayer. Lord, accept my prayer.

'Forgive me, Lord, and forgive my parents and all the faithful on the Day of Reckoning.'

Do not think that Allah is unaware of the wrongdoers' actions. He only gives them respite till the day on which all eyes will stare with consternation. They shall rush in terror with heads uplifted and hearts utterly vacant. They shall stare, but see nothing.

Forewarn mankind of the day when the scourge will 14:44 overtake them; when the wrongdoers will say: 'Lord, grant

1. Mecca.

us respite for a while. We will obey Your call, and follow Your apostles.'

14:45 But a voice will say to them: 'Did you not once swear that you would never cease to be? You lived in the dwellings of those who wronged their souls: yet you knew full well how We had dealt with them, and We had given you many a parable about them.'

They plot, but even if their plots can move mountains, Allah will balk them.

Do not think that Allah will break the pledge He gave to His Apostles. Mighty is Allah, and capable of revenge.

On the day when the earth is changed into a different earth and the heavens into new heavens, mankind shall stand before Allah, the One, the Almighty. On that day you shall see the guilty bound with chains, their garments blackened with pitch, and their heads covered with flames.

Allah will reward each soul according to its deeds. Swift is Allah's reckoning.

14:52 This is a warning to mankind. Let them take heed and know that Allah is one God. Let the wise bear this in mind.

FRIDAY,
OR THE DAY OF CONGREGATION

In the Name of Allah, the Compassionate, the Merciful

62:1 ALL that is in heaven and earth gives glory to Allah, the Sovereign Lord, the Holy One, the Almighty, the All-knowing.

It is He that has sent forth among the gentiles an apostle of their own to recite to them His revelations, to purify them, and to impart to them wisdom and knowledge of the Scriptures though they have hitherto been in gross error, together with others of their own kin who have not yet followed them. He is the Mighty, the Wise One.

Such is the grace of Allah: He bestows it on whom He will. His grace is infinite.

62:5 Those to whom the burden of the Torah was entrusted

and yet refused to bear it are like a donkey laden with books. Wretched is the example of those who deny Allah's revelations. Allah does not guide the wrongdoers.

Say to the Jews: 'If your claim be true that of all men you *62:6* alone are Allah's friends, then you should wish for death!' But, because of what their hands have done, they will never wish for death. Allah knows the wrongdoers.

Say: 'The death from which you shrink is sure to over-take you. Then you shall be sent back to Him who knows the visible and the unseen, and He will declare to you all that you have done.'

Believers, when you are summoned to Friday prayers hasten to the remembrance of Allah and cease your trading. That would be best for you, if you but knew it. Then, when the prayers are ended, disperse and go in quest of Allah's bounty. Remember Allah always, so that you may prosper.

Yet no sooner do they see some merchandise or merri- *62:11* ment than they flock to it eagerly, leaving you[1] standing all alone.

Say: 'That which Allah has in store is far better than any merchandise or merriment. Allah is the Most Munificent Giver.'

BATTLE ARRAY

In the Name of Allah, the Compassionate, the Merciful

ALL that is in heaven and earth gives glory to Allah. *61:1* He is the Mighty, the Wise One.

Believers, why do you profess what you never do? It is most odious in Allah's sight that you should say one thing and do another.

Allah loves those who fight for His cause in ranks as firm as a mighty edifice.

Tell of Moses, who said to his people: 'Why do you seek *61:5* to harm me, my people, when you know that I am sent to you by Allah?' And when they went astray Allah led their very hearts astray. He does not guide the evil-doers.

1. Mohammed.

61:6 And of Jesus, who said to the Israelites: 'I am sent forth to you by Allah to confirm the Torah already revealed and to give news of an apostle that will come after me whose name is Ahmed.'[1] Yet when he did miracles before them, they said: 'This is plain magic.'

And who is more wicked than the man who invents a falsehood about Allah when called upon to submit to Him? Allah does not guide the wrongdoers.

They seek to extinguish the light of Allah with their mouths; but Allah will perfect His light, much as the unbelievers may dislike it.

It is He who has sent His apostle with guidance and the Faith of Truth, so that He may exalt it above all religions, much as the pagans may dislike it.

61:10 Believers! Shall I point out to you a profitable course that will save you from a woeful scourge? Have faith in Allah and His apostle and fight for His cause with your wealth and your persons. That would be best for you, if you but knew it.

He will forgive you your sins and admit you to gardens watered by running streams; He will lodge you in pleasant mansions in the gardens of Eden. That is the supreme triumph.

And He will bestow upon you other blessings which you desire: help from Allah and a speedy victory. Proclaim the good tidings to the faithful.

61:14 Believers, be Allah's helpers. When Jesus the son of Mary said to the disciples: 'Who will come with me to the help of Allah?' they replied: '*We* are Allah's helpers.'

Some of the Israelites believed in him while others did not. We aided the believers against their enemies and they triumphed over them.

1. Another name of Mohammed's, meaning 'The Praised One'.

IRON

In the Name of Allah, the Compassionate, the Merciful

ALL that is in heaven and earth gives glory to Allah. 57:1 He is the Mighty, the Wise One.

His is the kingdom of the heavens and the earth. He ordains life and death and has power over all things.

He is the first and the last, the visible and the unseen. He has knowledge of all things.

He created the heavens and the earth in six days and then mounted His throne. He knows all that goes into the earth and all that emerges from it, all that comes down from heaven and all that ascends to it. He is with you wherever you are. Allah is cognizant of all your actions.

His is the kingdom of the heavens and the earth. To Him shall all things return. He causes the night to pass into the day and the day into the night. He has knowledge of the inmost thoughts of men.

Have faith in Allah and His apostle and give in alms 57:7 of that which He has made your inheritance; for whoever of you believes and gives in alms shall be richly rewarded.

And what cause have you not to believe in Allah, when the Apostle calls on you to have faith in your Lord, who has made a covenant with you? Put your trust in Him then, if you are true believers.

It is He who brings down clear revelations to His servant, so that he may lead you out of darkness into the light. Allah is compassionate and merciful to you.

And why should you not give to the cause of Allah, when 57:10 He alone will inherit the heavens and the earth? Those of you that gave of their wealth before the victory and took part in the fighting shall receive greater honour than the others who gave and fought thereafter. Yet Allah has promised you all a good reward; He has knowledge of all your actions.

57:11 Who will give a generous loan to Allah? He will pay him back twofold and he shall receive a rich reward.

The day will surely come when you shall see the true believers, men and women, with their light shining before them and on their right hands, and a voice saying to them: 'Rejoice this day. You shall enter gardens watered by running streams in which you shall abide forever.' That is the supreme triumph.

On that day the hypocrites, both men and women, will say to the true believers: 'Wait for us, that we may borrow some of your light.' But they will answer: 'Go back and seek some other light!'

A wall with a gate shall be set before them. Inside there shall be mercy, and out, to the fore, the scourge of Hell. They will call out to them, saying: 'Were we not on your side?' 'Yes,' they will reply, 'but you tempted yourselves, you wavered, you doubted, and were deceived by your own desires until Allah's will was done and the Dissembler tricked you about Allah. Today no ransom shall be accepted from you or from the unbelievers. Hell shall be your home: you have justly earned it, a dismal end!'

57:16 Is it not time for true believers to submit to Allah's warning and to the truth He has revealed, so that they may not be like those who were given the Scriptures before this, whose days were prolonged but whose hearts were hardened? Many of them were evil-doers.

Know that Allah restores the earth to life after its death. We have made plain to you Our revelations that you may grow in wisdom.

Those that give alms, be they men or women, and those that give a generous loan to Allah, shall be repaid twofold. They shall receive a noble recompense.

Those that believe in Allah and His apostles are the truthful men who shall testify in their Lord's presence. They shall have their guerdon and their light. But those that disbelieve Our revelations and deny them are the heirs of Hell.

57:20 Know that the life of this world is but a sport and a pastime, a show and an empty vaunt among you, a quest for greater riches and more children. It is like the plants that flourish after rain: the husbandman rejoices to see them grow; but then they wither and turn yellow, soon becoming worthless stubble. In the life to come a woeful punishment awaits you – or the forgiveness of Allah and His pleasure. The life of this world is but a vain provision.

Therefore strive emulously for the pardon of your Lord, 57:21 and for a Paradise as vast as heaven and earth, prepared for those who believe in Allah and His apostles. Such is the grace of Allah: He bestows it on whom He will. His grace is infinite.

Every misfortune that befalls the earth, or your own persons, is ordained before We bring it into being. That is easy for Allah: so that you may not grieve for the good things you miss or be overjoyed at what you gain. Allah does not love the haughty, the vainglorious; nor those who, being niggardly themselves, enjoin others to be niggardly also. He that gives no heed to this should know that Allah alone is self-sufficient and worthy of praise.

We have sent Our apostles with veritable signs and 57:25 brought down with them scriptures and the scales of justice, so that men might conduct themselves with fairness. We have sent down iron, with its mighty strength and diverse uses for mankind, so that Allah may know those who aid Him, though unseen, and help His apostles. Powerful is Allah, and mighty.

We sent forth Noah and Abraham, and bestowed on their offspring prophethood and the Scriptures. Some were rightly guided, but many were evil-doers. After them We sent other apostles, and after those Jesus the son of Mary. We gave him the Gospel and put compassion and mercy in the hearts of his followers. As for monasticism, they instituted it themselves (for We had not enjoined it on them), seeking thereby to please Allah; but they did not observe it faithfully. We rewarded only those who were true believers; for many of them were evil-doers.

Believers, have fear of Allah and put your trust in His 57:28 apostles. He will grant you a double share of His mercy, He will bestow on you a light to walk in, and will forgive you: Allah is forgiving and merciful.

57:29   Let the People of the Book know that they have no control over the gifts of Allah; that these gifts are in His hands alone, and that He vouchsafes them to whom He will. Allah's bounty is infinite.

THAT WHICH IS COMING

In the Name of Allah, the Compassionate, the Merciful

56:1   WHEN that which is coming comes – and no soul shall then deny its coming – some shall be abased and others exalted.

When the earth shakes and quivers and the mountains crumble away and scatter abroad into fine dust, you shall be divided into three multitudes: those on the right (blessed shall be those on the right!); those on the left (damned shall be those on the left!); and those to the fore (foremost shall be those!). Such are they that shall be brought near to their Lord in the gardens of delight: a whole multitude from the men of old, but only a few from the later generations.

56:15   They shall recline on jewelled couches face to face, and there shall wait on them immortal youths with bowls and ewers and a cup of purest wine (that will neither pain their heads nor take away their reason); with fruits of their own choice and flesh of fowls that they relish. And theirs shall be the dark-eyed houris, chaste as hidden pearls: a guerdon for their deeds.

There they shall hear no idle talk, no sinful speech, but only the greeting, 'Peace! Peace!'

Those on the right hand – happy shall be those on the right hand! They shall recline on couches raised on high in the shade of thornless sidrahs and clusters of talh;[1] amidst gushing waters and abundant fruits, unforbidden, never-ending.

56:36   We created the houris and made them virgins, loving

1. Probably the banana fruit.

companions for those on the right hand: a multitude from *56:38*
the men of old, and a multitude from the later generations.

As for those on the left hand (wretched shall be those on
the left hand!) they shall dwell amidst scorching winds and
seething water: in the shade of pitch-black smoke, neither
cool nor refreshing. For they have lived in comfort and
persisted in the heinous sin,[1] saying: 'When we are once
dead and turned to dust and bones, shall we, with all our
forefathers, be raised to life?'

Say: 'This present generation, as well as the generations
that passed before it, shall be brought together on an appointed day. As for you sinners who deny the truth, you
shall eat the fruit of the Zaqqum-tree and fill your bellies
with it. You shall drink boiling water: yet you shall drink it
as the thirsty camel drinks.'

Such shall be their fare on the Day of Reckoning. *56:56*

We created you: will you not believe then in Our power?

Behold the semen you discharge: did you create it, or
We?

It was We that ordained death among you. Nothing can
hinder Us from replacing you by others like yourselves or
transforming you into beings you know nothing of.

You surely know of the first creation. Why, then, do you
not reflect? Consider the seeds you grow. Is it you that give
them growth or We? If We pleased We could turn your
harvest into chaff, so that, filled with wonderment, you
would exclaim: 'We are laden with debts! Surely we have
been robbed!'

Consider the water which you drink. Was it you that
poured it from the cloud or We? If We pleased We could
turn it bitter. Why then do you not give thanks?

Observe the fire which you light. Is it you that create its
wood, or We? We have made it a reminder for man, and
for the traveller a comfort.

Praise then the name of your Lord, the Supreme One.

I swear by the shelters of the stars (a mighty oath, if you
but knew it) that this is a glorious Koran, inscribed in a *56:78*

1. Idolatry.

56:79 hidden book which none may touch except the purified; a revelation from the Lord of all creatures.

Would you scorn a scripture such as this and make it your daily task to deny it?

When under your very eyes a man's soul is about to leave him (We are nearer to him than you, although you cannot see Us), why do you not restore it, if you will not be judged hereafter? Answer this, if what you say be true!

Thus, if he is favoured, his lot will be repose and plenty and a garden of delights. If he is one of those on the right hand he will be greeted with, 'Peace be to you!' by those on the right hand.

But if he is an erring disbeliever his welcome will be scalding water and he will burn in Hell.

56:96 This is the indubitable truth. Praise then the name of your Lord, the Supreme One.

THE MOON

In the Name of Allah, the Compassionate, the Merciful

54:1 THE Hour of Doom is drawing near, and the moon is cleft in two. Yet when they see a sign the unbelievers turn their backs and say: 'Ingenious magic!'

They deny the truth and follow their own fancies. But in the end all issues shall be settled.

Admonitory news, profound in wisdom, has come to them: but warnings are unavailing.

Let them be. On the day when the Crier summons them to the dread account, they shall come out from their graves with downcast eyes and rush towards him like scattered locusts. The unbelievers will cry: 'This is indeed a woeful day!'

Long before them the people of Noah denied Our signs. They disbelieved Our servant and called him madman. Rejected and condemned, he cried out, saying: 'Help me, Lord, I am overcome!'

54:11 We opened the gates of heaven with pouring rain and

caused the earth to burst with gushing springs, so that the 54:12
waters met for a predestined end. We carried Noah in a
vessel built with planks and nails, which drifted on under
Our eye: a recompense for him who had been disbelieved.

We made the flood a sign: but will any take heed? I
warned them, and then how stern was My punishment!

We have made the Koran easy to remember: but will any
take heed?

Aad, too, denied their apostle. I warned them, and then
how stern was My punishment! On a day of unremitting
woe We let loose on them a howling wind which snatched
them off as though they were trunks of uprooted trees. I
warned them, and then how stern was My punishment!

We have made the Koran easy to remember: but will any
take heed?

Thamoud, too, disbelieved Our warnings. They said:
'Are we to follow a mortal who stands alone among us?
That would surely be error and madness. Did he alone
among us receive this warning? He is indeed a foolish liar.'

To him We said: 'Tomorrow they shall know who is the 54:26
foolish liar. We are sending to them a she-camel, that We
may put them to the proof. Observe them closely and have
patience. Tell them that they must share their drink with
her and that for every draught they must attend in person.'

They called their friend, who took a knife and slew her.
I warned them, and then how stern was My punishment!
A single cry was heard, and they became like the dry twigs
of the sheep-fold builder.

We have made the Koran easy to remember: but will any
take heed?

The people of Lot disbelieved Our warning. We let loose
on them a stone-charged whirlwind which destroyed them
all, except the house of Lot, whom We saved at dawn
through Our mercy. Thus We reward the thankful.

Lot had warned them of Our vengeance, but they
doubted his warnings. They demanded his guests of him.
But We put out their sight and said: 'Taste My punishment,
now that you have heard My warning.' And at daybreak a 54:38

54:39 heavy scourge overtook them. 'Taste My punishment, now that you have heard My warning!'

We have made the Koran easy to remember: but will any take heed?

To Pharaoh's people also came the warning. But they disbelieved all Our signs and We smote them with the scourge of the Mighty One, the All-powerful.

Are your unbelievers better men than these? are you given immunity in the Scriptures?

54:44 Do they say: 'We are a victorious army'? Their army shall be routed and put to flight.

The Hour of Doom is their appointed time. More calamitous, and more doleful, shall that Hour be than all their worldly trials.

Yet the wrongdoers persist in error and madness. On the day when they are dragged into the Fire with faces downwards, We shall say to them: 'Feel the touch of Hell!'

We have made all things according to a fixed decree. We command but once: Our will is done in the twinkling of an eye.

We have destroyed many a nation like yourselves. Will you not take warning?

All their deeds are in Our books: every action, small or great, is noted down. The righteous shall dwell in gardens 54:55 where rivers flow, honourably seated in the presence of a Mighty King.

THE STAR

In the Name of Allah, the Compassionate, the Merciful

53:1 By the declining star, your compatriot[1] is not in error, nor is he deceived!

He does not speak out of his own fancy. This is an 53:6 inspired revelation. He is taught by one who is powerful and mighty.[2]

1. Mohammed.   2. Gabriel.

He stood on the uppermost horizon; then, drawing near, *53:7*
he came down within two bows' length or even closer, and
revealed to his servant that which he revealed.

His[1] own heart did not deny his vision. How can you,[2]
then, question what he sees?

He beheld him once again at the sidrah-tree, beyond
which no one may pass. (Near it is the Garden of Repose.)

When that tree was covered with what covered it, his
eyes did not wander, nor did they turn aside: for he saw
some of his Lord's greatest signs.

Have you thought on Al-Lat and Al-Uzzah, and, thirdly,
on Manat?[3] Is He to have daughters and you sons? This is
indeed an unfair distinction!

They are but names which you and your fathers have invented: Allah has vested no authority in them. The unbelievers follow vain conjectures and the whims of their
own souls, although the guidance of their Lord has come
to them.

Is man to attain all that he desires? It is Allah who *53:24*
ordains the present and the hereafter.

Numerous are the angels in the heavens; yet their intercession shall avail nothing until Allah gives leave to whom
He accepts and chooses.

Those that disbelieve in the life to come call the angels by
the names of females. Yet of this they have no knowledge:
they follow mere conjecture, and conjecture is no substitute
for truth.

Give no heed, then, to those who ignore Our warning
and seek only the life of this world. This is the sum of their
knowledge. Your Lord knows best who have strayed from
His path, and who are rightly guided.

His is what the heavens and the earth contain. He will
requite the evil-doers according to their deeds, and bestow
a good reward on those who do good works.

To those who avoid the grossest sins and indecencies and *53:32*

1. Mohammed's.   2. The unbelievers.
3. Names of Arabian idols, claimed by the pagans of Mecca to be
daughters of Allah.

commit only small offences, Allah will show abundant
mercy. He knew you well when He created you of earth
and when you were hidden in your mothers' wombs. Do
not pretend to purity; He knows best those who guard
themselves against evil.

53:33   Have you considered him who turns his back upon the
Faith, giving little at first and then nothing at all? Does he
know, and can he see, what is hidden? Has he not heard of
what is preached in the Book of Moses and Abraham, who
fulfilled his duty: that no soul shall bear another's burden
and that each man shall be judged by his own labours; that
his labours shall be scrutinized and that he shall be justly
requited for them; that all things shall in the end return to
Allah; that it is Allah who moves to weeping and laughter
and ordains life and death; that Allah created the sexes, the
male and the female, from a drop of ejected semen, and will
create all things anew; that it is He who bestows and enriches, He who is the Lord of Sirius;[1] that it was He who
destroyed Thamoud and ancient Aad, sparing no one, and
before them the people of Noah who were more wicked
and more rebellious. The Mu'tafikah[2] He also ruined, so
that there fell on them what fell on them.

Which then of your Lord's blessings would you deny?
The Prophet who warns you now is not unlike the prophets
of old. That which is coming is near at hand; none but
Allah can disclose its hour.

Do you marvel then at this revelation and laugh light-
53:62 heartedly instead of weeping? Rather prostrate yourselves
before Allah and worship Him.

1. The Dog-star, worshipped by the pagan Arabs.
2. The Ruined Cities, where Lot's people had lived.

THE MOUNTAIN

In the Name of Allah, the Compassionate, the Merciful

B Y the Mountain,[1] and by the Scripture penned on un- *52:1*
rolled parchment; by the Visited House,[2] the Lofty
Vault,[3] and the swelling sea, your Lord's punishment shall surely come to pass! No power shall ward it off.

On that day the heaven will shake and reel, and the mountains crumble away and cease to be. On that day woeful shall be the plight of the unbelievers, who now divert themselves with vain disputes.

On that day they shall be sternly shoved into the fire of Hell, and a voice will say to them: 'This is the fire which you denied. Is this magic, or do you not see? Burn in its flames. It is alike whether you are patient or impatient. You shall be rewarded according to your deeds.'

But in fair gardens the righteous shall dwell in bliss, rejoicing in what their Lord will give them. He will shield them from the scourge of Hell. He will say: 'Eat and drink in joy. This is the reward of your labours.'

They shall recline on couches ranged in rows. To dark- *52:20*
eyed houris We shall wed them.

(We shall unite the true believers with those of their descendants who follow them in their faith, and shall not deny them the reward of their good works: each man is the hostage of his own deeds.)

Fruits We shall give them, and such meats as they desire. They will pass from hand to hand a cup inspiring no idle talk, no sinful urge; and there shall wait on them young boys of their own as fair as virgin pearls.

They will converse with one another. 'When we were living among our kinsfolk,' they will say, 'we were troubled by many fears. But Allah has been gracious to us; He has *52:27*

1. Mount Sinai.   2. The Ka'ba.   3. The sky.

52:28 preserved us from the scourge of Hell, for we have prayed to Him. He is the Beneficent One, the Merciful.'

Therefore give warning. By the grace of Allah, you are neither soothsayer nor madman.

Do they say: 'He is a poet: we are waiting for some misfortune to befall him'? Say: 'Wait if you will; I too am waiting.'

Does their reason prompt them to say this? Or is it merely that they are wicked men?

Do they say: 'He has invented it[1] himself'? Indeed, they have no faith. Let them produce a scripture like it, if what they say be true!

Were they created out of the void? Or were they their own creators?

Did *they* create the heavens and the earth? Surely they have no faith!

Do they hold the treasures of your Lord or have control over them?

52:38 Have they a ladder by means of which they overhear Him? Let their eavesdropper bring a positive proof!

Is He to have daughters and you[2] sons?

Are you[3] demanding payment of them, that they should fear to be weighed down with debts?

Have they knowledge of what is hidden? Can they write it down?

Are they seeking to ruin you? They themselves shall be ruined.

Have they a god other than Allah? Exalted be He above their idols!

If they saw a part of heaven falling down, they would still say: 'It is but a mass of clouds!'

Let them be, until they face the day when they shall stand dumbfounded; the day when their designs will avail them nothing and none will help them.

52:47 And besides this a punishment awaits the wrongdoers, though most of them do not know it.

1. The Koran.   2. The unbelievers.
3. Mohammed.

Therefore wait the judgement of your Lord: We are watching over you. Give glory to your Lord when you waken; in the night-time praise Him, and at the setting of *52:49* the stars.

THE WINDS

In the Name of Allah, the Compassionate, the Merciful

BY the dust-scattering winds and the heavily-laden *51:1* clouds; by the swiftly-gliding ships, and by the angels who deal out blessings to all men; that with which you are threatened shall be fulfilled and the Last Judgement shall surely come to pass!

By the heaven with its starry highways, you contradict yourselves! None but the perverse turn away from the true faith. Cursed are the liars who dwell in darkness and are heedless of the life to come.

'When will the Day of Judgement be?' they ask. On that day they shall be scourged in the fire of Hell, and a voice will say to them: 'Taste this, the punishment which you have sought to hasten!'

The righteous shall dwell amidst gardens and fountains, and shall receive what their Lord will give them. For they have done good works, sleeping but little in the night-time, praying at dawn for Allah's pardon, and sharing their goods with the beggars and the destitute.

On earth, and in yourselves, there are signs for firm *51:20* believers. Can you not see?

Heaven holds your sustenance and all that you are promised. I swear by the Lord of heaven and earth that this is true, as true as you are speaking now!

Have you heard the story of Abraham's honoured guests?

They went in to him and said: 'Peace!' 'Peace!' he answered and, seeing that they were strangers, betook himself to his family and returned with a fatted calf. He set it before them, saying: 'Will you not eat?'

He grew afraid of them, but they said, 'Have no fears,' *51:28* and told him that he was to have a son blessed with wisdom.

51:29 His wife came crying and beating her face. 'Surely I am a barren old woman,' she said.

'Such is the will of your Lord,' they replied. 'He is the Wise One, the All-knowing.'

'Messengers,' said Abraham, 'what is your errand?'

They replied: 'We are sent forth to a wicked nation, so that we may bring down on them a shower of clay-stones marked by your Lord for the destruction of the sinful.'

We saved all the faithful in the town – We found in it but one household of true believers – and left therein a sign for those who fear Our woeful punishment.

In Moses, too, there was a sign. We sent him forth to Pharaoh with clear authority, but he turned his back, he and his nobles, saying: 'He is either a sorcerer or a madman.' So We seized him and his warriors and cast them into the sea. Indeed, Pharaoh was an evil-doer.

In the fate of Aad there was another sign. We let loose on them a blighting wind which blew into dust all that it swept before it.

51:43 And in the people of Thamoud. They were allowed to take their ease awhile, but they disobeyed the commandments of their Lord. The thunderbolt struck them whilst they were looking on; they could not rise up from their fall, nor could they save themselves.

And before them We destroyed the people of Noah. They too were impious men.

We built the heaven with Our might, giving it a vast expanse, and stretched the earth beneath it. Gracious is He who spread it out. And all things We made in pairs, so that you may give thought.

Therefore seek Allah. I come from Him to warn you plainly. Set up no other god besides Allah. I come from Him to warn you plainly.

51:52 Thus whenever an apostle came to those that flourished before them[1] they cried: 'Sorcerer!' or 'Madman!' Have

1. The Meccans.

they handed down this cry from one generation to the 51:53 next? Surely they are transgressors all.

Give no heed to them; you shall incur no blame. But admonish the true believers: admonition will help them.

I created mankind and the jinn in order that they might worship Me. I demand no livelihood of them, nor do I ask that they should feed Me.

Allah alone is the Munificent Giver, the Mighty One, the Invincible. Those that now do wrong shall meet their predecessors' doom. Let them not challenge Me to hurry it on. Woe to the unbelievers when the threatened day arrives! 51:60

QAF

In the Name of Allah, the Compassionate, the Merciful

QAF. By the Glorious Koran! 50:1
They marvel that a prophet of their own has arisen amongst them. The unbelievers say: 'This is indeed a strange thing. When we are dead and turned to dust . . .?[1] Such a return is most improbable!'

We know all that the earth consumes of them. We hold a book in which all things are written.

Yes. They denied the truth when it was preached to them, and now they are perplexed. Have they never observed the sky above them and marked how We built it up and furnished it with ornaments, leaving no crack in its expanse?

We spread out the earth and set upon it immovable mountains. We brought forth in it all kinds of delectable plants. A lesson and an admonition to penitent men.

We send down blessed water from the sky with which We bring forth gardens and the harvest grain, and tall palm-trees laden with clusters of dates, a sustenance for 50:11 men; thereby giving new life to some dead land. Such shall be the Resurrection.

1. '. . . shall we be raised to life?'

50:12 Long before these the people of Noah and the dwellers of Ar-Raas[1] denied the truth; and so did Thamoud and Aad, Pharaoh and the compatriots of Lot, the dwellers of the Forest[2] and the people of Tobba:[3] all disbelieved their apostles and thus brought down upon themselves My threatened scourge.

Were We worn out by the first creation? Yet they are in doubt about a new creation.[4]

We created man. We know the promptings of his soul, and are closer to him than the vein of his neck.

When the two Keepers receive him, the one seated on his right, the other on his left, each word he utters shall be noted down by a vigilant guardian.

And when the agony of death justly overtakes him, they will say: 'This is the fate you have striven to avoid.' And the Trumpet shall be sounded. Such is the threatened day.

50:21 Each soul shall come attended by one who will testify against it and another who will drive it on. One of them will say: 'Of this you have been heedless. But now we have removed your veil. Today your sight is keen.' And his comrade will say: 'My testimony is ready.'

Then a voice will cry: 'Cast into Hell every hardened unbeliever, every opponent of good works, and every doubting transgressor who has set up another god besides Allah. Hurl him into the fierce, tormenting flames!'

His companion[5] will say: 'Lord, I did not mislead him. He was already gone far astray.'

Allah will say: 'Do not dispute in My presence. I gave you warning beforehand. My word cannot be changed, nor am I unjust to My servants.'

50:30 On that day We shall ask Hell: 'Are you full?' And Hell will answer: 'Are there any more?'

1. Commentators are disagreed as to the identity of this place-name. Some say it is a town in Yamamah, others a well in Midian.
2. The people of Midian.
3. The people of Hamyar, whose kings bore the title of Tobba.
4. The Resurrection.
5. The devil who is chained to him.

And not far thence Paradise shall be brought close to the 50:31 righteous. We shall say to them: 'Here is all that you were promised. It is for every penitent and faithful man, who fears the Merciful, though He is unseen, and comes before Him with a contrite heart. Enter it in peace. This is the day of immortality.'

There they will have all that they desire, and We shall give them more.

How many generations, far greater in prowess, have We destroyed before them! They searched the entire land: but could they find a refuge? Surely in this there is a lesson for every man who has a heart and ears and eyes.

In six days We created the heavens and the earth and all that lies between them; nor were We ever wearied.

Bear then with what they[1] say. Give glory to your Lord before sunrise and before sunset. Praise Him in the night, and make the additional prostrations.

Listen on the day when the Crier will call from near; the day when men will hear the fateful cry. On that day they will rise up from their graves.

It is We who ordain life and death. To Us all shall return.

On that day the earth will be rent asunder and they shall rush from it in haste. To assemble them all is no difficult task for Us.

We well know what they say. You shall not use force 50:45 with them. Admonish with this Koran whoever fears My warning.

MOHAMMED

In the Name of Allah, the Compassionate, the Merciful

ALLAH will bring to nothing the deeds of those who 47:1 disbelieve and debar others from His path. As for the faithful who do good works and believe in what is revealed to Mohammed – which is the truth from their Lord – He will forgive them their sins and ennoble their state.

1. The unbelievers.

47:3 This, because the unbelievers follow falsehood, while the faithful follow the truth from their Lord. Thus Allah coins their sayings for mankind.

When you meet the unbelievers in the battlefield strike off their heads and, when you have laid them low, bind your captives firmly. Then grant them their freedom or take ransom from them, until War shall lay down her armour.

Thus shall you do. Had Allah willed, He could Himself have punished them; but He has ordained it thus that He might test you, the one by the other.

As for those who are slain in the cause of Allah, He will not allow their works to perish. He will vouchsafe them guidance and ennoble their state; He will admit them to the Paradise He has made known to them.

Believers, if you help Allah, Allah will help you and make you strong. But the unbelievers shall be consigned to perdition. He will bring their deeds to nothing. Because they have opposed His revelations, He will frustrate their works.

47:10 Have they never journeyed through the land and seen what was the end of those who have gone before them? Allah destroyed them utterly. A similar fate awaits the unbelievers, because Allah is the protector of the faithful: because the unbelievers have no protector.

Allah will admit those who embrace the true faith and do good works to gardens watered by running streams. The unbelievers take their fill of pleasure and eat as the beasts eat: but Hell shall be their home.

How many cities were mightier than your own city, which has cast you¹ out! We destroyed them all, and there was none to help them.

Can he who follows the guidance of his Lord be compared to him who is led by his appetites and whose foul deeds seem fair to him?

47:15 This is the Paradise which the righteous have been promised. There shall flow in it rivers of unpolluted water, and rivers of milk for ever fresh; rivers of delectable wine and

1. Mohammed.

rivers of clearest honey. They shall eat therein of every fruit and receive forgiveness from their Lord. Is this like the lot of those who shall abide in Hell for ever and drink scalding water which will tear their bowels?

Some of them indeed listen to you, but no sooner do *47:16* they leave your presence than they ask those to whom knowledge has been given: 'What did he say just now?' Such are the men whose hearts are sealed by Allah and who follow their base desires.

As for those who follow the right path, Allah will increase their guidance and teach them to guard themselves against evil.

Are they waiting for the Hour of Doom to overtake them unawares? Its portents have already come. But how will they be warned when it overtakes them?

Know that there is no god but Allah. Implore Him to forgive your sins and to forgive the true believers, men and women. Allah knows your busy haunts and resting-places.

The faithful say: 'If only a Chapter were revealed!' But *47:20* when a forthright Chapter is revealed and war is mentioned in it, you see the infirm of heart looking towards you as though they were fainting away for fear of death. Yet obedience and courteous speech would become them more. Indeed, should war be decided upon, it would be better for them to be true to Allah.

If you[1] renounced the Faith you would surely do evil in the land and violate the ties of blood. Such are those on whom Allah has laid His curse, leaving them bereft of sight and hearing.

Will they not ponder on the Koran? Are there locks upon their hearts?

Those who return to unbelief after Allah's guidance has been revealed to them are seduced by Satan and inspired by him. That is because they say to those who abhor the word *47:26* of Allah: 'We shall obey you in *some* matters.' Allah knows their secret talk.

1. The hypocrites.

47:27   What will they do when the angels carry away their souls and strike them on their heads and backs?

That is because they follow what has incurred the wrath of Allah and abhor what pleases Him. He will surely bring their works to nothing.

Do the feeble-hearted think that Allah will not reveal their malice? If We pleased, We could point them out to you and you would recognize them promptly by their looks. But you will surely know them from the tenor of their words. Allah has knowledge of all your actions.

We shall put you to the proof until We know the valiant and the resolute among you and test all that is said about you.

The unbelievers who debar others from the path of Allah and disobey the Apostle after they have seen the light shall in no way harm Allah. He will bring their works to nothing.

Believers, obey Allah and His apostle and never let your labours go in vain.

47:34   Those that disbelieve and debar others from Allah's path and in the end die unbelievers shall not be shown forgiveness by Allah. Therefore do not falter or sue for peace when you have gained the upper hand. Allah is on your side and will not grudge you the reward of your labours.

The life of this world is but a sport and a pastime. Allah will reward you if you believe in Him and guard yourselves against evil. He does not ask for all your wealth. If he demanded all and strongly pressed you, you would grow niggardly and this would show your ill-feelings.

47:38   You are called upon to give to the cause of Allah. Some of you are ungenerous; yet whoever is ungenerous to this cause is ungenerous to himself. Indeed, Allah does not need you, but you need Him. If you give no heed, He will replace you by others different from you.

AL-AHQAF

In the Name of Allah, the Compassionate, the Merciful

HA *mim*. This Book is revealed by Allah, the Mighty 46:1
One, the Wise One.

It was to manifest the truth that We created the heavens and the earth and all that lies between them; We created them to last for an appointed term. Yet the unbelievers give no heed to Our warning.

Say: 'Have you pondered on those whom you invoke besides Allah? Show me what part of the earth they have created! Have they a share in the heavens? Bring me a scripture revealed before this or some other vestige of divine knowledge, if what you say be true.'

Who is in greater error than the man who prays to idols which will never hear him till the Day of Resurrection – which are, indeed, unconscious of his prayers? When mankind are gathered upon the Judgement-day, their idols will become their enemies and will disown their worship.

When Our clear revelations are recited to them, the un- 46:7
believers say: 'This is plain magic.' Such is their description of the truth when it is declared to them.

Do they say: 'He has invented it himself?'

Say: 'If I have indeed invented it,[1] then there is nothing that you can do to save me from Allah's wrath. He well knows what you say about it. He is our all-sufficient witness. He is the Benignant One, the Merciful.'

Say: 'I am no prodigy among the apostles; nor do I know what will be done with me or you. I follow only what is revealed to me, and my only duty is to give plain warning.'

Say: 'Think if this Koran is indeed from Allah and you reject it; if an Israelite[2] has vouched for its divinity and accepted Islam, while you yourselves deny it with scorn. Truly, Allah does not guide the wrongdoers.'

The unbelievers say of the faithful: 'Had there been any 47:11

1. The Koran.   2. Abdullah bin Salam.

good in this book they would not have believed in it before us.' And since they reject its guidance they say: 'This is an ancient falsehood.'

46:12 Yet before it the Book of Moses was revealed, a guide and a blessing to all men. This Book confirms it. It is revealed in the Arabic tongue to forewarn the wrongdoers and to give good news to the righteous.

Those that say: 'Our God is Allah,' and follow the straight path shall have nothing to fear or to regret. They shall for ever dwell in Paradise as a reward for their labours.

We have enjoined man to show kindness to his parents. With much pain his mother bears him, and with much pain she brings him into the world. He is born and weaned in thirty months. When he grows to manhood and attains his fortieth year, let him say: 'Inspire me, Lord, to give thanks for the favours You have bestowed on me and on my parents, and to do good works that will please You. Grant me good descendants. To You I turn and to You I surrender myself.'

46:16 Such are those from whom We will accept their noblest works and whose misdeeds We shall overlook. We shall admit them among the heirs of Paradise: true is the promise that has been given them.

But he that rebukes his parents and says to them: 'For shame! Do you threaten me with a resurrection when entire generations have passed away before me?' – he that, when they pray for Allah's help and say: 'Woe to you! Have faith. The promise of Allah is true,' replies: 'This is but a fable of the ancients,' – shall justly deserve the fate of bygone nations of men and jinn: he shall assuredly be lost.

There are rewards for all, according to their deeds, so that Allah may duly requite them for their works. They shall not be wronged.

46:20 On the day when the unbelievers are brought before the fire of Hell, We shall say to them: 'You squandered away your precious gifts in your earthly life and took your fill of pleasure. An ignominious punishment shall be yours this day, because you behaved with pride and injustice on the earth and committed evil.'

Tell of Aad's compatriot who warned his people in the *46:21* Valley of Al-Ahqaf (and there have been other apostles before and since his time), saying: 'Serve none but Allah. Beware of the torment of a fateful day.'

They replied: 'Have you come to turn us away from our own gods? Bring down the scourge with which you threaten us, if what you say be true!'

He said: 'Allah knows when it will come. I am here to declare to you my message. But I can see that you are ignorant men.'

And when they saw a cloud heading for their valley they said: 'Here is a passing cloud that will bring us rain.'

'By no means!' he replied. 'It is that which you have sought to hasten: a hurricane bringing a woeful scourge. It will destroy you all at the bidding of its Lord.'

And when morning came there was nothing to be seen besides their ruined dwellings. Thus We reward the wrongdoers.

We had made them more powerful than you[1] and given *46:26* them ears and eyes and hearts. Yet nothing did their ears, their eyes, or their hearts avail them since they denied the revelations of Allah. The scourge at which they scoffed encompassed them.

We destroyed the cities which once flourished around you, and made plain Our revelations to their people so that they might return to the right path. Why did their gods not help them, the gods they had set up besides Allah to bring them close to Him? Indeed, they utterly forsook them. Such were their lies and such their false inventions.

Tell how We sent to you a band of jinn who, when they came and listened to the Koran, said to each other: 'Hush! Hush!' As soon as it was ended they betook themselves to their people and gave them warning. 'Our people,' they *46:30* said, 'we have just been listening to a scripture revealed since the time of Moses, confirming previous scriptures and

1. The Meccans.

129

46:31 directing to the truth and to a straight path. Our people, answer the call of Allah's summoner and believe in him! He will forgive you your sins and deliver you from a woeful punishment. Those that give no heed to Allah's summoner shall not escape His judgement on this earth, nor shall any one protect them besides Him. They are in gross error.'

Do they not see that Allah who created the heavens and the earth and was not wearied by their creation can raise the dead to life? Yes. He has power over all things.

On the day when the unbelievers are brought before the fire of Hell they shall be asked: 'Is this not real?' 'Yes, by the Lord,' they will answer. 'Then taste Our punishment,' He will reply, 'for you were unbelievers.'

46:35 Bear up then with patience, as did the steadfast apostles before you, and do not seek to hurry on their doom. On the day when they behold the scourge with which they are threatened, their life on earth will seem to them no longer than an hour.

That is a warning. Shall any perish except the evil-doers?

KNEELING

In the Name of Allah, the Compassionate, the Merciful

45:1 HA *mim.* This Book is revealed by Allah, the Mighty One, the All-knowing.
Surely in the heavens and the earth there are signs for the faithful; in your own creation, and in the beasts that are scattered far and near, signs for true believers; in the alternation of night and day, in the sustenance Allah sends down from heaven with which He revives the earth after its death, and in the marshalling of the winds, signs for men of understanding.

Such are the revelations of Allah. We recite them to you in all truth. But in what scripture will they believe, if they deny Allah Himself and all His signs?

45:8 Woe to the lying sinner! He hears the revelations of Allah recited to Him and then, as though he never heard them,

persists in scorn. Forewarn him of a woeful doom. Those *45:9*
that deride Our revelations when they have scarcely heard
them shall be put to a shameful punishment.

Hell is behind them. Their gains shall not avail them, nor
shall the gods they serve besides Allah. A dreadful punishment awaits them.

Such is Our guidance. Those that deny the revelations of
their Lord shall suffer the torment of a hideous scourge.

It is Allah who has subdued to you the ocean, so that
ships may sail upon it at His bidding; so that you may seek
His bounty and render thanks to Him.

He has subjected to you what the heavens and the earth
contain; all is from Him. Surely there are signs in this for
thinking men.

Tell the believers to pardon those who dread the days of
victory,[1] the day when Allah will reward men according to
their deeds. He that does what is right does it to his own
advantage; and he that commits evil does so at his own
peril. To your Lord you shall all return.

We gave the Scriptures to the Israelites and bestowed on *45:16*
them wisdom and prophethood. We provided them with
good things and exalted them above the nations. We gave
them plain commandments: yet it was not till knowledge
had been vouchsafed them that they disagreed among themselves from evil motives. On the Day of Resurrection your
Lord Himself will judge their differences.

And now We have set you on the right path. Follow it
and do not yield to the lust of ignorant men; for they can in
no way protect you from the wrath of Allah. The wrongdoers are patrons to each other; but the righteous have
Allah Himself for their patron.

This is an admonition to mankind. It is a guide and a
blessing to true believers.

Do the evil-doers think that they are equal in Our sight
with the believers who do good works, so that their lives
and deaths shall be alike? How ill they judge!

Allah created the heavens and the earth to reveal the truth *45:22*

1. Lit., the Days of Allah.

and to reward each soul according to its deeds. None shall be wronged.

45:23 Think! Who, besides Allah, can guide the man who makes his lust his god, the man whom Allah deliberately misleads, setting a seal upon his ears and heart and drawing a veil over his eyes? Will you not take heed?

They say: 'There is this life and no other. We live and die; nothing but Time destroys us.' Surely of this they have no knowledge. They are merely guessing.

And when Our clear revelations are recited to them, their only argument is: 'Bring back to us our fathers, if what you say be true!'

Say: 'It is Allah who gives you life and later causes you to die. It is He who will gather you all on the Day of Resurrection. Of this there is no doubt; yet most men do not know it.'

Allah's is the kingdom of the heavens and the earth. On the day when the Hour of Doom arrives, those who have denied His revelations will assuredly be lost.

45:28 You shall see all the nations on their knees. Each nation shall be summoned to its book and a voice will say to them: 'You shall this day be rewarded for your deeds. This book of Ours speaks with truth against you. We have recorded all your actions.'

As for those who have faith and do good works, their Lord will admit them into His mercy. Theirs shall be a glorious triumph.

To the unbelievers a voice will say: 'Were My revelations not declared to you? Did you not scorn them and commit evil? When it was said to you: "Allah's promise is true: the Hour of Doom is sure to come," you replied: "We know nothing of the Hour of Doom. It is but a vain conjecture, nor are we convinced."'

The evil of their deeds will manifest itself to them and the scourge at which they scoffed will encompass them. We shall say: 'We will today forget you as you yourselves forgot that you would meet this day. Hell shall be your home *45:35* and none will help you. That is because you scoffed at

Allah's revelations and were seduced by your earthly life.'

On that day there shall be no way out for them; nor shall they be asked to make amends.

Praise, then, be to Allah, the Lord of the heavens and the earth, the Lord of the Creation. Glory be His in heaven and *45:37* earth. He is the Mighty One, the All-knowing.

HOUD

In the Name of Allah, the Compassionate, the Merciful

ALIF *lam ra*. This Book is a revelation from Him who *11:1* is wise and all-knowing. Its verses are imbued with wisdom and set forth with clarity:

Serve none but Allah. I am sent to you by Him to warn you and to give you good news.

Seek forgiveness of your Lord and turn to Him in repentance. He will make a goodly provision for you till an appointed day and will bestow His grace upon the righteous. But if you give no heed, then beware of the torment of a fateful day. To Allah you shall all return. He has power over all things.

They cover up their breasts to conceal their thoughts from Him. But when they put on their garments, does He not know what they hide and what they reveal? He knows their inmost thoughts.

There is not a creature on the earth whose sustenance is not provided by Allah. He knows its dwelling and its resting-place. All is recorded in a glorious book.

Throned above the waters, He made the heavens and the earth in six days, to find out which of you would best acquit himself.

When you[1] say: 'After death you shall be raised to life,' the unbelievers declare: 'It is nothing but plain magic.' And if We put off their punishment till an appointed time, *11:8* they ask: 'Why is it delayed?'

1. Mohammed.

On the day when it overtakes them, they shall not escape it. The terrors at which they scoffed will encompass them.

11:9 If We show man Our mercy and then withhold it from him, he yields to despair and becomes ungrateful. And if after adversity We bestow favours upon him, he says: 'Gone are my sorrows from me,' and grows jubilant and boastful.

Not so the steadfast who do good works. They shall have forgiveness and a rich reward.

You may chance to omit a part of that which is revealed to you and be distressed because they say: 'Why has no treasure been sent to him? Why has no angel come with him?'

But your mission is only to give warning. Allah is the guardian of all things. If they say: 'He has invented it[1] himself,' say to them: 'Invent ten chapters like it. Call on whom you will of your idols, if what you say be true. But if they fail you, know that it is revealed with Allah's knowledge, and that there is no god but Him. Will you then accept Islam?'

11:15 Those that desire the life of this world with all its frippery shall be rewarded for their deeds in their own lifetime: nothing shall be denied them. These are the men who in the world to come shall be rewarded with Hell-fire. Fruitless are their deeds, and vain are all their works.

Are they to be compared with those that have received a veritable word from their Lord, recited by a witness from Him and heralded by the Book of Moses, a guide and a blessing? These have faith in it, but the factions who deny it shall be consigned to the flames of Hell. Therefore do not doubt it. It is the truth from your Lord: yet most men have no faith.

And who is more wicked than the man who invents a falsehood about Allah? Such men shall be brought before their Lord, and witnesses will say: 'These are they who lied about Allah.'

11:19 Allah's curse is on the wrongdoers, who debar others

1. The Koran.

from His path and seek to make it crooked, and who deny
the life to come. These shall not escape in this world; there *11:20*
is none to protect them besides Allah. Their punishment
shall be doubled, for they could neither see nor hear.

Such are those who shall forfeit their souls. Their false
devices shall vanish from them, and in the life to come they
shall be lost indeed.

As for those that have faith and do good works and
humble themselves before their Lord, they are the heirs of
Paradise, and there they shall abide for ever.

Can the blind and the deaf be compared to those that can
see and hear? Such are the unbelievers compared to the
faithful. Will you not take heed?

Long ago We sent forth Noah to his people. He said: 'I *11:25*
have come to warn you plainly. Serve none but Allah.
Beware of the torment of a woeful day.'

The unbelieving elders of his people replied: 'We regard
you as a mortal like ourselves. Nor can we find any among
your followers but men of hasty judgement, the lowliest of
our tribe. We see no virtue in you: indeed we know that you
are lying.'

He said: 'Think, my people! If my Lord has revealed to
me His will and bestowed on me His grace, though it be
hidden from you, can we compel you to accept it against
your will? I seek of you no recompense for this, my people;
for none can reward me but Allah. Nor will I drive away the
faithful, for they will surely meet their Lord. But I can see
that you are ignorant men. Were I to drive them away, my
people, who would protect me from Allah? Will you not
take heed?

'I do not say that I possess Allah's treasures, or that I
know what is hidden. I do not claim to be an angel, nor do
I say to those whom you disdain that Allah will not be
bountiful to them – He knows best what is in their hearts –
for then I should become a wrongdoer.'

'Noah,' they replied, 'you have argued, and argued too *11:32*
much, with us. Bring down the scourge with which you
threaten us, if what you say be true!'

11:33   He said: 'Allah will visit His scourge upon you when He pleases: you shall not escape it. Nor will my counsel profit you if Allah seeks to mislead you, willing though I am to guide you. He is your Lord, and to Him you shall return.'

If they declare: 'He has invented it himself,' say: 'If I have indeed invented it, then may I be punished for my sin! I am innocent of your crimes.'

Allah's will was revealed to Noah, saying: 'None of your people will believe in you save those who have already believed. Do not grieve at their misdeeds. Build an ark under Our watchful eyes, according to Our bidding. Do not plead with Me for the wrongdoers: they shall all be drowned.'

11:38   So he built the ark. And whenever the elders of his people passed by him they jeered at him. He said: 'Mock if you will. Just as you now mock us, so we shall mock you. You shall know who will be punished and put to shame, and who will be afflicted by an everlasting scourge.'

And when Our will was done and water welled out from the Oven, We said to Noah: 'Take into the Ark a pair from every species, your tribe (except those already doomed), and all the true believers.' But none save a few believed with him.

Noah said: 'Embark in it. It will set sail in the name of Allah, and in the name of Allah it will cast anchor. My Lord is forgiving and merciful.'

And as the Ark moved on with them amidst the mountainous waves, Noah cried out to his son, who stood apart: 'Embark with us, my child,' he said. 'Do not stay with the unbelievers!'

He replied: 'I shall seek refuge in a mountain, which will protect me from the flood.'

Noah cried: 'None shall be secure this day from Allah's judgement, except those to whom He will show mercy!' And thereupon the billows rolled between them, and Noah's son was drowned.

11:44   A voice cried out: 'Earth, swallow up your waters. Heaven, cease your rain!' The floods abated and Allah's will was done. The Ark came to rest upon Al-Judi, and there was heard a voice saying: 'Gone are the evil-doers.'

Noah called out to his Lord, saying: 'Lord, my son was *11:45* my own flesh and blood. Your promise was surely true. You are the most just of judges.'

'Noah,' He replied, 'he was no kinsman of yours: he was an evil-doer. Do not question Me about things you know nothing of. I admonish you lest you become an ignorant man.'

'Forgive me, Lord, for my presumption,' said Noah. 'Pardon me and have mercy on me, or I shall surely be lost.'

'Noah,' He replied, 'go ashore in peace. Our blessings are upon you and on *some* of the descendants of those that are with you. As for the others, We will suffer them to take their ease in this world and then visit upon them a woeful scourge.'

That which We have now revealed to you is secret his- *11:49* tory: it was unknown to you and to your people. Have patience; the righteous shall have a joyful end.

To Aad We sent their compatriot Houd. He said: 'Serve Allah, my people; you have no god but Him. False are the idols you worship. I demand of you no recompense, my people, for none can reward me, except my Creator. Will you not understand?

'My people, seek forgiveness of your Lord and turn to Him in repentance. He will send from heaven abundant rain upon you; He will add strength to your strength. Do not turn away from Him with wrongdoing.'

They replied: 'You have given us no proof of your mission. We will not forsake our gods at your behest, nor will we believe in you. We can only suppose that our gods have afflicted you with madness.'

He said: 'Allah is my witness, and so are you, that I am done with your idols. Scheme against me if you will and give me no respite. I have put my trust in Allah, my Lord *11:56* and your Lord. There is not a living creature on the earth whose destiny He does not control. Straight is the path of my Lord.

11:57 'I have made known to you my message. If you give no heed, my Lord will replace you by other men. You can do Him no harm. My Lord is watching over all things.'

And when Our judgement came to pass, We delivered Houd through Our mercy, together with those who shared his faith. We delivered them from a woeful scourge.

Such were Aad. They denied the revelations of their Lord, disobeyed His apostles, and did the bidding of every rebellious reprobate. They were cursed in this world, and cursed they shall be on the Day of Resurrection.

Aad denied their Lord. Gone are Aad, the people of Houd.

And to Thamoud We sent their compatriot Saleh. He said: 'Serve Allah, my people; you have no god but Him. It was He who made you from the earth and gave you dwellings upon it. Seek forgiveness of Him and turn to Him in repentance. My Lord is near at hand; He will hear your prayers.'

11:62 'Saleh,' they replied, 'great were the hopes we placed in you. Would you now forbid us to serve the gods our fathers worshipped? Truly, we strongly doubt the faith to which you call us.'

He said: 'Think, my people! If my Lord has revealed to me His will and bestowed on me His grace, who would protect me from Allah if I rebelled against Him? You surely wish to ruin me.

'My people, here is Allah's she-camel, a veritable sign for you. Leave her to graze at will in Allah's own land and do not molest her lest an instant scourge should fall upon you.'

Yet they slew her. He said: 'You have but three days to live in your dwellings. This prophecy shall be fulfilled.'

And when Our judgement came to pass, We delivered Saleh through Our mercy from the ignominy of that day, together with those who shared his faith. Mighty is your Lord and all-powerful. A dreadful cry rang above the evil-doers, and when morning came they were prostrate in their *11:68* dwellings; they might never have prospered there.

Thamoud denied their Lord. Gone are they all.

Our messengers came to Abraham with good news. They *11:69* said: 'Peace!' 'Peace!' he answered, and hastened to bring them a roasted calf. But when he saw that they did not touch it, he mistrusted them and was afraid of them. But they said: 'Do not be alarmed. We are sent forth to the people of Lot.'

His wife, who was waiting on them, rejoiced. We told her that she would give birth to Isaac, and that Isaac would beget Jacob.

'Alas!' she replied. 'How shall I bear a child when I am old and my husband is well-advanced in years? This is indeed a strange thing.'

They replied: 'Do you marvel at the ways of Allah? May Allah's blessings and mercy be upon you, dear hosts! Glorious is He, and worthy of praise.'

And when he heard the good news and was no longer frightened, Abraham pleaded with Us for the people of Lot; for he was a gracious, compassionate, and tender-hearted man.

We said: 'Abraham, plead no more. Your Lord's decree *11:76* must be fulfilled. Irrevocable is the scourge which shall smite them.'

And when Our messengers came to Lot, he grew anxious about them, for he was unable to offer them protection. He thought: 'This is indeed a day of woe.'

His people, long addicted to evil practices, came running towards him. 'My people,' he said, 'here are my daughters: they are more lawful to you. Have fear of Allah and do not humiliate me by wronging my guests. Is there not one good man amongst you?'

They replied: 'You know we have no need of your daughters. You know full well what we are seeking.'

He cried: 'Would that I had strength enough to overcome you, or could find refuge in some mighty man!'

They said: 'Lot, we are the messengers of your Lord: *11:81* they shall not touch you. Depart with your kinsfolk in the dead of night and let none of you turn back. As for your wife, she shall suffer the fate of the others. In the morning their hour will come. Is not the morning near?'

11:82   And when Our judgement came to pass, We laid their town in ruins, and let loose upon it a shower of clay-stones bearing the tokens of your Lord. The punishment of the unjust was not far off.

And to the people of Midian We sent their compatriot Shoaib. He said: 'Serve Allah, my people; you have no god but Him. Do not give short weight or measure. Prosperous though you are, beware of the torment of a fateful day!

'My people, give just weight and measure in all fairness. Do not defraud others of their possessions and do not corrupt the land with evil. Better for you is Allah's reward, if you are true believers. I am no guardian over you.'

'Shoaib,' they replied, 'did your prayers teach you that we should renounce the gods of our fathers and that we ought not to conduct our affairs in the manner we pleased? Truly, you are a wise and gracious man!'

11:88   He said: 'Think, my people! If my Lord has revealed to me His will and bestowed on me a noble gift, should I not guide you? I do not wish to argue with you, nor will I stoop to that which I forbid you. I seek only to reform you: and to do this I shall strive with all my power. Allah will guide me. In Him I have put my trust and to Him I have turned in repentance.

'Let your disagreement with me not bring upon you the doom which overtook the peoples of Noah, Houd, and Saleh; nor is it long since the tribe of Lot was punished. Seek forgiveness of your Lord and turn to Him in repentance. My Lord is loving and merciful.'

They replied: 'Most of what you say is meaningless to us. We know how weak you are in this city. But for your tribe, we should have stoned you. You shall on no account prevail against us.'

He said: 'Have you more reverence for my tribe than for Allah? Dare you turn your backs upon Him? My Lord has *11:93* knowledge of all your actions. Do what you will, my people, and so will I. You shall know who will be punished and put to shame, and who is lying. Wait if you will; I too am waiting.'

And when Our judgement was executed We delivered 11:94 Shoaib through Our mercy, together with those who shared his faith. A dreadful cry rang above the evil-doers, and when morning came they were prostrate in their dwellings: they might never have prospered there. Like Thamoud, gone are the people of Midian.

We sent forth Moses with Our signs and with illustrious power to Pharaoh and his nobles. But they followed the behests of their master; evil were Pharaoh's behests. He shall stand at the head of his people on the Day of Resurrection and lead them into the fire of Hell. Dismal is the place to which they shall be led.

A curse followed them in this world, and a curse shall follow them on the Day of Resurrection. Evil is the gift they shall receive.

We have recounted to you the histories of these nations: some have survived, while others were annihilated. We did 11:101 not wrong them, but they wronged themselves. Their false gods availed them nothing: they only hastened their ruin.

Such was the scourge which your Lord has visited upon the sinful nations. His punishment is stern and harrowing.

Surely in this there is a sign for him that dreads the terrors of the life to come. On that day all men shall be assembled. That shall be a fateful day.

We shall defer it to its appointed hour. And when it comes, no man shall speak but by His leave. Some shall be damned, and others blessed. The damned shall be cast into the fire of Hell where, groaning and wailing, they shall abide as long as the heavens and the earth endure, unless your Lord ordains otherwise: your Lord accomplishes what He will. As for the blessed, they shall dwell in Paradise as long as the heavens and the earth endure, unless your Lord ordains otherwise. Theirs shall be an endless recompense.

Have no doubt as to what they worship. They serve the 11:109 idols which their fathers served before them. We shall requite them in full measure.

11:110 We gave the Scriptures to Moses, but his people disgreed about them. Had your Lord not deferred their punishment, their fate would have long been settled. Yet they strongly doubt this.

Your Lord will reward all men according to their deeds. He has knowledge of all their actions. Follow then the right path as you are bidden, together with those who have repented with you, and do not transgress. He is watching over all your actions.

Put no trust in the wrongdoers, lest you incur the punishment of Hell. None but Allah can protect or help you.

Recite your prayers morning and evening, and in the night-time too. Good deeds make amends for sins. That is an admonition for thoughtful men. Therefore have patience; the righteous shall not lose their reward.

Were there among the generations that have gone before you any upright men who preached against evil, except the few whom We delivered from among them? The wrongdoers pursued their worldly pleasures and thus became
11:117 guilty. Your Lord would not have ruined those cities, without just cause, had their inhabitants been righteous men.

Had your Lord pleased, He would have united all mankind. But only those whom He has shown mercy will cease to differ. For this end He has created them. The word of your Lord shall be fulfilled: 'I will fill the pit of Hell with jinn and men.'

We recount to you the histories of these apostles to put courage into your heart. Through this the truth is revealed to you, with precepts and admonitions for true believers.

Say to the infidels: 'Do whatever lies within your power, and so shall we. Wait if you will; we too are waiting.'
11:123 Allah alone has knowledge of what is hidden in the heavens and the earth; to Him all shall return. Serve Him, and put your trust in Him. Your Lord is watching over all your actions.

THUNDER

In the Name of Allah, the Compassionate, the Merciful

ALIF *lam mim ra*. These are the verses of the Book. *13:1* That which is revealed to you from your Lord is the truth, yet men have no faith.

It was Allah who raised the heavens without visible pillars. He ascended His throne and forced the sun and the moon into His service, each pursuing an appointed course. He ordains all things. He makes plain His revelations so that you may firmly believe in meeting your Lord.

It was He who spread out the earth and placed upon it rivers and immovable mountains. He gave all plants their male and female parts and drew the veil of night over the day. Surely in these there are signs for thinking men.

And in the land there are adjoining plots: vineyards and cornfields and groves of palm, the single and the clustered. Their fruits are nourished by the same water: yet We give each a different taste. Surely in this there are signs for men of understanding.

If anything could make you marvel, then you should *13:5* surely marvel at those who say: 'When we are dust, shall we be raised to life again?'

Such are those who deny their Lord. Their necks shall be bound with chains and in the fire of Hell they shall abide for ever.

They bid you hasten evil rather than good. Yet many were those who were punished before them. Your Lord is merciful to men, despite their sins: yet stern is He in retribution.

The unbelievers ask: 'Why has no sign been given him by his Lord?' But your mission is only to give warning. Every nation has its mentor.

Allah knows what every female bears: He knows of *13:8* every change within her womb. He plans all things.

13:9   He knows the visible and the unseen. He is the Supreme One, the Most High.

It is alike whether you whisper or speak aloud, whether you hide under the cloak of night or walk about in broad day. Each has guardian angels before him and behind him, who watch him by Allah's command.

Allah does not change a people's lot unless they change what is in their hearts. If He seeks to afflict them with a misfortune, none can ward it off. Besides Him, they have no protector.

It is He who makes the lightning flash upon you, inspiring you with fear and hope, as He gathers up the heavy clouds. The thunder sounds His praises, and the angels, too, for awe of Him. He hurls His thunderbolts at whom He pleases. Yet the unbelievers wrangle about Allah. Stern is His punishment.

13:14   His is the true prayer. The idols to which the pagans pray give them no answer. They are like a man who stretches out his hands to the water and bids it rise to his mouth: it cannot reach it! Vain are the prayers of the unbelievers.

All who dwell in the heavens and on earth shall prostrate themselves before Allah, some willingly and some by force; their very shadows shall bow to Him morning and evening.

Say: 'Who is the Lord of the heavens and the earth?'

Say: 'Allah.'

Say: 'Why then have you chosen other gods besides Him, who, even to themselves, can do neither harm nor good?'

Say: 'Are the blind and the seeing alike? Does darkness resemble the light?'

Have their idols brought into being a creation like His, so that both creations appear to them alike?

Say: 'Allah is the Creator of all things. He is the One, the Almighty.'

13:17   He sends down water from the sky which fills the riverbeds to overflowing, so that their torrents bear a swelling foam, akin to that which rises from smelted ore when men make ornaments and tools. Thus Allah depicts truth and falsehood. The scum is cast away, but that which is of use to man remains behind. Thus Allah coins His parables.

Rich is the reward of those that obey Allah. But those 13:18 that disobey Him – if they possessed all that the earth contains, and as much besides, they would gladly offer it for their ransom. Theirs shall be an evil reckoning. Hell shall be their home, a dismal resting-place.

Is then he who knows the truth of what has been revealed to you by your Lord, like him who is blind?

Truly, none will take heed but the wise: those who keep faith with Allah and do not break their pledge; who join together what He has bidden to be united; who fear their Lord and dread the terrors of Judgement-day; who for the sake of Allah endure with fortitude, attend to their prayers, and give alms in private and in public; and who ward off evil with good. These shall have a blissful end. They shall enter the Gardens of Eden, together with the righteous among their fathers, their wives, and their descendants. From every gate the angels will come to them, saying: 'Peace be to you for all that you have steadfastly endured. Blessed is the reward of Paradise.'

As for those who break Allah's covenant after accepting 13:25 it, who part what He has bidden to be united and commit evil in the land, a curse shall be laid on them, and they shall have an evil end.

Allah gives abundantly to whom He will and sparingly to whom He pleases. The unbelievers rejoice in this life: but brief indeed is the comfort of this life compared to the life to come.

The unbelievers ask: 'Why has no sign been given him by his Lord?'

Say: 'Allah leaves in error whom He will, and guides those who repent and have faith; whose hearts find comfort in the remembrance of Allah. Surely in the remembrance of Allah all hearts are comforted. Blessed are those who have faith and do good works; blissful their end.'

Thus We have sent you forth to a nation before whom 13:30 many others have passed away, that you may recite to them

Our revelations. Yet they deny the Lord of Mercy. Say: 'He is my Lord. There is no god but Him. In Him I have put my trust, and to Him I shall return.'

13:31 And what if this Koran were to move mountains, rend the earth asunder, and make the dead speak? All things are subject to Allah's will. Do the faithful doubt that Allah, had he pleased, could have guided all mankind?

As for the unbelievers, because of their misdeeds ill-fortune shall not cease to afflict them or crouch at their very doorstep until Allah's promise is fulfilled. Allah will not fail His promise.

Other apostles were mocked before you: but though I bore long with the unbelievers My scourge at length over-took them. And how terrible was My scourge!

Who is it that watches over every soul and all its actions? Yet they set up other gods besides Allah. Say: 'Name them. Would you tell Allah of that which is unknown to Him? Or are they but empty words?'

Indeed, their foul devices seem fair to the unbelievers, for they are debarred from the right path. None can guide those whom Allah has led astray. They shall be punished in this life: but more painful is the punishment of the life to come. None shall protect them from Allah.

13:35 This is the Paradise which the righteous have been promised: it is watered by running streams: eternal are its fruits, and eternal are its shades. Such is the reward of the righteous. But the reward of the unbelievers is the fire of Hell.

Those to whom the Scriptures were given rejoice in what is revealed to you, while some factions deny a part of it. Say: 'I am commanded to serve Allah and to associate none with Him. To Him I pray, and to Him I shall return.'

Thus We have revealed it, a code of judgements in the Arabic tongue. If you succumb to their desires after all the knowledge you have been given, none shall save or protect you from Allah.

13:38 We have sent forth other apostles before you and given them wives and children. Yet none of them could work miracles except by the will of Allah. Every age has its scripture. Allah confirms or abrogates what He pleases. His *13:39* is the Eternal Book.

Whether We let you witness the punishment with which We threaten them, or cause you to die before it is fulfilled, your mission is only to give warning: it is for Us to do the reckoning.

Do they not see how We invade their land and shrink its borders? If Allah decrees a thing, none can reverse it. Swift is His reckoning.

Those who have gone before them also plotted, but Allah is the master of every plot: He knows the deserts of every soul. The unbelievers shall know for whom is the reward of Paradise.

They say: 'You are no true apostle.' Say: 'Allah is our all- *13:43* sufficient witness, and those too who know the Scriptures.'

SMOKE

In the Name of Allah, the Compassionate, the Merciful

HA *mim*. We swear by the Glorious Book that We *44:1* revealed the Koran on a blessed night. We revealed it to warn mankind, on a night when every precept was made plain as a commandment from Ourself. We sent it down as a blessing from your Lord, who hears all and knows all.

He is the Lord of the heavens and the earth and all that lies between them. (Mark this, if you are true believers!) There is no god but Him. He ordains life and death. He is your God and the God of your forefathers. Yet they divert themselves with doubts.

Wait for the day when the sky will pour down blinding smoke, enveloping all men: a dreadful scourge. Then they will say: 'Lord, lift up this scourge from us. We are now believers.' But how will their new faith help them, when an undoubted prophet had come to them and they denied him, saying: 'A madman, taught by others!'

Yet if We slightly relieve their affliction they will return *44:15*

44:16 to unbelief. But on that day We will inflict on them the sternest punishment and avenge Ourself.

We tested Pharaoh's people long before that. A gracious apostle came to them, saying: 'Surrender to me the servants of Allah. I am a truthful messenger. Do not hold yourselves above Allah. I bring you veritable proofs. I adjure you by Him who is my Lord and your Lord not to stone me. If you have no faith in me, do not harm me.'

Then he cried out to his Lord, saying: 'These are sinful men.'

His Lord answered: 'Set forth with My servants by night, for the Egyptians will pursue you. Then cross the parted sea. Pharaoh's legions shall be drowned.'

How many gardens, how many fountains, they left behind them! Cornfields, and noble palaces, and good things in which they took delight. All this they left; and that which once belonged to them We gave to other men. Neither heaven nor earth shed tears for them; nor were they reprieved. We saved the Israelites from a degrading scourge, from Pharaoh, who was a tyrant and a transgressor, and exalted them advisedly above the nations. We showed them miracles which tested them beyond all doubt.

44:34 Yet the unbelievers say: 'We shall die but one death, nor shall we ever be raised to life. Bring back to us our fathers, if what you say be true.'

Are they better than the people of Tobba[1] and those who thrived before them? We destroyed them all, for they too were wicked men.

It was not in sport that We created the heavens and the earth and all that lies between them. We created them to reveal the truth. But of this most men have no knowledge.

The Day of Judgement is the appointed time for all. On that day no man shall help his friend; none shall be helped save those on whom Allah will have mercy. He is the Mighty One, the Merciful.

The fruit of the Zaqqum-tree shall be the sinner's food.
44:46 Like dregs of oil, like scalding water, it shall simmer in his

1. The people of Hamyar, in Arabia.

belly. A voice will cry: 'Seize him and drag him into the   *44:47*
depth of Hell. Then pour out boiling water over his head,
saying: "Taste this, illustrious and honourable man! This
is the punishment which you doubted."'

As for the righteous, they shall dwell in peace together
amidst gardens and fountains, arrayed in rich silks and fine
brocade. Yes, and We shall wed them to dark-eyed houris.
Secure against all ills, they shall call for every kind of fruit;
and, having died once, they shall die no more. Your Lord
will through His mercy shield them from the scourge of
Hell. That will be the supreme triumph.

We have revealed this to you in your own tongue so that
they may take heed. Wait, then, as they themselves are wait-   *44:59*
ing.

ORNAMENTS OF GOLD

In the Name of Allah, the Compassionate, the Merciful

HA *mim*. By the Glorious Book!   *43:1*
We have revealed the Koran in the Arabic
tongue that you may grasp its meaning. It is a
transcript of Our eternal book, sublime, and full of wisdom.

Should We ignore you because you are a sinful nation?
Many a prophet did We send forth to the ancients: but
they scoffed at each prophet that arose amongst them. We
utterly destroyed them, though they were mightier than
these.[1]

Such then, is the example of the ancients. Yet, if you ask
them[1] who created the heavens and the earth, they are
bound to answer: 'The Almighty, the All-knowing, created
them.'

It is He who has made the earth a resting-place for you
and traced out routes upon it that you may find your way;
who sends down water from the sky in due measure and
thereby quickens the dead land (even thus you shall be
raised to life); who has created all living things in pairs and   *43:12*

1. The Meccans.

made for you the ships and beasts on which you ride, so
43:13 that, as you mount upon their backs, you may recall the
goodness of your Lord and say: 'Glory to Him who has
subjected these to us. But for Him we could not be their
masters. To our Lord we shall all return.'

Yet they assign to Him offspring from among His servants! Surely man is monstrously ungrateful. Would Allah
choose daughters for Himself and sons for you?[1]

Yet when the birth of a daughter is announced to one of
them[1] his face darkens and he is filled with gloom. Would
they ascribe to Allah females who adorn themselves with
trinkets and are powerless in disputation?

They regard as females the angels who are Allah's servants. Did they witness their creation? Their claims shall
be noted down. They shall be closely questioned.

They say: 'Had it been Allah's will, we should never
have worshipped them.' Surely of this they have no knowledge: they are lying.

Have We given them a scripture before this, so that they
should hold fast to it?

They say: 'This was the faith our fathers practised. We
are merely walking in their footsteps.'

43:23   Thus, whenever, before you, We sent an apostle to warn
a nation, those who lived in comfort said: 'This was the
faith our fathers practised; we are merely walking in their
footsteps.'

Each apostle said: 'What if I bring you a religion more
enlightened than your fathers'?' But they replied: 'We deny
the message you have brought.' So We took vengeance on
them. Consider the fate of those who disbelieved Our
warning.

Tell of Abraham, who said to his father and to his
people: 'I renounce your gods except Him who created me,
43:28 for He will rightly guide me.' He made this an abiding
precept among his descendants, so that they might turn to
none but Allah.

1. The pagan Arabs believed that the angels, and their own god-
desses, were daughters of Allah.

I allowed these men and their fathers to live in comfort 43:29
until there came to them the truth and an apostle giving
them guidance. But now that the truth has come to them,
they say: 'It is witchcraft. We will not believe in it.' They
also say: 'Why was this Koran not revealed to some mighty
man from the two towns?'[1]

Are they the distributors of your Lord's blessings? It is
We who deal out to them their livelihoods in this world,
exalting some in rank above others, so that the one may
take the other into his service. Better is your Lord's mercy
than all their hoarded treasures.

But for the fear that all mankind might have become one
race of unbelievers, We would have given those who deny
the Lord of Mercy dwellings with silver roofs, and gates
and stairs of silver; silver couches to recline upon and ornaments of gold: for all these are but the fleeting comforts of
this life. It is the life to come that Allah reserves for those
who fear Him.

He that does not heed the warning of the Merciful shall 43:36
have a devil for his companion (devils turn men away from
the right path, though they may think themselves rightly
guided). And when he comes before Us, he shall say:[2]
'Would that we were as far apart as the east is from the
west.' Truly, Satan is an evil companion.

But because you have done wrong, that others will share
your punishment will not avail you on that day.

You cannot make the deaf hear, nor can you guide the
blind or those who are in gross error. Whether We take you
hence or let you live to see Our threats fulfilled, We shall
surely take vengeance on them: for We have absolute
power over them.

Therefore hold fast to that which is revealed to you: you
are on the right path. It is an admonition to you and to
your people. You shall be questioned all.

Ask those of Our apostles whom We sent before you if
We ever appointed gods to be worshipped besides Allah.

We sent forth Moses with Our signs to Pharaoh and his 43:46

1. Mecca and Medina.   2. To his companion.

nobles. He said: 'I am the apostle of the Lord of the
43:47 Creation.' But when he showed them Our signs they laughed at them: yet each fresh sign We revealed to them was
mightier than the one that came before it. Therefore We let
loose Our scourge upon them, so that they might return to
the right path.

'Magician,' they said, 'pray to your Lord for us and invoke the promise He has made you. We accept your guidance.'

But when We had relieved their affliction they broke
their pledge.

Pharaoh made a proclamation among his people. 'My
people,' said he, 'is the kingdom of Egypt not mine, and
are these rivers which flow at my feet not mine also? Can
you not see? Am I not mightier than this despicable wretch,
who can scarcely make his meaning plain? Why have no
bracelets of gold been given him, or angels sent down with
him?'

43:54   Thus he incited his people. They obeyed him, for they
were degenerate men. And when they provoked Us, We
took vengeance on them and drowned them all, as a lesson
and an example to those who succeeded them.

When Mary's son is cited as an instance, your people
laugh and say: 'Is he better than our own gods?' They cite
him to you merely to provoke you. Truly, they are a contentious nation.

Jesus was no more than a mortal whom We favoured and
made an example to the Israelites. Had it been Our will We
could have replaced you with angels to succeed you on the
earth. He is a portent of the Hour of Doom. Have no doubt
about its coming and follow Me. This is the right path: let
Satan not mislead you, for he is your sworn enemy.

And when Jesus worked his miracles, he said: 'I have
to give you wisdom and to make plain to you some of
the things about which you differ. Fear Allah and follow
43:64 me. Allah is my Lord and your Lord: therefore serve Him.
That is the right path.'

Yet the factions disagreed among themselves. But when 43:65 the Day of Judgement comes, woe to the wrongdoers, for they shall be sternly punished.

Are they waiting for the Hour of Doom to overtake them unawares, without warning? On that day friends shall become enemies, except the God-fearing.

But you, My servants, who have believed in My revelations and surrendered yourselves, shall on that day have nothing to fear or to regret. Enter Paradise, you and your spouses, in all delight. You shall be served with golden dishes and golden cups. Abiding there for ever, you shall find all that your souls desire and all that your eyes rejoice in.

Such is the Paradise you shall inherit by virtue of your good deeds. Your sustenance shall be abundant fruit.

But the evil-doers shall endure for ever the torment of Hell. Their punishment will never be lightened and they shall be speechless with despair. We do not wrong them, but they wrong themselves.

'Malek,'[1] they will call out, 'let your Lord make an end 43:77 of us!' But he will answer: 'Here you shall remain!'

We have made known to you the truth, but most of you abhor the truth.

If they are resolved to ruin you,[2] We are resolved to ruin them. Do they think We cannot hear their secret talk and private converse? Yes! Our angels, who are at their side, record it all.

Say:[3] 'If the Lord of Mercy had a son, I would be the first to worship him.'

Exalted be the Lord of the heavens and the earth, the Lord of the Throne, above their falsehoods! Let them blunder, let them play, until they face the day with which they are threatened.

He is God in heaven and God on earth; He is the Wise One, the All-knowing. Blessed be He to whom belongs 43:85

1. One of the keepers of Hell.
2. Mohammed.
3. To the Christians.

the kingdom of the heavens and the earth and all that lies between them! He alone has knowledge of the Hour of Doom. To Him you shall all return.

The gods to whom they pray besides Him have not the power to intercede for them. None can intercede for them save him who knows the truth and testifies to it.

Yet if you ask them who created them, they will promptly reply that it was Allah. How then can they turn away from Him?

The Apostle says: 'Lord, these men are unbelievers.'

43:89   Bear with them and wish them peace. They shall before long know their error.

COUNSEL

In the Name of Allah, the Compassionate, the Merciful

42:1   HA *mim: ain sin qaf.* Thus Allah, the Mighty One, the Wise One, inspires you as He inspired others before you.

His is what the heavens and the earth contain. He is the Most High, the Supreme One.

The heavens above well-nigh break apart as the angels give glory to their Lord and beg forgiveness for those on earth. Allah is the Benignant One, the Merciful.

As for those that serve other masters besides Him, Allah Himself is watching over them. You are not accountable for what they do.

Thus We have revealed to you an Arabic Koran, that you may warn the mother-city[1] and those who dwell around it; that you may forewarn them of the day which is sure to come: when all mankind are brought together, some in Paradise and some in Hell.

42:8   Had it been Allah's will, He could have made them all of one religion. But Allah brings whom He will into His mercy; the wrongdoers have none to befriend or help them.

1. Mecca.

Have they set up other guardians besides Him? Surely *42:9*
Allah alone is the Guardian. He brings back the dead to life
and has power over all things.

Whatever the subject of your disputes, the final word
belongs to Allah. Such is Allah, my Lord. In Him I have
put my trust, and to Him I turn in repentance.

Creator of the heavens and the earth, He has given you
wives from among yourselves to multiply you, and cattle
male and female. Nothing can be compared with Him. He
alone hears all and sees all.

His are the keys of the heavens and the earth. He gives
abundantly to whom He will and sparingly to whom He
pleases. He has knowledge of all things.

He has ordained for men the faith He has revealed to you *42:13*
and formerly enjoined on Noah and Abraham, on Moses
and Jesus, saying: 'Observe this Faith and be united in it.'
But that to which you call them is unacceptable to the
idolators. Allah chooses for it whom He will, and guides to
it those that repent.

Yet men divided themselves through their own wickedness only after knowledge had been given them. And had
Allah not deferred their punishment to an appointed time,
they would surely have been punished in this life. Those
who inherited the Scriptures after them have their grave
doubts too.

Therefore call men to the true faith, and follow the
straight path as you are bidden. Do not be led by their
desires, but say: 'I believe in all the scriptures that Allah
has revealed. I am commanded to exercise justice among
you. Allah is our Lord and your Lord. We have our own
works and you have yours; let there be no argument
between us. Allah will bring us all together, for to Him
we shall return.'

As for those who argue about Allah after pledging Him
obedience, their arguments will have no weight with their
Lord, and His wrath will fall upon them. They shall be
sternly punished.

It is Allah who has revealed the Book with truth and *42:17* justice. And who can tell? The Hour of Doom may be fast approaching.

42:18 Those who deny it seek to hurry it on; but the true believers dread its coming and know it is the truth. Indeed, those who doubt the Hour are in the grossest error.

Benign is Allah towards His servants. He is bountiful to whom He will. He is the Invincible One, the Almighty.

Whoever seeks the harvest of the world to come, to him We will give in great abundance; and whoever desires the harvest of this world, a share of it shall be his: but in the hereafter he shall have no share at all.

Have they idols which in the practice of their faith have made lawful to them what Allah has not allowed? Had the decisive word not been pronounced already, their fate would surely have been settled in this life. The wrongdoers shall endure a harrowing torment.

42:22 On that day you shall see the wrongdoers aghast at their own deeds, for then Our scourge will surely smite them. But those that have faith and do good works shall dwell in the fair gardens of Paradise and receive from their Lord all that they desire. Surely this is the supreme boon.

Such is Allah's promise to true believers who do good works. Say: 'For this I demand of you no recompense. I ask you only to love your kindred. He that does a good deed shall be repaid many times over. Allah is forgiving and bountiful in His rewards.'

Do they say: 'He has framed a falsehood about Allah?' But if Allah pleased He could seal your heart. He will bring falsehood to nothing and vindicate the truth by His words. He knows the secret thoughts of men.

He accepts the repentance of His servants and pardons their sins. He has knowledge of all their actions.

He hears the prayer of those who have faith and do good works, and enriches them through His bounty. But a woeful punishment awaits the unbelievers.

42:27 Had Allah bestowed abundance upon His servants, they would have filled the earth with evil. He gives them what He will in due measure; He knows and observes His servants.

It is He who sends down rain for them when they have **42:28** lost all hope, and spreads abroad His blessings. He is the Glorious Guardian.

Among His signs is the creation of the heavens and the earth and the living things which He has dispersed over them. If He will, He can gather them all together.

If a misfortune befalls you, it is the fruit of your own labours. He forgives much.

On this earth you cannot escape Him, nor is there any besides Allah to protect or help you.

And upon His signs are the ships which sail like banners[1] upon the ocean. If He will, He calms the wind so that they lie motionless upon its bosom (surely there are signs in this for steadfast men who render thanks); or causes them to founder as a punishment for their misdeeds.[2] Yet many are the sins that He forgives.

Those who dispute Our revelations shall know that they **42:35** have no escape.

That which you have been given is but the fleeting comfort of this life. Better and more enduring is Allah's reward to those who believe and put their trust in Him; who avoid gross sins and indecencies and, when angered, are willing to forgive; who obey their Lord, attend to their prayers, and conduct their affairs by mutual consent; who bestow in alms a part of that which We have given them and, when oppressed, seek to redress their wrongs.

Let evil be rewarded with like evil. But he that forgives and seeks reconcilement shall be rewarded by Allah. He does not love the wrongdoers.

Those who avenge themselves when wronged incur no guilt. But great is the guilt of those who oppress their fellowmen and conduct themselves with wickedness and injustice. These shall be sternly punished.

To endure with fortitude and to forgive is a duty incumbent on all. He whom Allah leads astray has none to **42:44** protect him.

When they face their punishment, you shall see the

1. Or *mountains*.   2. The misdeeds of those who sail in them.

42:45 wrongdoers exclaim: 'Is there no way back?' You shall see them brought before the Fire. Humbled by shame, they shall look upon it with furtive glances. The true believers will say: 'Great indeed is the loss of those who forfeited their souls and all their kindred on the Day of Resurrection.'

The wrongdoers shall suffer an everlasting punishment. They shall have no friend to help them besides Allah. He whom Allah leads astray shall be lost indeed.

Obey your Lord before that day arrives which none can defer against the will of Allah. For on that day there shall be no refuge for you, nor shall you be able to deny your sins.

42:48 If they give no heed, know that We have not sent you[1] to be their keeper. Your only duty is to warn them.

When We bestow a blessing on man, he rejoices in it; but when through his own fault evil befalls him he is ungrateful.

To Allah belongs the kingdom of the heavens and the earth. He creates what He will. He gives daughters to whom He will and sons to whom He pleases. To some He gives both sons and daughters, and to others He gives none at all. Mighty is Allah and all-knowing.

It is not vouchsafed to any mortal that Allah should speak to him except by revelation, or from behind a veil, or through a messenger sent and authorized by Him to make known His will. He is exalted and wise.

Thus We have inspired you with a spirit of Our will when you knew nothing of faith or scripture, and made it a light whereby We guide those of Our servants whom We please.

42:53 You shall surely guide them to the right path: the path of Allah, to whom belongs all that the heavens and the earth contain. All things shall in the end return to Him.

1. Mohammed.

REVELATIONS WELL EXPOUNDED

In the Name of Allah, the Compassionate, the Merciful

HA *mim*. This is revealed by the Compassionate, the **41:1** Merciful: a Book of revelations well expounded, an Arabic Koran for men of understanding.

It is good news and a warning: yet most men turn their backs and give no heed. They say: 'That to which you call us cannot reach our hearts, for they are well protected. Our ears are stopped and a thick veil stands between us. Do as you please, and so will we.'

Say: 'I am no more than a mortal like yourselves. It is revealed to me that your God is one God. Therefore take the right path to Him and implore Him to forgive you. Woe to those who serve other gods besides Him; who give no alms and disbelieve in the life to come. As for those who have faith and do good works, a lasting reward awaits them.'

He set upon the earth mountains towering high above it. **41:10** He pronounced His blessing upon it and in four days provided it with sustenance for all alike. Then He made His way to the sky, which was but a cloud of vapour, and to it and to the earth He said: 'Will you obey me willingly, or shall I compel you?'

'Willingly,' they answered. In two days He formed the sky into seven heavens, and to each heaven He assigned its task. We decked the lowest with brilliant stars and guardian comets. Such is the design of the Mighty One, the All-knowing.

If they give no heed, say: 'I have given you warning of the scourge which overtook Thamoud and Aad. When their apostles came to them from every side, saying: "Serve none but Allah," they answered: "Had it been Allah's will He would have sent down angels. We will never believe in your message."'

Arrogant and unjust were the men of Aad. 'Who is **41:15** mightier than we?' they used to say. Could they not see that

Allah, who had created them, was mightier than they? Yet they denied Our revelations.

41:16 So, over a few ill-omened days, We let loose on them a howling gale, that they might taste a dire punishment in this life; but more terrible will be the punishment of the life to come. They shall have none to help them.

As for Thamoud, We offered them Our guidance, but they preferred blindness to guidance. Therefore a hideous scourge overtook them as a punishment for their misdeeds; and We delivered the believers and those who feared Allah.

Forewarn them of the day when Allah's opponents will be gathered together and driven into Hell, so that when they reach it, their eyes, their ears, and their very skins will testify to their misdeeds. 'Why did you speak against us?' they will say to their skins, and their skins will reply: 'Allah, who gives speech to all things, has made us speak. It was He who in the beginning created you, and to Him you shall all

41:22 return. You did not hide yourselves, so that your eyes and ears and skins could not observe you. Yet you thought that Allah had no knowledge of what you did. It is this illusion that has ruined you, so that you are now among the lost.'

If they resign themselves, Hell shall still be their home: and if they sue for pardon, their suit shall not be granted.

We have given them companions who make their past and present, for all its foulness, seem fair and right to them. Well have they deserved the fate which overtook the jinn and men who have gone before them. They shall assuredly be lost.

The unbelievers say: 'Give no heed to this Koran. Interrupt its reading with booing and laughter, so that you may defeat it.'

We will sternly punish the unbelievers and pay them back for the worst of their misdeeds. Thus shall the enemies of Allah be rewarded. They shall abide in Hell for ever, because they have denied Our revelations.

41:29 The unbelievers will say: 'Lord, show us the jinn and men who led us astray. We will trample them under our feet and bring them low.'

As for those who say: 'Our God is Allah,' and take the 41:30
right path to Him, the angels will descend to them, saying:
'Let nothing alarm or grieve you. Rejoice in the Paradise
you have been promised. We are your guardians in this
world and in the next. You shall find there all that your
souls desire and all that you can ask for: a rich provision
from a benignant and merciful God.'

And who speaks better than he who calls others to the
service of Allah, does what is right, and says: 'I am a
Muslim'?

Good and evil deeds are not alike. Requite evil with
good, and he who is your enemy will become your dearest
friend. But none will attain this save those who endure with
fortitude and are greatly favoured by Allah.

If Satan tempts you, seek refuge in Allah. He hears all and
knows all.

Among His signs are the night and the day, and the sun
and the moon. But do not prostrate yourselves before the
sun or the moon; rather prostrate yourselves before Allah,
who created them both, if you would truly serve Him.

If they¹ disdain His service, let them remember that 41:38
those who dwell with Allah give glory to Him day and
night and are never wearied.

And among His signs is the resurrection of the earth.
You see it dry and barren: but when He sends down rain
upon it, it stirs and swells. He that gives it life will raise
the dead to life. Allah has power over all things.

Those that deny Our revelations are not hidden from Our
view. The man who emerges safe on the Day of Resurrection shall surely fare better than the one who is cast into
the Fire. Do as you will, Allah is watching over all your
actions.

Those who deny Our word when it is preached to them
shall be sternly punished. This is a mighty scripture. Falsehood cannot reach it from before or behind. It is a revelation from a wise and glorious God.

Nothing is said to you that has not been said to other 41:43

1. The Pagans.

apostles before you. Your Lord is forgiving, but stern in retribution.

41:44   Had We revealed the Koran in a foreign tongue they would have said: 'If only its verses were expounded! Why in a foreign tongue, when the Prophet is Arabian?'

Say: 'To true believers it is a guide and a healing balm. But those who deny it are deaf and blind. They are like men whom you call from far.'

We gave the Torah to Moses, but before long men disagreed about it. And had your Lord not deferred their punishment, He would have punished them in this life, grave though their doubts were about it.

He that does good, does it for his own soul; and he that commits evil does so at his own peril. Your Lord is never unjust to His servants.

He alone has knowledge of the Hour of Doom. No fruit is borne, no female conceives or is delivered, but with His knowledge.

On a certain day He will call mankind to Him and say: 'Where are those fellow-gods of Mine?'

'We confess,' they will reply, 'that none of us can vouch *41:48* for them.' The idols to which they had once prayed will vanish from them, and they shall know that there is no escape.

Man never wearies of praying for good things. But when evil befalls him he loses hope and grows despondent. And if after affliction We vouchsafe him Our favour, he is sure to say: 'This is my own. I do not think the Hour of Doom will ever come. And even if I return to my Lord, He will surely reward me well.' We shall tell the unbelievers what they did and visit upon them a stern chastisement.

When We show favour to man, he turns his back and holds aloof; but when evil befalls him he is loud in prayer.

Say: 'Think: if this Koran is indeed from Allah and you deny it, who can err more than the man who openly defies Him?'

41:53   We will show them Our signs in all the regions of the earth and in their own souls, until they clearly see that this is the truth. Does it not suffice that Allah is watching over all things?

Yet they still doubt that they will ever meet their Lord. *41:54* Surely Allah encompasses all things.

THE FORGIVING ONE

In the Name of Allah, the Compassionate, the Merciful

HA *mim.* This Book is revealed by Allah, the Mighty *40:1* One, the All-knowing, who forgives sin and accepts repentance; the Bountiful One, whose punishment is stern.

There is no god but Him. All shall return to Him. None but the unbelievers dispute the revelations of Allah. Do not be deceived by their prosperous dealings in the land. Long before them the people of Noah denied Our revelations, and so did the factions after them. Every nation strove to kill their apostle, seeking with false arguments to refute the truth; but when I smote them, how stern was My punishment! Thus the word of your Lord shall be fulfilled concerning the unbelievers: they are the heirs of Hell.

Those who bear the Throne and those who stand around it give glory to their Lord and believe in Him. They implore forgiveness for the faithful, saying: 'Lord, Your mercy and Your knowledge embrace all things. Forgive those that repent and follow Your path. Shield them from the scourge of Hell. Admit them, Lord, to the gardens of Eden which You have promised them, together with all the righteous among their fathers, their wives, and their descendants. You are the Almighty, the Wise One. Deliver them from all evil. He whom You will deliver from evil on that day will surely earn Your mercy. That is the supreme triumph.'

But to the unbelievers a voice will cry: 'Allah's abhorrence of you is greater than your hatred of yourselves. You were called to the Faith, but you denied it.'

They shall say: 'Lord, twice you have made us die, and *40:11* twice you have given us life. We now confess our sins. Is there no escape from Hell?'

40:12 They shall be answered: 'You have incurred this fate because when Allah was invoked alone, you disbelieved; but when you were bidden to serve other gods besides Him you believed in them. Today judgement rests with Allah, the Most High, the Supreme One.'

It is He who reveals to you His signs and sends down for you sustenance from the sky. Yet none takes heed except the repentant. Pray, then, to Allah and worship none but Him, however much the unbelievers dislike it.

Exalted and throned on high, He lets the Spirit descend at His behest on those of His servants whom He chooses, that He may warn them of the day when they shall meet Him; the day when they shall rise up from their graves with nothing hidden from Allah. And who shall reign supreme on that day? Allah, the One, the Mighty.

On that day every soul shall be paid back what it has earned. On that day none shall be wronged. Swift is Allah's reckoning.

40:18 Forewarn them of the approaching day, when men's hearts will leap up to their throats and choke them; when the wrongdoers will have no friend, no intercessor who will be heard. Allah knows the furtive look and the secret thought. He will judge men with fairness, but the idols to which they pray besides Him can judge nothing at all. Allah hears and observes all men.

Have they never journeyed through the land and seen what was the end of those who have gone before them, nations far greater in prowess and in splendour? Allah scourged them for their sins, and they had none to protect them from Allah. That was because their apostles had come to them with clear revelations and they denied them. So Allah punished them. Mighty is Allah, and stern His retribution.

We sent forth Moses with Our signs and with clear 40:24 authority to Pharaoh, Haman, and Korah. But they said: 'This man is a magician, an imposter.'

And when he brought them the truth from Ourself, they *40:25* said: 'Put to death the sons of those who uphold this faith, and spare their daughters.' Futile were the schemes of the unbelievers.

Pharaoh said: 'I will kill Moses, then let him invoke his god! I fear that he will change your religion and spread disorder in the land.'

Moses said: 'I take refuge in my Lord and in your Lord from every proud man who denies the Day of Reckoning.'

But one of Pharaoh's kinsmen, who in secret was a true believer, said: 'Would you kill a man merely because he says: "My Lord is Allah"? He has brought you veritable signs from your Lord. If he is lying, may his lie be on his head; but if he is speaking the truth, a part at least of what he threatens will smite you. Allah does not guide the lying transgressor. Today you are the masters, my people, illustrious throughout the earth. But who will save us from Allah's wrath when it falls upon us?'

Pharaoh said: 'I have told you what I think. I will surely guide you to the right path.'

He who was a true believer said: 'I warn you, my people, against the fate which overtook the factions: the people of Noah, Aad, and Thamoud, and those that came after them. Allah does not seek to wrong His servants.

'I warn you, my people, against the day when men will *40:32* cry out to one another, when you will turn and flee, with none to protect you from Allah. He whom Allah misleads shall find none to guide him. Long before this, Joseph came to you with veritable signs, but you never ceased to doubt them; and when he died you said: "Allah will never send another apostle after him." Thus Allah misleads the doubting transgressor. Those who dispute Allah's signs without proof are held in abhorrence by Allah and by the faithful. Thus Allah seals up the heart of every scornful tyrant.'

Pharaoh said to Haman: 'Build me a tower that I may reach the paths of heaven and look upon the god of Moses. *40:37* I am convinced that he is lying.'

Thus Pharaoh's foul deeds seemed fair to him, so that

he was turned away from the truth. His plot ended in ruin.

40:38 He who was a true believer said: 'Follow me, my people, that I may rightly guide you. The life of this world, my people, is a fleeting comfort, but the life to come is an everlasting mansion. Those that do evil shall be rewarded with like evil; but those that have faith and do good works, both men and women, shall enter the gardens of Paradise and receive blessings without number.

'My people, see how I call you to salvation and how you call me to Hell-fire. You bid me deny Allah and serve other gods of whom I know nothing; while I exhort you to serve the Almighty, the Benignant One. Indeed, the gods to whom you call me can be invoked neither in this world nor in the next. We shall all return to Allah. The transgressors are the Heirs of Hell.

'Bear in mind what I have told you. To Allah I commend myself. He is cognizant of all His servants.'

40:45 Allah delivered him from the evils which they planned, and a grievous scourge fell on Pharaoh's people. They shall be brought before the Fire morning and evening, and when the Last Day comes, a voice will cry: 'Let the people of Pharaoh be sternly punished!'

And when they argue in Hell, the humble will say to the haughty: 'We have been your followers: will you now ward off from us a part of our punishment?' But those who were haughty will reply: 'All of us are now in Hell. Allah has judged His servants.'

And the dwellers of Hell will say to its keepers: 'Implore your Lord to relieve Our torment for one day!'

'But did your apostles not come to you with undoubted signs?' they will ask.

'Yes,' they will answer. And their keepers will say: 'Then cry for help.' But vain shall be the cries of the unbelievers.

We shall help Our apostles and the true believers both in this world and on the day when the witnesses rise to testify. 40:52 On that day no excuse will help the evil-doers. Our curse, and an evil home, await them.

We gave Moses Our guidance and the Israelites the Book 40:53
to inherit: a guide and an admonition to men of understanding. Therefore have patience; Allah's promise is true.
Implore Him to forgive your sins, and celebrate His praise
morning and evening.

As for those who dispute the revelations of Allah without
proof, there is nothing in their hearts but ambitions which
they shall never attain. Therefore seek refuge in Allah; He
hears all and knows all.

The creation of heaven and earth is greater than the
creation of man; yet most men do not know it.

The blind and the seeing are not alike, nor are the wicked
equal with those that have faith and do good works. Yet
you seldom think.

The Hour of Doom is sure to come: yet most men do not
believe in it.

Your Lord has said: 'Call on me and I will hear you.
Those that disdain My service shall enter Hell disgraced.'

It was Allah who made for you the night to rest in and 40:61
the day to give you light. Allah is bountiful to men, yet
most men do not give thanks.

Such is Allah your Lord, the Creator of all things. There
is no god but Him. How then can you turn away from
Him? Yet even thus the men who deny His revelations
turn away from Him.

It is Allah who has given you the earth for a dwelling-
place and the sky for a ceiling. He has moulded your bodies
into a comely shape and provided you with good things.

Such is Allah, your Lord. Blessed be Allah, Lord of the
Creation.

He is the Living One; there is no god but Him. Pray to
Him, then, and worship none besides Him. Praise be to
Allah, Lord of the Creation!

Say: 'I am forbidden to serve your idols, now that clear
proofs have been given me from my Lord. I am commanded to surrender myself to the Lord of the Creation.'

It was He who created you from dust, making you a little 40:67
germ, and then a clot of blood. He brings you infants into

the world; you reach manhood, then decline into old age (though some of you die young), so that you may complete your appointed term and grow in wisdom.

40:68 He ordains life and death. If He decrees a thing, He need only say: 'Be,' and it is.

Do you not see how those who dispute the revelations of Allah turn away from the right path? Those who have denied the Scriptures and the message with which We have sent Our apostles shall know the truth hereafter: when with chains and shackles round their necks they shall be dragged through boiling water and burnt in the fire of Hell.

A voice will say to them: 'Where are the gods whom you have served besides Allah?'

'They have forsaken us,' they will reply. 'Indeed, they were nothing, those gods to whom we used to pray.' Thus Allah confounds the unbelievers.

And the voice will say: 'This you shall suffer because you rejoiced in wickedness and led a wanton life. Enter the gates of Hell and stay therein for ever. Evil is the home of the arrogant.'

Therefore have patience: Allah's promise is true. Whether We let you[1] witness a part of that with which We threaten them or cause you to die before it is fulfilled, to Us they shall all return.

40:78 We have sent forth other apostles before you; of some you have already heard, of others We have told you nothing. Yet none of these could work a miracle except by Allah's leave. And when Allah's will is done, justice will prevail and those who have denied His signs will come to grief.

It is Allah who has provided you with beasts, that you may ride on some and eat the flesh of others. You put them to many uses; they take you where you please, carrying you by land as ships carry you by sea.

He reveals to you His signs. Which of Allah's signs do you deny?

40:82 Have they never journeyed through the land and seen

1. Mohammed.

what was the end of those who have gone before them? More numerous were they and far greater in prowess and in splendour; yet all their labours were of no use to them.

When their apostles brought them veritable signs they *40:83* proudly boasted of their own knowledge; but soon the scourge at which they scoffed encompassed them. And when they saw Our punishment they said: 'We now believe in none but Allah. We deny the idols we used to serve besides Him.'

But their new faith was of no use to them, when they *40:85* beheld Our punishment.

That was how Allah dealt with the bygone generations. Lost were the unbelievers.

THE RANKS

In the Name of Allah, the Compassionate, the Merciful

I SWEAR by those who range themselves in ranks, by *37:1* those who cast out demons, and by those who recite Our Word, that your God is One: the Lord of the heavens and the earth and all that lies between them: the Lord of the Eastern Regions.

We have decked the lower heaven with constellations. They guard it against rebellious devils, so that they may not hear the words of those on high. Meteors are hurled at them from every side; then, driven away, they are consigned to an eternal scourge. Eavesdroppers are pursued by fiery comets.

Ask the unbelievers if they hold themselves of a nobler make than the rest of Our creation. Of coarse clay We created them.

You marvel, while they scoff. When they are warned they take no warning. When they are shown a sign they mock at it and say: 'This is plain magic. What! When we are dead and turned to dust and bones, shall we be raised to life, we and our forefathers?'

Say: 'Yes. And you shall be held to shame.' *37:18*

37:19 One blast will sound and they shall see the Resurrection. 'Woe to us!' they will exclaim. 'This is the Day of Reckoning. This is the Judgement-day which you denied.'

But We shall say: 'Call the sinners, their wives, and the idols which they worshipped besides Allah, and lead them to the path of Hell. Keep them there for questioning – But what has come over you that you cannot help one another?'

On that day they will all submit to Allah. They will reproach each other, saying: 'You have imposed upon us!' – 'No! It was you who would not be believers. We had no power over you: you were sinners all. Just is the verdict which Our Lord has passed upon us; we shall surely taste His punishment. We misled you, but we ourselves have been misled.'

On that day they will all share Our punishment. Thus We shall deal with the evil-doers, for when it was said to them: 'There is no god but Allah,' they replied with scorn: 'Are we to renounce our gods for the sake of a mad poet?'

Surely he has brought the truth, confirming those who were sent before him. You shall all be sternly punished: you shall be rewarded according to your deeds.

37:40 But the true servants of Allah shall be well provided for, feasting on fruit, and honoured in the gardens of delight. Reclining face to face upon soft couches, they shall be served with a goblet filled at a gushing fountain, white, and delicious to those who drink it. It will neither dull their senses nor befuddle them. They shall sit with bashful, dark-eyed virgins, as chaste as the sheltered eggs of ostriches.

They will put questions to each other. One of them will say: 'I had a friend who used to ask: "Do you really believe in the Resurrection? When we are dead and turned to dust and bones, shall we be brought to judgement?"' And he will say to those around him: 'Come, let us look down.' He will look down and see his friend in the midst of Hell. 'By the Lord,' he will say to him, 'you almost ruined me! But 37:57 for the grace of Allah I should have surely been driven into Hell.'

The blessed will ask: 'Shall we not die a second time, or *37:58*
be punished at all?'

Surely that is the supreme triumph. Let every man labour
to achieve it.

Is this not a better welcome than the Zaqqum-tree? We
have made this tree a scourge for the wrongdoers. It grows
in the nethermost part of Hell, bearing fruit like devils'
heads: on it they shall feed, and with it they shall cram
their bellies, together with draughts of scalding water.
Then to Hell they shall return.

They found their fathers erring, yet they eagerly followed
in their footsteps. Most of the ancients had gone astray
before them, though We had sent apostles to give them
warning. Consider the fate of those whom We have warned:
they perished all, except Allah's true servants.

Noah prayed to Us, and his prayers were graciously
answered. We delivered him and all his tribe from the
mighty scourge, so that his descendants were the sole sur-
vivors. We bestowed on him the praise of later generations:
'Peace be on Noah among all men!'

Thus We reward the righteous: he was one of Our *37:80*
believing servants. The others We overwhelmed with the
Flood.

Abraham was of the self-same faith and came to his Lord
with a pure heart. He said to his father and to his people:
'What are these that you worship? Would you serve false
gods instead of Allah? What do you think of the Lord of
the Creation?'

He lifted up his eyes to the stars and said: 'I am sick!'
And his people turned their backs and went off.

He stole away to their idols and said to them: 'Will you
not eat your offerings? Why do you not speak?' With that
he fell upon them, striking them down with his right hand.

The people came running to the scene. 'Would you worship that which you have made with your own hands,' he
said, 'when it was Allah who created you and all that you
have made?'

They replied: 'Build up a pyre and cast him into the *37:97* blazing flames.' Thus they schemed against him: but We balked their schemes.

37:99　He said: 'I will take refuge with my Lord; He will guide me. Grant me a son, Lord, and let him be a righteous man.'

We gave him news of a gentle son. And when he reached the age when he could work with him his father said to him: 'My son, I dreamt that I was sacrificing you. Tell me what you think.'

He replied: 'Father, do as you are bidden. Allah willing, you shall find me faithful.'

And when they had both surrendered themselves to Allah's will, and Abraham had laid down his son prostrate upon his face, We called out to him, saying: 'Abraham, you have fulfilled your vision.' Thus did We reward the righteous. That was indeed a bitter test. We ransomed his son with a noble sacrifice and bestowed on him the praise of later generations. 'Peace be on Abraham!'

Thus are the righteous rewarded. He was one of Our believing servants.

37:112　We gave him Isaac, whom We made a saintly prophet, and blessed them both. Among their offspring were some who did good works and others who clearly sinned against their souls.

We showed favour to Moses and Aaron and delivered them, with all their people, from a mighty scourge. We succoured them, and they became victorious. We gave them the glorious Scriptures and guided them to the right path. We bestowed on them the praise of later generations: 'Peace on Moses and Aaron!'

Thus We reward the righteous. They were two of Our believing servants.

We also sent forth Elias, who said to his people: 'Have you no fear of Allah? Would you invoke Baal and forsake the Most Gracious Creator? Allah is your Lord and the Lord of your forefathers.'

But they denied him, and thus incurred Our punishment, except Allah's true servants. We bestowed on him the
37:130　praise of later generations: 'Peace on Elias!'

Thus We reward the righteous. He was one of Our 37:131
believing servants.

Lot, too, was an apostle. We delivered him and all his
kinsfolk, except for an old woman who stayed behind, and
utterly destroyed the others. You pass by their ruins morning and evening: will you not take heed?

Jonah, too, was one of Our apostles. He fled to the laden
ship, cast lots with the crew, and was condemned. A whale
swallowed him, for he had done amiss; and had he not de-
voutly praised Allah he would have stayed in its belly till
the Day of Resurrection. We threw him, gravely ill, upon a
desolate shore and caused a gourd-tree to grow over him.
Thus We sent him to a nation a hundred thousand strong or
more. They believed in him and We let them live in ease
awhile.

Ask the unbelievers if it be true that Allah has daughters,
while they themselves choose sons. Did We create the
angels females? And were they present at their creation?
Surely they lie when they declare: 'Allah has begotten
children.'

Would He choose daughters instead of sons? What has 37:153
come over you that you should judge so ill?

Will you not take heed? Have you a positive proof?
Show us your scriptures, if what you say be true!

They assert kinship between Him and the jinn. But the
jinn well know that they will all be brought before Him,
except Allah's true servants. Exalted be Allah above their
imputations!

Neither you nor your idols shall deceive any about Allah
save him who is destined for Hell. We each have our
appointed place.[1] We range ourselves in adoration and give
glory to Him.

They say: 'Had we received an admonition from the ancients, we would have become true servants of Allah.' Yet
they disbelieve in the Koran. They shall before long know 37:170
the truth.

1. These words, say the commentators, were spoken by the Angel
Gabriel.

37:171 Long ago We promised the apostles who served Us that they would receive Our help and that Our armies would be victorious. So give no heed to them awhile: you shall surely see their downfall as they shall see your triumph.

Do they wish to hurry Our punishment? Dismal shall be that morning when Our vengeance smites them in their courtyards, forewarned though they have been.

So give no heed to them awhile. You shall surely see their downfall as they shall see your triumph. Exalted be your Lord, the Lord of Glory, above their imputations!

37:182 Peace be on the apostles, and praise to Allah, Lord of the Creation!

YA SIN

In the Name of Allah, the Compassionate, the Merciful

36:1 YA *sin.* I swear by the Wise Koran that you are sent upon a straight path.

This is revealed by the Mighty One, the Merciful, so that you may warn a nation who, because their fathers were not warned before them, live in heedlessness. Most of them deserve Our punishment, for they are unbelievers.

We have bound their necks with chains of iron reaching to their chins, so that they cannot bow their heads. We have put barriers before them and behind them and covered them over, so that they cannot see.

It is alike whether or not you forewarn them: they will never have faith.

You shall admonish none but those who observe Our precepts and fear the Merciful, though they cannot see Him. To these give news of pardon and a rich reward.

It is We who will bring back the dead to life. We record the deeds of men and the marks they leave behind: We note all things in a glorious book.

Recount to them the story of the city[1] to whose inhabit-
36:14 ants We sent Our messengers. At first We sent to them two

1. Probably Antioch, to which, we are told, Jesus sent two disciples, and then a third.

messengers, but when they rejected both We strengthened them with a third. They said: 'We have been sent to you by Allah.' But the people replied: 'You are mortals like our- 36:15 selves. The Merciful has revealed nothing: you are surely lying.'

They said: 'Our Lord knows that we are true apostles. Our only duty is to warn you plainly.'

The people answered: 'Your presence bodes nothing but evil. Desist, or we will stone you or inflict on you a painful punishment.'

They said: 'The evil you forebode can come only from yourselves. Will you not take heed? Surely you are great transgressors.'

Thereupon a man came running from the far side of the city. 'My people,' he said, 'follow those who have been sent by Allah. Follow those who ask no reward of you and are rightly guided. Why should I not serve Him who has created me and to whom you shall all be recalled? Should I serve other gods than Him? If it is the will of the Merciful to afflict me, their intercession will avail me nothing, nor will they save me. Indeed, I should then be in certain error. Messengers, I believe in your Lord. Countrymen, heed my counsel.'

We said to him: 'Come to Paradise,' and he exclaimed: 36:26 'Would that my people knew how gracious my Lord has been to me, how highly He has exalted me!'

But when he was gone We sent down no host from heaven against his people: this We never do. One shout was heard – and they fell down lifeless.

Alas for My bondsmen! They laugh to scorn every apostle that comes to them. Do they not see how many generations We have destroyed before them? Never shall they return to them: all shall be brought before Us.

Let the once-dead earth be a sign to them. We gave it life, and from it produced grain for their sustenance. We planted it with the palm and the vine and watered it with gushing springs, so that men might feed on its fruit. It was not their 36:35 hands that made all this. Should they not give thanks?

36:36   Glory be to Him who made His creatures male and female: the plants of the earth, mankind themselves, and the living things they know nothing of.

The night is another sign for men. From the night We lift the day – and they are plunged in darkness.

The sun hastens to its resting-place: its course is laid for it by the Mighty One, the All-knowing.

We have ordained phases for the moon, which daily wanes and in the end appears like a bent and withered twig.

The sun is not allowed to overtake the moon, nor does the night outpace the day. Each in its own orbit runs.

We gave them yet another sign when We carried their offspring in the laden Ark. And similar vessels We have made for them to voyage in. We drown them if We will: none can help or rescue them, except through Our mercy and unless We please to prolong their lives awhile.

36:45   When it is said to them: 'Have fear of that which is before you and behind you, so that Allah may show you mercy,' they give no heed. Indeed, they turn away from every sign you give them.

And when it is said to them: 'Give alms of that which Allah has given you,' the unbelievers say to the faithful: 'Are we to feed those whom Allah can feed if He chooses? Surely you are in undoubted error.'

They also say: 'When will this promise be fulfilled, if what you say be true?'

They must be waiting for the Trumpet's blast, which will overtake them whilst they are disputing. They will make no will, nor shall they return to their kinsfolk.

And when the Trumpet sounds, they shall rise up from their graves and rush forth to their Lord. 'Woe to us!' they will say. 'Who has roused us from our resting-place? This is what the Lord of Mercy promised: the apostles have preached the truth!' And with one shout they shall be gathered all before Us.

36:54   On that day no soul shall suffer the least injustice. You shall be rewarded according only to your deeds.

On that day the dwellers of Paradise shall think of *36:55* nothing but their bliss. Together with their wives, they shall recline in shady groves upon soft couches. They shall have fruits and all that they desire.

'Peace!' shall be the word spoken by a merciful God. But to the guilty He will say: 'Away with you this day! Sons of Adam, did I not charge you never to serve Satan, your acknowledged foe, but to worship Me? Surely that was the right path. Yet he has led many of you astray. Had you no sense? This is the Hell with which you have been threatened. Burn therein this day as a punishment for your unbelief.'

On that day We shall seal their mouths. Their hands will speak, and their very feet will testify to their misdeeds. Had it been Our will We could have put out their sight: yet even then they would have rushed along their wonted path. For how could they have seen their error?

Had it been Our will We could have transfixed them where they stood, so that they could neither go forward nor retrace their steps.

We reverse the growth of those to whom We give long *36:68* life. Can they not understand?

We have taught Mohammed no poetry, nor does it become him to be a poet. This is but a warning: an eloquent Koran to admonish the living and to pass judgement on the unbelievers.

Do they not see how among the things Our hands have made We have created for them the beasts of which they are masters? We have subjected these to them, that they may ride on some and eat the flesh of others; they drink their milk and put them to other uses. Will they not give thanks?

They have set up other gods besides Allah, hoping that they may help them. They cannot help them: yet their worshippers stand like warriors ready to defend them.

Let their words not grieve you. We have knowledge of all they hide and all that they reveal.

Is man not aware that We created him from a little germ? *36:77*

36:78 Yet he openly disputes Our power. He answers back with arguments, and forgets His own creation. He asks: 'Who will give life to rotten bones?'

Say: 'He who created them at first will give them life again: He has knowledge of every creature; He who gives you from the green tree a fire with which you light your fuel.'

Has He who created the heavens and the earth no power to create their like? That He surely has. He is the all-knowing Creator. When He decrees a thing He need only say: 'Be,' and it is.

36:83 Glory be to Him who has control of all things. To Him you shall all return.

THE CREATOR

In the Name of Allah, the Compassionate, the Merciful

35:1 PRAISE be to Allah, the Creator of heaven and earth! He sends forth the angels as His messengers, with two, three or four pairs of wings. He multiplies His creatures according to His will. Allah has power over all things.

The blessings Allah bestows on man none can withhold; and what He withholds none can bestow. He is the Mighty, the Wise One.

Men, bear in mind Allah's goodness towards you. Is there any other creator who provides for you from heaven and earth? There is no god but Him. How then can you turn away from Him?

If they deny you, other apostles have been denied before you. To Allah shall all things return.

Men, the promise of Allah is true. Let the life of this world not deceive you, nor let the Dissembler trick you about Allah. Satan is your enemy: therefore treat him as an enemy. He tempts his followers so that they may become the heirs of Hell.

35:7 The unbelievers shall be sternly punished, but those that accept the true faith and do good works shall be forgiven and richly rewarded.

Is he whose foul deeds seem fair to him like the man who 35:8 is rightly guided? Allah leaves in error whom He will and guides whom He pleases. Do not fret yourself[1] to death on their account: Allah has knowledge of all their actions.

Allah sends forth the winds which set the clouds in motion. We drive them on to some dead land and give fresh life to its barren soil. Such is the Resurrection.

If any one seeks glory, let him know that glory is Allah's alone. The good word is heard by Him and the good deed exalted. But those that plot evil shall be sternly punished; He will bring their plots to nothing.

Allah created you from dust, then from a little germ. Into two sexes He divided you. No female conceives or is delivered without His knowledge. No man grows old or has his life cut short but in accordance with His decree. All this is easy for Him.

The two seas are not alike. The one is fresh, sweet, and 35:12 pleasant to drink from, while the other is salt and bitter. From both you eat fresh fish and bring up ornaments to deck yourselves with. See how the ships plough their course through them as you sail away to seek His bounty. Perchance you will give thanks.

He causes the night to pass into the day and the day into the night. He has forced the sun and the moon into His service, each running for an appointed term. Such is Allah, your Lord. His is the sovereignty. The idols whom you invoke besides Him have power over nothing. If you pray to them they cannot hear you, and even if they hear you they cannot answer. None can guide you like the One who is all-knowing.

Men, it is you who stand in need of Allah. He is all-sufficient and glorious. He can destroy you if He will and replace you with a new creation; this is no impossible thing for Allah.

No soul shall bear another's burden. If a laden soul cries 35:18

1. Mohammed.

179

out for help, not even a near relation shall share its burden.

You shall admonish none but those who fear their Lord though they cannot see Him, and are steadfast in prayer. He that purifies himself has much to gain. To Allah shall all things return.

35:19 The blind and the seeing are not alike, nor are the darkness and the light. The shade and the heat are not alike, nor are the living and the dead. Allah can cause whom He will to hear Him, but you cannot make those who are in their graves hear you.

Your only duty is to give warning. We have sent you with the truth to proclaim good news and to warn your people; for there is no nation that has not been warned by an apostle. If they disbelieve you, know that those who have gone before them also disbelieved. Their apostles came to them with veritable signs, with scriptures, and with the light-giving Book. But in the end I smote the unbelievers: and how terrible was My punishment!

35:27 Did you not see how Allah sent down water from the sky and brought forth fruits of different hues? In the mountains there are canyons streaked with various shades of red and white, and jet-black rocks. Men, beasts, and cattle have their different colours, too.

From among His servants, only those fear Allah who know that Allah is mighty and forgiving.

Those who recite the Book of Allah and attend to their prayers and give alms in private and in public may hope for imperishable gain. Allah will give them their rewards and enrich them from His own abundance. He is forgiving and bountiful in His rewards.

What We have revealed to you in the Book is the truth confirming previous scriptures. Allah knows and observes His servants.

35:32 We have bestowed the Book on those of Our servants whom We have chosen. Some of them sin against their souls, some follow a middle course, and some, by Allah's leave, vie with each other in charitable works: this is the supreme virtue.

They shall enter the gardens of Eden, where they shall be 35:33
decked with pearls and bracelets of gold, and arrayed in
robes of silk. They shall say: 'Praise be to Allah who has
taken away all our sorrows from us. Our Lord is forgiving
and bountiful in His rewards. Through His grace He has
admitted us to the Eternal Mansion, where we shall know
no toil, no weariness.'

As for the unbelievers, the fire of Hell awaits them.
Death shall not deliver them, nor shall its torments be ever
lightened for them. Thus shall the thankless be rewarded.

There they will cry out: 'Lord, remove us hence! We will
live a good life and will not do as we have done.' But He will
answer: 'Did We not make your lives long enough for any
one who would be warned to take warning? Besides, Our
apostle *did* come to you; taste then the torment of Hell.
None shall help the wrongdoers.'

Allah knows the mysteries of heaven and earth. He 35:38
knows the hidden thoughts of men.

It is He who has given you the earth to inherit. He that
denies Him shall bear the burden of his unbelief. In denying
Him the unbelievers earn nothing but odium in the sight of
Allah; their unbelief gets them nothing but perdition.

Say: 'Behold your other gods on whom you call besides
Allah. Show me what part of the earth they have created!
Have they a share in the heavens?'

Have We given the idolaters a scripture affording proofs
of their gods' divinity? Truly, vain are the promises the
wrongdoers give one another.

It is Allah who keeps the heavens and the earth from
falling. Should they fall, none could hold them back but
He. Benignant is Allah, and forgiving.

They solemnly swore by Allah that if a prophet should
come to them they would accept his guidance more readily
than did other nations. Yet when an apostle was sent to
them they turned away from him with abhorrence, be-
having arrogantly in the land and plotting evil. But evil 35:43
shall recoil on those that plot evil.

What end are they awaiting, except the end which

overtook the ancients? In the ways of Allah you will find no change or alteration.

Have they never journeyed through the land and seen the fate of those who went before them, nations far mightier than they?

There is nothing in heaven or earth beyond the power of Allah. Mighty is He and all-knowing.

35:45 If it was Allah's will to punish men for their misdeeds, not one creature would be left alive on the earth's surface. He respites them till an appointed time. And when their hour comes, they shall know that Allah has been watching over all His servants.

SHEBA

In the Name of Allah, the Compassionate, the Merciful

34:1 PRAISE be to Allah, to whom belongs all that the heavens and the earth contain! Praise be to Him in the world to come. He is the Wise One, the All-knowing.

He has knowledge of all that goes into the earth and all that springs up from it; all that comes down from heaven and all that ascends to it. He is the Forgiving One, the Merciful.

The unbelievers declare: 'The Hour of Doom will never come.' Say: 'By the Lord, it is surely coming! He knows all that is hidden. Not an atom's weight in heaven or earth escapes Him; nor is there anything smaller or greater but is recorded in His glorious book. He will surely reward those who have faith and do good works; they shall be forgiven and a generous provision shall be made for them. But those who strive to confute Our revelations shall suffer the torment of a harrowing scourge.'

Those to whom knowledge has been given can see that what is revealed to you from your Lord is the truth, leading to the path of the Almighty, the Glorious One.

34:7 The unbelievers say: 'Shall we show you a man[1] who

1. Mohammed.

claims that when you have been mangled into dust you will be raised to life again? Has he invented a lie about Allah, or *34:8* is he mad?' Truly, those who deny the life to come are doomed, for they have grossly erred.

Do they not see what is before them and behind them in heaven and earth? If We will, We can cave in the earth under their feet or let a part of the sky fall upon them. Surely there is a sign in this for every penitent man.

On David We bestowed Our favours. We said: 'Mountains, and you birds, echo his songs of praise.' We made hard iron pliant to him, saying: 'Make coats of mail and measure their links with care. Do what is right: I am watching over all your actions.'

To Solomon We subdued the wind, travelling a month's *34:12* journey morning and evening. We gave him a spring flowing with molten brass, and jinn who served him by leave of his Lord. Those of them who did not do Our bidding We shall punish in the fire of Hell. They made for him whatever he pleased: shrines and statues, basins as large as watering-troughs, and built-in cauldrons. We said: 'Give thanks, House of David.' Yet few of My servants are truly thankful.

And when We had decreed his death, they did not know that he was dead until they saw a worm eating away his staff. And when his corpse fell down, the jinn realized that had they had knowledge of what was hidden they would not have continued in their abject servitude.

For the natives of Sheba there was indeed a sign in their dwelling-place: a garden on their left and a garden on their right. We said to them: 'Eat of what your Lord has given you and render thanks to Him. Pleasant is your land and forgiving is your Lord.'

But they gave no heed. So We unloosed upon them the waters of the dams and replaced their gardens by two others bearing bitter fruit, tamarisks, and a few nettle shrubs. Thus We punished them for their ingratitude: for We punish none save the ungrateful.

Between them and the cities that We have blessed, we *34:18* placed roadside hamlets so that they could journey to and fro in measured stages. We said: 'Travel through them by day and night in safety.'

34:19 But they said: 'Lord, make our journeys longer.' They sinned against their souls; so We made their fate a byword and scattered them throughout the land. Surely there is a sign in this for every steadfast, thankful man.

Satan had judged them rightly; they followed him all, except for a band of true believers. Yet he had no power over them: Our only aim was to know those who believed in the life to come and those who were in doubt about it. Your Lord takes cognizance of all things.

Say: 'Call on those whom you deify besides Allah. They do not control an atom's weight in heaven or earth, nor have they any share in either. Nor has Allah any helpers among them.'

34:23 None can intercede with Allah save him who has received His sanction. When fear is banished from their hearts they shall ask each other: 'What has your Lord ordained?' 'The truth,' they shall answer. 'He is the Most High, the Supreme One.'

Say: 'Who provides for you from heaven and earth?'

Say: 'Allah. We cannot both be right: either you or we are in evident error.'

Say: 'You are not accountable for our sins, nor are we accountable for your actions.'

Say: 'Our Lord will bring us all together, then He will rightly judge between us. He is the All-knowing Judge.'

Say: 'Show me those whom you have named with Him as partners. His partners they are not. Allah alone is wise and mighty.'

We have sent you forth to all mankind, so that you may give them good news and warn them. But most men have no knowledge. They ask: 'When will this promise be fulfilled, if what you say be true?'

34:30 Say: 'Your day is already appointed. Not for one hour can you hold it back, nor can you go before it.'

The unbelievers say: 'We will never believe in this 34:31
Koran, nor in the Scriptures which came before it.'

If only you could see the wrongdoers when they are
brought before their Lord! Bandying charges with one
another, the weak will say to the mighty: 'But for you, we
would have been believers.'

Then the mighty will say to the weak: 'Was it we who debarred you from Allah's guidance when it was given you?
No. You yourselves were wrongdoers.'

'By no means,' the weak will rejoin. 'You have plotted,
day and night, bidding us disbelieve in Allah and worship
other deities.'

And when they see their punishment they will repent in
secret. Chains shall be placed round the necks of the unbelievers. For shall We not reward them according to their
deeds?

We have sent no apostle to any nation whose message 34:34
was not denied by those of them that lived in comfort. The
unbelievers say: 'We have been given more wealth and
children than the faithful. Surely we shall never be punished.'

Say: 'My Lord gives abundantly to whom He will and
sparingly to whom He pleases. But most men do not know
it.'

Neither your riches nor your children shall bring you a
jot nearer to Us. Those that have faith and do what is right
shall be doubly rewarded for their deeds: they shall dwell in
peace in the pavilions of Paradise. But those that strive to
confute Our relevations shall be brought for punishment.

Say: 'My Lord gives abundantly to whom He will and
sparingly to whom He pleases. Whatever you give in alms
He will pay you back for it. He is the most munificent
Giver.'

On the day when He gathers them all together, He will
say to the angels: 'Was it you that these men worshipped?'

'Allah forbid!' they will answer. 'Defend us from them! 34:41
They worshipped jinn, and it was in jinn that most of them
believed.'

34:42 On that day you shall have no power to help or harm one another. To the wrongdoers We shall say: 'Taste the torment of Hell, which you persistently denied.'

When Our clear revelations are recited to them, they say: 'This man would turn you away from the gods of your forefathers.' Others say: 'This[1] is an invented falsehood.' While yet others, who denied the truth when it was first made known to them, declare: 'This is plain magic.'

Yet We have given them no scriptures to study, nor have We sent before you any apostle to warn them.

Those who have gone before them likewise denied Our revelations. They were ten times as prosperous and mighty: yet they denied My apostles. And then how terrible was My vengeance!

Say: 'One thing I would ask you: stand up before Allah in pairs or singly and ponder whether your compatriot[2] is truly mad. He is sent forth to warn you against a dreadful scourge.'

34:47 Say: 'I demand no recompense of you: keep it for yourselves. None can reward me except Allah. He is watching over all things.'

Say: 'My Lord reveals the truth. He has knowledge of all that is hidden.'

Say: 'Truth has come. Falsehood has vanished and shall return no more.'

Say: 'If I am in error, the loss is surely mine; but if I am in the right, it is thanks to that which my Lord has revealed to me. He hears all and is near at hand.'

If you could only see the unbelievers when they are seized with terror! They shall not escape, but shall be taken from their graves. They will say: 'We believe in Him.' But how will they attain the Faith when they are far away, since they at first denied it, and sneered at the unseen when they were far away?

34:54 They shall be prevented from attaining that which they desire, as were their likes before them, who disbelieved and doubted.

1. The Koran.   2. Mohammed.

ADORATION

ALIF *lam mim*. This Book is beyond doubt revealed 32:1
by the Lord of the Creation.

Do they say: 'He[1] has invented it himself?'

It is the truth from your Lord, which He has bestowed upon you so that you may forewarn a nation, whom none has warned before you, and that they may be rightly guided.

It was Allah who in six days created the heavens and the earth and all that lies between them, and then ascended His throne. You have no guardian or intercessor besides Him. Will you not take heed?

He governs the creation from heaven to earth. And in the end it will ascend to Him in one day, a day whose space is a thousand years by your reckoning.

He knows the visible and the unseen. He is the Mighty 32:6 One, the Merciful, who excelled in the making of all things. He first created man from clay, then bred his offspring from a drop of paltry fluid. He moulded him and breathed into him of His spirit. He gave you eyes and ears and hearts: yet you are seldom thankful.

They say: 'When we are once lost into the earth, shall we be restored to life?' Indeed, they deny that they will ever meet their Lord.

Say: 'The angel of death, who has been given charge of you, will carry off your souls. Then to your Lord you shall all return.'

Would that you could see the wrongdoers when they hang their heads before their Lord! They will say: 'Lord, we now see and hear. Send us back and we will never do wrong again. We are firm believers.'

Had it been Our Will, We could have guided every soul. 32:13 But My word shall be fulfilled: 'I will fill the pit of Hell with jinn and men.'

1. Mohammed.

32:14 We shall say to them: 'Taste Our punishment, for you forgot this day. We, too, will forget you. Taste Our eternal scourge, which you have earned by your misdeeds.'

None believes in Our revelations save those who, when reminded of them, prostrate themselves in adoration and give glory to their Lord in all humility; who forsake their beds to pray to their Lord in fear and hope; who give in charity of that which We have bestowed on them. No mortal knows what bliss is in store for these as a reward for their labours.

Can he, then, who is a true believer, be compared to him who is an evil-doer? Surely they are not alike.

Those that have faith and do good works shall be received in the gardens of Paradise, as a reward for that which they have done. But those that do evil shall be cast into the Fire. Whenever they try to get out of Hell they shall be driven back, and a voice will say to them: 'Taste the torment of Hell-fire, which you have persistently denied.'

32:21 But We will inflict on them the lighter punishment of this world before the supreme punishment of the world to come, so that they may return to the right path. And who is more wicked than the man who gives no heed to the revelations of his Lord when he is reminded of them? We will surely take vengeance on the evil-doers.

We gave the Scriptures to Moses (never doubt that you[1] will meet him) and made it a guide for the Israelites. And when they grew steadfast and firmly believed in Our revelations, We appointed leaders from among them who gave guidance at Our bidding. On the Day of Resurrection your Lord will resolve for them their differences.

Do they not know how many generations We have destroyed before them? They walk among their ruined dwellings. Surely in this there are veritable signs. Have they no ears to hear with?

32:27 Do they not see how We drive the rain to the parched lands and bring forth crops of which they and their cattle eat? Have they no eyes to see with?

1. Mohammed.

They ask: 'When will this judgement come, if what you say be true?'

Say: 'On the Day of Judgement the unbelievers will gain nothing from their faith (for then they will surely believe) nor shall they be respited.'

Therefore give no heed to them, and wait as they are *32:30* waiting.

LUQMAN

In the Name of Allah, the Compassionate, the Merciful

ALIF *lam mim.* These are the revelations of the Wise *31:1* Book, a guide and a blessing to the righteous, who attend to their prayers, pay the alms-tax, and firmly believe in the life to come. These are rightly guided by their Lord and will surely prosper.

Some there are who would gladly pay for a frivolous tale, so that in their ignorance they may mislead others from the path of Allah and make fun of it. For these We have prepared a shameful punishment.

When Our revelations are recited to them, they turn *31:7* their backs in scorn, as though they never heard them: as though their ears were sealed. To these proclaim a woeful scourge.

But those that have faith and do good works shall enter the gardens of delight, where they shall dwell for ever. Allah's promise shall be fulfilled: He is the Mighty, the Wise One.

He raised the heavens without visible pillars and set immovable mountains on the earth lest it should shake with you. He dispersed upon it all manner of beasts, and sent down water from the sky with which He caused all kinds of goodly plants to grow.

Such is Allah's creation: now show me what your other gods created. Truly, the unbelievers are in the grossest error.

We bestowed wisdom on Luqman,[1] saying: 'Give thanks *31:12*

---

1. A sage who, we are told, was a grandson of a sister or an aunt of Job.

to Allah. He that gives thanks to Him has much to gain, but if any one denies His favours, Allah is self-sufficient and glorious.'

31:13 Luqman admonished his son. 'My son,' he said, 'serve no other god instead of Allah, for idolatry is an abominable sin.'

(We enjoined man to show kindness to his parents, for with much pain his mother bears him and he is not weaned before he is two years of age. We said: 'Give thanks to Me and to your parents. To Me shall all things return. But if they press you to serve, besides Me, what you know nothing of do not obey them. Be kind to them in this world, and turn to Me with all devotion. To Me you shall all return, and I will declare to you all that you have done.')

'My son, Allah will bring all things to light, be they as small as a grain of mustard seed, be they hidden inside a rock or in heaven or earth. Allah is wise and all-knowing.

31:17 'My son, be steadfast in prayer, enjoin justice, and forbid evil. Endure with fortitude whatever befalls you. That is a duty incumbent on all.

'Do not treat men with scorn, nor walk proudly on the earth: Allah does not love the arrogant and the vain-glorious. Rather let your gait be modest and your voice low: the harshest of voices is the braying of the ass.'

Do you not see how Allah has subjected to you all that the heavens and the earth contain and lavished on you both His visible and unseen favours? Yet some would argue about Allah without knowledge or guidance or illuminating scriptures.

When it is said to them: 'Follow what Allah has revealed,' they reply: 'We will follow nothing but the faith of our fathers.' Yes, even though Satan is inviting them to the scourge of Hell.

He that surrenders himself to Allah and leads a righteous life stands on the firmest ground. To Allah shall all things 31:23 return. As for those that disbelieve, let their unbelief not vex you. To Allah they shall return and He will declare to them all that they have done. Allah has knowledge of their inmost thoughts.

We suffer them to take their ease awhile, and then will 31:24 sternly punish them.

If you ask them: 'Who has created the heavens and the earth?' they will reply: 'Allah.' Say: 'Praise, then, be to Allah!' But most of them are ignorant men.

His is what the heavens and the earth contain. He is self-sufficient and worthy of praise.

If all the trees in the earth were pens, and the sea, with seven more seas to replenish it, were ink, the writing of Allah's words could never be finished. Mighty is Allah and wise.

He created you as one soul, and as one soul He will bring you back to life. Allah hears all and observes all.

Do you not see how Allah causes the night to pass into the day and the day into the night? He has forced the sun and the moon into His service, each running for an appointed term. Allah is cognizant of all your actions, for you must know that He is the truth, while that which they invoke besides Him is false. Allah is the Most High, the Supreme One.

Do you not see how the ships speed upon the ocean by 31:31 Allah's grace, so that He may reveal to you His wonders? Surely there are signs in this for every steadfast, thankful man.

When the waves, like giant shadows, envelop them, they pray to Allah with all devotion. But no sooner does He bring them safe to land than some of them falter between faith and unbelief. Truly, only the treacherous and the ungrateful deny Our revelations.

Men, fear your Lord, and fear the day when no parent shall avail his child nor any child his parent. Allah's promise is surely true. Let the life of this world not deceive you, nor let the Dissembler trick you concerning Allah.

Allah alone has knowledge of the Hour of Doom. He 31:34 sends down the rain and knows what every womb conceals.

No mortal knows what he will earn tomorrow; no mortal knows where he will breathe his last. Allah alone is wise and all-knowing.

THE GREEKS

In the Name of Allah, the Compassionate, the Merciful

30:1 ALIF *lam mim.* The Greeks have been defeated[1] in a neighbouring land. But in a few years they shall themselves gain victory: such being the will of Allah before and after.

On that day the believers will rejoice in Allah's help. He gives victory to whom He will. He is the Mighty One, the Merciful.

That is Allah's promise; to His promise He will never be untrue. Yet most men do not know it.

They care for the outward show of this life, but of the life to come they are heedless. Have they not considered that Allah created the heavens and the earth and all that lies between them for a worthy end, to last for an appointed term? Yet most men deny that they will ever meet their Lord.

30:9 Have they never journeyed through the land and seen what was the fate of their forebears? Far mightier were they; they tilled the land and built upon it more than these have built. And to them, too, their apostles came with undoubted signs. Allah did not wrong them but they wronged themselves. Evil was the end of the evil-doers, because they had denied the revelations of Allah and scoffed at them.

Allah brings His creatures into being and then He reproduces them. To Him He will recall you all.

On the day when the Hour of Doom overtakes them, the wrongdoers will be speechless with despair. None of their idols will intercede for them: indeed, they shall deny their idols.

On the day when the Hour of Doom overtakes them, 30:15 mankind will be divided. Those who have embraced the

1. By the Persians, in Syria – A.D. 615. Mohammed's sympathies were with the Christians, not with the idolatrous Persians.

faith and done good works shall rejoice in a fair garden; but those who have disbelieved and denied Our revelations 30:16 and the life to come, shall be delivered up for punishment.

Therefore give glory to Allah morning and evening. Praise be to Him in the heavens and the earth, at twilight and at noon.

He brings forth the living from the dead, and the dead from the living: the lifeless earth is quickened by Him. Likewise you shall be raised to life.

By one of His signs He created you from dust; you became men and multiplied throughout the earth. By another sign He gave you wives from among yourselves, that you might live in joy with them, and planted love and kindness in your hearts. Surely there are signs in this for thinking men.

Among His other signs are the creation of heaven and earth and the diversity of your tongues and colours. Surely there are signs in this for all mankind.

By another sign of His you sleep at night and seek by day His bounty. Surely there are signs in this for those who hear.

Lightning is yet another of His signs, a source of fear 30:24 and hope. He sends down water from the sky and with it He quickens the dead earth. Surely in this there are signs for men of understanding.

By another sign heaven and earth stand firm at His bidding. And when with one shout He will summon you out of the earth you shall go out to Him.

His is what the heavens and the earth contain. All are obedient to Him.

He conceives Creation, then renews it: that is easier for Him.

His is the most exalted attribute in heaven and earth. He is the Mighty, the Wise One.

Listen to this comparison, drawn from your own lives. 30:28 Do your slaves share with you on equal terms the riches which We have given you? Do you fear them as you fear one another? Thus We make plain Our revelations to men of understanding.

30:29 Indeed, the wrongdoers are led unwittingly by their own appetites. And who can guide those whom Allah has led astray? There shall be none to help them.

Therefore stand firm in your devotion to the true faith, the upright nature with which Allah has endowed man. Allah's creation cannot be changed. This is surely the true religion, although most men do not know it.

Turn to Allah and fear Him. Be steadfast in prayer and serve no other god besides Him. Do not split up your religion into sects, each exulting in its own beliefs.

When evil befalls men they turn in prayer to their Lord. But no sooner does He show them mercy than some of them take to idol-worship, showing no gratitude for what We give them. Enjoy yourselves awhile, but in the end you shall know your error.

Have We revealed to them a sanction enjoining them to serve idols?

When We bestow a favour on men they rejoice in it, but when evil befalls them through their own fault, they grow despondent. Do they not know that Allah gives abundantly to whom He will and sparingly to whom He pleases? Surely there are signs in this for true believers.

30:38 Give their due to the near of kin, to the needy, and to the wayfarers. That is best for those that strive to please Allah; such men will surely prosper.

That which you seek to increase by usury will not be blessed by Allah; but the alms you give for His sake shall be repaid to you many times over.

It is Allah who has created you and given you your daily bread. He will cause you to die hereafter and will then bring you back to life. Can any of your idols do the least of these? Allah forbid! Exalted be He above your false gods!

Evil has become rife on land and sea as a result of man's misdeeds. Allah has ordained it thus for men, so that they may taste the fruit of their own works and mend their ways.

30:42 Say: 'Roam the earth and see what was the end of those who flourished before you. Most of them worshipped idols instead of Allah.'

Therefore stand firm in your devotion to the true faith be- 30:43
fore that day arrives which none may put off against the will
of Allah. On that day mankind will be divided. The unbelievers will answer for their unbelief, while the righteous
will make ready for their blissful home: for then Allah will
in His bounty reward those who have embraced the faith
and done good works. Allah does not love the unbelievers.

By another sign He sends the winds as bearers of good
tidings so that you may rejoice in His mercy and your
ships may sail at His bidding; so that you may seek His
bounty and render thanks to Him.

We sent before you other apostles to their peoples and
they showed them veritable signs. We took vengeance on
the guilty, and rightly succoured the true believers.

It is Allah who drives the winds that raise the clouds.
He spreads them as He will in the heaven and breaks them
up, so that you can see the rain falling from their midst.
When He sends it down upon His servants they are filled
with joy, though before its coming they may have lost all
hope.

Behold then the tokens of Allah's mercy; how He gives 30:50
fresh life to the dead earth. Likewise, He will bring back
the dead to life. He has power over all things.

Yet if We let loose on them a searing wind they would
return to unbelief.

The dead can never hear you, nor can you make the deaf
hear your call if they turn their backs and give no heed; nor
can you guide the blind out of their error. None shall give
ear to you save those who believe in Our revelations, and
are submissive to Our will.

Allah creates you weak: after weakness He gives you
strength, and after strength infirmity and grey hairs. He
creates whatever He will. He is the All-knowing, the
Almighty.

When the Hour of Doom overtakes them, the wrongdoers will swear that they had stayed away but one hour.
Thus they are ever deceived.

But those to whom knowledge and faith have been given 30:56

will say: 'You have stayed away till the Day of Resurrection, as was decreed by Allah. *This* is the Day of Resurrection: yet you did not know it.'

On that day their pleas shall not avail the wrongdoers nor shall they be asked to make amends.

In this Koran we have set forth for men all manner of arguments. Yet if you recite to them a single verse, the unbelievers will surely say: 'You are preaching lies.' Thus Allah seals the hearts of ignorant men.

30:60 Therefore, have patience. Allah's promise is true. Let not those who doubt drive you to despair.

THE SPIDER

In the Name of Allah, the Compassionate, the Merciful

29:1 ALIF *lam mim*. Do men think that once they say: 'We are believers', they will be left alone and not be tried with affliction?

We put to the proof those who have gone before them. Allah knows those who are truthful and those who are lying.

Or do the evil-doers think that they will escape Our punishment? How ill they judge!

He that hopes to meet his Lord must know that Allah's appointed hour is sure to come. He alone hears all and knows all.

He that fights for Allah's cause fights for himself. Allah does not need His creatures' help. As for those that have faith and do good works, We shall cleanse them of their sins and reward them according to their noblest deeds.

We have enjoined man to show kindness to his parents. But if they bid you serve besides Me what you know nothing of, do not obey them. To Me you will all return, and I shall declare to you all that you have done. Those that accept the true faith and do good works shall be admitted among the righteous.

29:10 Some profess to believe in Allah, yet when they suffer in

His cause they confound the persecution of man with the punishment of Allah. But if your Lord gives you victory, they say: 'We were on your side.'

Does Allah not know the thoughts of men? He knows *29:11* the true believers and the hypocrites.

The unbelievers say to the faithful: 'Follow us, and we will bear the burden of your sins.' But they will bear none of their sins. They are surely lying.

They shall bear their own burdens, and other burdens besides. On the Day of Resurrection they shall be questioned about their falsehoods.

We sent forth Noah to his people, and he dwelt amongst them for nine hundred and fifty years. Then in their sinfulness the Flood overwhelmed them. But We delivered him and all who were in the Ark, and made the event a sign to mankind.

And tell of Abraham. He said to his people: 'Serve Allah and fear Him. That would be best for you, if you but knew it. You worship idols besides Allah and invent falsehoods. Those whom you serve besides Him can give you nothing. Therefore seek the bounty of Allah, and worship Him. Give thanks to Him, for to Him you shall return.

'If you deny me, likewise other nations before you denied *29:18* their apostles. An apostle's duty is but to give plain warning.'

Do they not see how Allah conceives Creation, and then renews it? That is easy enough for Allah.

Say: 'Roam the earth and see how Allah conceived Creation. Then Allah will create the Second Creation. Allah has power over all things; He punishes whom He will and shows mercy to whom He pleases. To Him you shall be recalled.'

Neither on earth nor in heaven shall you escape His reach: nor have you any besides Allah to protect or help you.

Those that disbelieve His revelations and deny that they will ever meet Him shall despair of My mercy. Theirs shall be a woeful punishment.

Abraham's people replied: 'Kill him! Burn him!' *29:24*

But from the fire Allah delivered him. Surely in this there are signs for true believers.

29:25　Abraham said: 'You have chosen idols instead of Allah, but your love of them will last only in this life. On the Day of Resurrection you shall disown and curse one another. Hell shall be your home and none shall help you.'

Lot believed in him. He said: 'I will fly this land and go where Allah has bidden me. He is the Mighty One, the All-knowing.'

We gave him Isaac and Jacob and bestowed on his descendants prophethood and the Scriptures. We gave him his reward in this life, and in the life to come he shall dwell among the righteous.

And We sent forth Lot to his people. He said to them: 'You commit indecent acts which no other nation has committed before you. You lust after men and assault them on your highways. You turn your very gatherings into orgies.'

But his people's only reply was: 'Bring down Allah's scourge upon us, if what you say be true.'

'Lord,' said he, 'deliver me from these degenerate men.'

And when Our messengers brought Abraham the good news[1] they said: 'We are about to destroy the people of this town, for they are wicked men.'

29:32　Abraham said: 'Lot dwells in it.'

'We well know who live in it,' they replied. 'We shall deliver him and all his kinsfolk, except his wife, who shall remain behind.'

And when Our messengers came to Lot, he grew anxious about their safety, for he could not protect them. But they said: 'Have no fears, nor distress yourself. You shall be delivered with all your kinsfolk, except your wife, who shall remain behind. We shall bring down a scourge from heaven upon the people of this town to punish them for their sins.'

Surely the ruins of that city are a veritable sign for men of understanding.

29:36　And to the people of Midian We sent their compatriot

1. The birth of a son in his old age.

Shoaib. He said: 'Serve Allah, my people. Look forward to the Last Day. Do not corrupt the earth with wickedness.'

But they denied him. The earth shook beneath their feet 29:37 and when morning came they were prostrate in their dwellings.

Aad and Thamoud We also destroyed. This is vouched for by their ruins. Satan had made their foul deeds seem fair to them and debarred them from the right path, keen-sighted though they were.

And Korah, Pharaoh, and Haman! Moses came to them with veritable signs, but they conducted themselves with insolence, powerless though they were to escape Us: and in their sinfulness We smote them. On some We sent down a violent whirlwind; others were seized by the Dreadful Cry; some were swallowed up by the earth, and yet others were overwhelmed by the Flood. Allah did not wrong them but they wronged themselves.

The false gods which the idolators serve besides Allah 29:41 may be compared to the spider's cobweb. Surely the spider's is the frailest of all dwellings, if they but knew it. Allah knows what they invoke besides Him; He is the Mighty, the Wise One.

We coin these similes for the instruction of men; but none will grasp their meaning except the wise.

Allah has created the heavens and the earth to establish the truth. Surely in this there is a sign for true believers.

Proclaim the portions of the Book that are revealed to you and be steadfast in prayer. Prayer fends away indecency and evil. But your foremost duty is to remember Allah. Allah has knowledge of all your actions.

Be courteous when you argue with the People of the Book, except with those among them who do evil. Say: 'We believe in that which is revealed to us and which was revealed to you. Our God and your God is one. To Him we surrender ourselves.'

Thus We have revealed the Book to you. Those to whom 29:47 We gave the Scriptures believe in it, and so do some of your own people. Only the unbelievers deny Our revelations.

29:48 Never have you[1] read a book before this, nor have you ever transcribed one with your right hand. Had you done either of these, the unbelievers might have justly doubted. But to those who are endowed with knowledge it is an undoubted sign. Only the wrongdoers deny Our signs.

They ask: 'Why has no sign been given him by his Lord?' Say: 'Signs are in the hands of Allah. My mission is only to give plain warning.'

Is it not enough for them that We have revealed to you the Book for their instruction? Surely in this there is a blessing and an admonition to true believers.

Say: 'Allah is our all-sufficient witness. He knows all that the heavens and the earth contain. Those who believe in falsehood and deny Allah shall surely be lost.'

They challenge you to hurry on the scourge. Had there not been a time appointed for it, the scourge would have long since overtaken them. But it will suddenly come, and overtake them unawares. But the day will surely come when Hell will encompass the unbelievers; when Our scourge will assail them from above and from beneath, and Allah will say to them: 'Taste the reward of your own deeds.'

29:56 You that are true believers among My servants, My earth is vast. Therefore serve Me. Every soul shall taste death, and in the end you shall return to Us.

Those that embrace the true faith and do good works shall be for ever lodged in the mansions of Paradise, where rivers will roll at their feet. Blessed is the reward of those who labour patiently and put their trust in Allah.

Countless are the beasts that cannot fend for themselves. Allah provides for them, as He provides for you. He alone hears all and knows all.

If you ask them who it is that has created the heavens and the earth and subjected the sun and the moon, they will say: 'Allah'. How then can they turn away from Him?

29:62 Allah gives abundantly to those of His servants whom He will and sparingly to whom He pleases. He has knowledge of all things.

1. Mohammed.

If you ask them who it is that sends down water from the 29:63
sky and thereby quickens the dead earth, they will reply:
'Allah'. Say: 'Praise, then, be to Allah!' But most of them
are senseless men.

The life of this world is but a sport and a pastime. It is the
life to come that is the true life: if they but knew it.

When they embark they pray to Allah with all fervour;
but when He brings them safe to land, they serve other
gods besides Him, showing ingratitude for Our favours
and revelling in wanton ease. They shall before long know
their folly.

Do they not see how We have given them a sanctuary of
safety,[1] while all around them terror holds its reign? Would
they believe in falsehood and deny Allah's goodness?

And who is more wicked than the man who invents a
falsehood about Allah and denies the truth when it is declared to him? Is there not a home in Hell for the unbelievers?

Those that fight for Our cause We will surely guide to 29:69
Our own paths. Allah is with the righteous.

THE POETS

In the Name of Allah, the Compassionate, the Merciful

TA *sin mim.* These are the verses of the Glorious Book: 26:1
You will perhaps fret yourself to death on account
of their unbelief. If We will, We can reveal to them a
sign from heaven before which they will bow their heads in
utter humility.

They deny and turn their backs on each fresh warning
they receive from the Merciful: but the truth of that which
they have laughed to scorn will surely dawn upon
them.

Do they not see the earth, how We have brought forth
in it all kinds of beneficial plants? Surely in this there is a 26:8
sign; yet most of them do not believe.

1. At the Ka'ba.

26:9 Your Lord is the Mighty One, the Merciful. He called to Moses, saying: 'Go to those wicked people, the people of Pharaoh. Will they not have fear of Me?'

'Lord,' he replied, 'I fear they will deny me. I may become impatient and stammer in my speech. Send for Aaron. They hold a charge[1] against me and I fear that they may put me to death.'

'Have no fears,' said He. 'Go both of you with Our signs; We shall be with you and shall hear all. Go to Pharaoh and say to him: "We are messengers from the Lord of all men. Let the Israelites depart with us."'

Pharaoh said to Moses: 'Did We not bring you up when you were an infant? And have you not spent several years of your life amongst us? Yet you have done what you have done; surely you are ungrateful.'

26:20 Moses replied: 'I did that when I was a misguided youth. I fled from you because I feared you. But my Lord has given me wisdom and made me His apostle. And this is the favour with which you taunt me: you have made the Israelites your bondsmen.'

'Who is the Lord of all men?' asked Pharaoh.

Moses replied: 'He is the Lord of the heavens and the earth and all that lies between them. If only you had faith!'

'Do you hear?' said Pharaoh to those around him.

'He is your Lord,' went on Moses, 'and the Lord of your forefathers.'

Pharaoh said: 'The apostle who has been sent to you is surely possessed!'

'He is the Lord of the East and the West,' said Moses, 'and all that lies between them. If only you could understand!'

'If you serve any other god but myself,' replied Pharaoh, 'you shall be thrown into prison.'

'Even if I showed you a convincing sign?' said Moses.

26:31 Pharaoh replied: 'Show us your sign, if what you say be true.'

---

1. Moses had killed an Egyptian.

Moses threw down his staff and thereupon it changed to a   *26:32*
veritable serpent. Then he drew out his hand, and it appeared white to all who saw it.

'This man,' said Pharaoh to his nobles, 'is a skilled enchanter who seeks to drive you from your land by his witchcraft. What is your counsel?'

They replied: 'Put them off awhile, him and his brother, and send forth heralds to your cities to summon every skilled magician to your presence.'

They gathered the magicians on the appointed day, and the people were asked if they had all assembled. 'Yes,' they replied. 'We will follow the magicians if they win the day.'

And when the magicians came to Pharaoh, they said: 'Shall we be rewarded if we win?'

'Yes,' he answered, 'and you shall become my favoured friends.'

Moses said to them: 'Throw down all that you wish to   *26:43*
throw.'

They cast down their ropes and staffs, saying: 'By Pharaoh's glory, we shall surely win!'

Then Moses threw down his staff and it swallowed their false devices. The magicians prostrated themselves in adoration, saying: 'We believe in the Lord of the Creation, the Lord of Moses and Aaron.'

Pharaoh said: 'Do you dare believe in Him without my consent? This man must be your master, who has taught you witchcraft. But you shall see. I will cut off your hands and feet on alternate sides and crucify you all.'

'That cannot harm us,' they replied, 'for to our Lord we shall return. We trust that He will forgive us our sins, since we are the first who have believed.'

Then We revealed Our will to Moses, saying: 'Set forth with My servants by night, for you will be pursued.'

Pharaoh sent forth heralds to all the cities. 'These,' they said, 'are but a puny band, who have provoked us much. But we are a numerous army, well-prepared.'

Thus We made them leave their gardens and their foun-   *26:57*

26:58 tains, their treasures and their sumptuous dwellings. Even thus; and we gave the like to the Israelites.

At sunrise the Egyptians followed them. And when the two bands came in view of each other, Moses' companions said: 'We have surely been overtaken!'

'No,' replied Moses, 'my Lord is with me and He will guide me.'

We bade Moses strike the sea with his staff, and the sea was cleft asunder, each part as high as a massive mountain. In between We led the others. We delivered Moses and those who were with him, and drowned Pharaoh and all his men.

Surely in that there was a sign; yet most men do not believe. Truly, your Lord is the Mighty One, the Merciful.

Recount to them the story of Abraham. He said to his father and to his people: 'What is that which you worship?'

They replied: 'We worship idols and pray to them with all fervour.'

'Do they hear you when you call on them?' he asked. 'Can they help you or do you harm?'

They replied: 'This was what our fathers did before us.'

26:75 He said: 'Do you see those which you and your fathers worship? They are enemies to me. Not so the Lord of the Creation, who has made me; who gives me guidance, food and drink; who, when I am sick, restores me; who will cause me to die and bring me back to life hereafter; who, I pray, will forgive me my sins on the Day of Judgement.

'Lord, bestow on me wisdom and let me dwell among the righteous. Give me renown among posterity and place me amongst the heirs of the Blissful Garden. Forgive my father, for he has gone astray. Do not hold me to shame on the Day of Resurrection; the day when wealth and children will avail nothing and when none shall be saved except him who comes before his Lord with a pure heart; when Paradise shall be brought in sight of the righteous and Hell be revealed to the erring. A voice will say to them: "Where are your idols now? Can they help you or even help them-
26:94 selves?" And into Hell they shall be hurled, they and those

who misled them, and Satan's legions all. "By Allah," they *26:95* will say to their idols, as they contend with them, "we erred indeed when we made you equals with the Lord of the Creation. It was the evil-doers who led us astray. We have no intercessors now, no loving friend. Could we but live our lives again we would be true believers." '

Surely in that there was a sign, yet most of them do not believe.

Your Lord is the Mighty One, the Merciful. The people of Noah, too, denied their apostles. 'Will you have no fear of Allah?' said Noah, their compatriot, to them. 'I am indeed your true apostle. Fear Allah, then, and follow me. For this I demand of you no recompense, for none can reward me except the Lord of the Creation. Have fear of Allah and follow me.'

They replied: 'Are we to believe in you when the lowest of the low are your followers?'

'I have no knowledge of what they may have done,' said *26:112* Noah. 'My Lord alone can bring them to account. Would that you understood! I will not drive away the true believers. I am sent only to give plain warning.'

'Noah' they replied, 'desist, or you shall be stoned to death.'

He said: 'Lord, my people have denied me. Judge rightly between us. Save me and the believers who are with me.'

We delivered him and those who were with him in the laden Ark, and overwhelmed the others with the Flood.

Surely in that there was a sign; yet most of them do not believe.

Your Lord is the Mighty One, the Merciful. Aad, too, disbelieved their apostles. Their compatriot Houd had said to them: 'Will you not have fear of Allah? I am indeed your true apostle. Fear Allah then and follow me. For this I demand of you no recompense; none can reward me except the Lord of the Creation. Will you build a monument on every hill? Vain is your work. You raise strong fortresses, hoping that you may last for ever. When you exercise your *26:130*

26:131 power, you act like cruel tyrants. Have fear of Allah, and follow me. Fear Him who has given you all the things you know. He has given you flocks and children, gardens and fountains. Beware of the torment of a fateful day.'

They replied: 'We care nothing whether you preach or not. That with which you threaten us is but a legend of the ancients. Surely we shall never be punished.'

They denied him, and thus We utterly destroyed them. Surely in that there was a sign; yet most of them do not believe.

Your Lord is the Mighty One, the Merciful. Thamoud, too, disbelieved their apostles. Their compatriot Saleh said to them: 'Will you not have fear of Allah? I am indeed your true apostle. Fear Allah and follow me. For this I demand of you no recompense; none can reward me except the Lord of the Creation. Are you to be left safe in this land, amidst gardens and fountains, cornfields and palm-trees laden with fine fruit, hewing your dwellings in the mountains and leading a wanton life? Have fear of Allah and follow me. Do not do the bidding of transgressors who commit evil in the earth and reform nothing.'

26:153 They replied: 'Surely you are bewitched. You are but a mortal like ourselves. Show us a sign, if what you say be true.'

'Your sign,' he said, 'is this she-camel. She shall have her share of water as you have yours, each drinking on an appointed day. Do not molest her, or the scourge of a fateful day shall fall upon you.'

Yet they slew her, and then repented of their deed. The scourge overtook them.

Surely in that there was a sign. Yet most of them do not believe.

Your Lord is the Mighty One, the Merciful. Lot's people, too, disbelieved their apostles. Their compatriot Lot said to them: 'Will you not have fear of Allah? I am indeed your true apostle. Fear Allah then and follow me. *26:164* I demand of you no recompense for this; none can reward

me except the Lord of the Creation. Will you fornicate with   *26:165*
males and leave your wives, whom Allah has created for
you? Surely you are great transgressors.'

'Lot,' they replied, 'desist or you shall be banished.'

He said: 'I abhor your ways. Lord, preserve me and my
kinsfolk from their evil doings.'

We delivered Lot and all his kinsfolk, save for one old
woman who stayed behind, and the rest We utterly destroyed. We pelted them with rain, and evil was the rain
which fell on those who had been warned.

Surely in that there was a sign. Yet most of them do not
believe.

Your Lord is the Mighty One, the Merciful. The dwellers of the Forest,[1] too, disbelieved their apostles. Shoaib
had said to them: 'Will you not have fear of Allah? I am indeed your true apostle. Fear Allah, then, and follow me. I
demand of you no recompense: none can reward me except
the Lord of the Creation. Give just measure and defraud
none. Weigh with even scales and do not cheat others of
what is rightly theirs; nor corrupt the land with evil. Fear
Him who created you and those who have gone before you.'

They replied: 'You are surely bewitched. You are but a   *26:185*
mortal like ourselves. Indeed, we believe that you are
lying. Bring down upon us a part of heaven if what you say
be true.'

He said: 'My Lord has full knowledge of all your actions.' They disbelieved him, and thus the scourge of the
Day of Darkness smote them; the punishment of a fateful
day.

Surely in that there was a sign; yet most of them do not
believe.

Your Lord is the Mighty One, the Merciful. This Book
is revealed by the Lord of the Creation. The faithful Spirit
brought it down into your heart, that you might warn mankind in plain Arabic speech. It was foretold in the scriptures
of the ancients. Is it not sufficient proof for them that the   *26:197*

1. The people of Midian.

26:198 doctors of the Israelites recognize it? If We had revealed it to a foreign man, and he had recited it to them, they still would not have believed. We thus put unbelief in the hearts of the evil-doers: they shall not believe in it until they see the woeful scourge which in their heedlessness will suddenly smite them. And then they will say: 'Shall we never be reprieved?'

Do they wish to hasten Our punishment? Think! If We let them live in ease for many years, and then the scourge with which they are threatened falls upon them, of what avail will their past enjoyments be to them?

Never have We destroyed a nation whom We did not warn and admonish beforehand. We are never unjust.

It was not the devils who brought down this Koran: it is neither in their interest nor in their power. Indeed, they are *26:213* too far away to overhear it.

Call on no other god besides Allah, lest you incur His punishment. Admonish your nearest kinsfolk and show kindness to the believers who follow you. If they disobey you, say: 'I am not accountable for what you do.'

Put your trust in the Mighty One, the Merciful, who observes you when you stand upright and when you walk among the worshippers. He hears all and knows all.

Shall I tell you on whom the devils descend? They descend on every lying sinner. They eagerly listen, but most of them are liars.

Poets are followed by none save erring men. Behold how aimlessly they rove in every valley, preaching what they *26:227* never practise. Not so the true believers who do good works and remember Allah and defend themselves when wronged. The wrongdoers will see what a come-back they shall have.

AL-FURQAN[1]

In the Name of Allah, the Compassionate, the Merciful

BLESSED be He who has revealed Al-Furqan to His **25:1**
servant, that he may warn mankind; the Lord of the
heavens and the earth, who has begotten no children
and has no partner in His kingdom; who has created all
things and ordained their destinies.

Yet the unbelievers serve, besides Him, other gods
which can create nothing and were themselves created:
idols which can neither help nor harm themselves, and
which have no power over life or death, or the raising of
the dead.

The unbelievers say: 'This[2] is but a forgery of his own
invention, in which others have helped him.' Unjust is
what they say and false.

And they say: 'Fables of the ancients he has written:
they are dictated to him morning and evening.'

Say: 'It is revealed by Him who knows the secrets of
heaven and earth. He is forgiving and merciful.'

They also say: 'How is it that this apostle eats and walks **25:7**
about the market-squares? Why has no angel been sent
down with him to warn us? Why has no treasure been
given him, no garden to provide his sustenance?'

And the wrongdoers say: 'The man you follow is surely
bewitched.'

See what epithets they bestow upon you![3] Surely they
have gone astray and cannot return to the true path.

Blessed be He who, if He wills, can give you better things
than these; palaces and gardens watered by running streams.

They deny the Hour of Doom. For those who deny that
hour We have prepared a blazing fire. From a long distance **25:12**

---

1. 'The distinction between right and wrong; also one of the names of
the Koran.' The word has puzzled Muslim commentators, but, clearly, it
is identical with the Aramaic *porqan* (salvation).

2. The Koran.

3. Mohammed.

25:13 they shall hear it raging and roaring. And when, chained together, they are flung into some narrow space, they will earnestly call for death. But the angels will say to them: 'Do not call today for one death; call for many deaths!'

Say: 'Which is better, this or the Paradise of Immortality which the righteous have been promised? It is their recompense and their retreat. Abiding there for ever, they shall find in it all that they desire. That is a promise which Allah must needs fulfil.'

On the day when He assembles them with all their idols, He will say: 'Was it you who misled My servants, or did they wilfully go astray?'

They will answer: 'Allah forbid that we should choose other guardians besides You. You gave them and their fathers the good things of life, so that they forgot Your warning and thus incurred destruction.'

Then to the idolaters Allah will say: 'Your idols have denied your charges. They cannot avert your doom, nor can they help you. Those of you who have done wrong shall be sternly punished.'

25:20 We have sent no apostles before you who did not eat or walk about the market-squares. We test you by means of one another. Will you not have patience? Your Lord observes all.

Those who do not hope to meet Us ask: 'Why have no angels been sent to us? Why can we not see our Lord?' How arrogant they are, and how great their transgression!

On the day when they behold the angels, the evil-doers will not rejoice. The angels will say to them: 'You shall never cross that barrier.' Then We shall turn to that which they have done and render it as vain as scattered dust.

As for the heirs of Paradise, they shall lodge in a more auspicious dwelling on that day and in a cooler resting-place.

On that day the sky with all its clouds shall be rent *25:26* asunder and the angels sent down in their ranks. On that day the Merciful will truly reign supreme. A day of woe it shall be to the unbelievers.

On that day the wrongdoer will bite his hands and say: 25:27
'Would that I had walked in the Apostle's path! Oh,
would that I had never chosen so-and-so for my companion! It was he that made me disbelieve in Allah's warning after it had reached me. Satan is ever treacherous to
man.'

The Apostle says: 'Lord, my people have denied this
Koran.' Thus to every prophet We have appointed adver-
saries among the wrongdoers: but you need none besides
your Lord to guide and help you.

The unbelievers ask: 'Why was the Koran not revealed
to him entire in a single revelation?'

We have revealed it thus so that We may strengthen your
faith. We have imparted it to you by gradual revelation. No
sooner will they come to you with an argument than We
shall reveal to you the truth and properly explain it. Those
who will be dragged headlong into Hell shall have an evil
place to dwell in, for they have strayed far from the right
path.

We revealed the Scriptures to Moses and gave him his 25:35
brother Aaron to help him. We sent them to those who had
denied Our signs, and utterly destroyed them.

As for Noah's people, We drowned them when they
denied their apostles and made of them an example to all
men. For the wrongdoers We have prepared a stern chastisement.

The tribes of Thamoud and Aad were also destroyed,
and so were those who dwelt at Raas, and many generations
in between. To each of them We gave warnings, and each
of them We exterminated.

The unbelievers have doubtless passed by the city which
was destroyed by the fatal rain: have they never seen its
ruins? Yet they have no faith in the Resurrection.

Whenever they see you they scoff at you, saying: 'Is this
the man whom Allah has sent as His apostle? Had we not 25:42
stood firm he would have turned us away from our deities '
But when they face their punishment they shall know who
has been more grossly misled.

25:43   Have you seen those who have made gods of their own appetites? Would you be a guardian over them?

Do you think that they can hear or understand? They are like beasts, and even more misguided.

Do you not see how your Lord lengthens the shadows? Had it been His will He could have made them constant. But He makes the sun their guide; little by little He shortens them.

It is He who has made the night a mantle for you and sleep a rest. He makes each day a resurrection.

It is He who drives the winds as harbingers of His mercy, and sends down pure water from the sky, so that He may give life to dead lands and quench the thirst of man and beast.

We have made plain to them Our revelations so that they may take heed. Yet most men decline to render thanks.

Had it been Our will, We could have raised a prophet in every nation. Do not yield to the unbelievers, but fight them strenuously with this Koran

25:53   It was He who sent the two seas rolling, the one sweet and fresh, the other salt and bitter, and set a rampart between them, an insurmountable barrier.

It was He who created man from water and gave him kindred of blood and of marriage. Your Lord is all-powerful.

Yet the unbelievers worship idols which can neither help nor harm them. Surely the unbeliever is his Lord's enemy.

We have sent you only to proclaim good news and to give warning. Say: 'I demand of you no recompense for this. Let him who will take the right path to his Lord.'

Put your trust in the Ever-living who never dies. Celebrate His praise: He well knows all His servants' sins. In six days He created the heavens and the earth and all that lies between them, and then ascended His throne. He is the Lord of Mercy. Ask those who know, concerning Him.

25:60   When it is said to them: 'Prostrate yourselves before the Merciful,' they ask: 'Who is the Merciful? Would you have us worship whatever you will?' And they grow more and more rebellious.

Blessed be He who decked the sky with constellations 25:61 and set in it a lamp and a shining moon. He makes the night succeed the day: a sign to those who would take heed and render thanks.

The true servants of the Merciful are those who walk humbly on the earth and say: 'Peace!' to the ignorant who accost them; who pass the night standing and on their knees in adoration of their Lord; who say: 'Lord, ward off from us the punishment of Hell, for its punishment is everlasting: an evil dwelling and an evil resting-place'; who are neither extravagant nor niggardly but keep the golden mean; who invoke no other god besides Allah and do not kill except for a just cause (manslaughter is forbidden by Him); who do not commit adultery (he that does this shall meet with evil: his punishment shall be doubled on the Day of Resurrection and in disgrace he shall abide for ever – unless he repent and believe and do good works, for then Allah will change his sins to good actions: Allah is forgiving and merciful: he that repents and does good works truly returns 25:72 to Allah); who do not bear false witness and do not lose their dignity when listening to profane abuse; who do not turn a blind eye and a deaf ear to the revelations of their Lord when they are reminded of them; who say: 'Lord, give us joy in our wives and children and make us examples to those who fear you.' These shall be rewarded with Paradise for their fortitude. There they shall find a welcome and a greeting, and there they shall abide for ever: a blessed dwelling and a blessed resting-place.

Say to the unbelievers: 'Little cares my Lord if you do 25:77 not invoke Him. Now that you have denied His revelations His punishment is bound to overtake you.'

In the Name of Allah, the Compassionate, the Merciful

24:1 WE have revealed this Chapter and sanctioned it, proclaiming in it clear revelations, so that you may take heed.

The adulterer and the adulteress shall each be given a hundred lashes. Let no pity for them cause you to disobey Allah, if you truly believe in Allah and the Last Day; and let their punishment be witnessed by a number of believers.

The adulterer may marry only an adulteress or an idolatress; and the adulteress may marry only an adulterer or an idolater. True believers are forbidden such marriages.

Those that defame honourable women and cannot produce four witnesses shall be given eighty lashes. No testimony of theirs shall be admissible, for they are great transgressors – except those among them that afterwards repent and mend their ways. Allah is forgiving and merciful.

24:6 If a man accuses his wife but has no witnesses except himself, he shall swear four times by Allah that his charge is true, calling down upon himself the curse of Allah if he is lying. But if his wife swears four times by Allah that his charge is false and calls down His curse upon herself if it be true, she shall receive no punishment.[1]

But for Allah's grace and mercy, His wisdom and forgiveness, this would never have been revealed to you.

Those who invented that slander[2] were a number of your own people. Do not regard it as a misfortune, for it has proved an advantage. Each one of them shall be punished according to his crime. As for him who had the greater share in it, his punishment shall be terrible indeed.

24:12 When you heard it, why did the faithful, men and women, not think well of their own people, and say: 'This

1. Cf. Numbers v, 11–31.
2. The reference is to the scandal involving Mohammed's wife Aisha with Safwan ibn-el-Moattel.

is an evident falsehood'? Why did they not produce four 24:13
witnesses? If they could not produce any witnesses, then
they were surely lying in the sight of Allah.

But for Allah's grace and mercy towards you in this life
and in the next, you would have been sternly punished for
what you did. You carried with your tongues and uttered
what your mouths did not know. You may have thought
it a trifle, but in the sight of Allah it was a grave offence.

When you heard it, why did you not say: 'It is not right
for us to speak of this. Allah forbid! This is a monstrous
slander'?

Allah bids you never again to lend your ears to such
scandals, if you are true believers. Allah makes plain to you
His revelations. He is wise and all-knowing.

Those who delight in spreading slanders against the
faithful shall be sternly punished in this life and in the next.
Allah knows them all, but you do not.

But for Allah's grace and mercy, His compassion and 24:20
forgiveness, you would have long since been punished.

You that are true believers, do not walk in the footsteps
of Satan. He that walks in Satan's footsteps is incited to
indecency and evil. But for Allah's grace and mercy, none
of you would have been cleansed of sin. Allah purifies
whom He will; He hears all and knows all.

Let the rich and honourable among you not swear to
withhold their gifts from their kindred, the poor, and those
who have fled their homes for the cause of Allah. Rather
let them pardon and forgive. Do you not wish Allah to
forgive you? He is forgiving and merciful.

Those who defame honourable but careless believing
women shall be cursed in this world and in the next. Theirs
shall be a woeful punishment on the day when their own
tongues, hand, and feet will testify to what they did. On
that day Allah will justly requite them. They shall know
that Allah is the Glorious Truth.

Unclean women are for unclean men, and unclean men 24:26
for unclean women. But good women are for good men,
and good men for good women. These shall be cleared of

calumny; they shall be shown forgiveness, and a generous provision shall be made for them.

24:27 Believers, do not enter the dwellings of other men until you have asked their owners' permission and wished them peace. That will be best for you. Perchance you will take heed.

If you find no one in them, do not go in till you are given leave. If you are refused admission, it is but right that you should go away. Allah has knowledge of all your actions.

It shall be no offence for you to seek shelter in empty dwellings. Allah knows what you hide and what you reveal.

Enjoin believing men to turn their eyes away from temptation and to restrain their carnal desires. This will make their lives purer. Allah has knowledge of all their actions.

24:31 Enjoin believing women to turn their eyes away from temptation and to preserve their chastity; to cover their adornments (except such as are normally displayed); to draw their veils over their bosoms and not to reveal their finery except to their husbands, their fathers, their husbands' fathers, their sons, their step-sons, their brothers, their brothers' sons, their sisters' sons, their women-servants, and their slave-girls; male attendants lacking in natural vigour, and children who have no carnal knowledge of women. And let them not stamp their feet in walking so as to reveal their hidden trinkets.

Believers, turn to Allah in repentance, that you may prosper.

Take in marriage those among you who are single and those of your male and female slaves who are honest. If they are poor, Allah will enrich them from His own abundance. Allah is munificent and all-knowing.

24:33 Let those who cannot afford to marry live in continence until Allah enriches them. As for those of your slaves who wish to buy their liberty, free them if you find in them any promise and bestow on them a part of the riches which Allah has given you.

You shall not force your slave-girls into prostitution in order that you may make money, if they wish to preserve their chastity. If any one compels them, Allah will be forgiving and merciful to them.

We have sent down to you revelations showing you the 24:34 right path. We have given you an account of those who have gone before you and an admonition to righteous men.

Allah is the light of the heavens and the earth. His light may be compared to a niche that enshrines a lamp, the lamp within a crystal of star-like brilliance. It is lit from a blessed olive tree neither eastern nor western. Its very oil would almost shine forth, though no fire touched it. Light upon light; Allah guides to His light whom He will.

Allah coins metaphors for men. He has knowledge of all things.

His light is found in temples which Allah has sanctioned 24:36 to be built for the remembrance of His name. In them morning and evening His praise is sung by men whom neither trade nor profit can divert from remembering Him, from offering prayers, or from giving alms; who dread the day when men's hearts and eyes shall writhe with anguish; who hope that Allah will requite them for their noblest deeds and lavish His grace upon them. Allah gives without measure to whom He will.

As for the unbelievers, their works are like a mirage in a desert. The thirsty traveller thinks it is water, but when he comes near he finds that it is nothing. He finds Allah there, who pays him back in full. Swift is Allah's reckoning.

Or like darkness on a bottomless ocean spread with clashing billows and overcast with clouds: darkness upon darkness. If he stretches out his hand he can scarcely see it. Indeed the man from whom Allah withholds His light shall find no light at all.

Do you not see how Allah is praised by those in heaven and earth? The very birds praise Him as they wing their flight. He notes the prayers and praises of all His creatures, and has knowledge of all their actions.

To Allah belongs the kingdom of the heavens and the earth. To Him shall all things return.

Do you not see how Allah drives the clouds, then gathers 24:43

them and piles them up in masses which pour down torrents of rain? From heaven's mountains He sends down hail, pelting with it whom He will and turning it away from whom He pleases. The flash of His lightning almost snatches off men's eyes.

24:44 He makes the night succeed the day: surely in this there is a lesson for clear-sighted men.

Allah created every beast from water. Some creep upon their bellies, others walk on two legs, and others on four. Allah creates what He pleases. He has power over all things.

We have sent down revelations showing the truth. Allah guides whom He will to a straight path.

They declare: 'We believe in Allah and His apostle and obey them both.' But no sooner do they utter these words than some of them turn their backs. Surely these are no believers.

24:48 And when they are called to Allah and His apostle that he may judge between them, some turn away. Had justice been on their side they would have come to him in all obedience.

Is there a sickness in their hearts, or are they full of doubt? Do they fear that Allah and His apostle may deny them justice? Surely these are wrongdoers.

But when true believers are called to Allah and His apostle that he may pass judgement upon them, their only reply is: 'We hear and obey.' Such men shall surely prosper.

Those that obey Allah and His apostles, those that revere Allah and fear Him, shall surely triumph.

They solemnly swear by Allah that if you order them to fight they will obey you. Say: 'Do not swear: your obedience, not your oaths, will count. Allah is cognizant of all your actions.'

Say: 'Obey Allah and obey His apostle. If you do not, he is still bound to fulfil his duty, as you yourselves are bound to fulfil yours. If you obey him, you shall be guided. The duty of an apostle is only to give plain warning.'

24:55 Allah has promised those of you who believe and do good works to make them masters in the land as He had made their ancestors before them, to strengthen the Faith

He chose for them, and to change their fears to safety. Let them worship Me and serve no other gods besides Me. Wicked indeed are they who after this deny Me.

Attend to your prayers, pay the alms-tax, and obey the 24:56 Apostle, so that you may be shown mercy.

Never think that the unbelievers will escape the wrath of Allah in this world. Hell shall be their home. An evil fate awaits them.

Believers, let your slaves and children ask your leave when they come in to see you before the morning prayer, when you have put off your garments in the heat of noon, and after the evening prayer. These are the three occasions when none may intrude upon you. At other times, when some of you go round to visit others, they shall be free to enter your chambers without leave. Thus Allah makes plain to you His revelations: He is wise and all-knowing.

And when they have reached the age of puberty, let your 24:59 children still ask your leave as their elders do. Thus Allah makes plain to you His revelations: He is wise and all-knowing.

It shall be no offence for old spinsters who have no hope of marriage to discard their cloaks without revealing their adornments. Better if they do not discard them. Allah hears all and knows all.

It shall be no offence for the blind, the lame, and the sick, to eat at your table. Nor shall it be an offence for you to eat in the houses of your own children, your fathers, your mothers, your brothers, your sisters, your paternal uncles, your paternal aunts, your maternal uncles, your maternal aunts, or your friends; or in houses with the keys of which you are entrusted. It shall be equally lawful whether you eat together or apart.

When you enter a house, salute one another in the name of Allah, and let your greeting be devout and kindly. Thus Allah makes clear to you His revelations so that you may grow in wisdom.

They only are true believers who have faith in Allah and 24:62 His apostle, and who, when gathered with him upon a grave occasion, do not depart till they have begged his leave. The men who ask your leave are those who truly believe in Allah and His apostle. When they ask your leave to go away on any business of their own, grant it to whomever you please and implore Allah to forgive them; Allah is forgiving and merciful.

Do not address the apostle in the manner you address one another. Allah knows those of you who steal away, concealing themselves behind others. Let those who disobey his orders beware, lest some affliction or some woeful scourge be visited upon them.

24:64 To Allah belongs what the heavens and the earth contain. He has knowledge of all your thoughts and actions. On the day when they return to Him He will declare to them all that they have done. He has knowledge of all things.

THE BELIEVERS

In the Name of Allah, the Compassionate, the Merciful

23:1 BLESSED are the believers, who are humble in their prayers; who avoid profane talk, and give alms to the destitute; who restrain their carnal desires (except with their wives and slave-girls, for these are lawful to them) and do not trangress through lusting after other women; who are true to their trusts and promises and never neglect their prayers. These are the heirs of Paradise; they shall abide in it for ever.

We first created man from an essence of clay: then placed him, a living germ, in a safe enclosure.[1] The germ We made a clot of blood, and the clot a lump of flesh. This We fashioned into bones, then clothed the bones with flesh, thus bringing forth another creation. Blessed be Allah, the noblest of creators!

You shall surely die hereafter, and be restored to life on *23:17* the Day of Resurrection. We have created seven heavens above you; of Our creation We are never heedless.

1. The womb.

We sent down water from the sky in due measure, and 23:18
lodged it into the earth. But if We please, We can take it all
away.

With it We caused vineyards and palm-groves to spring up,
yielding abundant fruit for your sustenance. The tree[1] which
grows on Mount Sinai gives oil and a condiment for men.

In the beasts, too, you have an example of Our power.
You drink of that which is in their bellies, you eat their
flesh, and gain other benefits from them besides. By them,
as by the ships that sail the sea, you are carried from place
to place.

We sent forth Noah to his people. 'Serve Allah, my
people,' he said, 'for you have no god but Him. Will you
not take heed?'

The unbelieving elders of his people said: 'This man is 23:24
but a mortal like you, feigning himself your superior. Had
Allah willed, He could have sent down angels. Nor did such
a thing happen to our forefathers. He is surely possessed.
Keep an eye on him awhile.'

Noah said: 'Help me, Lord. They will not believe me.'

We revealed Our will to him, saying: 'Build an ark under
Our watchful eye, according to Our instructions. When
Our judgement comes to pass and water wells out from the
Oven, take abroad a pair from every species and the mem-
bers of your household, except those of them already
doomed. Do not plead with me for those who have done
wrong: they shall be drowned. And when you and all your
followers have gone aboard, say: "Praise be to Allah who
has delivered us from a sinful nation. Lord, let my landing
from this ark be blessed. You alone can make me land in
safety."'

Surely that was a veritable sign. Thus We put mankind
to the proof.

Then We raised a new generation and sent forth to them
an apostle of their own. 'Serve Allah,' he said, 'for you
have no god but Him. Will you not take heed?'

But the unbelieving elders of his people, who denied the 23:33

1. The olive.

221

life to come and on whom We had bestowed the good things of this life, said: 'This man is but a mortal like your-

23:34 selves, nourished by the same food and drink. If you obey a mortal like yourselves, you shall be lost. Does he threaten you that when you are dead and turned to dust and bones, you will be raised to life? A foolish threat, indeed. There is no other life but this, our earthly life: we live and die, never to live again. This man is but an impostor who tells of Allah what is untrue. We will never believe him.'

He said: 'Help me, Lord, they will not believe me.'

We replied: 'Before long they shall rue it.' Our scourge overtook them in all justice and We swept them away like withered leaves. Gone are those wicked men.

After them We raised other generations – no people can delay their doom or go before it – and sent forth Our apostles in succession. Yet time after time they disbelieved their apostles, so that We destroyed them one by one and made them a byword for iniquity. Gone are the unbelievers.

23:45 Then We sent Moses and his brother Aaron with Our signs and clear authority to Pharaoh and his nobles. But they received them with scorn, for they were arrogant men. 'What!' they said. 'Are we to believe in two mortals like yourselves, whose people are our bondsmen?' They denied them, and thus incurred destruction. And We gave Moses the Torah, so that his people might be rightly guided.

We made the son of Mary and his mother a sign to mankind and gave them a shelter on a peaceful hill-side watered by a fresh spring.

Apostles! Eat of that which is wholesome and do good works: I have knowledge of all your actions. Your religion is but one religion, and I am your only Lord: therefore fear Me.

Yet men have divided themselves into different sects, each rejoicing in its own doctrines. Leave them in their error till death overtakes them.

Do they think that in giving them wealth and children

23:56 We are solicitous for their welfare. By no means! They cannot see.

Those who walk in fear of their Lord; who believe in the 23:57
revelations of their Lord; who worship none besides their
Lord; who give alms with their hearts filled with awe,
knowing that they will return to their Lord: these vie with
each other for salvation and are the first to attain it.

We charge no soul with more than it can bear. Our Book
records the truth: none shall be wronged.

But the unbelievers are blind to all this; their deeds are
unlike those of the faithful. But when We visit Our scourge
upon those of them that live in comfort, they will cry out
for help. We shall say: 'Do not howl this day, for from Us
you shall receive no help. My revelations were recited to
you many a time, but you turned your backs in scorn,
reviling them by day and night.'

Should they not heed the Word of Allah?

Was anything revealed to them that had not been revealed to their forefathers?

Or is it because they do not know their apostle that they 23:69
deny him?

Do they say he is possessed?

He has proclaimed to them the truth. But most of them
abhor the truth. Had the truth followed their appetites, the
heavens, the earth, and all who dwell in them, would have
surely been corrupted. We have given them their scriptures: yet to their scriptures they pay no heed.

Are you seeking a reward of them? Your Lord's recompense is better. He is the most munificent Giver.

You have called them to a straight path, but those who
deny the life to come will ever stray from the right path.

If We showed them mercy and relieved their misfortunes,
they would still blunder about in their evil ways. We punished them once, but they neither besought their Lord nor
humbled themselves towards Him. And when We smote
them with a dreadful scourge, they yielded to utter despair.

It was He who gave you ears, eyes, and hearts: yet you
are seldom thankful.

It was He who placed you on the earth, and before Him 23:79
you shall all be assembled.

23:80   It is He who ordains life and death and He who controls the night and the day. Can you not understand?

They say what the ancients said before them. 'When we are bones and dust,' they say, 'shall we be raised to life? This we have been promised before, we and our fathers. It is but an old fictitious tale.'

Say: 'Whose is the earth and all that it contains? Tell me, if you know the truth.'

'Allah's,' they will reply.

Say: 'Then will you not take heed?'

Say: 'Who is the Lord of the seven heavens, and of the Glorious Throne?'

'Allah,' they will reply.

Say: 'Will you keep from evil, then?'

Say: 'In whose hands is the sovereignty of all things, protecting all, while against Him there is no protection? Tell me, if you know the truth.'

'In Allah's,' they will reply.

Say: 'How then can you be so bewitched?'

23:90   We have revealed to them the truth, but they are liars all.

Never has Allah begotten a son, nor is there any other god besides Him. Were this otherwise, each god would govern his own creation, each holding himself above the other. Exalted be Allah above their falsehoods!

He knows alike the visible and the unseen. Exalted be He above the gods they serve besides Him!

Say: 'Lord, if You let me witness the punishment with which they are threatened, do not abandon me among this sinful nation.' Indeed, We have power enough to let you see the punishment with which they are threatened.

Requite evil with good. We are fully aware of all their slanders. And say: 'Lord, I seek refuge in You from the promptings of the devils. Lord, I seek refuge in You from their presence.'

When death comes to a wrongdoer, he will say: 'Lord, *23:100* let me go back, that I may do good works in the world I have left behind.'

Never! These are the very words which he will speak.

Behind them there shall stand a barrier till the Day of Resurrection. And when the Trumpet is sounded, on that 23:101 day their ties of kindred shall be no more, nor shall they ask help of one another.

Those whose scales are heavy shall triumph but those whose scales are light shall forfeit their souls and abide in Hell for ever. Its flames will scorch their faces and they will writhe with pain.

We shall say: 'Were My revelations not recited to you, and did you not deny them?'

'Lord,' they will reply, 'fortune betrayed us and we went astray. Lord, deliver us from Hell. If we return to sin, then we shall indeed be wicked men.'

He will say: 'Stay here in shame and do not plead with Me. Among My servants there were those who said: "Lord, we believe in You. Forgive us and have mercy on us: You are most merciful." But you derided them until they caused you to forget My warning. Today I shall reward them for 23:111 their fortitude, for it is they who have triumphed.'

And He will ask: 'How many years did you live on earth?'

They will reply: 'A day, or possibly less. Ask those who have kept count.'

He will say: 'Brief indeed was your sojourn, if you but knew it! Did you think that We had created you in vain and that you would never be recalled to Us?'

Exalted be Allah, the True King. There is no god but Him, the Lord of the Glorious Throne.

He that invokes another god besides Allah – a god of whose divinity he has no proof – his Lord will bring him to account. The unbelievers shall never prosper.

Say: 'Lord, forgive and have mercy. You are the best 23:118 of those that show mercy.'

TA HA

In the Name of Allah, the Compassionate, the Merciful

20:1 TA *ha.*

It was not to distress you that We revealed the Koran, but to admonish the God-fearing. It is a revelation from Him who has created the earth and the lofty heavens, the Merciful who sits enthroned on high.

His is what the heavens and the earth contain, and all that lies between them and underneath the soil. You have no need to speak aloud; for He has knowledge of all that is secret and all that is hidden.

He is Allah. There is no god but Him. His are the most gracious names.

Have you heard the story of Moses?

When he saw a fire, he said to his people: 'Stay here, for I can see a fire. Perchance I can bring you a lighted torch or find a guide hard by.'

When he came near, a voice called out to him: 'Moses, I am your Lord. Take off your sandals, for you are now in the sacred valley of Towah.

20:13 'Know that I have chosen you. Therefore listen to what shall be revealed.

'I am Allah. There is no god but Me. Serve Me, and recite your prayers in My remembrance.

'The Hour of Doom is sure to come. But I choose to keep it hidden, so that every soul may be rewarded for its labours. Let those who disbelieve in it and yield to their desires not turn your thoughts from it, lest you perish. What is it you are carrying in your right hand, Moses?'

He replied: 'It is my staff; upon it I lean and with it I beat down the leaves for my flock. It has other uses besides.'

He said: 'Moses, cast it down.'

Moses threw it down, and thereupon it turned into a scurrying serpent.

20:21 'Take it up and do not be alarmed,' He said. 'We will

change it back to its former state. Now put your hand 20:22
under your armpit. It shall come out white, although
unharmed. This shall be another sign.

'But before long We shall show you the most wondrous
of all Our signs. Go to Pharaoh; he has transgressed all
bounds.'

'Lord,' said Moses, 'put courage into my heart, and do
not beset my task with hardships. Free my tongue from its
impediment, that men may understand my speech. Appoint
for me a counsellor from among my kinsmen, Aaron my
brother. Grant me strength through him and let him share
my task, so that we may give glory to You and remember
You always. You are surely watching over us.'

He replied: 'Your request is granted, Moses. We had
already shown you favour when We revealed Our will to
your mother, saying: "Put your child in the ark and let him
be carried away by the river. The river will cast him on to
the bank, and he shall be taken up by an enemy of his and
Mine." I lavished My love on you, so that you might be
reared under My watchful eye.

'Your sister went to them and said: "Shall I bring you 20:40
one who will nurse him?"'

'Thus We restored you to your mother, so that her mind
might be set at ease and that she might not grieve.

'And when you killed a man We delivered you from
affliction and then proved you by other trials.

'You stayed among the people of Midian for many years,
and at length came here as I ordained. I have chosen you
for Myself. Go, you and your brother, with My signs, and
do not cease to remember Me. Go both of you to Pharaoh,
for he has transgressed all bounds. Speak to him with
gentle words; he may yet take heed and fear Our punishment.'

'Lord,' they said, 'we dread his malevolence and tyran-
ny.'

He replied: 'Have no fears. I shall be with you. I see all
and hear all. Go to him and say: "We are the messengers of 20:47
your Lord. Let the Israelites depart with us, and oppress

them no more. We have come to you with a revelation from your Lord: blessed is he that follows the guidance of his Lord. It is revealed to us that His scourge will fall on those who deny His signs and give no heed to them.'''

20:48

Pharaoh said: 'And who is your Lord, Moses?'

'Our Lord,' he replied, 'is He that gave all creatures their distinctive form and then rightly guided them.'

'How was it, then, with the ancients?' asked Pharaoh.

He answered: 'My Lord alone has knowledge of that; it is recorded in His book. He does not err, nor does He forget. It is He who has made the earth your cradle and traced on it paths for you to walk on. It is He who sends down water from the sky with which He brings forth every kind of plant, saying: "Eat and feed your cattle. Surely in this there are signs for men of understanding. From the earth We have created you, and to the earth We will restore you; and from it We will bring you back to life."'

20:56

We showed Pharaoh Our signs, but he denied them and gave no heed. He said to Moses: 'Have you come to drive us from our land with your sorcery? Know that we will confront you with magic as powerful as yours. Appoint a day when both of us can meet, and a place accessible to you and to ourselves.'

He replied: 'Meet me on the day of the Feast, and let all the people assemble before noon.'

Pharaoh gathered his magicians and took them to Moses. 'Woe to you!' said Moses. 'Invent no falsehoods against Allah, or He will destroy you with His scourge. Liars will surely fail.'

The magicians conferred among themselves, whispering to one another. They said to Pharaoh: 'These two are sorcerers who intend to drive you from your land by their magic and abuse your best ideals. Muster all your forces and array them in their ranks; those who win today shall surely triumph.'

To Moses they said: 'Will you first throw down your gear, or shall we?'

20:66

'Throw down yours,' he answered.

And by the power of their magic their cords and staffs appeared to Moses' eyes as though they were running.

Moses was much alarmed. But We said to him: 'Have no 20:67 fear; you shall surely triumph. Throw that which is in your right hand. It will swallow up their devices, for their devices are but the deceitful show of witchcraft. Magicians shall not prosper, whatever they do.'

The magicians prostrated themselves, crying: 'We believe in the Lord of Aaron and Moses.'

'Do you dare believe in Him without my consent?' said Pharaoh. 'This man must be your master, who taught you witchcraft. I will cut off your hands and feet on alternate sides and crucify you on the trunks of palm-trees. You shall know whose punishment is more terrible, and more lasting.'

They replied: 'Obey you we cannot. Rather will we obey 20:72 the miracles which we have witnessed and Him who has created us. Therefore do your worst; you can punish us only in this present life. We have put our faith in our Lord so that He may forgive us our sins and the witchcraft you have forced us to practise. Better is the reward of Allah, and more lasting. He that comes before his Lord laden with sin shall be consigned to Hell, where he shall neither live nor die. But he that comes before Him with true faith and good works shall be exalted to the highest rank. He shall abide for ever in the gardens of Eden, in gardens watered by running streams. Such shall be the recompense of those that purify themselves.'

Then We revealed Our will to Moses, saying: 'Set forth with My servants in the night and strike for them a dry path across the sea. Have no fear of being overtaken, nor let anything dismay you.'

Pharaoh pursued them with his legions, but the waters overwhelmed them. For Pharaoh misled his people: he did not guide them.

Children of Israel! We delivered you from your enemies and made a covenant with you on the right flank of the Mountain. We sent down manna and quails for you. 'Eat of 20:81

the wholesome things with which We have provided you
and do not transgress, lest you should incur My wrath,' We
20:82 said. 'He that incurs My wrath shall assuredly be lost, but he
that repents and believes in Me, does good works and
follows the right path, shall be forgiven. But, Moses, why
have you come with such haste from your people?'

Moses replied: 'They are close behind me. I hastened to
You so that I might earn Your pleasure.'

Allah said: 'We proved your people in your absence, but
the Samiri[1] has led them astray.'

Angry and sorrowful, Moses went back to them. 'My
people,' he said, 'did your Lord not make you a gracious
promise? Did my absence seem too long to you, or was it
to incur your Lord's anger that you failed me?'

They replied: 'We failed you through no fault of ours.
We were made to carry the people's trinkets and throw
20:87 them into the fire. The Samiri did the same, and forged a
calf for them, an image with a hollow sound. "This," they
said, "is your god and the god of Moses whom he has forgotten."'

Did they not see that it returned them no answer, and
that it could neither help nor harm them?

Aaron had said to them: 'My people, this is but a test for
you. Your Lord is the Merciful. Follow me and do as I bid
you.' But they had replied: 'We will worship it until
Moses returns.'

Moses said to Aaron: 'Why did you not seek me out
when you saw them doing evil? Why did you disobey
me?'

'Son of my mother,' he replied, 'let go, I pray you, of
my head and beard. I was afraid that you might say: "You
have sown discord among the Israelites and did not wait
for my orders."'

'Samiri,' cried Moses, 'what had come over you?'

20:96 He replied: 'I saw what they did not see. I took a handful
of dust from the trail of the Messenger and flung it away:
thus did my soul prompt me.'

1. It is not clear who the Samiri is.

'Begone!' cried Moses. 'You are an outcast in this life, *20:97* nor shall you escape, in the life to come, your appointed doom. Behold this idol which you have served with such devotion: we will burn it to cinders and scatter its ashes over the sea.'

Your God is Allah, besides whom there is no other god. He has knowledge of all things.

Thus We recount to you the history of past events. A Scripture of Our own We have given you: those that reject it shall bear a heavy burden on the Day of Resurrection. They shall bear it for ever: an evil burden on the Day of Resurrection, the day when the Trumpet shall be sounded.

On that day We shall assemble all the sinners. Their eyes will become dim with terror and they shall murmur among themselves: 'You have stayed away but ten days.'

We know full well what they will say. The most upright among them will declare: 'You have stayed away but one day.'

They ask you about the mountains. Say: 'My Lord will *20:105* crush them to fine dust and leave them a desolate waste, with no hollows nor jutting mounds.'

On that day men will follow their truthful summoner, their voices hushed before the Lord of Mercy; and you shall hear no sound except the light tread of marching feet. On that day none shall have power to intercede for them except him that has received the sanction of the Merciful and whose word is acceptable to Him. He knows what is before them and behind them, but they themselves have no knowledge of it.

They will hang their heads with awe before the Living One, the Ever-existent.[1] Those who are burdened with sin shall come to grief: but those who have believed and done good works shall fear neither inequity nor injustice.

Thus We have revealed the Koran in the Arabic tongue and proclaimed in it warnings and threats so that they may take heed and guard themselves against evil. Exalted be *20:114* Allah, the True King!

1. The phrase is similar to *Hai we Qayyam*, in the Old Testament.

231

Do not be quick to recite the Koran before its revelation is completed, but rather say: 'Lord, increase my knowledge.'

20:115 We made a covenant with Adam, but he forgot and showed himself lacking in steadfastness. And when We said to the angels: 'Prostrate yourselves before Adam,' they all prostrated themselves except Satan, who refused.

'Adam,' We said, 'Satan is an enemy to you and to your wife. Let him not turn you out of Paradise and plunge you into affliction. Here you shall not hunger or be naked; you shall not thirst, or feel the scorching heat.'

But Satan whispered to him, saying: 'Shall I show you the Tree of Immortality and an everlasting kingdom?'

They both ate of its fruit, so that they beheld their nakedness and began to cover themselves with leaves. Thus Adam disobeyed his Lord and went astray.

Then his Lord had mercy on him; He relented towards him and rightly guided him.

20:123 'Go hence,' He said, 'and may your offspring be enemies to each other. When My guidance is revealed to you, he that follows it shall neither err nor be afflicted; but he that gives no heed to My warning shall live in woe and come before Us blind on the Day of Resurrection.' 'Lord,' he will say, 'why have You brought me blind before You when in my life-time I was blessed with sight?'

He will answer: 'Because Our revelations were declared to you and you forgot them. This day you are yourself forgotten.'

Thus do We reward the transgressor who denies the revelations of his Lord. But the punishment of the life to come is more terrible and more lasting.

Do they not see how many generations We have destroyed before them? They walk amidst the very ruins in which they dwelt. Surely in this there are signs for men of judgement.

Had your Lord not already fixed their term and deferred their punishment, their destruction in this life would have 20:130 been certain. Therefore bear with what they say. Give glory to your Lord before sunrise and before sunset. Praise Him day and night and you shall find comfort.

Do not regard with envy the worldly benefits We have 20:131 bestowed on some of them, for with these We seek only to try them. Your Lord's reward is better and more lasting.

Enjoin prayer on your people and be diligent in its observance. We demand nothing of you: We shall Ourself provide for you. Blessed shall be the end of the devout.

They say: 'Why does he give us no sign from his Lord?' Have they not been given sufficient proof in previous scriptures?

Had We destroyed them before his[1] coming they would have said: 'Lord, if only You had sent us an apostle! We would have followed Your revelations before we were humbled and disgraced.'

Say: 'All are waiting: so wait if you will. You shall know 20:135 who has followed the right path and who has been rightly guided.'

THE NIGHT JOURNEY

In the Name of Allah, the Compassionate, the Merciful

GLORY be to Him who made His servants go by night 17:1 from the Sacred Temple[2] to the farther Temple[3] whose surroundings We have blessed, that We might show him some of Our signs. He alone hears all and observes all.

We gave Moses the Scriptures and made them a guide for the Israelites, saying: 'Take no other guardian than Myself. You are the descendants of those whom We carried in the Ark with Noah. He was a truly thankful servant.'

In the Scriptures We solemnly declared to the Israelites: 'Twice you shall commit evil in the land. You shall become 17:4 great transgressors.'

1. Mohammed's.   2. Of Mecca.

3. Of Jerusalem (and thence to the Throne of Allah, accompanied by the Angel Gabriel). Some Muslim commentators give a literal interpretation to this passage, others regard it as a vision.

17:5   And when the prophecy of your first transgression came to be fulfilled, We sent against you a formidable army[1] which ravaged your land and carried out the punishment with which you had been threatened.

Then We granted you victory over them and multiplied your riches and your descendants, so that once again you became a numerous people. We said: 'If you do good, it shall be to your own advantage; but if you do evil, you shall sin against your own souls.'

And when the prophecy of your second transgression came to be fulfilled, We sent another army[2] to afflict you and to enter the Temple as the former entered it before, utterly destroying all that they laid their hands on.

17:8   We said: 'Allah may yet be merciful to you. If you again transgress, you shall again be scourged. We have made Hell a prison-house for the unbelievers.'

This Koran will guide men to that which is most upright. It promises the believers who do good works a rich reward, and threatens those who deny the life to come with a grievous scourge. Yet man prays for evil as fervently as he prays for good. Truly, man is ever impatient.

We made the night and the day twin marvels. We enshrouded the night with darkness and gave light to the day, so that you might seek the bounty of your Lord and learn to compute the seasons and the years. We have made all things manifestly plain to you.

The fate of each man We have bound about his neck. On the Day of Resurrection We shall confront him with a book spread wide open, saying: 'Here is your book: read it. Enough for you this day that your own soul should call you to account.'

He that seeks guidance shall be guided to his own advantage, but he that errs shall err at his own peril. No soul shall bear another's burden. Nor do We punish a nation until We have sent forth an apostle to warn them.

17:16   When We resolve to annihilate a people, We first warn those of them that live in comfort. If they persist in sin, We

1. The Assyrians.   2. The Romans.

234

rightly pass Our judgement and utterly destroy them.

How many generations have We destroyed since Noah's *17:17* time! Your Lord is well aware of His servants' sins: He observes them all.

He that desires this fleeting life shall before long receive in it whatever We will: We bestow Our gifts on whom We please. But We have prepared Hell for him; he will burn in it despised and helpless.

As for him that desires the life to come and strives for it with all his soul, being a true believer, his endeavours shall be rewarded by Allah.

We bestow Our bounty on all men: none shall be denied the bounty of your Lord.

See how We have exalted some above others. Yet the life *17:21* to come has greater honours and is more exalted.

Serve no other gods besides Allah, lest you incur disgrace and ruin. Your Lord has enjoined you to worship none but Him, and to show kindness to your parents. If either or both of them attain old age in your dwelling, show them no sign of impatience, nor rebuke them; but speak to them kind words. Treat them with humility and tenderness and say: 'Lord, be merciful to them. They nursed me when I was an infant.'

Your Lord best knows what is in your hearts; He knows if you are good. He will forgive those that turn to Him.

Give to the near of kin their due, and also to the destitute and to the wayfarers. Do not squander your substance wastefully, for the wasteful are Satan's brothers; and Satan is ever ungrateful to his Lord. But if, while waiting for your Lord's bounty, you lack the means to assist them, then at least speak to them kindly.

Be neither miserly nor prodigal, for then you should either be reproached or be reduced to penury.

Your Lord gives abundantly to whom He will and sparingly to whom He pleases. He knows and observes His servants.

You shall not kill your children for fear of want.[1] We will *17:31*

1. In allusion to the pre-Islamic custom of burying alive unwanted newborn girls.

provide for them and for you. To kill them is a great sin.

17:32 You shall not commit adultery, for it is foul and indecent.

You shall not kill any man whom Allah has forbidden you to kill, except for a just cause. If a man is slain unjustly, his heir is entitled to satisfaction. But let him not carry his vengeance too far, for his victim will in turn be assisted and avenged.

Do not interfere with the property of orphans except with the best of motives, until they reach maturity. Keep your promises; you are accountable for all that you promise.

Give full measure, when you measure, and weigh with even scales. That is fair, and better in the end.

Do not follow what you do not know. Man's eyes, ears, and heart – each of his senses shall be closely questioned.

17:37 Do not walk proudly on the earth. You cannot cleave the earth, nor can you rival the mountains in stature.

All this is evil; odious in the sight of your Lord.

These injunctions are but a part of the wisdom with which your Lord has inspired you.[1] Serve no other god besides Allah, lest you should be cast into Hell, despised and helpless.

What! Has your Lord blessed *you*[2] with sons and Himself adopted daughters from among the angels? A monstrous blasphemy is that which you utter.

We have made plain Our revelations in this Koran so that the unbelievers may take warning. Yet it has only added to their unbelief. Say: 'If, as you affirm, there were other gods besides Allah, they would surely seek to dethrone Him.'

Glory to Him! Exalted be He, high above their falsehoods!

17:44 The seven heavens, the earth, and all who dwell in them give glory to Him. All creatures celebrate His praises. Yet you cannot understand their praises. Benignant is He and forgiving.

1. Mohammed.   2. The unbelievers.

When you recite the Koran, We place between you and 17:45
those who deny the life to come a hidden barrier. We cast
a veil upon their hearts and make them hard of hearing,
lest they understand it. That is why on hearing mention
of your One and Only Lord, they turn their backs in flight.

We well know what they wish to hear when they listen
to you, and what they say when they converse in private;
when the wrongdoers declare: 'The man you follow is
surely bewitched.'

Behold what epithets they bestow upon you. They have
surely gone astray and cannot find the right path.

'What!' they say. 'When we are turned to bones and
dust, shall we be restored to life?'

Say: 'You shall; whether you turn to stone or iron, or 17:50
any other substance which you may think unlikely to be
given life.'

They will ask: 'Who will restore us?'

Say: 'He that created you at first.'

They will shake their heads and ask: 'When will this be?'

Say: 'It may be near at hand. On that day He will
summon you all, and you shall answer Him with praises.
You shall think that you have stayed away but for a little
while.'

Tell My servants to be courteous in their speech. Satan
would sow discord among them; He is the sworn enemy of
man.

Your Lord knows you best. He will show you mercy if
He will, and punish you if He pleases.

We have not charged you to be their guardian. Your Lord
is best aware of all who dwell in heaven and earth.

We have exalted some prophets above others. To David
We gave the Psalms.

Say: 'Pray if you will to those whom you deify besides
Him.[1] They cannot relieve your distress, nor can they
change it.'

Those to whom they pray, themselves seek to approach 17:57
their Lord, vying with each other to be near Him. They

---

1. The allusion is to saint-worship.

crave for His mercy and fear His punishment; for your Lord's punishment is terrible indeed.

17:58 There is no nation but shall be destroyed or sternly punished before the Day of Resurrection. That is decreed in the Eternal Book.

Nothing hinders us from giving signs except that the ancients disbelieved them. To Thamoud We gave the she-camel as a visible sign, yet they laid violent hands on her. We give signs only by way of warning.

We have told you that your Lord controls all men. We have made the vision which We showed you, as well as the tree[1] cursed in the Koran, a test for men's faith. We seek to put fear in their hearts, but their wickedness increases.

When We said to the angels: 'Prostrate yourselves before Adam,' they all prostrated themselves, except Satan, who replied: 'Shall I bow to him whom You have made of clay?
17:62 Do You see this being whom You have exalted above me? If You give me respite till the Day of Resurrection, I will exterminate all but a few of his descendants.'

'Begone!' said He. 'Hell is your reward, and the reward of those that follow you. An ample reward it shall be. Rouse with your voice whomever you are able. Muster against them all your forces. Be their partner in their riches and in their offspring. Promise them what you will. (Satan promises them only to deceive them.) But over My true servants you shall have no power. Your Lord will be their all-sufficient Guardian.'

It is your Lord who drives your ships across the ocean, so that you may sail in them in quest of His abundance. Your Lord is merciful towards you.

When at sea a misfortune befalls you, all but He of those to whom you pray forsake you; yet when He brings you safe to dry land you turn your backs upon Him. Truly, man is ever thankless.

17:68 Are you confident that He will not cave in the earth beneath you, or let loose a deadly sand-storm upon you? Then you shall find none to protect you.

1. The Zaqqum tree.

Are you confident that when again you put to sea He will 17:69
not smite you with a violent tempest and drown you for
your thanklessness? Then you shall find none to help you.

We have bestowed blessings on Adam's children and
guided them by land and sea. We have provided them with
good things and exalted them above many of Our creatures.

The day will surely come when We shall summon every
nation with its apostle. Those who are given their books in
their right hands will read their recorded doings, and shall
not in the least be wronged. But those who have been blind
in this life, shall be blind in the life to come and go farther
astray.

They sought to entice you from Our revelations, hoping
that you might invent some other scripture in Our name,
and thus become their trusted friend. Indeed, had We not
strengthened your faith you might have made some com-
promise with them and thus incurred a double punishment
in this life and in the next. Then you should have found
none to protect your from Our wrath.

They sought to provoke you and thus drive you out of 17:76
the land. Had they succeeded, they would have scarcely
survived your departure.

Such was Our way with the apostles whom We sent
before you. You shall find no change in Our way.

Recite your prayers at sunset, at nightfall, and at dawn;
the dawn prayer has its witnesses. Pray during the night as
well, an additional duty for the fulfilment of which your
Lord may exalt you to an honourable station.

Say: 'Lord, grant me a goodly entrance and a goodly
exit, and sustain me with Your power.'

Say: 'Truth has come and Falsehood has been overthrown. Falsehood was bound to be discomfited.'

That which We have revealed in the Koran is a balm and
a blessing to true believers, though it adds nothing but ruin
to the evil-doers.

When We bestow favours on man, he turns his back and 17:83
holds aloof. But when evil befalls him, he grows despondent.

17:84 Say: 'Each man behaves after his own fashion. But your Lord best knows who is best guided.'

They put questions to you about the Spirit. Say: 'The Spirit is at my Lord's command. Little indeed is the knowledge vouchsafed to you.'

If We pleased We could take away that which We have revealed to you: then you should find none to plead with Us on your behalf. But your Lord is merciful to you. His goodness towards you is great indeed.

Say: 'If men and jinn combined to write the like of this Koran, they would surely fail to compose one like it, though they helped one another.'

We have set forth in this Koran all manner of arguments, yet most men persist in unbelief. They say: 'We will not believe in you until you make a spring gush from the earth
17:91 before our very eyes, or cause rivers to flow in a grove of palms and vines; until you cause the sky to fall upon us in pieces, as you have threatened to do, or bring down Allah and the angels in our midst; until you build a house of gold, or ascend to heaven: nor will we believe in your ascension until you have sent down for us a book which we can read.'

Say: 'Glory to my Lord! Surely I am no more than a human apostle.'

Nothing prevents men from having faith when guidance is revealed to them but the excuse: 'Could Allah have sent a human being as an apostle?'

Say: 'Had the earth been a safe place for angels to dwell in, We would have sent forth to them an angel from heaven as an apostle.'

Say: 'Sufficient is Allah as a judge between us. He knows and observes His servants.'

17:97 Those whom Allah guides are rightly guided; but those whom He misleads shall find no friend besides Him. We shall gather them all on the Day of Resurrection, prostrate upon their faces, deaf, dumb, and blind. Hell shall be their home: whenever its flames die down We will rekindle them into a greater fire.

Thus shall they be rewarded: because they disbelieved 17:98
Our revelations and said: 'When we are turned to bones
and dust, shall we be raised to life?'

Do they not see that Allah, who has created the heavens
and the earth, has power to create their like? Their fate is
pre-ordained beyond all doubt. Yet the wrongdoers persist
in unbelief.

Say: 'Had you possessed the treasures of my Lord's
mercy, you would have covetously hoarded them. How
niggardly is man!'

To Moses We gave nine clear signs. Ask the Israelites
how he first appeared amongst them.

Pharaoh said to him: 'Moses, I can see that you are
bewitched.'

'You know full well,' he replied, 'that none but the Lord
of the heavens and the earth has revealed these visible
signs. Pharaoh, you are doomed.'

Pharaoh sought to scare them out of the land: but We 17:103
drowned him, together with all who were with him. Then
We said to the Israelites: 'Dwell in this land. When the
promise of the hereafter comes to be fulfilled, We shall
assemble you all together.'

We have revealed the Koran with the truth, and with the
truth it has come down. We have sent you forth only to
proclaim good news and to give warning.

We have divided the Koran into sections so that you may
recite it to the people with deliberation. We have imparted
it by gradual revelation.

Say: 'It is for you to believe in it or to deny it. Those to
whom knowledge was given before its revelation prostrate
themselves when it is recited to them and say: "Glorious
is our Lord. His promise has been fulfilled." They fall down
upon their faces, weeping; and as they listen, their humility
increases.'

Say: 'It is the same whether you call on Allah or on the
Merciful: His are the most gracious names.'

Pray neither with too loud a voice nor in silence, but seek
between these extremes a middle course. Say: 'Praise be to 17:111

Allah who has never begotten a son; who has no partner in His Kingdom; who needs none to defend Him from humiliation.' Proclaim His greatness.

AL-HIJR

In the Name of Allah, the Compassionate, the Merciful

15:1 ALIF *lam ra*. These are the verses of the Book, the Glorious Koran:

The day will surely come when the unbelievers will wish that they were Muslims. Let them feast and make merry; and let their hopes beguile them. They shall know the truth.

Never have We destroyed a nation whose term of life was not ordained beforehand. Men cannot forestall their doom, nor can they retard it.

They say: 'You to whom the warning was revealed, you are surely possessed. Bring down the angels, if what you say be true.'

We shall send down the angels only when Our judgement has been passed. Then they shall never be reprieved.

15:9 It was We that revealed the Koran, and shall Ourself preserve it. We have sent forth apostles before you to the older nations: but they scoffed at each apostle We sent them. Thus We will put doubt in the hearts of the guilty: they will deny their apostle despite the example of the ancients.

If We opened for the unbelievers a gate in heaven and they ascended through it higher and higher, still they would say: 'Our eyes were dazzled: truly, we must have been bewitched.'

We have decked the heavens with constellations and guarded them from all accursed devils. Eavesdroppers are pursued by fiery comets.

We have spread out the earth and set upon it immovable mountains. We have planted it with every seasonable fruit, **15:20** thus providing sustenance for man and beast. We hold the store of every blessing and send it down in appropriate *15:21* measure. We let loose the fertilizing winds and bring down water from the sky for you to drink; its stores are beyond your reach.

We ordain life and death. We are the Heir of all things.

We know those who have gone before you, and those who will come hereafter. Your Lord will gather them all before Him. He is wise and all-knowing.

We created man from dry clay, from black moulded loam, and before him Satan from smokeless fire. Your Lord said to the angels: 'I am creating man from dry clay, from black moulded loam. When I have fashioned him and breathed of My spirit into him, kneel down and prostrate yourselves before him.'

All the angels prostrated themselves, except Satan. He refused to prostrate himself.

'Satan,' said Allah, 'why do you not prostrate your- *15:32* self?'

He replied: 'I will not bow to a mortal created of dry clay, of black moulded loam.'

'Begone,' said Allah, 'you are accursed. My curse shall be on you till Judgement-day.'

'Lord,' said Satan, 'reprieve me till the Day of Resurrection.'

He answered: 'You are reprieved till the Appointed Day.'

'Lord,' said Satan, 'since you have led me astray, I will seduce mankind on earth: I will seduce them all, except those that faithfully serve you.'

He replied: 'This is the right course for Me. You shall have no power over My servants, except the sinners who follow you. They are all destined for Hell. It has seven gates, and through these they shall come in separate bands. But the righteous shall dwell amongst gardens and fountains; in peace and safety they shall enter them. We shall remove all hatred from their hearts, and they shall recline on couches face to face, a band of brothers. Toil shall not weary them, nor shall they ever leave their Paradise.' *15:48*

15:49 Tell My servants that I am forgiving and merciful, and that My punishment is dire indeed.

Tell them of Abraham's guests. They went in to him and said: 'Peace be to you,' but he replied: 'I fear your intent.'

'Do not be alarmed,' they answered. 'We come to you with good news. You shall have a son blessed with wisdom.'

He said: 'Do you bring me such news in my old age? What news can this be?'

They replied: 'We have made known to you the truth. Do not despair.'

He said: 'Who but a sinner would despair of Allah's mercy? Messengers, what is your errand?'

They replied: 'We are sent to a wicked nation. The house of Lot alone shall be delivered, except his wife.' We had decreed that she should remain with those who were to stay behind.

And when Our envoys came to the house of Lot, he said to them: 'I do not know you.'

'No,' they replied. 'We bring you news of that concern-
15:64 ing which you are disputing. We bring you the truth, for what we say is true. Depart with your kinsfolk in the dead of night. Walk in their rear and let none of you turn round. Go where you are commanded.'

Such were the instructions We gave him; for the wrong-doers were to be utterly destroyed next morning.

The townsfolk came to him rejoicing. He said: 'These men are my guests; do not disgrace me. Have fear of Allah and do not shame me.'

They replied: 'Did we not forbid you to entertain strangers?'

He said: 'Here are my daughters: take them, if you are bent on evil.'

By your life, they were blundering in madness! When the sun rose a dreadful cry rang above them. We laid their town in ruin and rained clay-stones upon them.

15:76 Surely in this there are signs for prudent men. The road

on which their city stood is trodden still. Surely in this there *15:77*
is a sign for true believers.

The dwellers of the Forest[1] were also guilty. On them,
too, We took vengeance, and made of both a manifest
example.

The people of Hijr[2] also denied Our apostles. We gave
them signs, but they ignored them. They hewed their
dwellings into the mountains and lived in safety. But one
morning a dreadful cry brought down death upon them.
Nothing did their gains avail them.

It was to reveal the truth that We created the heavens and
the earth and all that lies between them. The Hour of Doom
is sure to come: therefore forgive them nobly. Your Lord is
the all-knowing Creator.

We have given you the seven oft-repeated verses[3] and the
Glorious Koran. Do not regard with envy the good things *15:88*
We have bestowed on some of them, nor grieve on their
account. Show kindness to the faithful, and say: 'It is for
me to warn men plainly.'

We will surely punish the schismatics, who have broken
up their scriptures into separate parts. By the Lord, We
will question them all about their actions.

Proclaim, then, what you are bidden and avoid the idolaters. We will Ourself sustain you against those that mock
you and serve other gods besides Allah. They shall before
long know the truth.

We know that you are vexed by what they say. Give glory
to your Lord and prostrate yourself before Him. Worship *15:99*
Him till certain death overtakes you.

1. The people of Midian.
2. Territory to the north of Medina, where Thamoud are supposed
to have dwelt.
3. The seven verses of the Fatihah, or Exordium.

In the Name of Allah, the Compassionate, the Merciful

7:1 ALIF *lam mim sad*. This Book is revealed to you: let your heart not be troubled about it. It is revealed to you that you may thereby warn the unbelievers and admonish the faithful.

Observe that which is brought down to you[1] from your Lord and do not follow other masters besides Him. But you seldom take warning.

How many cities have We laid in ruin! In the night Our scourge fell upon them, or at midday, when they were drowsing.

And when Our scourge fell upon them, their only cry was: 'We have indeed been wicked men.'

We will question those to whom Our message was sent, as We shall question Our messengers. With knowledge We will recount to them what they have done, for We are watching over all their actions.

7:8 On that day their deeds shall be weighed with justice. Those whose scales are heavy shall triumph, but those whose scales are light shall lose their souls, because they have denied Our revelations.

We have given you power on earth and provided you with a livelihood: yet you are seldom thankful.

We created you and gave you form. Then We said to the angels: 'Prostrate yourselves before Adam.' They all prostrated themselves except Satan, who refused.

'Why did you not prostrate yourself?' Allah asked.

'I am nobler than Adam,' he replied. 'You created me of fire and him of clay.'

He said: 'Begone from Paradise! This is no place for your contemptuous pride. Away with you! Henceforth you shall be humble.'

7:14 Satan replied: 'Reprieve me till the Day of Resurrection.'

1. The Meccans.

'You are reprieved,' said He.   7:15

'Because You have led me into sin,' said Satan, 'I will waylay Your servants as they walk on Your straight path, and spring upon them from the front and from the rear, from their right and from their left. Then you shall find the greater part of them ungrateful.'

'Begone!' said Allah. 'A despicable outcast you shall henceforth be. With those that follow you I shall fill the pit of Hell.'

To Adam He said: 'Dwell with your wife in Paradise, and eat of any fruit you please; but never approach this tree or you shall both become transgressors.'

But Satan tempted them, so that he might reveal to them their nakedness, which they had never seen before. He said: 'Your Lord has forbidden you to approach this tree only to prevent you from becoming angels or immortals.' Then he swore to them that he would give them friendly counsel.

Thus he cunningly seduced them. And when they had   7:22
eaten of the tree, their shame became visible to them, and they both covered themselves with the leaves of the garden.

Their Lord called out to them, saying: 'Did I not forbid you to approach that tree, and did I not warn you that Satan was your sworn enemy?'

They replied: 'Lord, we have wronged our souls. Pardon us and have mercy on us, or we shall surely be among the lost.'

He said: 'Go hence, and may your descendants be enemies to each other. The earth will for a while provide your sustenance and dwelling-place. There you shall live and there you shall die, and thence you shall be raised to life.'

Children of Adam! We have given you clothing with which to cover your nakedness, and garments pleasing to the eye, but the finest of all these is the robe of piety.

That is one of Allah's revelations. Perchance they will take heed.

Children of Adam! Let Satan not deceive you, as he   7:27
deceived your parents out of Paradise. He stripped them of

247

their garments to reveal to them their nakedness. He and his minions see you whence you cannot see them. We have made the devils guardians over the unbelievers.

7:28   When they commit an indecent act, they say: 'This is what our fathers used to do before us. Allah Himself enjoined it.'

Say: 'Allah does not enjoin what is indecent. Would you tell of Allah what you do not know?'

Say: 'My Lord has ordered you to act justly. Turn to Him wherever you kneel in prayer and call on Him with true devotion. You shall return to Him as He created you.'

Some He has guided and some He has justly led astray; for they had chosen the devils for their guardians instead of Allah and deemed themselves on the right path.

Children of Adam, dress well when you attend your mosques. Eat and drink, but avoid excess. He does not love the intemperate.

7:32   Say: 'Who has forbidden you to wear the decent clothes or to eat the good things which Allah has bestowed upon His servants?'

Say: 'These are for the enjoyment of the faithful in the life of this world, though shared by others; but they shall be theirs alone on the Day of Resurrection,'

Thus We make plain Our revelations to men of understanding.

Say: 'My Lord has forbidden all indecent acts, whether overt or disguised, sin, and wrongful oppression; He has forbidden you to worship that which is not sanctioned by Him, or to tell of Allah what you do not know.'

A space of time is fixed for every nation; when their hour is come, not for one moment shall they hold back, nor can they go before it.

Children of Adam, when apostles of your own come to proclaim to you My revelations, those that take warning and mend their ways will have nothing to fear or to regret; but those that deny and scorn Our revelations shall be the heirs of Hell, and there they shall remain for ever.

7:37   Who is more wicked than the man who invents a falsehood about Allah or denies His revelations? Such men shall have their destined share, and when Our angels come to carry off their souls they shall say to them: 'Where are your idols now, those whom you invoked besides Allah?' 'They have forsaken us,' they will answer, and will admit that they were unbelievers.

Allah will say: 'Enter the fire of Hell and join the nations *7:38* of jinn and men that have gone before you.'

As it enters every nation will curse the one that went before it, and when all are gathered there, the last of them will say of the first: 'These, Lord, are the men who led us astray. Let their punishment be doubled in Hell-fire.'

He will answer: 'You shall all be doubly punished, although you may not know it.'

Then the first will say to the last: 'You were no better than we. Taste the penalty of your misdeeds.'

The gates of heaven shall not be opened for those that have denied and scorned Our revelations; nor shall they enter the gates of Paradise until a camel shall pass through the eye of a needle. Thus shall the guilty be rewarded.

Hell shall be their couch, and sheets of fire shall cover *7:41* them. Thus shall the wicked be rewarded.

As for those that have faith and do good works – We never charge a soul with more than it can bear – they are the heirs of Paradise, and there they shall abide for ever.

We shall take away all hatred from their hearts. Rivers shall roll at their feet and they shall say: 'Praise be to Allah who has guided us hither. Had He not given us guidance we should have strayed from the right path. His apostles have surely preached the truth.' And a voice will cry out to them, saying: 'This is the Paradise which you have earned with your labours.'

Then the blessed will cry out to the damned: 'What our Lord promised we have found to be true. Have you, too, found the promise of your Lord to be true?'

'Yes,' they shall answer, and a herald will cry out among them: 'Cursed are the evil-doers who have debarred others *7:45* from the path of Allah and sought to make it crooked, and who had no faith in the life to come.'

7:46   A barrier shall divide the blessed from the damned, and on the Heights there shall stand men who will know each of them by his look. To the blessed they shall say: 'Peace be upon you!' But they shall not yet join them, though they long to do so.

And when they turn their eyes towards the heirs of the Fire they will cry: 'Lord, do not cast us among these wicked people!' Then they shall say to men whose looks they recognize: 'Nothing have your riches or your scornful pride availed you. Are these the men who you swore would never earn Allah's mercy?'

And again turning to the blessed they shall say: 'Dwell in Paradise. You have nothing to fear or to regret.'

7:50   The damned will cry out to the blessed: 'Give us some water, or some of that which Allah has given you.' But the blessed shall reply: 'Allah has forbidden both to the unbelievers, who made their religion a pastime and an idle sport, and who were seduced by their earthly life.'

On that day We will forget them as they forgot that day: for they denied Our revelations.

We have bestowed on them a Book which We have imbued with knowledge, a guide and a blessing to true believers. Are they waiting for its fulfilment? On the day when it is fulfilled, those that have forgotten it will say: 'Our Lord's apostles have surely preached the truth. Will no one plead on our behalf? Could we but live our lives again, we would not do as we have done.' They shall forfeit their souls, and that which they devised will fail them.

Your Lord is Allah, who in six days created the heavens and the earth and then ascended His throne. He throws the veil of night over the day. Swiftly they follow one another.

It was He who created the sun, the moon, and the stars, and forced them into His service. His is the creation, His the command. Blessed be Allah, the Lord of all creatures!

7:55   Pray to your Lord with humility and in secret. He does not love the transgressors.

Do not corrupt the earth after it has been purged of evil. 7:56
Pray to Him with fear and hope; His mercy is within reach
of the righteous.

He sends forth the winds as harbingers of His mercy, and
when they have gathered up a heavy cloud, He drives it on
to some dead land and lets water fall upon it, bringing forth
all manner of fruit. Thus He will raise the dead to life. Perchance you will take heed.

Good soil yields fruit by Allah's will. But poor and scant
are the fruits which spring from barren soil. Thus We make
plain Our revelations to those who render thanks.

Long ago We sent forth Noah to his people. He said:
'Serve Allah, my people, for you have no god but Him. Beware of the torment of a fateful day.'

But the elders of his people said: 'We can see that you 7:60
are in palpable error.'

'I am not in error, my people,' he replied. 'I am sent
forth by the Lord of the Creation to make known to you
His will and to give you friendly counsel, for I know of
Allah what you do not know. Do you think it strange that a
warning should come to you from your Lord through a
mortal like yourselves, and that He should exhort you to
guard yourselves against evil so that Allah may show you
mercy?'

They did not believe him. So We saved Noah and all who
were with him and drowned those that denied Our revelations. Surely they were blind men.

And to the tribe of Aad We sent their compatriot Houd.
He said: 'Serve Allah, my people, for you have no god
but Him. Will you not be warned?'

The unbelievers among the elders of his tribe said: 'We
can see you are a foolish man, and what is more, we think
that you are lying.'

'I am not foolish, my people,' he replied. 'I am sent forth
by the Lord of the Creation to make known to you His will
and to give you honest counsel. Do you think it strange 7:69
that an admonition should come to you from your Lord
through a mortal like yourselves and that he should warn

you? Remember that He has made you the heirs of Noah's people and endowed you with greater power than He has given to other men. Remember the favours of Allah, so that you may prosper.'

7:70 They said: 'Would you have us serve Allah only and renounce the gods which our fathers worshipped? Bring down the scourge with which you threaten us if what you say be true.'

He answered: 'Your Lord's punishment and wrath have already visited you. Would you dispute with me about names which you and your fathers have invented and for which no sanction has been revealed from Allah? Wait if you will; I too am waiting.'

We delivered Houd and all who were with him through Our mercy, and annihilated those that disbelieved Our revelations. They were unbelievers all.

7:73 And to Thamoud We sent their compatriot Saleh. He said: 'Serve Allah, my people, for you have no god but Him. A veritable proof has come to you from your Lord. Here is Allah's she-camel: a sign for you. Leave her to graze at will in Allah's land and do not molest her, lest you incur a woeful punishment. Remember that He has made you the heirs of Aad, and provided you with dwellings in this land. You have built mansions on its plains and hewed out houses among its mountains. Remember Allah's favours and do not corrupt the earth with wickedness.'

The haughty elders of his people said to the believers whom they oppressed: 'Do you really believe that Saleh is sent forth from his Lord?'

They answered: 'We believe in the message with which he has been sent.'

Those who were scornful said: 'We deny all that you believe in.' They slaughtered the she-camel and defied the commandment of their Lord, saying to Saleh: 'Bring down the scourge with which you threaten us if you truly are an apostle.'

Thereupon an earthquake felled them, and when morn-
7:79 ing came they were prostrate in their dwellings. Saleh left

them, saying:'I conveyed to you, my people, the message of my Lord and gave you counsel; but you had no love for those who sought to guide you.'

Remember the words of Lot, who said to his people: 7:80 'Will you persist in these indecent acts which no other nation has committed before you? You lust after men instead of women. Truly, you are a degenerate people.'

Their only answer was: 'Banish him from your city, him and all his followers. They are men who would keep chaste.'

We delivered Lot and all his kinsfolk, except his wife, who stayed behind, and let loose a shower upon them. Consider the fate of the evil-doers.

And to Midian We sent their compatriot Shoaib. He said: 'Serve Allah, my people, for you have no god but Him. A veritable sign has come to you from your Lord. Give just weight and measure and do not defraud others of their possessions. Do not corrupt the land after it has been purged of evil. That is best for you, if you are true believers.

'Do not squat in every road, threatening believers and 7:86 debarring them from the path of Allah, nor seek to make that path crooked. Remember how He multiplied you when you were few in number. Consider the fate of the evil-doers.

'If there are some among you who believe in my message and others who disbelieve it, be patient until Allah shall judge between us. He is the best of judges.'

The haughty elders of his tribe said: 'Return to our fold, Shoaib, or we will banish you from our city, you and all your followers.'

'Even though we abhor your creed?' he replied. 'If we returned to the faith from which Allah has delivered us, we should be false to our Lord; nor can we turn to it again except by the will of Allah, our Lord. He has knowledge of all things, and in Him we have put our trust. Lord, judge rightly between us and our people; You are the best of judges.'

But the infidel chiefs said to their people: 'If you follow 7:90 Shoaib, you shall assuredly be lost.'

7:91   Thereupon an earthquake felled them, and when morning came they were prostrate in their dwellings. Those that spurned Shoaib might never have lived there. Lost were those who disbelieved him.

Shoaib left them, saying: 'I conveyed to you, my people, the message of my Lord and gave you good counsel. How can I grieve for the unbelievers?'

Whenever We sent a prophet to a city We afflicted its people with calamities and misfortunes to humble them. Then We changed adversity to good fortune, so that in the hour of prosperity they said: 'Our fathers also had their joys and sorrows.' And in their heedlessness Our vengeance smote them.

Had the people of those cities believed and kept from evil, We would have showered upon them the riches of heaven and earth. But they denied their apostles, and We punished them for their misdeeds.

7:97   Were the people of those cities secure from Our vengeance when it overtook them in the night whilst they were sleeping?

Were they secure from Our wrath when it overtook them in the morning at their play?

Did they feel themselves secure from Allah's profound machinations? None feels secure from them except those who shall be lost.

Is it not plain to the present generation that if We pleased, We could punish them for their sins and set a seal upon their hearts, leaving them bereft of hearing?

We have recounted to you the history of those peoples. Their apostles came to them with veritable proofs, yet they persisted in their unbelief. Thus Allah seals up the hearts of the unbelievers.

We found the larger part of them untrue to their covenants; indeed, We found most of them evil-doers.

After those We sent forth Moses with Our signs to Pharaoh and his nobles, but they too disbelieved them. Consider the fate of the evil-doers.

7:104   Moses said: 'Pharaoh, I am an apostle from the Lord of

the Creation, and may tell nothing of Allah but what is true. 7:105
I bring you an undoubted sign from your Lord. Let the
Children of Israel depart with me.'

Pharaoh answered: 'Show us your sign, if what you say
be true.'

Moses threw down his staff, and thereupon it changed
to a veritable serpent. Then he drew out his hand and it appeared white to all who saw it.

The elders of Pharaoh's people said: 'This man is a
skilled enchanter who seeks to drive you from your kingdom. What would you have us do?'

Others said: 'Put them off awhile, him and his brother,
and send forth heralds to your cities to summon every
skilled magician to your presence.'

The magicians came to Pharaoh. They said: 'Shall we be
rewarded if we win?'

'Yes,' he answered. 'And you shall become my closest
friends.'

They said: 'Moses, will you first throw down your staff, 7:115
or shall we?'

'Throw down yours,' he replied.

And when the magicians threw down their staffs, they bewitched the people's eyes and terrified them by a display of
great wonders.

Then We said to Moses: 'Now throw down your staff.'
And thereupon his staff swallowed up their false devices.

Thus the truth prevailed and their doings proved vain.
Pharaoh and his men were defeated and put to shame, and
the enchanters prostrated themselves in adoration, saying:
'We believe in the Lord of the Creation, the Lord of Moses
and Aaron.'

Pharaoh said: 'Do you dare believe in Him without my
consent? This is a plot which you have contrived in order
to turn my people out of their city. But you shall see. I will
cut off your hands and feet on alternate sides and then
crucify you all!'

They replied: 'We shall surely return to our Lord. You
would punish us only because we believed in His signs 7:126

255

when they were shown to us. Lord, give us patience and let us die in submission.'

7:127   The elders of Pharaoh's nation said: 'Will you allow Moses and his people to commit evil in the land and to forsake you and your gods?'

He replied: 'We will put their sons to death and spare their daughters. We shall yet triumph over them.'

Moses said to his people: 'Seek help in Allah and be patient. The earth is Allah's; He gives it to those of His servants whom He chooses. Happy shall be the lot of the righteous.'

They replied: 'We were oppressed before you came to us, and oppressed we still remain.'

He said: 'Your Lord will perchance destroy your enemies and make you rulers in the land. Then He will see how you conduct yourselves.'

We afflicted Pharaoh's people with dearth and famine so 7:131 that they might take heed. When good things came their way, they said: 'It is our due,' but when evil befell them they ascribed it to Moses and his people. Yet it was Allah who had ordained their ill fortune, though most of them did not know it.

They said to Moses: 'Whatever miracles you may work to confound us, we will not believe in you.'

So We plagued them with floods and locusts, with lice and frogs, and with blood. All these were clear miracles, yet they scorned them, for they were a wicked people.

And when each plague smote them, they said: 'Moses, pray to your Lord for us: invoke the promise He has made you. If you lift the plague from us, we will believe in you and let the Israelites go with you.'

But when We had lifted the plague from them and the appointed time had come, they broke their promise. So We took vengeance on them and drowned them in the sea, for they had denied Our signs and gave no heed to them.

7:137   We gave the persecuted people dominion over the eastern and western lands which We had blessed. Thus your Lord's gracious word was fulfilled for the Israelites, because they had endured with fortitude; and We destroyed the edifices and towers of Pharaoh and his people.

We led the Israelites across the sea, and they came upon a *7:138* people zealously devoted to idols which they had. They said to Moses: 'Make us a god like their gods.'

Moses replied: 'You are indeed an ignorant people. The religion which these idolaters follow is doomed and all their works are vain. Should I seek any god for you but Allah? He has exalted you above the nations and delivered you from Pharaoh's people, who had oppressed you cruelly, putting your sons to death and sparing your daughters. Surely that was a great trial from your Lord.'

We promised Moses that We would speak with him after thirty nights, to which We added ten nights more: so that the meeting with his Lord took place after forty nights.

Moses said to Aaron his brother: 'Take my place among my people. Do what is right and do not follow the path of the wrongdoers.'

And when Moses came at the appointed time and His *7:143* Lord communed with him, he said: 'Lord, reveal Yourself to me, that I may look upon You.'

He replied: 'You shall not see Me. But look upon the Mountain; if it remains firm upon its base, then only shall you see Me.'

And when his Lord revealed Himself to the Mountain, He crushed it to fine dust. Moses fell down senseless, and when he came to himself said: 'Glory be to You! Accept my repentance. I am the first of believers.'

He said: 'I have chosen you of all mankind to make known My messages and My commandments. Take therefore what I have given you, and be thankful.'

We inscribed for him upon the Tablets all manner of precepts, and instructions concerning all things, and said to him: 'Observe these steadfastly, and enjoin your people to observe what is best in them. I shall show you the home of the wicked. I will turn away from My signs the arrogant *7:146* and the unjust, so that even if they witness each and every sign they shall deny them. If they see the right path, they shall not walk upon it: but if they see the path of error, they shall choose it for their path; because they disbelieved Our signs and gave no heed to them.

7:147 'Vain are the deeds of those who disbelieve in Our signs and in the life to come. Shall they not be rewarded according to their deeds?'

In his absence the people of Moses made a calf from their ornaments, an image with a hollow sound. Did they not see that it could neither speak to them nor give them guidance? Yet they worshipped it and thus committed evil.

But when they repented and realized that they had sinned they said: 'If our Lord does not have mercy on us and pardon us, we shall be lost.'

And when Moses returned to his people, angry and sorrowful, he said: 'Evil is the thing you have done in my absence! Would you hasten the retribution of your Lord?'

He threw down the Tablets and, seizing his brother by the hair, dragged him towards him.

'Son of my mother,' cried Aaron, 'the people overpowered me and almost did me to death. Do not let my enemies gloat over me; do not number me among the wrongdoers.'

7:151 'Lord,' said Moses, 'forgive me and forgive my brother. Admit us to Your mercy, for You are most merciful.'

Those that worshipped the calf incurred the wrath of their Lord and disgrace in this life. Thus shall the faithless be rewarded. As for those that do evil and later repent and have faith, they shall find your Lord forgiving and merciful.

When his anger was allayed, Moses took up the Tablets, upon which was inscribed a pledge of guidance and of 7:155 mercy to those that fear their Lord. He chose from among his people seventy men for Our meeting, and when the earth shook beneath their feet, Moses said: 'Had it been Your will, Lord, You could have destroyed us long ago. But would You destroy us for that which the fools amongst us did? That trial was ordained by You, to mislead whom You willed and to guide whom You pleased. You alone are our guardian. Forgive us and have mercy on us: You are the noblest of those who forgive. Ordain for us what is 7:156 good, both in this life and in the hereafter. To You alone we turn.'

He replied: 'I will visit My scourge upon whom I please: yet My mercy encompasses all things. I will show mercy to those that keep from evil, give alms, and believe in Our signs; and to those that shall follow the Apostle – the Unlettered Prophet[1] – whom they shall find described in the Torah and the Gospel. He will enjoin righteousness upon them and forbid them to do evil. He will make good things lawful to them and prohibit all that is foul. He will relieve them of their burdens and of the shackles that weigh upon them. Those that believe in him and honour him, those that aid him and follow the light to be sent forth with him, shall surely triumph.'

Say to your people:[2] 'I am sent forth to you all by Allah. 7:158 His is the kingdom of the heavens and the earth. There is no god but Him. He ordains life and death. Therefore have faith in Allah and His apostle, the Unlettered Prophet, who believes in Allah and His Word. Follow him so that you may be rightly guided.'

Yet among the people of Moses there were some who preached the truth and acted justly. We divided them into twelve tribes, each a nation. And when his people demanded drink of him, We said to Moses: 'Strike the rock with your staff.' Thereupon twelve springs gushed from the rock and each tribe knew its drinking-place.

We caused the clouds to draw their shadow over them and sent down for them manna and quails, saying: 'Eat of the good things We have given you.' Indeed, they did Us no wrong, but they wronged themselves.

When it was said to them: 'Dwell in this city, and eat of whatever you please; pray for forgiveness and enter the gates adoring: We will forgive you your sins and give abundance to the righteous,' – the wicked amongst them 7:162 altered these words. Therefore We let loose upon them a scourge from heaven as a punishment for their misdeeds.

1. Mohammed.   2. These words are addressed to Mohammed.

7:163   Ask them about the city¹ which overlooked the sea and what befell its people when they broke the Sabbath. Each Sabbath the fish used to appear before them floating on the water, but on week-days they never came near them. Thus We tempted the people because they had done wrong.

When some asked: 'Why do you admonish men whom Allah will destroy or sternly punish?' they replied: 'We admonish them so that we may be free from blame in the sight of your Lord, and that they may guard themselves against evil.' Therefore, when they forgot the warning they had been given, We delivered those who had admonished them, and sternly punished the wrongdoers for their misdeeds. And when they had scornfully persisted in what they had been forbidden, We changed them into detested apes.

7:167   Then your Lord declared that He would raise against them others who would oppress them cruelly till the Day of Resurrection. Swift is the retribution of your Lord, yet He is forgiving and merciful.

We dispersed them through the earth in multitudes – some were righteous men, others were not – and tested them with blessings and misfortunes so that they might desist from sin. Then others succeeded them who inherited the Scriptures and availed themselves of the good things of this nether life. 'We shall be forgiven our sins,' they said – and persisted in their evil ways.

Are they not committed in the Scriptures, which they have studied well, to tell nothing of Allah but what is true? Surely the world to come is a better prize for those that guard themselves against evil. Have you no sense?

As for those that strictly observe the Scriptures and are steadfast in prayer, their reward shall not be lost.

7:171   We suspended the Mountain over them as though it were a shadow (they feared that it was falling down on them) and said: 'Hold fast to that which We have given you and bear in mind what it contains, so that you may keep from evil.'

1. Eylat, on the Red Sea.

Your Lord brought forth descendants from the loins of 7:172
Adam's children, and made them testify against themselves.
He said: 'Am I not your Lord?' They replied: 'We bear
witness that you are.' This He did, lest you[1] should say on
the Day of Resurrection: 'We had no knowledge of that,'
or: 'Our forefathers were, indeed, idolaters; but will You
destroy us, their descendants, on account of what the followers of falsehood did?'

Thus We make plain Our revelations so that they may return to the right path.

Tell them of the man to whom We vouchsafed Our signs
and who turned away from them: how Satan overtook him
as he was led astray. Had it been Our will, We would have
exalted him through Our signs: but he clung to this earthly
life and succumbed to his desires. He was like the dog
which lolls out its tongue whether you chase it away or let
it alone. Such are those that deny Our revelations. Recount
to them these parables, so that they may take thought.

Dismal is the tale of those that denied Our revelations; 7:177
they were unjust to their own souls.

The man whom Allah guides is rightly guided, but he
who is led astray by Allah shall surely be lost.

We have predestined for Hell many jinn and many men.
They have hearts, yet they cannot understand; eyes, yet
they do not see; and ears, yet they do not hear. They are
like beasts – indeed, they are less enlightened. Such are the
heedless.

Allah has the Most Excellent Names. Call on Him by
His names and keep away from those that pervert them.
They shall be punished for their misdeeds.

Among those whom We created there are some who give
true guidance and act justly. As for those that deny Our
revelations, We will lead them step by step to ruin, whence
they cannot tell; for though I bear with them, My stratagem
is sure.

Has it never occurred to them that their compatriot[2] is no
madman, but one who gives plain warning? Will they not 7:185

1. Mankind.   2. Mohammed.

ponder upon the kingdom of the heavens and the earth, and all that Allah created, to see whether their hour is not drawing near? And in what other revelation will they believe, those that deny this?

7:186   None can guide the people whom Allah leads astray. He leaves them blundering·about in their wickedness.

They ask you about the Hour of Doom and when it is to come. Say: 'None knows except my Lord. He alone will reveal it at the appointed time. A fateful hour it shall be, both in the heavens and on earth. It will come without warning.'

They will put questions to you as though you had full knowledge of it. Say: 'None knows about it save Allah, though most men are unaware of this.'

Say: 'I have not the power to acquire benefits or to avert evil from myself, except by the will of Allah. Had I possessed knowledge of what is hidden, I would have availed myself of much that is good and no harm would have touched me. But I am no more than one who gives warning and good news to true believers.'

7:189   It was He who created you from a single being. From that being He created his mate, so that he might find comfort in her. And when he had lain with her, she conceived, and for a time her burden was light. She carried it with ease, but when it grew heavy, they both cried to Allah their Lord: 'Grant us a goodly child and we will be truly thankful.'

Yet when He had granted them a goodly child, they set up other gods besides Him in return for what He had given them. Exalted be He above their idols!

Will they worship that which can create nothing, but is itself created? They cannot help them, nor can they help themselves.

If you call them to the right path they will not follow you. It is the same whether you call to them or hold your peace.

7:194   Those whom you invoke besides Allah are, like yourselves, His servants. Call on them, and let them answer you, if what you say be true!

Have they feet to walk with? Have they hands to hold 7:195 with? Have they eyes to see with? Have they ears to hear with?

Say: 'Call on your false gods and scheme against me. Give me no respite. My guardian is Allah, who has revealed this Book. He is the guardian of the righteous. Those to whom you pray besides Him cannot help you, nor can they help themselves.'

If you call them to the right path, they will not hear you. You find them looking towards you, but they cannot see you.

Show forgiveness, speak for justice, and avoid the ignor- 7:199 ant. If Satan tempts you, seek refuge in Allah; He hears all and knows all.

If those that guard themselves against evil are tempted by Satan, they have but to recall Allah's precepts and they shall see the light. As for their brothers, they shall be kept long in error, nor shall they ever desist.

When you do not recite to them a revelation they say: 'Have you not yet invented one?' Say: 'I follow only what is revealed to me by my Lord. This Book is a veritable proof from your Lord, a guide and a blessing to true believers.'

When the Koran is recited, listen to it in silence so that Allah may show you mercy. Remember your Lord deep in your soul with humility and reverence, and without ostentation: remember Him morning and evening, and do not be negligent.

Those who dwell with your Lord do not disdain His 7:206 service. They give glory to Him and prostrate themselves before Him.

THE ELEPHANT

In the Name of Allah, the Compassionate, the Merciful

105:1 HAVE you not considered how Allah dealt with the Army of the Elephant?[1]

Did He not foil their strategem and send against them flocks of birds which pelted them with clay-stones, so 105:5 that they became like plants cropped by cattle?

QURAYSH[2]

In the Name of Allah, the Compassionate, the Merciful

106:1 FOR the protection of Quraysh: their protection in their summer and winter journeyings.

Therefore let them worship the Lord of this House 106:4 who fed them in the days of famine and shielded them from all perils.

FIBRE

In the Name of Allah, the Compassionate, the Merciful

111:1 MAY the hands of Abu-Lahab[3] perish! May he himself perish!

Nothing shall his wealth and gains avail him. He shall be burnt in a flaming fire,[4] and his wife, laden with 111:5 faggots, shall have a rope of fibre round her neck!

1. The allusion is to the expedition of Abraha, the Christian King of Ethiopia, against Mecca, said to have taken place in the year of Mohammed's birth.

2. Mohammed's own clan. Some commentators connect this chapter with the preceding one.

3. The Prophet's uncle, and one of his staunchest opponents.

4. A pun on the meaning of Abu-Lahab, *father of flame.*

UNITY

In the Name of Allah, the Compassionate, the Merciful

SAY: 'Allah is One, the Eternal God. He begot none, 112:1
nor was He begotten. None is equal to Him.' 112:4

THE JINN

In the Name of Allah, the Compassionate, the Merciful

SAY: 'It is revealed to me that a band of jinn listened to 72:1
Allah's revelations and said: "We have heard a wondrous discourse giving guidance to the right path. We
believed in it and shall henceforth serve none besides Our
Lord. He (exalted be the glory of our Lord!) has taken no
wife, nor has He begotten any children. The Blaspheming
One among us has uttered a wanton falsehood against
Allah, although we had supposed no man or jinnee could
tell of Him what is untrue."'

(Some men have sought the help of jinn, but they misled
them into further error. Like you they thought that Allah
could never raise the dead.)

'"We made our way to high heaven and found it filled
with mighty wardens and fiery comets. We sat eavesdrop- 72:9
ping, but eavesdroppers find flaming darts in wait for
them. We cannot tell if this bodes evil to those on earth or
whether their Lord intends to guide them.

'"Some of us are righteous, while others are not; we
follow different ways. We know we cannot escape on earth
from Allah, nor can we elude His grasp by flight. When we
heard His guidance we believed in Him: he that believes in
his Lord shall never be wronged or harmed.

'"Some of us are Muslims and some are wrongdoers.
Those that embrace Islam pursue the right path; but those
that do wrong shall become the fuel of Hell."'

If they[1] pursue the right path We shall vouchsafe them 72:16

1. The Meccans.

72:17 abundant rain, and thereby put them to the proof. He that gives no heed to his Lord's warning shall be sternly punished.

Temples are built for Allah's worship; invoke in them no other god besides Him. When His servant[1] rose to pray to Him, they pressed round him in multitudes.

Say: 'I will pray to my Lord and worship none besides Him.'

72:21 Say: 'I have no control over any good or evil that befalls you.'

Say: 'None can protect me from Allah, nor can I find any refuge besides Him. My mission is only to make known His messages; those that disobey Allah and His apostle shall abide for ever in the fire of Hell.'

When they behold the scourge with which they are threatened they shall know which side had the less powerful protector and which was fewer in numbers.

Say: 'I cannot tell whether the scourge with which you are threatened is imminent, or whether my Lord has set for it a far-off day. He alone has knowledge of what is hidden: His secrets He reveals to none, except to the apostles whom He elects. He sends down guardians who walk before them *72:28* and behind them, that He may know if they have indeed delivered His messages. He has knowledge of all their actions and takes count of all things.'

SHE WHO IS TESTED

In the Name of Allah, the Compassionate, the Merciful

60:1 BELIEVERS, do not make friends with those who are enemies of Mine and yours. Would you show them kindness when they have denied the truth that has been revealed to you and driven the Apostle and yourselves out of your city because you believe in Allah, your Lord?

If it was indeed to fight for My cause, and out of a desire to please Me that you left your city, how can you be friendly

1. Mohammed.

to them in secret? I well know all that you hide and all that you reveal. Whoever of you does this will stray from the right path.

If they gain ascendency over you, they will plainly show *60:2* themselves your enemies, and use their hands and tongues to harm you. They long to see you unbelievers.

On the Day of Resurrection neither your kinsfolk nor your children shall avail you. Allah will separate you. He is cognizant of all your actions.

You have a good example in Abraham and those who followed him. They said to their people: 'We disown you and the idols which you worship besides Allah. We renounce you: enmity and hate shall reign between us until you believe in Allah only.' (But do not emulate the words of Abraham to his father: 'I shall implore Allah to forgive you, although I have no power to save you from His punishment.') 'Lord, in You we have put our trust; to You we turn and to You we shall come at last. Lord, do not expose us to the designs of the unbelievers. Forgive us, Lord; You are the Mighty, the Wise One.'

Truly, in those men there is a good example for everyone who puts his hopes in Allah and in the Last Day. He that gives no heed to you should bear in mind that Allah alone is self-sufficient and worthy of praise.

It may well be that Allah will put good will between you *60:7* and those with whom you have hitherto been at odds. Allah is mighty. He is forgiving and merciful.

Allah does not forbid you to be kind and equitable to those who have neither made war on your religion nor driven you from your homes. Allah loves the equitable. But He forbids you to make friends with those who have fought against you on account of your religion and driven you from your homes or abetted others so to do. Those that make friends with them are wrongdoers.

Believers, when believing women seek refuge with you, *60:10* test them. Allah best knows their faith. If you find them true believers do not return them to the infidels; they are not lawful to the infidels, nor are the infidels lawful to them. But hand back to the unbelievers the dowries they gave them. Nor is it an offence for you to marry such women, provided you give them their dowries. Do not hold on to your marriages with unbelieving women: demand the dowries you have given them and let the infidels do the same. Such is the law which Allah lays down among you. Allah is wise and all-knowing.

60:11 If any of your wives go over to the unbelievers and you subsequently gain a victory over them, pay those whose wives have fled the equivalent of the dowries they have given them. Fear Allah, in whom you believe.

Prophet, if believing women come to you and pledge themselves to serve no other god besides Allah, to commit neither theft, nor adultery, nor child-murder, to utter no monstrous falsehoods of their own invention, and to disobey you in nothing just or reasonable, accept their allegiance and implore Allah to forgive them. Allah is forgiving and merciful.

60:13 Believers, do not make friends with those who have incurred the wrath of Allah. Such men despair of the life to come, just as the unbelievers despair of the buried dead.

EXILE

In the Name of Allah, the Compassionate, the Merciful

59:1 ALL that is in heaven and earth gives glory to Allah. He is the Mighty, the Wise One.

59:2 It was He that drove the unbelievers among the People of the Book out of their dwellings into the first exile.[1] You did not think that they would go; and they, for their part, fancied that their strongholds would protect them from Allah. But Allah's scourge fell upon them whence they did not expect it, casting such terror into their hearts that their dwellings were destroyed by their own hands as well as by the faithful. Learn from their examples, you that have eyes.

1. An allusion to Mohammed's expedition against the Jews of Nadhir in Arabia.

Had Allah not decreed exile for them He would have *59:3*
surely punished them in this world. But in the world to
come they shall be punished in Hell-fire, because they have
set themselves against Allah and His apostle; and he that
sets himself against Allah should know that Allah is stern
in retribution.

It was Allah who gave you leave to cut down or spare
their palm-trees, so that He might humiliate the evil-doers.
As for those spoils of theirs which Allah has assigned to
His apostle, you spurred neither horse nor camel to capture
them: but Allah gives His apostles authority over whom
He will. He has power over all things.

The spoils taken from the town-dwellers and assigned by *59:7*
Allah to His apostle belong to Allah, the Apostle and his kinsfolk, the orphans, the poor and the wayfarers; they shall not
become the property of the rich among you. Whatever the
Apostle gives you, accept it; and whatever he forbids you,
forbear from it. Have fear of Allah; He is stern in retribution.

A share of the spoils shall also fall to the poor *muhadjirs*[1]
who have been driven from their homes and possessions;
who seek Allah's grace and bounty and help Allah and His
apostle. These are the true believers.

The men who stayed in their own city[2] and embraced the *59:9*
Faith before them love those who have sought refuge with
them; they do not covet what they are given but rather prize
them above themselves, though they are in want. Those
that preserve themselves from their own greed shall surely
prosper.

Those that came to the Faith after them say: 'Forgive us,
Lord, and forgive our brothers who embraced the Faith before us. Do not put in our hearts any malice towards the
faithful. Lord, You are compassionate and merciful.'

Have you not seen the hypocrites? They say to their *59:11*
fellow-unbelievers among the People of the Book: 'If they
drive you out, we will go with you. We will never obey any
one who seeks to harm you. If you are attacked we will
certainly help you.'

1. Those who fled with Mohammed to Medina.   2. Medina.

19:12   Allah bears witness that they are lying. If they are driven out they will not go with them, nor, if they are attacked, will they help them. Indeed, if they go to their help they will turn their backs in flight and leave them in the lurch.

Their dread of you is more intense in their hearts than their fear of Allah: so devoid are they of understanding.

They will never fight against you in a body except in fortified cities and from behind high walls. Great is their valour among themselves; you think of them as one band, yet their hearts are divided. They are surely lacking in judgement.

Like those[1] who were but recently punished before them, they tasted the fruit of their own deeds: a grievous scourge awaits them.

The hypocrites may be compared to Satan, who, when he has ordered man to disbelieve and man has done his bidding says to him: 'I here and now disown you. I fear Allah, the Lord of the Creation.' They shall both end in Hell and remain therein for ever. Thus are the wrongdoers rewarded.

19:18   Believers, have fear of Allah. Let every soul look to what it offers for the morrow. Fear Allah, for He is cognizant of all your actions.

Do not act like those who have forgotten Allah so that He has caused them to forget themselves. Such men are evil-doers.

The dwellers of Paradise and the heirs of Hell shall not be held alike. The dwellers of Paradise alone shall be triumphant.

Had We brought down this Koran upon a mountain, you would have seen it humble itself and break asunder for fear of Allah.

Such are the sayings We coin for men, so that they may give thought.

He is Allah, besides whom there is no other god. He knows the visible and the unseen. He is the Compassionate, the Merciful.

19:23   He is Allah, besides whom there is no other god. He is

1. Probably the Jews of Kainoka, also reduced by Mohammed.

the Sovereign Lord, the Holy One, the Giver of Peace, the Keeper of Faith; the Guardian, the Mighty One, the All-powerful, the Most High! Exalted be He above their idols!

He is Allah, the Creator, the Originator, the Modeller. *59:24* His are the most gracious names. All that is in heaven and earth gives glory to Him. He is the Mighty, the Wise One.

SHE WHO PLEADED

In the Name of Allah, the Compassionate, the Merciful

ALLAH has heard the words of her[1] that pleaded with *58:1* you against her husband and made her plaint to Him. Allah has heard your conversation: He hears all and observes all.

Those of you who divorce their wives by declaring them to be their mothers should know that they are *not* their mothers. Their mothers are those only who gave birth to them. The words they utter are unjust and false: but Allah is forgiving and merciful.

Those that divorce their wives by so saying and afterwards retract their words shall free a slave[2] before they touch them again. This you are enjoined to do: Allah is cognizant of all your actions. He that has no slave shall fast *58:4* two successive months before he and his wife touch one another. If he cannot do this, he shall feed sixty of the poor. This is enjoined on you so that you may have faith in Allah and His apostle. Such are the laws of Allah. A grievous punishment awaits the unbelievers.

Those that oppose Allah and His apostle shall be brought low as have been those before them. We have sent down clear revelations. A shameful punishment awaits the unbelievers.

On the day when Allah restores them all to life He will *58:6* inform them of their actions. Allah has taken count of these,

1. Khaula, daughter of Tha'alaba, who had been divorced by the formula: 'Be to me as my mother's back,' which was accepted as a declaration of divorce among pagan Arabs.
2. As a penalty.

although they have forgotten them. Allah observes all things.

58:7 Are you not aware that Allah knows what the heavens and the earth contain? If three men talk in secret together, He is their fourth; if four, He is their fifth; if five, He is their sixth; whether fewer or more, wherever they be, He is with them. Then, on the Day of Resurrection, He will inform them of their doings. Allah has knowledge of all things.

Have you not seen those who, though forbidden to intrigue in secret, defiantly plot together in wickedness and enmity and disobedience to the Apostle? When they come to you they salute you in words with which Allah does not greet you and ask themselves: 'Why does Allah not punish us for what we say?' Hell is scourge enough for them: they shall burn in its flames, a wretched fate!

58:9 Believers, when you converse in private do not speak with wickedness and enmity and disobedience towards the Apostle, but with justice and with piety. Have fear of Allah, before whom you shall be brought together.

Intrigue is the work of Satan, who thereby seeks to annoy the faithful. Yet he can harm them not at all, except by the will of Allah. In Allah let the faithful put their trust.

Believers, make room[1] in your assemblies when you are bidden to do so: Allah will make room for you hereafter. Again, rise up when you are told to rise: Allah will raise to high ranks those that have faith and knowledge among you. He is cognizant of all your actions.

Believers, when you confer with the Apostle, give alms before such conference. That is best and purest for you. But if you lack the means, know that Allah is forgiving and merciful.

Do you hesitate to offer alms before you speak with him? If you do not (and Allah will pardon your offence), then at least recite your prayers and pay the alms-tax and show obedience to Allah and His apostle. Allah is cognizant of all your actions.

58:14 Do you see those that have befriended a people[2] with

1. For the Prophet.   2. The Jews.

whom Allah is angry? They belong neither to you nor to them. They knowingly swear to falsehoods. Allah has pre- *58:15* pared for them a grievous scourge. Evil indeed is that which they have done.

They use their faith as a disguise and debar others from the path of Allah. A shameful scourge awaits them.

Neither their wealth nor their children shall in the least protect them from Allah. They are the heirs of Hell, and there they shall abide for ever.

On the day when Allah restores them all to life, they will *58:18* swear to Him as they now swear to you, thinking that their oaths will help them. Surely they are liars all.

Satan has gained possession of them and caused them to forget Allah's warning. They are the confederates of Satan; Satan's confederates shall assuredly be lost.

Those that oppose Allah and His apostle shall be brought low. Allah has decreed: 'I will surely triumph, Myself and My apostles.' Powerful is Allah, and mighty.

You shall find no believers in Allah and the Last Day on *58:22* friendly terms with those who oppose Allah and His apostle, even though they be their fathers, their sons, their brothers, or their nearest kindred. Allah has inscribed the Faith on their very hearts and strengthened them with a spirit of His own. He will admit them to gardens watered by running streams, where they shall dwell for ever. Allah is well pleased with them and they with Him. They are the confederates of Allah: and Allah's confederates shall surely triumph.

THE CHAMBERS

In the Name of Allah, the Compassionate, the Merciful

BELIEVERS, do not behave presumptuously in the *49:1* presence of Allah and His apostle. Have fear of Allah: He hears all and knows all.

Believers, do not raise your voices above the voice of the Prophet, nor shout aloud when speaking to him as you do

to one another, lest your labours should come to nothing
49:3 without your knowledge. Those who speak softly in the presence of Allah's apostle are the men whose hearts Allah has inured to piety. They shall receive forgiveness and a rich reward.

Those who call out to you[1] whilst you are in your chambers are for the most part foolish men. If they waited until you went out to them it would be better for them. But Allah is forgiving and merciful.

Believers, if an evil-doer brings you a piece of news inquire first into its truth, lest you should wrong others unwittingly and then repent of what you have done.

49:7 Know that Allah's apostle is among you. If he obeyed you in many matters, you would surely come to grief. But Allah has endeared the Faith to you and beautified it in your hearts, making unbelief, wrongdoing, and disobedience abhorrent to you. Such are those who are rightly guided through Allah's grace and bounty. Allah is wise and all-knowing.

If two parties of believers take up arms the one against the other, make peace between them. If either of them commits aggression against the other, fight against the aggressors till they submit to Allah's judgement. When they submit make peace between them in equity and justice; Allah loves those who act in justice.

49:10 The believers are a band of brothers. Make peace among your brothers and fear Allah, so that you may be shown mercy.

Believers, let no man mock another man, who may perhaps be better than himself. Let no woman mock another woman, who may perhaps be better than herself. Do not defame one another, nor call one another by nicknames. It is an evil thing to be called by a bad name after embracing the true faith. Those that do not repent are wrongdoers.

49:12 Believers, avoid immoderate suspicion, for in some cases suspicion is a crime. Do not spy on one another, nor backbite one another. Would any of you like to eat the flesh of

1. Mohammed.

274

his dead brother? Surely you would loathe it. Have fear of Allah. He is forgiving and merciful.

Men, We have created you from a male and a female and *49:13* divided you into nations and tribes that you might get to know one another. The noblest of you in Allah's sight is he who fears Him most. Allah is wise and all-knowing.

The Arabs of the desert declare: 'We are true believers.' Say: 'You are not. Rather say: "We profess Islam," for faith has not yet found its way into your hearts. If you obey Allah and His apostle, He will not deny you the reward of your labours. Allah is forgiving and merciful.'

The true believers are those that have faith in Allah and His apostle and never doubt; and who fight for His cause with their wealth and persons. Such are those whose faith is true.

Say: 'Would you tell Allah of your religion, when Allah knows what the heavens and the earth contain? He has knowledge of all things.'

They regard it as a favour to you that they embraced Islam. Say: 'In accepting Islam you have conferred on me no favour. It was Allah who bestowed a favour on you in guiding you to the true faith. Admit this, if you are men of truth. Allah knows all that is hidden in the heavens and the *49:18* earth. He is watching over all your actions.'

VICTORY

In the Name of Allah, the Compassionate, the Merciful

WE have given you a glorious victory,[1] so that Allah *48:1* may forgive your past and future sins, and perfect His goodness to you; that He may guide you to the right path and bestow on you His mighty help.

It was He who sent down tranquillity[2] into the hearts of

1. The taking of Mecca, A.D. 630, or of Khaybar a year earlier.
2. This is the meaning of the Arabic word *sakeenah*, which, however, could well be related to *shekheenah* (the Holy Presence), in the Old Testament.

the faithful so that their faith might grow stronger. His are the legions of the heavens and the earth. Allah is wise and all-knowing.

48:5 He has caused you to do as you have done that He may bring the believers, both men and women, into gardens watered by running streams, there to abide for ever; that He may forgive them their sins (this, in Allah's sight, is a glorious triumph); and that He may punish the hypocrites and the idolaters, men and women, who think evil thoughts about Him. A turn of evil shall befall them, for Allah is angry with them. He has laid on them His curse and prepared for them the fire of Hell: an evil fate.

48:7 His are the legions of the heavens and the earth. Allah is mighty and wise.

We have sent you[1] forth as a witness and as a bearer of news and warnings, so that you[2] may have faith in Allah and His apostle and that you may assist him, honour him, and praise Him morning and evening.

Those that swear fealty to you swear fealty to Allah Himself. The Hand of Allah is above their hands. He that breaks his oath breaks it at his own peril, but he that keeps his pledge to Allah shall be richly rewarded.

48:11 The desert Arabs who stayed behind[3] will say to you: 'We were occupied with our goods and families. Implore Allah to pardon us.' They will say with their tongues what they do not mean in their hearts.

Say: 'Who can prevent Allah from punishing you or being gracious to you, if He is pleased to do either? Allah is cognizant of all your actions.'

No. You[4] thought the Apostle and the believers would never return to their people; and with this fancy your hearts were delighted. You harboured evil thoughts and thus incurred damnation.

For those that disbelieve in Allah and His apostle We 48:14 have prepared a blazing Fire. Allah's is the kingdom of the heavens and the earth. He pardons whom He will and

1. Mohammed.   2. The Meccans.   3. Away from the war.
4. The desert Arabs.

punishes whom He pleases. Allah is forgiving and merciful.

When you set forth to take the spoils those that stayed *48:15*
away will say: 'Let us come with you.'

They seek to change the word of Allah. Say: 'You shall
not come with us. So Allah has said beforehand.'

They will reply: 'You are jealous of us.' But how little
they understand!

Say to the desert Arabs who stayed behind: 'You shall be
called upon to fight a mighty nation, unless they embrace
Islam. If you prove obedient you shall receive a good reward from Allah. But if you run away, as you have done
before this, He will inflict on you a stern chastisement.'

It shall be no offence for the blind, the lame, and the sick *48:17*
to stay behind. He that obeys Allah and His apostle shall be
admitted to gardens watered by running streams; but he
that turns and flees shall be sternly punished.

Allah was well pleased with the faithful when they swore
allegiance to you under the tree. He knew what was in their
hearts. Therefore He sent down tranquillity[1] upon them and
rewarded them with a speedy victory and with the many
spoils which they have taken. Mighty is Allah and wise.

Allah has promised you rich booty and has given you
this[2] with all promptness. He has protected you from your
enemies, so that He may make your victory a sign to true
believers and guide you along a straight path.

And Allah knows of other spoils which you have not yet *48:21*
taken. Allah has power over all things.

If the unbelievers join battle with you, they shall be
put to flight. They shall find none to protect or help them.

Such were the ways of Allah in days gone by: and you
shall find that they remain unchanged.

It was He who made peace between you in the Valley of
Mecca[3] after He had given you victory over them. Allah
was watching over all your actions.

Those were the unbelievers who debarred you from the *48:25*
Sacred Mosque and prevented your offerings from reaching

1. See Note 2, p. 275.   2. The spoils taken at Khaybar.
3. The allusion is probably to the peace of Hudaybiyyah, A.D. 628.

their destination. But for the fear that you might have trampled under foot believing men and women unknown to you and thus incurred unwitting guilt on their account, Allah would have commanded you to fight it out with them; but He ordained it thus that He might bring whom He will into His mercy. Had the faithful stood apart from them, We would have sternly punished the unbelievers.

48:26 And while bigotry – the bigotry of ignorance – was holding its reign in the hearts of the unbelievers, Allah sent down His tranquillity[1] on His apostle and the faithful and made the word of piety binding on them, for they were most worthy and deserving of it. Allah has knowledge of all things.

Allah has in all truth fulfilled His apostle's vision, in which He had said: 'If Allah will, you shall enter the Sacred Mosque secure and fearless, with hair cropped or shaven.' He knew what you did not know; and what is more, He granted you a speedy victory.

It is He that has sent forth His apostle with guidance and the true faith, so that he may exalt it above all religions. Allah is the all-sufficient Witness.

48:29 Mohammed is Allah's apostle. Those who follow him are ruthless to the unbelievers but merciful to one another. You see them adoring on their knees, seeking the grace of Allah and His good will. Their marks[2] are on their faces, the traces of their prostrations. Thus they are described in the Torah and in the Gospel: they are like the seed which puts forth its shoot and strengthens it, so that it rises stout and firm upon its stalk, delighting the sowers. Through them Allah seeks to enrage the unbelievers. Yet to those of them who will embrace the Faith and do good works He has promised forgiveness and a rich reward.

1. See Note 2, p. 275.   2. Dust.

THE HORDES

In the Name of Allah, the Compassionate, the Merciful

THIS Book is revealed by Allah, the Mighty, the Wise 39:1
One. We have revealed to you the Book with the
truth: therefore serve Allah and worship none but
Him.

To Allah alone is true worship due. As for those who
choose other guardians besides Him, saying: 'We serve
them only that they may bring us nearer to Allah,' Allah
Himself will judge for them their differences. He does not
guide the untruthful disbeliever.

Had it been His will to take a son, He would have chosen
whom He pleased out of His own creation. But Allah forbid! He is Allah, the One, the Almighty.

It was to reveal the truth that He created the heavens 39:5
and the earth. He causes the night to succeed the day and the
day to overtake the night. He made the sun and the moon
obedient to Him, each running for an appointed term. He is
the Mighty, the Benignant One.

He created you from a single being, then from that being
He created its mate. He has given you four different pairs of
cattle.[1] He moulds you in your mothers' wombs by stages
in threefold darkness.

Such is Allah, your Lord. His is the Kingdom. There is
no god but Him. How, then, can you turn away from Him?

If you render Him no thanks, know that Allah does not 39:7
need you. Yet the ingratitude of His servants does not
please Him. If you are thankful, your thanks will please Him.

No soul shall bear another's burden. To Allah you shall
all return and He will declare to you what you have done.
He knows your inmost thoughts.

When evil befalls man, he prays to his Lord and turns to 39:8
Him in repentance; yet no sooner does He bestow on him
His favour than he forgets that for which he had prayed

1. Camels, cows, sheep, and goats.

279

before and worships other gods instead of Allah, in order to lead men away from His path.

Say: 'Enjoy your unbelief awhile; you shall surely be con-
39:9 signed to Hell. Can he who passes his night in adoration, standing or on his knees, who dreads the terrors of the life to come and hopes to earn the mercy of his Lord, be compared to the unbeliever? Are the wise and the ignorant equal?' Truly, none will take heed but men of understanding.

Say: 'Fear your Lord, you that serve Allah and are true believers. Those who do good works in this life shall receive a good reward. Allah's earth is vast. Those that endure with fortitude shall be requited without measure.'

Say: 'I am bidden to serve Allah and to worship none besides Him. I am bidden to be the first of those who shall submit to Him.'

Say: 'I will never disobey my Lord, for I fear the torment of a fateful day.'

39:14 Say: 'I will serve Allah and worship Him alone. As for yourselves, serve what you will besides Him.'

Say: 'They shall lose much, those who will forfeit their souls and all their kinsfolk on the Day of Resurrection. Their loss will be great indeed. They shall be covered with sheets of fire from above and from beneath. By this Allah puts fear into His servants' hearts.' Fear Me, then, My servants.

But let those rejoice who keep off from idol-worship and turn to Allah in repentance. Give good news to My servants, who listen to My precepts and follow what is best in them. These are they whom Allah has guided. These are they who are endued with understanding.

Can you save those who have rightly earned Our punishment and are doomed to burn in Hell? As for those who truly fear their Lord, they shall dwell in towering mansions set about with running streams. Such is Allah's promise: He will not fail His promise.

39:21 Do you not see how Allah sends down water from the sky which penetrates the earth and gathers in springs beneath? He brings forth plants of every kind. They wither, they turn yellow, and then He crumbles them to dust. Surely in this there is an admonition for men of understanding.

He whose heart Allah has opened to Islam shall receive *39:22* light from his Lord. But woe to those whose hearts are hardened against the remembrance of Allah! Truly, they are in the grossest error.

Allah has now revealed the best of scriptures, a book uniform in style proclaiming promises and warnings. Those who fear their Lord are filled with awe as they listen to its revelations, so that their hearts soften at the remembrance of Allah. Such is Allah's guidance: He bestows it on whom He will. But he whom Allah misleads shall have none to guide him.

Can he who shall face the terrors of the Resurrection be compared to the true believer? To the wrongdoers We shall say: 'Taste the punishment which you have earned.'

Those who have gone before them also denied their *39:25* apostles, so that Our scourge overtook them unawares. Allah disgraced them in this life, but the punishment of the life to come shall be more terrible, if they but knew it.

We have given mankind in this Koran all manner of arguments, so that they may take heed. We have revealed it in the Arabic tongue, a Koran free from all faults, that they may guard themselves against evil.

Consider this comparison. There are two men: the one has many masters who are ever at odds among themselves; the other has one master, to whom he is devoted. Are these two to be held alike? Allah forbid! But most of them have no knowledge.

You,[1] as well as they, are doomed to die. Then, on the Day of Resurrection, you[2] shall dispute in your Lord's presence with one another.

Who is more wicked than the man who invents a false- *39:32* hood about Allah and denies the truth when it is declared to him? Is there not a home in Hell for the unbelievers?

1. Mohammed.   2. The unbelievers.

39:33   Those who proclaim the truth, and those who accept the truth – they surely are the God-fearing. Their Lord will give them all that they desire. Thus shall the righteous be rewarded.

Allah will do away with their foulest deeds and reward them according to their noblest actions.

Is Allah not all-sufficient for His servant? Yet they threaten you with their idols. Truly, he whom Allah misleads has none to guide him. But he whom Allah guides none can lead astray. Is Allah not mighty and capable of revenge?

If you ask them who created the heavens and the earth, they will reply: 'Allah created them.' Say: 'Do you think then that, if Allah be pleased to afflict me, your idols could relieve my affliction; or that if He be pleased to show me mercy, they could withhold His mercy?'

Say: 'Allah is my all-sufficient patron. In Him let the faithful put their trust.'

39:39   Say: 'My people, do as best you can and so will I. You shall before long know who will receive a punishment shameful and everlasting.'

We have revealed to you the Book with the truth, for the instruction of mankind. He that follows the right path shall follow it to his own advantage; and he that goes astray shall do so at his own peril. You are not accountable for them.

Allah takes away men's souls upon their death, and the souls of the living during their sleep. Those that are doomed He keeps with Him and restores the others for a time ordained. Surely there are signs in this for thinking men.

Have they chosen others besides Allah to intercede for them? Say: 'Even though they have no power nor understanding?'

39:44   Say: 'Intercession is wholly in the hands of Allah. His is the kingdom of the heavens and the earth. To Him you shall all be recalled.'

When Allah alone is named, the hearts of those who deny **39:45** the hereafter shrink with aversion; but when their other gods are named, they are filled with joy.

Say: 'Lord, Creator of the heavens and the earth, who have knowledge of the visible and the unseen, You alone can judge the disputes of Your servants.'

If the wrongdoers had all the treasures of the earth and as much besides, they would gladly offer it on the Day of Resurrection to redeem themselves from the torment of Our scourge. For Allah will show them that with which they have never reckoned. Their evil deeds will become manifest to them, and what they scoffed at will encompass them.

When evil befalls man he calls upon Us; but when We vouchsafe him Our favour, he says: 'It is my due.' By no means! It is but a test: yet most men do not know it.

Those before them said the same: but they gained nothing from what they did, and the very evil of their deeds recoiled upon them.

The wrongdoers among these[1] shall also pay the penalty of their sins: nor shall they escape Our punishment.

Do they not know that Allah gives abundantly to whom **39:52** He will and sparingly to whom He pleases? Surely there are signs in this for true believers.

Say: 'Servants of Allah, you that have sinned against your souls, do not despair of Allah's mercy, for He forgives all sins. He is the Forgiving One, the Merciful. Turn in repentance to your Lord and surrender yourselves to Him before His scourge overtakes you; for then there will be none to help you. Follow the best of what is revealed to you from your Lord before His scourge overtakes you in your heedlessness, without warning; lest any man should say: "Alas! I have disobeyed Allah and scoffed at His revelations." Or: "If Allah had guided me I would have been a righteous man." Or, when he sees his punishment: "Could **39:58** I but live again, I would lead a righteous life." For Allah

---

1. The Meccans.

39:59 will say to him: "You heard My revelations, yet you denied them. You were arrogant and had no faith at all."'

On the Day of Resurrection you shall see those who uttered falsehoods about Allah with faces blackened. Is there not in Hell a home for the arrogant?

39:61 But Allah will deliver those who fear Him, for they have earned salvation. No harm shall touch them, nor shall they ever grieve.

Allah is the Creator of all things, and of all things He is the Guardian. His are the treasures of the heavens and the earth. Those that deny His revelations shall assuredly be lost.

Say: 'Ignorant men! Would you bid me serve a god other than Allah?'

You have been warned, you and those who have gone before you, that if you worshipped other gods besides Allah, your works would come to nothing and you would surely perish. Therefore serve Allah and render thanks to Him.

They underrate the might of Allah. But on the Day of Resurrection He will hold the entire earth in His grasp and fold up the heavens in His right hand. Glory be to Him! Exalted be He above their idols!

39:68 The Trumpet shall be sounded and all who are in heaven and earth shall fall down fainting, except those that shall be spared by Allah. Then the Trumpet will sound again and they shall rise and gaze around them. The earth will shine with the light of her Lord, and the Book will be laid open. The prophets and witnesses shall be brought in and all shall be judged with fairness: none shall be wronged. Every soul shall be paid back according to its deeds, for Allah knows of all their actions.

39:71 In hordes the unbelievers shall be led to Hell. When they draw near, its gates will be opened, and its keepers will say to them: 'Did there not come to you apostles of your own who proclaimed to you the revelations of your Lord and forewarned you of this day?'

'Yes,' they will answer. And thus the punishment which

the unbelievers have been promised shall be fulfilled. A 39:72
voice will say to them: 'Enter the gates of Hell and stay
there in for ever.' Evil is the dwelling-place of the arrogant.

But those who fear their Lord shall be led in bands to
Paradise. When they draw near, its gates will be opened,
and its keepers will say to them: 'Peace be to you; you
have been good men. Enter Paradise and dwell in it for
ever.'

They will say: 'Praise be to Allah who has made good to
us His promise and given us the earth to inherit, that we
may dwell in Paradise wherever we please.' Blessed is the
reward of the righteous.

You shall see the angels circling round the Throne, giving 39:75
glory to their Lord. Mankind shall be judged with fairness,
and all shall say: 'Praise be to Allah, Lord of the Creation!'

SAD

In the Name of Allah, the Compassionate, the Merciful

SAD. I swear by the renowned Koran that the unbeliev- 38:1
ers shall come to grief through their own arrogance
and internal strife.

How many generations We have destroyed before them!
They all cried out for mercy, when it was too late to escape.

They marvel that a prophet of their own should arise
amongst them. 'He is but a cunning enchanter,' say the unbelievers. 'Does he claim that all the gods are one god?
This is indeed a strange thing.'

Their leaders go about, saying: 'Pay no heed and stand
firm in the worship of your gods: it is a binding duty. We
have not heard of this[1] in the Christian Faith.[2] It is nothing
but a false invention. Was the word of Allah revealed to
him alone of all our countrymen?'

Yes, they are in doubt about My warning, for they have
not yet felt My punishment.

Do they possess the treasures of the blessings of your 38:9

1. Monotheism.   2. Lit., the *last faith*.

38:10 Lord, the Mighty, the Munificent One? Is theirs the kingdom of the heavens and the earth and all that lies between them? Then let them climb up to the sky by ropes!

Their faction is no more than a beaten army. The people of Noah, Aad, and Pharaoh, who impaled his victims upon the stake, Thamoud, the compatriots of Lot, and the dwellers of the Forest[1] – all denied their Lord and divided themselves into factions: all charged their apostles with imposture. But in the end My vengeance justly smote them.

Yet these wait for a single shout – the shout which none may retard – and say: 'Lord, hasten our doom before the Day of Reckoning comes!'

Bear with what they say, and remember Our servant David, who was both a mighty and a penitent man. We made the mountains[2] join with him in praise morning and evening, and the birds, too, in all their flocks; all were obedient to him. We made his kingdom strong and gave him wisdom and sound judgement.

38:21 Have you heard the story of the two litigants who entered his chamber by climbing over the wall? When they went in to him and saw that he was alarmed, they said: 'Have no fear. We are two litigants, one of whom has wronged the other. Judge rightly between us and do not be unjust; guide us to the right path.

'My brother here has ninety-nine ewes, but I have only one ewe.[3] He demanded that I should entrust it to him and got the better of me in the dispute.'

David replied: 'He has certainly wronged you in seeking to add your ewe to his flock. Many partners are unjust to one another; but not so those that have faith and do good works, and they are few indeed.'

David realized that this was a test for him. He sought forgiveness of his Lord and fell down penitently on his knees. We forgave him his sin, and in the world to come he shall be honoured and well received.

38:26 We said: 'David, We have made you master in the land.

1. The people of Midian.
2. Cf. Psalms 148, 9–10.　　　　3. The allusion is to Uriah's wife.

Rule with justice among men and do not yield to lust, lest it should turn you away from Allah's path. Because they forget the Day of Reckoning, those that stray from Allah's path shall be sternly punished.'

It was not in vain that We created the heavens and the 38:27 earth and all that lies between them. That is the fancy of the unbelievers. But woe to the unbelievers when they are cast into the fire of Hell!

Are We to treat alike those that have faith and do good works, and those that corrupt the earth with wickedness? Are We to treat the righteous as We treat the wicked?

We have revealed to you this Book with Our blessing, so that the wise might ponder its revelations and take warning.

We gave Solomon to David; and he was a good and faithful servant. When, one evening, his prancing steeds were ranged before him, he said: 'My love for the good things of life has caused me to forget my prayers; for now the sun has vanished behind the veil of darkness. Bring me back my chargers!' And with this he fell to hacking their legs and necks.

We put Solomon to the proof and placed a counterfeit 38:24 upon his throne, so that he at length repented. He said: 'Forgive me, Lord, and bestow upon me such power as shall belong to none after me. You are the Bountiful Giver.'

We subdued the wind to him, so that it blew softly at his bidding wherever he directed it; and the devils, too, among whom were builders and divers and others bound with chains. 'All this We give you,' We said. 'Bestow or withhold, without reckoning.' In the world to come he shall be honoured and well received.

And tell of Our servant Job. He called out to his Lord, saying: 'Satan has afflicted me with sorrows and misfortunes.'

We said: 'Stamp your feet against the earth, and a cool spring will gush forth. Wash and refresh yourself.'

We restored to him his people and as many more with 38:43 them: a blessing from Ourself and an admonition to prudent men.

38:44 We said to him: 'Take a bunch of twigs and beat your wife with it; do not break your oath.'[1] We found him full of patience. He was a good and faithful man.

And tell of Our servants Abraham, Isaac, and Jacob: men of might and vision whom We made pure with the thought of the hereafter. They shall dwell with Us among the righteous whom We have chosen.

And of Ishmael, Elisha, and Dhulkifl,[2] who were all just men.

This is but an admonition. The righteous shall return to a blessed retreat. They shall enter the gardens of Eden, whose gates shall open to receive them. Reclining there with bashful virgins for companions, they shall feast on abundant fruit and drink.

All this shall be yours on the Day of Reckoning; Our gifts shall never fail.

38:55 But doleful shall be the return of the transgressors. They shall burn in the fire of Hell, a dismal resting-place. There let them taste their drink: scalding water, festering blood, and other putrid things.

We shall say to their leaders: 'This band shall be thrown in headlong with you. No welcome awaits them; they shall be promptly cast into the Fire.'

And the damned will say to their leaders: 'No welcome for you either! It was you who prepared this for us, an evil plight.'

Then they will say: 'Lord, inflict on those who brought this fate upon us a twofold punishment in Hell. But why do we not see those whom we regarded as wicked men and whom we laughed to scorn? Or have our eyes missed them?'

38:64 All this shall come to pass. The dwellers of Hell will wrangle among themselves.

1. Job had sworn to give his wife a hundred blows. The oath was kept by his giving her one blow with a bunch of a hundred twigs. Commentators quote this passage as permitting any similar release from an oath rashly taken.

2. Probably the prophet Ezekiel.

Say: 'My mission is only to give warning. There is no *38:61* god but Allah, the One, the Almighty. He is the Lord of the heavens and the earth and all that lies between them: the Illustrious, the Benignant One.'

Say: 'This is a fateful message: yet you give no heed to it. I had no knowledge of the disputes of those on high. It was revealed to me, only that I might warn you plainly.'

Your Lord said to the angels: 'I am creating man from clay. When I have fashioned him and breathed of My spirit into him, kneel down and prostrate yourselves before him.'

The angels all prostrated themselves except Satan, who was too proud, for he was an unbeliever.

'Satan,' said Allah, 'why do you not bow to him whom My own hands have made? Are you too proud, or do you think he is beneath you?'

Satan replied: 'I am nobler than he. You created me *38:76* from fire, but him from clay.'

'Begone, you are accursed!' said He. 'My curse shall remain on you until the Day of Reckoning.'

Satan replied: 'Reprieve me, Lord, till the Day of Resurrection.'

Allah said: 'Reprieved you shall be till the Appointed Day.'

'I swear by Your glory,' said Satan, 'that I will seduce all men except your faithful servants.'

Allah replied: 'Learn the truth, then (and I speak nothing but the truth): I shall fill Hell with your offspring and the men who follow you.'

Say: 'For this I demand of you no recompense. Nor do I pretend to be what I am not. This is an admonition to mankind; you shall before long know its truth.' *38:88*

In the Name of Allah, the Compassionate, the Merciful

33:1 PROPHET, have fear of Allah and do not yield to the unbelievers and the hypocrites. Allah is wise and all-knowing.

Obey what is revealed to you from your Lord, for Allah is cognizant of all your actions, and put your trust in Him; He is your all-sufficient guardian.

Allah has never put two hearts within one man's body. He does not regard the wives whom you divorce as your mothers,[1] nor your adopted sons as your own sons. These are mere words which you utter with your mouths: but Allah declares the truth and guides to the right path.

33:5 Name your adopted sons after their fathers; that is more just in the sight of Allah. If you do not know their fathers, regard them as your brothers in the faith and as your wards. Your unintentional mistakes shall be forgiven, but not your deliberate errors. Allah is forgiving and merciful.

The Prophet has a greater claim on the faithful than they have on each other. His wives are their mothers.

Allah ordains that blood relations are closer to one another than to other believers or *muhadjirs*,[2] although you are permitted to do your friends a kindness.[3] That is decreed in Allah's Book.

We made a covenant with you as We did with the other prophets; with Noah and Abraham, with Moses and Jesus, the son of Mary. A solemn covenant We made with them, so that Allah might question the truthful about their truthfulness. But for the unbelievers He has prepared a woeful punishment.

33:9 Believers, remember Allah's goodness to you when you were attacked by your enemy's army. We unleashed against

1. In allusion to the formula: 'Be to me as my mother's back,' accepted among pagan Arabs as a declaration of divorce.
2. Mohammed's early followers who fled with him to Medina.
3. By leaving them bequests.

them a violent wind and invisible warriors: Allah saw all that you were doing.

They attacked you from above and from below, so that 33:10 your eyes were blurred, your hearts leapt to your throats, and your faith in Allah was shaken. There the faithful were put to the proof; there they were severely afflicted. The hypocrites and the faint-hearted said: 'Allah and His apostle have deceived us.' Others said: 'People of Yath-rib,[1] you cannot stand much longer. Go back to your city.' And yet others sought the Prophet's leave, saying: 'Our homes are defenceless,' whereas they were not. They only wished to flee.

Had the enemy invaded the city from every quarter and roused them to rebellion, they would have surely rebelled. But they would have occupied it only for a short while.

Before that they swore to Allah never to turn their backs in flight. They shall be questioned about their oath here-after.

Say: 'Nothing will your flight avail you. If you escaped 33:16 from death or slaughter you would enjoy this world only for a little while.'

Say: 'Who can protect you from Allah if it is His will to scourge you? And who can prevent Him from showing you mercy?' They shall find none besides Allah to protect or help them.

Allah well knows those of you who prevent others from following the Apostle; who say to their comrades: 'Join our side,' and seldom take part in the fighting, being ever reluctant to assist you. When fear overtakes them they look to you[2] for help, their eyes rolling as though they were on the point of death. But once they are out of danger they assail you with their sharp tongues, covetously demanding the richest part of the booty. Such men have no faith. Allah will bring their deeds to nothing. That is no difficult thing for Allah.

They thought the confederate tribes would never raise 33:20 the siege. Indeed, if they should come again, they would

1. The old name of Medina.   2. Mohammed.

sooner be in the desert among the wandering Arabs. There they would ask news of you, but were they with you they would take but little part in the fighting.

33:21 There is a good example in Allah's apostle for those who look to Allah and the Last Day and remember Allah always.

When the true believers saw the confederates they said: 'This is what Allah and His apostle have promised us; surely their promise has come true.' And this increased their faith and submission.

Among the believers there are men who have been true to Allah. Some have died, and others await their end, yielding to no change. Allah will surely reward the faithful for their faith and sternly punish the hypocrites – or show them mercy if He will: Allah is forgiving and merciful.

Allah turned back the unbelievers in their rage, and they went away empty-handed. He helped the faithful in the stress of war: mighty is Allah, and all-powerful.

33:26 He brought down from their strongholds those who had supported them from among the People of the Book[1] and cast terror into their hearts, so that some you slew and others you took captive.

He made you masters of their land, their houses, and their goods, and of yet another land[2] on which you had never set foot before. Truly, Allah has power over all things.

Prophet, say to your wives; 'If you seek this life and all its finery, come, I will make provision for you and release you honourably. But if you seek Allah and His apostle and the hereafter, know that Allah has prepared a rich reward for those of you who do good works.'

Wives of the Prophet! Those of you who commit a proven sin shall be doubly punished. That is no difficult thing for Allah. But those of you who obey Allah and His apostle and do good works shall be doubly rewarded; for them We have made a generous provision.

33:32 Wives of the Prophet, you are not like other women. If you fear Allah, do not be too complaisant in your speech,

1. The Jews of Beni Qurayza.   2. Khaybar.

lest the lecherous-hearted should lust after you. Show discretion in what you say. Stay in your homes and do not 33:33 display your finery as women used to do in the days of ignorance.[1] Attend to your prayers, give alms to the poor, and obey Allah and His apostle.

Women of the Prophet's household, Allah seeks only to remove uncleanness from you and to purify you. Commit to memory the revelations of Allah, and the wise sayings that are recited in your dwellings. Benignant is Allah and all-knowing.

Those who surrender themselves to Allah and accept the true faith; who are devout, sincere, patient, humble, charitable, and chaste; who fast and are ever mindful of Allah – on these, both men and women, Allah will bestow forgiveness and a rich reward.

It is not for true believers – men or women – to take their 33:36 choice in their affairs if Allah and His apostle decree otherwise. He that disobeys Allah and His apostle strays far indeed.

You[2] said to the man[3] whom Allah and yourself have favoured: 'Keep your wife and have fear of Allah.' You sought to hide in your heart what Allah was to reveal.[4] You were afraid of man, although it would have been more right to fear Allah. And when Zeid divorced his wife, We gave her to you in marriage, so that it should become legitimate for true believers to wed the wives of their adopted sons if they divorced them. Allah's will must needs be done.

No blame shall be attached to the Prophet for doing what is sanctioned for him by Allah. Such was the way of Allah with the prophets who passed away before him (Allah's decrees are pre-ordained); who fulfilled the mission with which Allah had charged them, fearing Allah and fearing none besides Him. Sufficient is Allah's reckoning.

Mohammed is the father of no man among you.[5] He is 33:40

1. Pre-Islamic days. 2. Mohammed.
3. Zeid, Mohammed's adopted son.
4. Your intention to marry Zeid's wife.
5. Mohammed left no male heirs.

the apostle of Allah and the Seal of the Prophets. Allah has knowledge of all things.

33:41 Believers, be ever mindful of Allah: praise Him morning and evening. He and His angels bless you, so that He may lead you from darkness to the light. He is merciful to true believers.

On the day they meet Him their greeting shall be: 'Peace!' A rich reward He has prepared for them.

Prophet, We have sent you forth as a witness, a bearer of good news, and a warner; one who shall call men to Allah by His leave and guide them like a shining light.

Tell the faithful that Allah has bounteous blessings in store for them. Do not yield to the unbelievers and the hypocrites: disregard their insolence. Put your trust in Allah; Allah is your all-sufficient guardian.

33:49 Believers, if you marry believing women and divorce them before the marriage is consummated, you are not required to observe a waiting period. Provide well for them and release them honourably.

Prophet, We have made lawful to you the wives to whom you have granted dowries and the slave-girls whom Allah has given you as booty; the daughters of your paternal and maternal uncles and of your paternal and maternal aunts who fled with you; and the other women who gave themselves to you and whom you wished to take in marriage.[1] This privilege is yours alone, being granted to no other believer.

We well know the duties We have imposed on the faithful concerning their wives and slave-girls. We grant you this privilege so that none may blame you. Allah is forgiving and merciful.

33:51 You may put off any of your wives you please and take to your bed any of them you please. Nor is it unlawful for you to receive any of those whom you have temporarily set aside. That is more proper, so that they may be contented and not vexed, and may all be pleased with what you give them.

1. At this time Mohammed had nine wives, apart from slave-girls.

Allah knows what is in your[1] hearts. He is benignant and all-knowing.

It shall be unlawful for you[2] to take more wives or to 33:52 change your present wives for other women, though their beauty please you, except where slave-girls are concerned. Allah takes cognizance of all things.

Believers, do not enter the houses of the Prophet for a meal without waiting for the proper time, unless you are given leave. But if you are invited, enter; and when you have eaten, disperse. Do not engage in familiar talk, for this would annoy the Prophet and he would be ashamed to bid you go; but of the truth Allah is not ashamed. If you ask his wives for anything, speak to them from behind a curtain. This is more chaste for your hearts and their hearts.

You must not speak ill of Allah's apostle, nor shall you ever wed his wives after him; this would be a grave offence in the sight of Allah. Whether you hide or reveal them, Allah has knowledge of all things.

It shall be no offence for the Prophet's wives to be seen 33:55 unveiled by their fathers, their sons, their brothers, their brothers' sons, their sisters' sons, their women, and their slave-girls. Women, have fear of Allah, for He observes all things.

The Prophet is blessed by Allah and His angels. Bless him, then, you that are true believers, and greet him with a worthy salutation.

Those who speak ill of Allah and His apostle shall be cursed by Allah in this life and in the life to come. He has prepared for them a shameful punishment.

Those who traduce believing men and believing women undeservedly shall bear the guilt of slander and a gross sin.

Prophet, enjoin your wives, your daughters, and the wives of true believers to draw their veils close round them. That is more proper, so that they may be recognized and not molested. Allah is forgiving and merciful.

If the hypocrites and those who have tainted hearts and 33:60 the scandal-mongers of Medina do not desist, We will

1. The believers.   2. Mohammed.

rouse you against them and their days in that city will be
33:61 numbered. Cursed wherever they are found, they will be
seized and put to death.

Such has been the way of Allah with those who have
gone before them. You shall find His ways unchanged.

People ask you about the Hour of Doom. Say: 'Allah
alone has knowledge of it. Who knows? It may well be that
it is near at hand.'

Allah has laid His curse upon the unbelievers and prepared for them a blazing Fire. Abiding there for ever, they
shall find none to protect or help them.

On the day when their heads will roll about in Hell, they
shall say: 'Would that we had obeyed Allah and the
33:67 Apostle!' And they shall say: 'Lord, We obeyed our masters and our great ones, but they led us away from the right
path. Lord, let their punishment be doubled; lay on them a
mighty curse.'

Believers, do not behave like those who slandered Moses.
Allah cleared him of their calumny and he was exalted by
Allah.

Believers, fear Allah and speak the truth. He will bless
your works and forgive you your sins. Those who obey
Allah and His apostle shall win a great victory.

We offered Our trust to the heavens, to the earth, and to
the mountains, but they refused the burden and were afraid
to receive it. Man undertook to bear it, but he has proved a
sinner and a fool.

33:73 Allah will surely punish the hypocrites and the idolaters,
both men and women; but to believing men and to believing women He shall show mercy. Allah is forgiving and
merciful.

THE PROPHETS

In the Name of Allah, the Compassionate, the Merciful

THE Day of Reckoning is drawing near, yet the people 21:1
heedlessly persist in unbelief. They listen flippantly
to each fresh warning that their Lord gives them:
their hearts are set on pleasure.

In private the unbelievers say to each other: 'Is this man
not a mortal like yourselves? Have you no eyes that you
should yield to witchcraft?'

Say: 'My Lord has knowledge of whatever is said in
heaven and earth. He hears all and knows all.'

Some say: 'It[1] is but a medley of dreams.' Others: 'He
has invented it himself.' And yet others: 'He is a poet: let
him show us some sign, as did the apostles in days gone
by.'

Yet though We showed them signs the nations whom We 21:6
destroyed never believed in them. Will *they* believe in them?

The apostles We sent before you were no more than men
whom We inspired. Let them ask the People of the Book if
they do not know this. The bodies We gave them could not
dispense with food, nor were they immortal. Then We fulfilled Our promise: We delivered them and those We willed,
and utterly destroyed the transgressors.

And now We have revealed a Book for your admonish-
ment. Will you give no heed?

We have destroyed many a sinful nation and replaced
them by other men. And when they felt Our might they
fled from their cities. Our angels said to them: 'Do not run
away. Return to your comforts and your dwellings. You
shall be questioned all.'

'Woe to us, we have done wrong!' was their reply. And
this they kept repeating until We mowed them down and
put out their light.

It was not in sport that We made the heavens and the 21:16

1. The Koran.

21:17 earth and all that lies between them. Had it been Our will to find a pastime, We could have found one near at hand.

We will hurl Truth at Falsehood, until Truth shall triumph and Falsehood be no more. Woe shall befall you, for all the falsehoods you have uttered.

His are all who dwell in the heavens and the earth. Those who stand in His presence do not disdain to worship Him, nor are they ever wearied. They praise Him day and night, unflaggingly.

Have they chosen earthly deities? And can these deities restore the dead to life? Had there been other gods in heaven or earth besides Allah, both heaven and earth would have been ruined. Exalted be Allah, Lord of the Throne, above their falsehoods!

21:23 None shall question Him about His works, but of *them* an account shall be demanded. Have they chosen other gods besides Him?

Say: 'Show us your proofs. Here are the Scriptures of today and those of long ago.' But most of them do not know the truth, and this is why they give no heed.

We inspired all the apostles whom We sent before you, saying: 'There is no god but Me. Therefore serve Me.'

They say: 'The Merciful has begotten children.' Allah forbid! They are but His honoured servants. They do not speak till He has spoken: they act by His command. He knows what is before them and behind them. They intercede for none save those whom He accepts, and tremble for awe of Him. Whoever of them declares: 'I am a god besides Him,' shall be requited with Hell-fire. Thus shall the sinners be rewarded.

Are the disbelievers unaware that the heavens and the earth were one solid mass which We tore asunder, and that We made every living thing of water? Will they not have faith?

21:31 We set firm mountains upon the earth lest it should move away with them, and hewed out highways in the rock so that they might be rightly guided.

We spread the heaven like a canopy and provided it with *21:32*
strong support: yet of its signs they are heedless.

It was He who created the night and the day, and the sun
and the moon: each moves swiftly in an orbit of its own.

No man before you[1] have We made immortal. If you
yourself are doomed to die, will they live forever?

Every soul shall taste death. We will prove you all with
good and evil. To Us you shall be recalled.

When the unbelievers see you they scoff at you, saying:
'Is this the man who fulminates against your gods?' They
deny all mention of the Merciful.

Impatience is the very stuff man is made of. You shall
before long see My signs: you need not ask Me to hasten
them.

They say: 'When will this promise be fulfilled, if what *21:38*
you say be true?'

If only the unbelievers knew the day when they shall be
powerless to shield their faces and their backs from the fire
of Hell; the day when none shall help them! It will overtake
them unawares and stupefy them. They shall have no
power to ward it off, nor shall they be reprieved.

Other apostles have been mocked before you; but those
who scoffed at them were smitten by the very scourge they
mocked.

Say: 'Who will protect you, by night and by day, from
the Lord of Mercy?' Yet they are unmindful of their Lord's
remembrance.

Have they other gods to defend them? Their idols shall
have no power over their own salvation, nor shall they be
protected from Our scourge.

We have bestowed good things upon these men and on
their fathers and made their lives too long. Can they not see
how We invade their land and shrink its borders? Is it they
who will triumph?

Say: 'I warn you only by that with which I am inspired.' *21:45*
But the deaf can hear nothing when they are warned.

1. Mohammed.

21:46 Yet if the lightest breath from the vengeance of your Lord touched them, they would say: 'Woe to us: we have done wrong!'

We shall set up just scales on the Day of Resurrection, so that no man shall in the least be wronged. Actions as small as a grain of mustard seed shall be weighed out. Our reckoning shall suffice.

We showed Moses and Aaron the distinction between right and wrong, and gave them a light and an admonition for righteous men: those who truly fear their Lord and dread the terrors of Judgement-day.

And in this[1] We have revealed a blessed counsel. Will you then reject it?

We bestowed guidance on Abraham, for We knew him well. He said to his father and to his people: 'What are these images to which you are so devoted?'

They replied: 'Our fathers worshipped them.'

21:54 He said: 'Then you and your fathers were in the grossest error.'

'Is it the truth that you are preaching,' they asked, 'or is this but a jest?'

'Know, then,' he answered, 'that your Lord is the Lord of the heavens and the earth. It was He that made them: to this I bear witness. By the Lord, I will overthrow your idols as soon as you have turned your backs.'

He broke them all in pieces, except their supreme god, so that they might return to Him.

'Who has done this to our deities?' asked some. 'He must surely be a wicked man.'

Others replied: 'We have heard a youth called Abraham speak of them.'

They said: 'Then bring him here in sight of all the people, that they may act as witnesses.'

'Abraham,' they said, 'was it you who did this to our deities?'

'No,' he replied. 'It was their chief who smote them. Ask
21:63 them, if they can speak.'

1. The Koran.

Thereupon they turned their thoughts to their own folly 21·64 and said to each other: 'Surely you are sinful men.'

But they soon returned to unbelief and said to Abraham: 'You know they cannot speak.'

He answered: 'Would you then worship that, instead of Allah, which can neither help nor harm you? Shame on you and on your idols! Have you no sense?'

They cried: 'Burn him and avenge your gods, if you must punish him!'

'Fire,' We said, 'be cool to Abraham and keep him safe.'

They sought to lay a snare for him, but they themselves were ruined. We delivered him and Lot, and brought them to the land which We had blessed for all mankind.

We gave him Isaac, and then Jacob for a grandson; and We made each a righteous man. We ordained them leaders to guide mankind at Our behest, and enjoined on them charity, prayer and almsgiving. They served none but Ourself.

To Lot We gave wisdom and knowledge and delivered 21:74 him from the Wicked City; for its inhabitants were men of iniquity and evil. We admitted him to Our mercy: he was a righteous man.

Before him Noah invoked Us and We heard his prayer. We saved him and all his kinsfolk from the great calamity, and delivered him from the people who had denied Our revelations. Evil men they were; We drowned them all.

And tell of David and Solomon: how they passed judgement regarding the cornfield in which strayed lambs had grazed by night. We gave Solomon insight into the case and bore witness to both their judgements.

We bestowed on them wisdom and knowledge, and caused the birds and mountains to join with David in Our praise. All this We have done.

We taught him the armourer's craft, so that you might have protection in your wars. Will you then give thanks?

To Solomon We subdued the raging wind: it sped at his 21:81 bidding to the land which We had blessed. We have knowledge of all things.

21:82   We assigned him devils who dived into the sea for him and performed other tasks besides. We kept a watchful eye over them.

And tell of Job: how he called on his Lord, saying: 'I am sorely afflicted: but of all those that show mercy You are the most merciful.'

We heard his prayer and relieved his affliction. We restored to him his family and as many more with them: a blessing from Ourself and an admonition to worshippers.

And you shall also tell of Ishmael, Idris,[1] and Dhulkifl,[2] who all endured with fortitude. To Our mercy We admitted them, for they were upright men.

And of Dhul-Nun:[3] how he went away in anger, thinking We had no power over him. But in the darkness he cried: 'There is no god but You. Glory be to You! I have done wrong.'

21:88   We heard his prayer and delivered him from affliction. Thus We shall save the true believers.

And of Zacharias, who invoked his Lord, saying: 'Lord, let me not remain childless, though of all heirs You are the best.'

We heard his prayer and gave him John, curing his wife of sterility. They vied with each other in good works and called on Us with piety, fear, and submission.

And of the woman who kept her chastity. We breathed into her of Our spirit, and made her and her son a sign to all men.

Your religion is but one religion, and I am Your only Lord. Therefore serve Me. Men have divided themselves into schisms, but to Us they shall all return. He that does good works in the fullness of his faith, his endeavours shall not be lost: We record them all.

It is ordained that no nation We have destroyed shall ever rise again. But when Gog and Magog are let loose and *21:97* rush headlong down every hill; when the true promise nears its fulfilment; the unbelievers shall stare in amaze-

1. Enoch.   2. Probably Ezekiel.   3. Jonah.

302

ment crying: 'Woe to us! Of this we have been heedless. We have done wrong.'

You and all your idols shall be the fuel of Hell; therein *21:98* you shall all go down. Were they true gods, your idols would not go there: but in it they shall abide for ever. They shall groan with pain and be bereft of hearing.

But those to whom We have already shown Our favour shall be far removed from Hell. They shall not hear its roar, but shall delight for ever in what their souls desire.

The Supreme Terror shall not grieve them, and the angels will receive them, saying: 'This is the day you have been promised.'

On that day We shall roll up the heaven like a scroll of *21:104* parchment. As We first created man, so will We bring him back to life. This is a promise We shall assuredly fulfil.

We wrote in the Psalms[1] after the Torah had been given: 'The righteous among My servants shall inherit the earth.' That is an admonition to those who serve Us.

We have sent you forth as a blessing to mankind. Say: 'It is revealed to me that your God is one God. Will you submit to Him?'

If they give no heed say: 'I have warned you all alike, though I cannot tell whether what you are threatened with is imminent or far off. Allah knows your spoken words and hidden thoughts. This may be a test for you and a short reprieve.'

Say: 'Lord, judge with fairness. Our Lord is the Merci- *21:112* ful, whose help We seek against your blasphemies.'

1. Psalm xxxvii, 29.

THE BEE

In the Name of Allah, the Compassionate, the Merciful

16:1   THE judgement of Allah will surely come to pass: do not seek to hurry it on. Glory to Him! Exalted be He above their idols!

By His will He sends down the angels with the Spirit to those of His servants whom He chooses, bidding them proclaim: 'There is no god but Me: therefore fear Me.'

He created the heavens and the earth to manifest the truth. Exalted be He above their idols!

He created man from a little germ: yet man openly disputes His judgement.

He created the beasts which provide you with warm clothing, food, and other benefits. How pleasant they look when you bring them home and when you lead them out to pasture!

They carry your burdens to far-off lands, which you could not otherwise reach except with painful toil. Compassionate is your Lord, and merciful.

16:8   He has given you horses, mules, and donkeys, which you may ride or use as ornaments; and He has created other things beyond your knowledge.

Allah alone can show the right path. Some turn aside from it, but had He pleased He would have guided you all aright.

It is He who sends down water from the sky, which provides drink for you and brings forth the crops on which your cattle feed. And thereby He brings up corn and olives, dates and grapes and other fruit. Surely in this there is a sign for thinking men.

16:12   He has forced the night and the day, and the sun and the moon, into your service: the stars also serve you by His leave. Surely in this there are signs for men of understanding.

On the earth He has fashioned for you objects of various 16:13
hues: surely in this there is a sign for prudent men.

It is He who has subjected to you the ocean, so that you
may eat of its fresh fish and bring up from it ornaments with
which to adorn your persons. Behold the ships ploughing
their course through it. All this He has created, that you
may seek His bounty and render thanks to Him.

He set firm mountains upon the earth lest it should move
away with you; and rivers, roads, and landmarks, so that
you may be rightly guided. By the stars, too, are men
directed.

Is He, then, who has wrought the creation, like him who
has created nothing? Will you not take heed?

If you reckoned up Allah's blessings you could not count 16:18
them. He is forgiving and merciful.

Allah has knowledge of all that you hide and all that you
reveal. But the false gods which infidels invoke create
nothing: they are themselves created. They are dead, not
living; nor do they know when they will be raised to life.

Your God is one God. Those that deny the life to come
have faithless hearts and are puffed up with pride. Allah
surely knows what they hide and what they reveal. He does
not love the proud.

When they are asked: 'What has your Lord revealed?'
they say: 'Old fictitious tales!' They shall bear the full brunt
of their burdens on the Day of Resurrection, together with
the burdens of those who in their ignorance were misled
by them. Evil is that which they shall bear.

Those who have gone before them also plotted. But
Allah smote their edifice at its foundations and its roof fell
down upon their heads. His scourge overtook them
whence they did not know.

He will disgrace them on the Day of Resurrection. He 16:27
will say: 'Where are your idols now, the subject of your
disputes?' And those to whom Knowledge has been given
will say: 'Misery and shame shall this day fall on the unbelievers.'

16:28   Those whom the angels will carry off while steeped in sin will offer submission, saying: 'We have done no wrong!' 'Indeed!' the angels will reply. 'Allah knows all that you have done. Enter the gates of Hell: there you shall abide for ever.' Dismal is the house where the proud shall dwell.

But when the righteous are asked: 'What has your Lord revealed?' they will reply: 'That which is best.' Good is the reward of those that do good works in this present life: but far better is the reward of the life to come. Blessed is the dwelling-place of the righteous. They shall enter the gardens of Eden. Rivers shall roll at their feet, and they shall be given all they desire. Thus shall the righteous be rewarded.

The angels will receive the souls of good men, saying: 'Peace be on you. Come in to Paradise, the reward of your labours.'

16:33   Are the unbelievers waiting for the angels to come down or for the fulfilment of your Lord's judgement? Those who have gone before them also waited. Allah did not wrong them, but they wronged themselves: the evil which they did recoiled upon them, and the scourge at which they scoffed encompassed them.

The idolaters say: 'Had Allah pleased, neither we nor our fathers would have served other gods besides Him; nor would we have forbidden anything without His sanction.' Such also was the plea of others before them. Yet what should apostles do but give plain warning?

We raised an apostle in every nation, saying: 'Serve Allah and avoid false gods.' Amongst them were some whom Allah guided, and others destined to go astray. Roam the world and see what was the end of the disbelievers!

Strive as you may to guide them, Allah will not guide those whom He misleads. There shall be none to help them.

They solemnly swear by Allah that He will never raise the dead to life. But Allah's promise shall surely be fulfilled, *16:39* though most men may not know it. He will manifest to them that which they dispute, and the unbelievers shall

know that they were lying. When We decree a thing, We 16:40
need only say: 'Be,' and it is.

As for those who have endured persecution and fled
their homes for the cause of Allah, bearing ills with patience and putting their trust in their Lord, We will provide
well for them in this life: but better is the reward of the life
to come, if they but knew it.

The apostles We sent before you were no more than
mortals whom We inspired with revelations and with writ-
ings. Ask the People of the Book, if you doubt this. To you
We have revealed the Koran, so that you may proclaim to
men what has been revealed for them, and that they may
give thought.

Are those who plot evil confident that Allah will not cave
in the earth beneath them, or that His scourge will not fall
upon them whence they do not know? Are they confident
that He will not smite them in the course of their journeys
when they cannot escape, or that He will not give them
over to slow destruction? Yet your Lord is compassionate
and merciful.

Do they not see how every object Allah created casts its 16:48
shadow right and left, prostrating itself before Him in all
humility? To Allah bow all the creatures of the heavens and
the earth, and the angels also. They are not disdainful; they
fear their Lord on high and do as they are bidden.

Allah has said: 'You shall not serve two gods, for He is
but one God. Revere none but Me.'

His is what the heavens and the earth contain. His is the
Faith everlasting. Would you then fear any but Allah?

His are all your blessings, and to Him you turn for help
when misfortune befalls you. Yet no sooner does He remove your ills than some of you set up other gods besides
Him, giving no thanks for what We grant them. Take your
pleasure, then, in this life; you shall before long know the
truth.

To idols of which they know nothing they assign a por- 16:56
tion of Our gifts. By Allah, you shall be questioned about
your false inventions!

16:57   They give daughters to Allah (glory be to Him!), but they themselves would have what they desire. When the birth of a girl is announced to one of them, his face grows dark and he is filled with inward gloom. Because of the bad news he hides himself from men: should he keep her with disgrace or bury her under the dust? How ill they judge!

Evil are the ways of those who deny the life to come. But most sublime are the ways of Allah. He is the Mighty, the Wise One.

If Allah punished men for their sins, not one creature would be left alive. He respites them to an appointed day; when their hour is come, not for one moment shall they stay behind: nor can they go before it.

They ascribe to Allah what they themselves dislike. They preach the lie that a good reward awaits them. But let them have no doubt: the fire of Hell awaits them, and there they shall be left.

16:63   By the Lord, We have sent apostles before you to other nations. But Satan made their foul deeds seem fair to them, and to this day He is their patron. Theirs shall be a woeful punishment.

We have revealed to you the Book only so that you may declare to them the truth concerning which they are disputing. It is a guide and a blessing to true believers.

Allah sends down water from the sky with which He quickens the dead earth. Surely in this there is a sign for prudent men.

In cattle too you have a worthy lesson. We give you to drink of that which is in their bellies, between the bowels and the blood-streams: pure milk, a pleasant beverage for those who drink it.

We give you the fruits of the palm and of the vine, from which you derive intoxicants and wholesome food. Surely in this there is a sign for men of understanding.

Your Lord inspired the bee, saying: 'Build your homes in the mountains, in the trees, and in the hives which men *16:69* shall make for you. Feed on every kind of fruit, and follow the trodden paths of your Lord.'

From its belly comes forth a fluid of many hues, a medicinal drink for men. Surely in this there is a sign for those who would give thought.

Allah created you, and He will cause you to die hereafter. 16:70 Some of you shall have their lives prolonged to abject old age, when all that they once knew they shall know no more. Mighty is Allah, and all-knowing.

To some of you Allah has given more than to others. Those on whom He has bestowed His bounty deny their slaves an equal share in their possessions. Would they deny Allah's goodness?

Allah has given you wives from among yourselves, and through them He has granted you sons and grandsons. He has provided you with good things: will they then believe in false gods and deny His favours?

They worship helpless idols which can confer on them no benefits from heaven or earth. Compare none with Allah: He has knowledge, but you have not.

Allah makes this comparison. On the one hand there is a 16:75 helpless slave, the property of his master. On the other, a man on whom We have bestowed Our bounty, so that he gives of it both in private and in public. Are the two alike? Allah forbid! Most men have no knowledge.

He also makes this comparison. Take a dumb and helpless man, a burden on his master: wherever he sends him he returns with empty hands. Is he equal with one who enjoins justice and follows the right path?

To Allah belong the secrets of the heavens and the earth. The business of the Final Hour shall be accomplished in the twinkling of an eye, or even less. Allah has power over all things.

Allah brought you out of your mothers' wombs devoid of all knowledge, and gave you ears and eyes and hearts, so that you may give thanks.

Do they not see the birds that wing their flight in heaven's vault? None sustains them but Allah. Surely in this there are signs for true believers.

Allah has given you houses to dwell in, and the skins of 16:80

beasts for tents, so that you may find them light in your wanderings and easy to pitch when you halt for shelter; while from their wool, fur, and hair, He has given you comforts and domestic goods.

16:81 By means of that which He created, Allah has given you shelter from the sun. He has given you refuge in the mountains. He has furnished you with garments to protect you from the heat, and with coats of armour to shield you in your wars. Thus He perfects His favours to you, so that you may submit to Him.

But if they[1] give no heed to you,[2] bear in mind that your mission is only to give plain warning.

They recognize the favours of Allah, yet they deny them. Truly, most of them are ungrateful.

On the day We call a witness from every nation, their pleas shall not avail the unbelievers, nor shall they be allowed to make amends. And when the guilty face their punishment, their torment shall never be allayed, nor shall they ever be reprieved.

16:86 When the pagans behold their idols, they shall say: 'Lord, these are the idols to whom we used to pray.' But their idols will retort: 'You are liars all!' They shall proffer submission on that day, and the gods of their own invention will forsake them.

As for those that disbelieve and debar others from the path of Allah, We shall sternly chastise them for their misdeeds.

The day will surely come when We shall call a witness from every nation to testify against it. We shall call *you* to testify against your people: for to you We have revealed the Book which manifests the truth about all things, a guide, a blessing, and good news to those who submit to Allah.

Allah enjoins justice, kindness and charity to one's kindred, and forbids indecency, wickedness and oppression. He admonishes you so that you may take heed.

16:91 Keep faith with Allah when you make a covenant with Him. Do not break your oaths after you have sworn them:

1. The Meccans   2. Mohammed.

for by swearing in His name you make Allah your surety. Allah has knowledge of all your actions.

Do not, like the woman who unravels to bits the thread *16:92* which she has firmly spun, take oaths with mutual deceit and break them on finding yourselves superior to others in numbers. In this Allah puts you to the proof. On the Day of Resurrection He will declare to you the truth of that over which you are now at odds.

Had Allah pleased, He would have united you into one nation. But He leaves in error whom He will and gives guidance to whom He pleases. You shall be questioned about all your actions.

Do not take oaths to deceive each other, lest your foot should slip after being rightly guided, and lest evil should befall you for debarring others from the path of Allah: for then indeed you should incur a grievous punishment.

Do not barter away the covenant of Allah for a trifling *16:95* price. His reward is better than all your gain, if you but knew it. Your worldly riches are transitory, but Allah's reward is everlasting.

We shall reward the steadfast according to their noblest deeds. Be they men or women, those that embrace the faith and do what is right We will surely grant a happy life; We shall reward them according to their noblest actions.

When you recite the Koran, seek refuge in Allah from accursed Satan: no power has he over believers who put their trust in their Lord. He has power only over those who befriend him and those who serve other gods besides Allah.

When We change one verse for another (Allah knows best what He reveals), they say: 'You[1] are an impostor.' Indeed most of them are ignorant men.

Say: 'The Holy Spirit brought it down from your Lord in truth to reassure the faithful, and to give guidance and good news to those that surrender themselves to Allah.'

We know that they say: 'A mortal taught him.' But the *16:103*

1. Mohammed.

man[1] to whom they allude speaks a foreign tongue, while this is eloquent Arabic speech.

16:104 Allah will not guide those who disbelieve His revelations. A grievous punishment awaits them.

None invents falsehoods save those who disbelieve the revelations of Allah: they alone are the liars.

Those who are forced to recant while their hearts remain loyal to the faith shall be absolved; but those who deny Allah after professing Islam and open their bosoms to unbelief shall incur the wrath of Allah and be sternly punished. For such men love the life of this world more than the life to come. Allah gives no guidance to the unbelievers.

Such are those whose hearts and ears and eyes are sealed by Allah; such are the heedless. In the life to come they shall assuredly be lost.

As for those who after great ordeals fled their homes and fought and remained constant to the last, your Lord will be forgiving and merciful to them on the day when every man will come pleading for himself; when every soul will be requited for its deeds. None shall be wronged.

16:112 Allah has made an example of the city[2] which was once safe and peaceful. Its provisions used to come in abundance from every quarter: but its people denied the favours of Allah. Therefore He afflicted them with famine and fear as a punishment for what they did.

An apostle of their own was sent to them, but they denied him. Therefore Our scourge smote them in their sinfulness.

Eat of the good and lawful things which Allah has bestowed on you and give thanks for His favours if you truly serve Him.

16:115 He has forbidden you carrion, blood, and the flesh of swine; also any flesh consecrated other than in the name of Allah. But whoever is constrained to eat any of these, not

1. Scholars differ as to the identity of this 'foreigner'. Some suppose him to be Salman the Persian, others Suheib bin Sinan, and yet others Addas the monk.
2. Mecca.

intending to sin or transgress, will find Allah forgiving and merciful.

Do not falsely declare: 'This is lawful, and this is for- 16:116
bidden,' in order to invent a falsehood about Allah. Those who invent falsehoods about Allah shall never prosper. Brief is their enjoyment of this life, and grievous the punishment that awaits them.

We have forbidden the Jews the foods We have already enumerated. We never wronged them, but they wronged themselves.

To those who commit evil through ignorance and afterwards repent and mend their ways your Lord is forgiving and merciful.

Abraham was a paragon of piety, an upright man obedient to Allah. He was no idolater. He rendered thanks for His favours, so that He chose him and guided him to a straight path. We blessed him in this world, and in the world to come he shall dwell amongst the righteous.

And now We have revealed to you Our will, saying: 16:123
'Follow the faith of saintly Abraham: He was no idolater.'

The Sabbath was ordained only for those who differed about it. On the Day of Resurrection your Lord will judge their disputes.

Call men to the path of your Lord with wisdom and kindly exhortation. Reason with them in the most courteous manner. Your Lord best knows those who stray from His path and those who are rightly guided.

If you punish, let your punishment be proportionate to the wrong that has been done you. But it shall be best for you to endure your wrongs with patience.

Be patient, then: Allah will grant you patience. Do not grieve for the unbelievers, nor distress yourself at their intrigues. Allah is with those who keep from evil and do 16:128
good works.

THE SPOILS[1]

In the Name of Allah, the Compassionate, the Merciful

8:1 THEY ask you about the spoils. Say: 'The spoils belong to Allah and the Apostle. Therefore have fear of Allah and end your disputes. Obey Allah and His apostle, if you are true believers.'

The true believers are those whose hearts are filled with awe at the mention of Allah, and whose faith grows stronger as they listen to His revelations. They are those who put their trust in their Lord, pray steadfastly, and bestow in alms of that which We have given them. Such are the true believers. They shall be exalted and forgiven by their Lord, and a generous provision shall be made for them.

Your Lord bade you leave your home to fight for justice, but some of the faithful were reluctant. They argued with you about the truth that had been revealed, as though they were being led to certain death.

8:7 Allah promised to grant you victory over one of the two bands, but you wished to fight the one that was unarmed.[2] He sought to fulfil His promise and to annihilate the unbelievers, so that Truth should triumph and falsehood be discomfited, though the wrongdoers wished otherwise.

When you prayed to your Lord for help, He answered: 'I am sending to your aid a thousand angels in their ranks.' By this good news Allah sought to reassure your hearts, for victory comes only from Allah; He is mighty and wise.

8:11 You were overcome by sleep, a token of His protection. He sent down water from the sky to cleanse you and to

1. Of the Battle of Badr, A.D. 624.

2. Mohammed's plan was to attack an unarmed caravan belonging to the Quraysh of Mecca on its way from Syria to that city. An army of Meccans marched to its assistance. Some of the Muslims wished to attack the caravan, others the Meccan army. Mohammed's forces, only 319 strong, routed the Meccans, who were nearly 1,000 in number.

purify you of Satan's filth, to strengthen your hearts and to steady your footsteps.

Allah revealed His will to the angels, saying: 'I shall be 8:12 with you. Give courage to the believers. I shall cast terror into the hearts of the infidels. Strike off their heads, maim them in every limb!

Thus We punished them because they defied Allah and His apostle. He that defies Allah and His apostle shall be sternly punished. We said to them: 'Feel Our scourge. Hellfire awaits the unbelievers.'

Believers, when you encounter the armies of the infidels do not turn your backs to them in flight. If anyone on that day turns his back to them, except it be for tactical reasons, or to join another band, he shall incur the wrath of Allah and Hell shall be his home: an evil fate.

It was not you, but Allah, who slew them. It was not you who smote them: Allah smote them so that He might richly reward the faithful. He hears all and knows all. He will surely thwart the designs of the unbelievers.

If you[1] were seeking a judgement, now has a judgement 8:19 come to you. If you desist it will be best for you. If you resume your war against the faithful, We will return to their assistance, and your forces, superior though they be in number, shall avail you nothing: for Allah is with the faithful.

Believers, obey Allah and His apostle, and do not forsake him. You have heard the truth. Do not be like those who say: 'We hear,' but give no heed to what they hear.

The meanest beasts in Allah's sight are those that are deaf, dumb, and devoid of reason. Had he perceived any virtue in them, He would have surely endowed them with hearing. But even if He had made them hear, they would have turned away and refused to listen.

Believers, obey Allah and the Apostle when he calls you 8:24 to that which gives you life. Know that Allah stands between man and his desires, and that in His presence you shall all be assembled.

1. The Meccans.

8:25   Guard yourselves against temptation. The wrongdoers among you are not the only men who will be tempted. Know that Allah's punishment is stern.

Remember how He gave you shelter when you were few in number and persecuted in the land, ever fearing the onslaught of your enemies. He made you strong with His help and bestowed great benefits upon you, so that you might give thanks.

Believers, do not betray Allah and the Apostle, nor knowingly violate your trust. Know that your children and your worldly goods are but a temptation, and that Allah's reward is great.

Believers, if you fear Allah He will give you guidance and cleanse you of your sins and forgive you. The bounty of Allah is great.

Remember how the unbelievers plotted against you.[1] They sought to take you captive or have you killed or banished. They plotted – but Allah plotted also. Allah is most profound in His machinations.

8:31   Whenever Our revelations are recited to them, they say: 'We have heard them. If we wished we could invent the like. They are but fables of the ancients.'

They also say: 'Lord, if this be Your revealed truth, rain down upon us stones from heaven or send some dreadful scourge to punish us.'

But Allah was not to punish them whilst you were dwelling in their midst. Nor would He punish them if they sought forgiveness of Him.

Yet it is but just that He should punish them; for they have debarred others from the Sacred Mosque, although they have no right to be its guardians. Its only guardians are those that fear Allah, though most of them do not know it.

Their prayers at the Sacred House are nothing but whistling and clapping of hands. They shall be punished for their unbelief.

8:36   The unbelievers expend their riches in debarring others from the path of Allah. Thus they dissipate their wealth: but

1. Mohammed.

they shall rue it, and in the end be overthrown. The unbelievers shall be driven into Hell.

Allah will separate the wicked from the just. He will heap *8:37*
the wicked one upon another and then cast them into Hell.
Such are those that shall be lost.

Tell the unbelievers that if they mend their ways their
past shall be forgiven; but if they persist in sin, let them
reflect upon the fate of their forefathers.

Make war on them until idolatry is no more and Allah's
religion reigns supreme. If they desist Allah is cognizant of
all their actions; but if they give no heed, know then that
Allah will protect you. He is the noblest Helper and Protector.

Know that to Allah, the Apostle, the Apostle's kinsfolk,
the orphans, the needy, and the wayfarers, shall belong one
fifth of your spoils: if you truly believe in Allah and what
We revealed to Our servant on the day of victory, the day
when the two armies met. Allah has power over all things.

You were encamped on this side of the valley and the un- *8:42*
believers on the farther side, with the caravan below. Had
they offered battle, you would have surely declined; but
Allah sought to accomplish what He had ordained, so that,
by a miracle, he that was destined to perish might die, and
he that was destined to live might survive. Allah hears all
and knows all.

Allah made them appear to you in a dream as a small
band. Had He showed them to you as a great army, your
courage would have failed you and discord would have
triumphed in your ranks. But this Allah spared you. He
knows your inmost thoughts.

And when you met them, he made each appear to the
other few in number, that He might accomplish what He
had ordained. To Allah shall all things return.

Believers, when you meet their army stand firm and pray
fervently to Allah, so that you may triumph. Obey Allah *8:46*
and His apostle and do not dispute with one another, lest
you should lose courage and your resolve weaken. Have
patience: Allah is with those that are patient.

8:47 Do not be like those who left their homes elated with insolence and vainglory. They debar others from the path of Allah: but Allah has knowledge of all their actions.

Satan made their foul deeds seem fair to them. He said: 'No man shall conquer you this day. I shall be at hand to help you.' But when the two armies came within sight of each other, he took to his heels, saying: 'I am done with you, for I can see what you cannot. I fear Allah. His punishment is stern.'

The hypocrites and the cowards said: 'Their religion has deceived them.' But he that puts his trust in Allah shall find Allah mighty and wise.

If you could see the angels when they carry off the souls of the unbelievers! They shall strike them on their faces and their backs, saying: 'Feel the torment of Hell-fire! This is your punishment for what your hands committed.' Allah is not unjust to His servants.

8:52 Like Pharaoh's people and those that have gone before them, they disbelieved Allah's revelations. Therefore Allah will smite them in their sinfulness. Mighty is Allah and stern His retribution.

Allah does not withhold His favours from men until they change what is in their hearts. Allah hears all and knows all.

Like Pharaoh's people and those who have gone before them, they disbelieved the revelations of their Lord. We will destroy them in their sinfulness as We drowned Pharaoh's people. They were wicked men all.

The basest creatures in the sight of Allah are the faithless who will not believe; those who time after time violate their treaties with you and have no fear of Allah. If you capture them in battle discriminate between them and those that follow them, so that their followers may take warning.

If you fear treachery from any of your allies, you may retaliate by breaking off your treaty with them. Allah does not love the treacherous.

Let the unbelievers not think that they will escape Us.
8:60 They have not the power to do so. Muster against them all the men and cavalry at your disposal, so that you may strike

terror into the enemies of Allah and the faithful, and others besides them. All that you give for the cause of Allah shall be repaid you. You shall not be wronged.

If they incline to peace, make peace with them, and put *8:61* your trust in Allah. He hears all and knows all. Should they seek to deceive you, Allah is all-sufficient for you. He has made you strong with His help and rallied the faithful round you, making their hearts one. If you had given away all the riches of the earth, you could not have so united them: but Allah has united them. He is mighty and wise.

Prophet, Allah is your strength and the faithful who *8:64* follow you.

Prophet, rouse the faithful to arms. If there are twenty steadfast men among you, they shall vanquish two hundred; and if there are a hundred, they shall rout a thousand unbelievers, for they are devoid of understanding.

Allah has now lightened your burden, for He knows that you are weak. If there are a hundred steadfast men among you, they shall vanquish two hundred; and if there are a thousand, they shall, by Allah's will, defeat two thousand. Allah is with those that are steadfast.

A prophet may not take captives until he has fought and triumphed in his land. You[1] seek the chance gain of this world, but Allah desires for you the world to come. He is mighty and wise. Had there not been a previous sanction *8:68* from Allah, you would have been sternly punished for what you have taken. Enjoy, therefore, the good and lawful things which you have gained in war, and fear Allah. He is forgiving and merciful.

Prophet, say to those you have taken captive: 'If Allah finds goodness in your hearts, He will give you that which is better than what has been taken from you, and He will forgive you. Allah is forgiving and merciful.'

But if they seek to betray you, know they had already *8:71* betrayed Allah. Therefore He has made you triumph over them. Allah is wise and all-knowing.

1. Mohammed's followers.

8:72   Those that have embraced the faith and fled their homes, and fought for the cause of Allah with their wealth and their persons; and those that sheltered them and helped them, shall be friends to each other.

Those that have embraced the faith but have not fled their homes shall in no way become your friends until they too leave their city. But if they seek your help in the cause of your religion, it is your duty to aid them, except against a people you have a treaty with. Allah is cognizant of all your actions.

8:73   The unbelievers give aid to one another. If you do not do the same, there will be persecution in the land and great corruption.

Those that have embraced the faith and fled their homes and fought for the cause of Allah, and those that have sheltered them and helped them – they are the true believers. They shall receive mercy and a generous provision.

8:75   Those that have since embraced the faith and fled their homes to fight with you – they too are your brothers; although according to the Book of Allah those who are bound by ties of blood are nearest to one another. Allah has knowledge of all things.

REPENTANCE[1]

9:1   A DECLARATION of immunity by Allah and His apostle to the idolaters with whom you have made agreements:

For four months you shall go unmolested in the land. But know that you shall not escape the judgement of Allah, and that Allah will humble the unbelievers.

A proclamation to the people by Allah and His apostle on the day of the greater pilgrimage:

Allah and His apostle are free from obligation to the

1. This is the only chapter in the Koran which does not begin with the invocation 'In the Name of Allah, etc.' Traditional commentators regard it as a continuation of 'The Spoils'.

idolaters. If you repent it will be well with you; but if you give no heed, know that you shall not escape His judgement.

Proclaim a woeful punishment to the unbelievers, except 9:4 those idolaters who have honoured their treaties with you and aided none against you. With these keep faith, until their treaties have run their term. Allah loves the righteous.

When the sacred months¹ are over slay the idolaters wherever you find them. Arrest them, besiege them, and lie in ambush everywhere for them. If they repent and take to prayer and pay the alms-tax, let them go their way. Allah is forgiving and merciful.

If an idolater seeks asylum with you, give him protection so that he may hear the Word of Allah, and then convey him to safety. For the idolaters are ignorant men.

Allah and His apostle repose no trust in idolaters, save those with whom you have made treaties at the Sacred Mosque. So long as they keep faith with you, keep faith with them. Allah loves the righteous.

How can you trust them? If they prevail against you they 9:8 will respect neither agreements nor ties of kindred. They flatter you with their tongues, but their hearts abhor you. Most of them are evil-doers.

They sell Allah's revelations for trifling gain and debar others from His path. Evil is what they do. They break faith with the believers and set at nought all ties of kindred. Such are the transgressors.

If they repent and take to prayer and pay the alms-tax, they shall become your brothers in the faith. Thus We make plain Our revelations for men of understanding.

But if, after coming to terms with you, they break their oaths and revile your faith, make war on the leaders of unbelief – for no oaths are binding with them – so that they may desist.

Will you not fight against those who have broken their 9:13 oaths and conspired to banish the apostle? They were the first to attack you. Do you fear them? Surely Allah is more worthy of your fear, if you are true believers.

1. Shawal, Dhul-Qa'ada, Dhul-Hajja, and Muharram.

9:14 Make war on them: Allah will chastise them through you and humble them. He will grant you victory over them and heal the spirit of the faithful. He will take away all anger from their hearts: He shows mercy to whom He pleases. He is wise and all-knowing.

Did you imagine that you would be forsaken before Allah has had time to know those of you who have fought valiantly and served none but Him and His apostle and the faithful? Allah is cognizant of all your actions.

It ill becomes the idolaters to visit the mosques of Allah, for they are self-confessed unbelievers. Vain shall be their works, and in the fire of Hell they shall abide for ever.

None should visit the mosques of Allah except those who believe in Allah and the Last Day, attend to their prayers and pay the alms-tax and fear none but Allah. These shall be rightly guided.

9:19 Do you pretend that he who gives a drink to the pilgrims and pays a visit to the Sacred Mosque is as worthy as the man who believes in Allah and the Last Day and fights for Allah's cause? These are not held equal by Allah. He does not guide the wrongdoers.

Those that have embraced the faith and fled their homes and fought for Allah's cause with their wealth and their persons are held in higher regard by Allah. It is they who shall triumph. Their Lord has promised them joy and mercy, and gardens of eternal bliss where they shall dwell for ever. Allah's reward is great indeed.

Believers, do not befriend your fathers or your brothers if they choose unbelief in preference to faith. Wrongdoers are those that befriend them.

Say: 'If your fathers, your sons, your brothers, your wives, your tribes, the property you have acquired, the merchandise you fear may not be sold, and the homes you love, are dearer to you than Allah, His apostle and His cause, then wait until Allah shall fulfil His decree. Allah does not guide the evil-doers.'

9:25 Allah has been with you on many a battle-field. In the

Battle of Hunain[1] you set great store by your numbers, but they availed you nothing: the earth, for all its vastness, seemed to close in upon you and you turned your backs and fled. Then Allah caused His tranquillity[2] to descend upon 9:26 His apostle and the faithful: He sent to your aid invisible warriors and sternly punished the unbelievers. Thus were the infidels rewarded.

Yet Allah will show mercy to whom He will. He is forgiving and merciful.

Believers, know that the idolaters are unclean. Let them not approach the Sacred Mosque after this year is ended. If you fear poverty, Allah, if He pleases, will enrich you through His bounty. He is wise and all-knowing.

Fight against such of those to whom the Scriptures were given as believe neither in Allah nor the Last Day, who do not forbid what Allah and His apostle have forbidden, and do not embrace the true faith, until they pay tribute out of hand and are utterly subdued.

The Jews say Ezra is the son of Allah, while the Christ- 9:30 ians say the Messiah is the son of Allah. Such are their assertions, by which they imitate the infidels of old. Allah confound them! How perverse they are!

They worship their rabbis and their monks, and the Messiah the son of Mary, as gods besides Allah; though they were ordered to serve one God only. There is no god but Him. Exalted be He above those whom they deify beside Him!

They would extinguish the light of Allah with their mouths: but Allah seeks only to perfect His light, though the infidels abhor it.

It is He who has sent forth His apostle with guidance and the true faith to make it triumphant over all religions, however much the idolaters may dislike it.

Believers, many are the rabbis and the monks who de- 9:34 fraud men of their possessions and debar them from the path

---

1. Fought in A.D. 630. The Muslim army was 12,000 strong, the Meccans 4,000.
2. See Note 2, p. 275.

of Allah. Proclaim a woeful punishment to those that hoard
9:35 up gold and silver and do not spent it in Allah's cause. The
day will surely come when their treasures shall be heated in
the fire of Hell, and their foreheads, sides, and backs
branded with them. Their tormentors will say to them:
'These are the riches which you hoarded. Taste then the
punishment which is your due.'

Allah ordained the months twelve in number when He
created the heavens and the earth. Of these four are sacred,
according to the true faith. Therefore do not sin against
yourselves by violating them. But you may fight against the
idolaters in all these months since they themselves fight
against you in all of them. Know that Allah is with the
righteous.

The postponement of sacred months is a grossly impious
practice, in which the unbelievers are misguided. They allow
it one year and forbid it in the next, so that they may make
up for the months which Allah has sanctified, thus making
lawful what Allah has forbidden. Their foul acts seem fair
to them: Allah does not guide the unbelievers.

9:38 Believers, why is it that when it is said to you: 'March in
the cause of Allah,' you linger slothfully in the land? Are
you content with this life in preference to the life to come?
Few indeed are the blessings of this life, compared to those
of the life to come.

If you do not fight He will punish you sternly and replace
you by other men. You will in no way harm Him: for Allah
has power over all things.

9:40 If you do not help him,[1] Allah will help him as He helped
him when he was driven out by the unbelievers with one
other.[2] In the cave he said to his companion: 'Do not despair. Allah is with us.' Allah caused His tranquillity[3] to
descend upon him and sent to his aid invisible warriors, so
that he routed the unbelievers and exalted the Word of
Allah. Allah is mighty and wise.

1. Mohammed.
2. Abu-Bakr, later the first of the Rightly-guided Caliphs.
3. See Note 2, p. 275.

Whether unarmed or well-equipped, march on and fight *9:41* for the cause of Allah, with your wealth and your persons. This will be best for you, if you but knew it.

Had the gain been immediate or the journey short, they would have followed you[1]: but the distance seemed too far to them. Yet they will swear by Allah: 'Had we been able, we would have marched with you.' They bring ruin upon themselves. Allah knows that they are lying.

Allah forgive you! Why did you give them leave to stay *9:43* behind before you knew those who spoke the truth from those who invented false excuses?

Those that believe in Allah and the Last Day will not beg you to exempt them from fighting with their wealth and their persons. Allah best knows the righteous. Only those seek exemption who disbelieve in Allah and the Last Day and whose hearts are filled with doubt. They waver in their disbelief.

Had they intended to set forth with you, they would have prepared themselves for war. But Allah wished them to linger behind and held them back. They were bidden to stay with the weaklings.

Had they taken the field with you, they would have only *9:47* added to your burden. They would have wormed their way through your ranks, seeking to sow discord among the faithful: and amongst you there were some who would have gladly listened to them. Allah knows the evil-doers.

They had sought before this to sow dissension, and thought out plots against you. But in the end justice was done and the will of Allah triumphed, much as they disliked it.

Some of them say: 'Give us leave to stay behind, and do not expose us to temptation.' Surely they have already succumbed to temptation. The fire of Hell shall engulf the unbelievers.

If you meet with success, it grieves them; but if a disaster befalls you, they say: 'We have taken our precautions.' And they turn away, rejoicing.

Say: 'Nothing will befall us except what Allah has *9:51*

1. Mohammed.

ordained. He is our Guardian. In Allah let the faithful put their trust.'

9:52 Say: 'Are you waiting for anything to befall us except victory or martyrdom? We are waiting for Allah's scourge to overtake you, direct from Him or through ourselves. Wait if you will; we too are waiting.'

Say: 'Whether you give willingly or with reluctance, your offerings shall not be accepted from you; for you are wicked men.'

9:54 Their offerings shall not be accepted from them because they have denied Allah and His apostle. They pray half-heartedly and grudge their contributions to the cause.

Let neither their riches nor their children rouse your envy. Through these Allah seeks to punish them in this life, so that they shall die unbelievers.

They swear by Allah that they are believers like you. Yet they are not. They are afraid of you. If they could find a cave or shelter, or any hiding-place, they would run in frantic haste to seek refuge in it.

There are some among them who speak ill of you[1] concerning the distribution of alms. If a share is given them, they are contented: but if they receive nothing, they grow resentful.

9:59 Would that they were satisfied with what Allah and His apostle have given them, and would say: 'Allah is all-sufficient for us. He will provide for us from His own abundance, and so will His apostle. To Allah we will submit.'

Alms shall be used only for the advancement of Allah's cause, for the ransom of captives and debtors, and for distribution among the poor, the destitute, the wayfarers, those that are employed in collecting alms, and those that are converted to the faith. That is a duty enjoined by Allah. He is wise and all-knowing.

9:61 And there are others among them who speak ill of the Prophet, saying: 'He believes everything he hears.' Say: 'He hears only what is good for you. He believes in Allah

1. Mohammed.

and puts his trust in the faithful. He is a blessing to the true believers among you. Those that wrong the apostle of Allah shall be sternly punished.'

They swear in the name of Allah in order to please you. 9:62 But it is more just that they should please Allah and the Apostle, if they are true believers.

Are they not aware that the man who defies Allah and His apostle shall abide for ever in the fire of Hell? That surely is the supreme humiliation.

The hypocrites are afraid lest a Chapter be revealed about them, telling them what is in their hearts. Say: 'Scoff if you will; Allah will surely bring to light what you are dreading.'

If you question them, they will say: 'We were only jesting and making merry.' Say: 'Would you mock at Allah, His revelations, and His apostle? Make no excuses. You have bartered away your faith for unbelief. If We forgive some of you, We will punish others, for they are guilty men.'

Be they men or women, the hypocrites are all alike. They 9:67 enjoin what is evil, forbid what is just, and tighten their purse-strings. They forsook Allah and Allah forsook them. Surely the hypocrites are evil-doers.

Allah has promised the hypocrites, both men and women, and the unbelievers, the fire of Hell. They shall abide in it for ever: a sufficient recompense. The curse of Allah is upon them; theirs shall be a lasting torment.

Your ways are like the ways of those who have gone before you. They were mightier than you, and were blessed with greater riches and more children. Like them, you have enjoyed your earthly lot and, like them, you have engaged in idle talk. But vain were their works in this life, and vain they shall be in the life to come. They shall assuredly be lost.

Have they not heard the histories of those who have gone 9:70 before them? The fate of Noah's people and of Thamoud and Aad; of Abraham's people and the people of Midian and the Ruined Cities? Their apostles showed them veritable signs. Allah did not wrong them, but they wronged themselves.

9:71 The true believers, both men and women, are friends to each other. They enjoin what is just and forbid what is evil; they attend to their prayers and pay the alms-tax and obey Allah and His apostle. On these Allah will have mercy. He is mighty and wise.

Allah has promised the men and women who believe in Him gardens watered by running streams, in which they shall abide for ever. He has promised them goodly mansions in the gardens of Eden. And what is more, they shall have grace in His sight. That is the supreme triumph.

9:73 Prophet, make war on the unbelievers and the hypocrites and deal rigorously with them. Hell shall be their home: an evil fate.

They swear by Allah that they said nothing. Yet they uttered the word of unbelief and renounced Islam after embracing it. They sought to do what they could not attain. Yet they had no reason to be spiteful; except perhaps because Allah and His apostle had enriched them through His bounty. If they repent, it will indeed be better for them; but if they give no heed, Allah will sternly punish them both in this world and in the world to come. They have none to protect or help them.

Some of them made a covenant with Allah, saying: 'If Allah is bountiful to us, we will give alms and live like righteous men.' But when Allah had bestowed His favours on them they grew niggardly and, turning their backs, *9:77* hurried away. He has caused hypocrisy to reign in their hearts till the day they meet Him, because they have been untrue to the promise they made Him and because they have invented falsehoods.

Are they not aware that Allah knows what they conceal and what they talk about in secret? Are they not aware that Allah knows what is hidden? As for those that taunt the believers who give freely, and scoff at those who give according to their means, Allah will scoff at them. Theirs shall be a woeful punishment.

9:80 It is the same whether or not you beg forgiveness for them. If seventy times you beg forgiveness for them Allah will not forgive them, for they have denied Allah and His apostle. Allah does not guide the evil-doers.

Those that stayed at home were glad that they were left 9:81 behind by Allah's apostle, for they had no wish to fight for the cause of Allah with their wealth and their persons. They said to each other: 'Do not go to war, the heat is fierce.'

Say to them: 'More fierce is the heat of Hell-fire!' Would that they understood!

They shall laugh but little and shed many tears. Thus shall they be rewarded for their misdeeds.

If Allah brings you back in safety and some of them ask leave to march with you, say: 'You shall not march with me, nor shall you fight with me against my enemies. You chose to remain at home on the first occasion; therefore you shall now stay with those who remain behind.'

You shall not pray for their dead, nor shall you attend their burial. For they denied Allah and His apostle and remained sinners to the last.

Let neither their riches nor their children rouse your 9:85 envy. Through these Allah seeks to punish them in this life, so that they shall die unbelievers.

Whenever a Chapter was revealed, saying: 'Believe in Allah and fight with His apostle,' the rich among them asked you to excuse them, saying: 'Leave us with those who are to stay behind.'

They were content to be with those who stayed behind: a seal was set upon their hearts, leaving them bereft of understanding. But the Apostle and the men who shared his faith fought with their goods and their persons. These shall be rewarded with good things. These shall surely prosper. Allah has prepared for them gardens watered by running streams, in which they shall abide for ever. That is the supreme triumph.

Some Arabs of the desert came with excuses, begging 9:90 leave to stay behind; whilst those who denied Allah and His apostle remained idle at home. A woeful scourge shall fall on those of them that disbelieved.

9:91   It shall be no offence for the disabled, the sick, and those lacking the means to contribute to the war, to stay behind, if they are true to Allah and His apostle. The righteous shall not be blamed: Allah is forgiving and merciful. Nor shall those be blamed who, when they came to you demanding conveyances to the battle-front and you could find none to carry them, went away in tears grieving that they could take no part.

The real offenders are those that seek exemption although they are men of wealth. They are content to remain with those who stay behind. Allah has set a seal upon their hearts; they are devoid of understanding.

9:94   When you return they will apologize to you. Say: 'Make no excuses: we will not believe you. Allah has revealed to us the truth about you. He and His apostle are watching over all your actions. You shall return to Him who knows alike the visible and unseen, and He will declare to you what you have done.'

When you return they will appeal to you in Allah's name to pardon them. Let them be: they are unclean. Hell shall be their home, the punishment for their misdeeds.

They will swear to you in order to please you. But if you accept them, Allah will not accept the evil-doers.

The desert Arabs surpass the town-dwellers in unbelief and hypocrisy, and have more cause to be ignorant of the laws which Allah has revealed to His apostle. But Allah is wise and all-knowing.

9:98   Some desert Arabs regard what they give for the cause of Allah as a compulsory fine and wait for some misfortune to befall you. May ill-fortune befall them! Allah hears all and knows all.

Yet there are others among them who believe in Allah and the Last Day, and regard their offerings as a means of bringing them close to Allah and to the prayers of the Apostle. Indeed, closer they shall be brought; Allah will admit them to His mercy. He is forgiving and merciful.

9:100   As for those who led the way, the first of the *muhadjirs*[1]

1. Mohammed's early followers who fled with him to Medina.

and the *ansar*,[1] and those who nobly followed them, Allah is pleased with them and they with Him. He has prepared for them gardens watered by running streams, where they shall dwell for ever. That is the supreme triumph.

Some of the desert Arabs around you are hypocrites, 9:101 and so are some of the citizens of Medina. You do not know them, but We do. Twice We will chastise them: then they shall be sent a harrowing torment.

Others there are who have confessed their sins; their good works had been intermixed with evil. Perchance Allah will turn to them in mercy. He is forgiving and merciful. Take alms from them, so that they may thereby be cleansed and purified, and pray for them: for your prayers will give them comfort. Allah hears all and knows all.

Do they not know that Allah accepts the repentance of His servants and takes their alms, and that Allah is the Forgiving One, the Merciful?

Say: 'Do as you will. Allah will behold your works, and 9:105 so will His apostle and the faithful; then you shall return to Him who knows alike the invisible and the unseen, and He will declare to you all that you have done.'

There are yet others who must await Allah's decree. He will either punish or pardon them. Allah is wise and all-knowing.

And there are those who built a mosque from mischievous motives to spread unbelief and disunite the faithful, in expectation of him[2] who had made war on Allah and His apostle. They swear that their intentions were good, but Allah bears witness that they are lying. You shall not set foot in it. It is more fitting that you should pray in a mosque founded on piety from the very first. There you shall find men who would keep pure. Allah loves those that purify themselves.

Who is a better man, he who founds his house on the 9:109 fear of Allah and His good pleasure, or he who builds on the brink of a crumbling precipice, so that his house will

1. Mohammed's supporters in Medina.
2. Abu Amir.

fall with him into the fire of Hell? Allah does not guide the wrongdoers.

9:110 The edifice which they have built shall ever inspire their hearts with doubt, until their hearts are cut in pieces. Allah is wise and all-knowing.

Allah has purchased of the faithful their lives and worldly goods and in return has promised them the Garden. They will fight for His cause, slay, and be slain. Such is the true pledge which He has made them in the Torah, the Gospel and the Koran. And who is more true to his promise than Allah? Rejoice then in the bargain you have made. That is the supreme triumph.

Those that repent and those that serve Allah and praise Him; those that fast and those that kneel and prostrate themselves before Him; those that enjoin justice, forbid evil, and observe the commandments of Allah, shall be richly rewarded. Proclaim the good tidings to the faithful.

9:113 It is not for the Prophet or the believers to beg forgiveness for idolaters, even though they be related to them, after it has become manifest that they have earned the punishment of Hell. Abraham prayed for his father only to fulfil a promise he had made him. But when he realized he was an enemy of Allah, he disowned him. Yet Abraham was a compassionate and tender-hearted man.

Nor will Allah lead men astray after He has given them guidance until He has made plain to them all that they should avoid. Allah has knowledge of all things.

His is the kingdom of the heavens and the earth; He ordains life and death. You have none besides Allah to protect or help you.

Allah turned in mercy to the Prophet, the *muhadjirs* and the *ansar*, who stood by him in the hour of adversity, when some of them were on the point of losing heart. He turned to them in mercy. He took pity on them and was merciful.

9:118 He was also merciful to the three who had been left behind. So despondent were they that the earth, for all its vastness, and their own souls, seemed to close in upon them. They knew there was no refuge from Allah except in Him.

Therefore He turned to them in mercy, so that they might repent. Allah is the Forgiving One, the Merciful.

Believers, have fear of Allah and stand with those who 9:119 uphold the cause of truth. No cause have the people of Medina and the desert Arabs who dwell around them to forsake Allah's apostle or to jeopardize his life so as to safeguard their own; for they do not expose themselves to thirst or hunger or to any ordeal on account of the cause of Allah, nor do they stir a step which may provoke the unbelievers. Each loss they suffer at the enemy's hands shall be counted as a good deed in the sight of Allah: He will not deny the righteous their recompense. Each sum they give, be it small or large, and each journey they undertake, shall be noted down, so that Allah may requite them for their noblest deeds.

It is not right that all the faithful should go to war at once. 9:122 A band from each community should stay behind to instruct themselves in religion and admonish their men when they return, so that they may take heed.

Believers, make war on the infidels who dwell around you. Deal courteously with them. Know that Allah is with the righteous.

Whenever a Chapter is revealed, some of them ask: 'Whose faith will this increase?' It will surely increase the faith of the believers and give them joy. As for those whose hearts are diseased, it will add to their disbelief so that they shall die unbelievers.

Do they not see how every year they were afflicted once or twice? Yet they neither repent nor take warning. Whenever a Chapter is revealed, they glance at each other, asking: 'Is any one watching?' Then they turn away. Allah has turned away their hearts, for they are senseless men.

There has now come to you an apostle of your own, one who grieves at your sinfulness and is solicitous over you; one who is compassionate and merciful to true believers.

If they give no heed, say: 'Allah is all-sufficient for me. 9:129 There is no god but Him. In Him I have put my trust. He is the Lord of the Glorious Throne.'

THE COW

2:1 ALIF *lam mim*. This Book is not to be doubted. It is a guide for the righteous, who have faith in the unseen and are steadfast in prayer; who bestow in charity a part of what We have given them; who trust what has been revealed to you[1] and to others before you, and firmly believe in the life to come. These are rightly guided by their Lord; these shall surely triumph.

As for the unbelievers, whether you forewarn them or not, they will not have faith. Allah has set a seal upon their hearts and ears; their sight is dimmed and a grievous punishment awaits them.

2:8 There are some who declare: 'We believe in Allah and the Last Day,' yet they are no true believers. They seek to deceive Allah and those who believe in Him: but they deceive none save themselves, though they may not perceive it. There is a sickness in their hearts which Allah has increased: they shall be sternly punished for their hypocrisy.

When it is said to them: 'Do not commit evil in the land,' they reply: 'We do nothing but good.' But it is they who are the evil-doers, though they may not perceive it.

And when it is said to them: 'Believe as others believe,' they reply: 'Are we to believe as fools believe?' It is they who are the fools, if they but knew it!

2:14 When they meet the faithful, they declare: 'We, too, are believers.' But when they are alone with their devils they say to them: 'We follow none but you: we were only mocking.' Allah will mock at them and keep them long in sin, blundering blindly along.

Such are those that barter away guidance for error: they 2:17 profit nothing, nor are they on the right path. They are like one who kindled a fire, but as soon as it lit up all around him Allah put it out and he was left darkling: they do not see.

1. Mohammed.

Deaf, dumb, and blind, they shall never return to the right 2:18
path.

Or like those who, beneath a dark storm-cloud charged
with thunder and lightning, thrust their fingers in their ears
at the sound of every thunder-clap for fear of death (Allah
thus encompasses the unbelievers). The lightning almost
takes away their sight: whenever it flashes upon them they
walk on, but as soon as it darkens they stand still. Indeed,
if Allah pleased, He could take away their sight and hearing:
He has power over all things.

Men, serve your Lord, who has created you and those 2:21
who have gone before you, so that you may guard yourselves against evil; who has made the earth a bed for you and
the sky a dome, and has sent down water from the sky to
bring forth fruits for your sustenance. Do not knowingly
set up other gods beside Him.

If you doubt what We have revealed to Our servant, produce one chapter comparable to this Book. Call upon your
idols to assist you, if what you say be true. But if you fail (as
you are sure to fail) then guard yourselves against the fire
whose fuel is men and stones, prepared for the unbelievers.

Proclaim good tidings to those who have faith and do
good works. They shall dwell in gardens watered by running streams: whenever they are given fruit to eat they will
say: 'This is what we used to eat before,' for they shall be
given the like. Wedded to chaste virgins, they shall abide
there for ever.

Allah does not disdain to give a parable about a gnat or a 2:26
larger creature. The faithful know that it is the truth from
their Lord, but the unbelievers ask: 'What could Allah
mean by this parable?'

By such parables Allah misleads many and enlightens
many. But He misleads none except the evil-doers, who
break His covenant after accepting it and divide what he
has bidden to be united and commit evil in the land. Truly
these shall have much to lose.

How can you deny Allah? Did He not give you life 2:28
when you were dead, and will He not cause you to die

and then restore you to life? Will you not return to Him at last? He created for you all that the earth contains; then, ascending to the sky, fashioned it into seven heavens. He has knowledge of all things.

2:29

When your Lord said to the angels: 'I am placing on the earth one that shall rule as My deputy,' they replied: 'Will You put there one that will do evil and shed blood, when we have for so long sung Your praises and sanctified Your name?'

He said: 'I know what you do not know.'

He taught Adam the names of all things and then set them before the angels, saying: 'Tell Me the names of these, if what you say be true.'

2:32

'Glory to You,' they replied, 'we have no knowledge except that which You have given us. You alone are wise and all-knowing.'

Then said He to Adam: 'Tell them their names.' And when Adam had named them, He said: 'Did I not tell you that I know the secrets of heaven and earth, and all that you hide and all that you reveal?'

And when We said to the angels: 'Prostrate yourselves before Adam,' they all prostrated themselves except Satan, who in his pride refused and became an unbeliever.

To Adam We said: 'Dwell with your wife in Paradise and eat of its fruits to your hearts' content wherever you will. But never approach this tree or you shall both become transgressors.'

But Satan made them fall from Paradise and brought about their banishment. 'Go hence,' We said, 'and may your offspring be enemies to each other. The earth will for a while provide your sustenance and dwelling-place.'

2:37

Then Adam received commandments from his Lord, and his Lord relented towards him. He is the Forgiving One, the Merciful.

'Go down hence, all,' We said. 'When Our guidance is revealed those that accept it shall have nothing to fear or to regret; but those that deny and reject Our revelations shall be the heirs of Hell, and there they shall abide for ever.'

2:39

Children of Israel, remember the favours I have be- 2:40
stowed upon you. Keep your covenant, and I will be true to
Mine. Revere Me. Have faith in My revelations, which confirm your Scriptures, and do not be the first to deny them.
Fear Me, and do not sell My revelations for a paltry price.
Do not confound truth with falsehood, nor knowingly hide
the truth. Attend to your prayers, pay the alms-tax, and
worship with the worshippers. Would you enjoin righteousness on others and forget it yourselves? Yet you read
the Scriptures. Have you no sense?

Fortify yourselves with patience and prayer. This may
indeed be an exacting discipline, but not to the devout, who
know that they will meet their Lord and that to Him they
will return.

Children of Israel, remember the blessing I have be- 2:47
stowed on you, and that I have exalted you above the
nations. Guard yourselves against the day when every soul
will stand alone: when neither intercession nor ransom
shall be accepted from it, nor any help be given it.

Remember how We delivered you from Pharaoh's
people, who had oppressed you cruelly, slaying your sons
and sparing your daughters. Surely that was a great trial
from your Lord. We parted the sea for you and, taking you
to safety, drowned Pharaoh's men before your very eyes.
We communed with Moses for forty nights, but in his
absence you took up the calf and worshipped it, thus
committing evil. Yet after that We pardoned you, so that
you might give thanks.

We gave Moses the Scriptures and knowledge of right
and wrong, so that you might be rightly guided. Moses 2:54
said to his people: 'You have wronged yourselves, my
people, in worshipping the calf. Turn in repentance to your
Creator and slay the culprits. That will be best for you in
His sight.' And He relented towards you. He is the Forgiving One, the Merciful.

When you said to Moses: 'We will not believe in you
until we see Allah with our own eyes,' a thunderbolt struck
you whilst you were looking on. Then We revived 2:56

you from your stupor, so that you might give thanks.

2:57   We caused the clouds to draw their shadow over you and sent down for you manna and quails, saying: 'Eat of the good things We have given you.' Indeed, they[1] did not wrong Us, but they wronged themselves.

'Enter this city,' We said, 'and eat where you will to your hearts' content. Make your way reverently through the gates, saying: "We repent." We shall forgive you your sins and bestow abundance on the righteous among you.' But the wrongdoers perverted Our words and We let loose on them a scourge from heaven as a punishment for their misdeeds.

When Moses demanded water for his people We said to him: 'Strike the Rock with your staff.' Thereupon twelve springs gushed from the Rock, and each tribe knew their drinking-place. We said: 'Eat and drink of that which Allah has provided and do not corrupt the land with evil.'

2:61   'Moses,' you[1] said, 'we will no longer put up with this monotonous diet. Call on your Lord to give us some of the varied produce of the earth, green herbs and cucumbers, corn and lentils and onions.'

'What!' he answered. 'Would you exchange that which is good for what is worse? Go back to Egypt. There you shall find all that you have asked for.'

Shame and misery were stamped upon them[1] and they incurred the wrath of Allah; because they disbelieved His signs and slew His prophets unjustly; because they were rebels and transgressors.

Believers, Jews, Christians, and Sabaeans – whoever believes in Allah and the Last Day and does what is right – shall be rewarded by their Lord; they have nothing to fear or to regret.

2:63   We made a covenant with you[1] and raised the Mount above you, saying: 'Receive what We have given you with earnestness and bear in mind its precepts, that you may

1. The Israelites.

guard yourselves against evil.' Yet after that you turned 2:64
away, and but for Allah's grace and mercy you would have
surely been among the lost.

You have heard of those of you that broke the Sabbath.
We said to them: 'You shall be changed into detested apes.'
We made their fate an example to their own generation and
to those who followed them, and a lesson to the righteous.

When Moses said to his people: 'Allah commands you to
sacrifice a cow,' they replied: 'Are you making game of us?'

'Allah forbid that I should be so foolish!' he rejoined.

'Call on your Lord,' they said, 'to make known to us
what kind of cow she shall be,'

Moses replied: 'Your Lord says: "Let her be neither an
old cow nor a young heifer, but in between." Do, therefore, as you are bidden.'

'Call on your Lord,' they said, 'to make known to us
what her colour shall be.'

Moses replied: 'Your Lord says: "Let the cow be yellow,
a rich yellow pleasing to the eye."'

'Call on your Lord,' they said, 'to make known to us the 2:70
exact type of cow she shall be; for to us cows look all alike.
If Allah wills we shall be rightly guided.'

Moses replied: 'Your Lord says: "Let her be a healthy
cow, not worn out with ploughing the earth or watering
the field; a cow free from any blemish."'

'Now you have told us all,' they answered. And they
slaughtered a cow, after they had nearly failed to do so.

And when you slew a man and then fell out with one
another concerning him, Allah made known what you
concealed. We said: 'Strike the corpse with a piece of it.'
Thus Allah restores the dead to life and shows you His
signs, that you may grow in understanding.

Yet after that your hearts became as hard as rock or even 2:74
harder; for from some rocks rivers take their course: some
break asunder and water gushes from them: and others
tumble down through fear of Allah. Allah is not unaware
of what you do.

2:75 Do you[1] then hope that they[2] will believe in you, when some of them have already heard the Word of Allah and knowingly perverted it, although they understood its meaning?

When they meet the faithful they declare: 'We, too, are believers.' But when alone they say to each other: 'Must you preach to them what Allah has revealed to you? They will only dispute with you about it in your Lord's presence. Have you no sense?'

Do they not know that Allah has knowledge of all they hide and all that they reveal?

There are illiterate men among them who, ignorant of the Scriptures, know of nothing except lies and vague fancies. Woe to those that write the Scriptures with their own hands and then declare: 'This is from Allah,' in order to gain some paltry end. Woeful shall be their fate, because of what their hands have written, because of that which they have gained!

2:80 They declare: 'The Fire will never touch us – except for a few days.' Say: 'Did Allah make you such a promise – Allah will not break His promise – or do you assert about Him what you have no means of knowing?'

Truly, those that commit evil and become engrossed in sin are the heirs of Hell; in it they shall remain for ever. But those that have faith and do good works are the heirs of Paradise; for ever they shall abide in it.

When We made a covenant with the Israelites We said: 'Serve none but Allah. Show kindness to your parents, to your kinsfolk, to the orphans, and to the destitute. Exhort men to righteousness. Attend to your prayers and pay the alms-tax.' But you all broke your covenant except a few, and gave no heed.

And when We made a covenant with you We said: 'You shall not shed your kinsmen's blood or turn them out of their dwellings.' To this you consented and bore witness.
2:85 Yet there you were, slaying your own kinsfolk, and turning a number of them out of their dwellings, and helping

1. The believers are here addressed.　　2. The Jews.

others against them with sin and enmity in your hearts. Though had they come to you as captives, you would have ransomed them. Surely their expulsion was unlawful. Can you believe in one part of the Scriptures and deny another?

Those of you that act thus shall be rewarded with disgrace in this world and with a grievous punishment on the Day of Resurrection. Allah is watching over all your actions.

Such are they who buy the life of this world at the price *2:86* of the life to come. Their punishment shall not be lightened, nor shall they be helped.

To Moses We gave the Scriptures and after him We sent other apostles. We gave Jesus the son of Mary veritable signs and strengthened him with the Holy Spirit. Will you then scorn each apostle whose message does not suit your fancies, charging some with imposture and slaying others?

They say: 'Our hearts are sealed.' But Allah has cursed them for their unbelief. They have but little faith.

And now that a Book confirming their own has come to them from Allah, they deny it, although they know it to be the truth and have long prayed for help against the unbelievers. May Allah's curse be upon the infidels! Evil is *2:90* that for which they have bartered away their souls. To deny Allah's own revelation, grudging that He should reveal His bounty to whom He chooses from His servants! They have incurred Allah's most inexorable wrath. An ignominious punishment awaits the unbelievers.

When it is said to them: 'Believe in what Allah has revealed,' they reply: 'We believe in what was revealed to *us*.' But they deny what has since been revealed, although it is the truth, corroborating their own scriptures.

Say: 'Why did you kill the prophets of Allah, if you are true believers? Moses came to you with veritable signs, but in his absence you worshipped the calf and committed evil.'

When We made a covenant with you and raised the *2:93* Mount above you, saying: 'Take what We have given you

341

with willing hearts and hear Our commandments,' you[1] replied: 'We hear but disobey.'

For their unbelief they were made to drink the calf into their very hearts.[2] Say: 'Evil is that to which your faith prompts you if you are indeed believers.'

2:94   Say: 'If Allah's Everlasting Mansions are for you alone, to the exclusion of all others, then you must long for death if your claim be true!'

But they will never long for death, because of what they did; for Allah knows the evil-doers. Indeed, you will find that they love this life more than other men: more than the pagans do. Each one of them would willingly live a thousand years.

But even if their lives were indeed prolonged, that will surely not save them from Our scourge. Allah is watching over all their actions.

Say: 'Whoever is an enemy of Gabriel' (who has by Allah's grace revealed to you[3] the Koran as a guide and joyful tidings for the faithful, confirming previous scrip-
2:98   tures) 'whoever is an enemy of Allah, His angels, or His apostles, or of Gabriel or Michael, shall make Allah Himself his enemy: Allah is the enemy of the unbelievers.'

We have sent down to you clear revelations: none will deny them except the evil-doers. What! Whenever they make a covenant, must some of them cast it aside? Most of them are unbelievers.

And now that an apostle has come to them from Allah confirming their own Scriptures, some of those to whom the Scriptures were given cast off the Book of Allah behind
2:102   their backs as though they know nothing and accept what the devils tell of Solomon's kingdom. Not that Solomon was an unbeliever: it is the devils who are unbelievers. They teach men witchcraft and that which was revealed to the angels Harut and Marut in Babylon. Yet they never instruct any man without saying to him beforehand: 'We have been sent to tempt you; do not renounce your faith.'

1. Lit., they.   2. Cf. Exodus xxxii, 20.   3. Mohammed.

From these two, men learn a charm by which they can create discord between husband and wife, although they can harm none with what they learn except by Allah's leave. They learn, indeed, what harms them and does not profit them; yet they know full well that anyone who engaged in that traffic would have no share in the life to come. Vile is that for which they have sold their souls, if they but knew it! Had they embraced the Faith and kept from evil, far better for them would His reward have been, if they but knew it. *2:103*

Believers, do not say to Our apostle *Ra'ina*, but say *Undhurna*.[1] Take heed; the unbelievers shall be sternly punished.

The unbelievers among the People of the Book, and the pagans, resent that any blessings should have been sent down to you from your Lord. But Allah chooses whom He will for His mercy. His grace is infinite.

If We abrogate any verse or cause it to be forgotten We will replace it by a better one or one similar. Do you not know that Allah has power over all things? Do you not know that it is to Allah that the kingdom of the heavens and the earth belongs, and that there is none besides Him to protect or help you? *2:107*

Would you demand of your apostle that which was once demanded of Moses? He that barters faith for unbelief has surely strayed from the right path.

Many of the People of the Book wish, through envy, to lead you back to unbelief, now that you have embraced the faith and the truth has been made plain to them. Forgive them and bear with them until Allah makes known His will. He has power over all things.

Attend to your prayers and pay the alms-tax. Your good works shall be rewarded by Allah. He is watching over all your actions.

They declare: 'None but Jews and Christians shall be *2:111*

1. These words mean 'Listen to us' and 'Look upon us' respectively; but in Hebrew the sound of the first conveys the sense, 'Our evil one'. Jewish Arabs used the expression as a derisive pun.

admitted to Paradise.' Such are their wishful fancies. Say: 2:112 'Let us have your proof, if what you say be true.' Indeed, those that surrender themselves to Allah and do good works shall be rewarded· by their Lord: they shall have nothing to fear or to regret.

The Jews say the Christians are misguided, and the Christians say it is the Jews who are misguided. Yet they both read the Scriptures. And the pagans say the same of both. Allah will judge their disputes on the Day of Resurrection.

Who is more wicked than the men who seek to destroy the mosques of Allah and forbid His name to be mentioned in them, when it behoves these men to enter them with fear in their hearts? They shall be held to shame in this world and sternly punished in the next.

2:115 To Allah belongs the east and the west. Whichever way you turn there is the face of Allah. He is omnipresent and all-knowing.

They say: 'Allah has begotten a son.' Allah forbid! His is what the heavens and the earth contain; all things are obedient to Him. Creator of the heavens and the earth! When He decrees a thing, He need only say 'Be,' and it is.

The ignorant ask: 'Why does Allah not speak to us or give us a sign?' The same demand was made by those before them: their hearts are all alike. But to those whose faith is firm We have already revealed Our signs.

2:119 We have sent you forth to proclaim the truth and to give warning. You shall not be questioned about the heirs of Hell.

You will please neither the Christians nor the Jews unless you follow their faith. Say: 'The guidance of Allah is the only guidance.' And if after all the knowledge you have been given you yield to their desires, there shall be none to 2:121 help or protect you from the wrath of Allah. Those to whom We have given the Book, and who read it as it ought to be read, truly believe in it; those that deny it shall assuredly be lost.

Children of Israel, remember that I have bestowed fav- 2:122
ours upon you and exalted you above the nations. Fear the
day when every soul shall stand alone: when neither intercession nor ransom shall be accepted from it, nor any help
be given it.

When his Lord put Abraham to the proof by enjoining
on him certain commandments and Abraham fulfilled
them, He said: 'I have appointed you a leader of mankind.'

'And what of my descendants?' asked Abraham.

'My covenant,' said He, 'does not apply to the evil-
doers.'

We made the House¹ a resort and a sanctuary for man- 2:125
kind, saying: 'Make the place where Abraham stood a
house of worship.' We enjoined Abraham and Ishmael to
cleanse Our House for those who walk round it, who
meditate in it, and who kneel and prostrate themselves.

'Lord,' said Abraham, 'make this a land of peace and bestow plenty upon its people, those of them that believe in
Allah and the Last Day.'

'As for those that do not,' He answered, 'I shall let them
live awhile and then drag them to the scourge of Hell. Evil
shall be their fate.'

Abraham and Ishmael built the House and dedicated it, 2:127
saying: 'Accept this from us, Lord. You hear all and You
know all. Lord, make us submissive to You; make of our
descendants a nation that will submit to You. Teach us our
rites of worship and turn to us mercifully; You are forgiving and merciful. Lord, send forth to them an apostle of
their own who shall declare to them Your revelations and
instruct them in the Scriptures and in wisdom and purify
them of sin. You are the Mighty, the Wise One.'

Who but a foolish man would renounce the faith of
Abraham? We chose him in this world, and in the world to
come he shall dwell among the righteous. When his Lord 2:131
said to him: 'Submit,' he answered: 'I have submitted
to the Lord of the Creation.'

1. The Ka'ba at Mecca.

2:132   Abraham enjoined the faith on his children, and so did Jacob, saying: 'My children, Allah has chosen for you the true faith. Do not depart this life except as men who have submitted to Him.'

Were you present when death came to Jacob? He said to his children: 'What will you worship when I am gone?' They replied: 'We will worship your God and the God of your forefathers Abraham and Ishmael and Isaac: the One God. To Him we will surrender ourselves.'

That nation have passed away. Theirs is what they did, and yours what you have done. You shall not be questioned about their actions.

2:135   They say: 'Accept the Jewish or the Christian faith and you shall be rightly guided.'

Say: 'By no means! We believe in the faith of Abraham, the upright one. He was no idolater.'

Say: 'We believe in Allah and that which is revealed to us; in what was revealed to Abraham, Ishmael, Isaac, Jacob, and the tribes; to Moses and Jesus and the other prophets by their Lord. We make no distinction amongst any of them, and to Allah we have surrendered ourselves.'

If they accept your faith they shall be rightly guided; if they reject it, they shall surely be in schism. Against them Allah is your all-sufficient defender. He hears all and knows all.

We take on Allah's own dye. And who has a better dye than Allah's? Him will we worship.

2:139   Say: 'Would you dispute with us about Him, who is our Lord and your Lord? We shall both be judged by our works. To Him alone we are devoted.'

Do you claim that Abraham, Ishmael, Isaac, Jacob, and the tribes, were all Jews or Christians? Do you know better than Allah Himself? Who is more wicked than the man who hides a testimony which he has received from Allah? He is watching over all your actions.

2:141   That nation have passed away. Theirs is what they did and yours what you have done. You shall not be questioned about their actions.

The foolish will ask: 'What has made them change their 2:142
qiblah?'[1]

Say: 'The east and the west are Allah's. He guides whom
He will to the right path.'

We have made you a just nation, so that you may testify
against mankind and that your own apostle may testify
against you. We decreed your former *qiblah* only in order
that We might know the Apostle's true adherents and
those who were to disown him. It was indeed a hard test,
but not to those whom Allah guided. He was not to make
your faith fruitless. He is compassionate and merciful to
men.

Many a time We have seen you turn your face towards 2:144
heaven. We will make you turn towards a *qiblah* that will
please you. Turn towards the Holy Mosque; wherever you
be face towards it.

Those to whom the Scriptures were given know this to
be the truth from their Lord. Allah is watching over all
their actions. But even if you gave them every proof they
would not accept your *qiblah*, nor would you accept theirs;
nor would any of their sects accept the *qiblah* of the other.
If after all the knowledge you have been given you yield to
their desires, then you will surely become an evil-doer.

Those to whom We gave the Scriptures know Our apostle
as they know their own sons. But some of them deliberately
conceal the truth. This is the truth from your Lord: therefore never doubt it.

Each one has a goal towards which he turns. But wherever you be, emulate one another in good works. Allah
will bring you all before Him. He has power over all things.

Whichever way you depart, face towards the Holy
Mosque. This is surely the truth from your Lord. Allah is
never heedless of what you do.

Whichever way you depart, face towards the Holy
Mosque: and wherever you are, face towards it, so that men 2:150
will have no cause to reproach you, except the evil-doers

1. The direction which the Muslim faces in prayer. At first the believers were ordered to turn towards Jerusalem, afterwards to Mecca.

among them. Have no fear of them; fear Me, so that I may perfect My favour to you and that you may be rightly guided.

2:151   Thus We have sent forth to you an apostle of your own who will recite to you Our revelations and purify you of sin, who will instruct you in the Book and in wisdom and teach you that of which you have no knowledge. Remember Me, then, and I will remember you. Give thanks to Me and never deny Me.

Believers, fortify yourselves with patience and prayer. Allah is with those that are patient. Do not say that those who were slain in the cause of Allah are dead; they are alive, although you are not aware of them.

We shall test your steadfastness with fear and famine, with loss of life and property and crops. Give good news to 2:156 those who endure with fortitude; who in adversity say: 'We belong to Allah, and to Him we shall return.' On such men will be Allah's blessing and mercy; such men are rightly guided.

Safa and Marwa[1] are beacons of Allah. It shall be no offence for the pilgrim or the visitor to the Sacred House to walk around them. He that does good of his own accord shall be rewarded by Allah. Allah has knowledge of all things.

Those that hide the clear proofs and the guidance We have revealed after We have proclaimed them in the Scriptures, shall be cursed by Allah and man; except those that repent and mend their ways and make known the truth. Towards them I shall relent. I am the Relenting One, the Merciful. But the infidels who die unbelievers shall incur the curse of Allah, the angels, and those who invoke damnation. Under it they shall remain for ever; their punishment shall not be lightened, nor shall they be reprieved.

Your God is one God. There is no god but Him. He is the Compassionate, the Merciful.

2:164   In the creation of the heavens and the earth; in the alternation of night and day; in the ships that sail the ocean

1. Two hills near Mecca, held in reverence by pagan Arabs.

with cargoes beneficial to man; in the water which Allah sends down from the sky and with which He revives the dead earth, dispersing over it all manner of beasts; in the movements of the winds, and in the clouds that are driven between earth and sky: surely in these there are signs for rational men.

Yet there are some who worship idols, bestowing on 2:165 them the adoration due to Allah (though the love of Allah is stronger in the faithful). But when they face their punishment the wrongdoers will know that might is His alone and that Allah is stern in retribution. When they face their punishment the leaders will disown their followers, and the bonds which now unite them will break asunder. Those who followed them will say: 'Could we but live again, we would disown them as they have now disowned us.'

Thus Allah will show them their own works. They shall sigh with remorse, but shall never come out of the Fire.

Men, eat of what is lawful and wholesome on the earth 2:168 and do not walk in Satan's footsteps, for he is your sworn enemy. He enjoins you to commit evil and indecency and to assert about Allah what you do not know.

When it is said to them: 'Follow what Allah has revealed,' they reply: 'We will follow that which our fathers practised,' even though their fathers were senseless men lacking in guidance.

In preaching to the unbelievers the Apostle may be compared to one who calls on beasts that can hear nothing except a shout and a cry. Deaf, dumb, and blind, they understand nothing.

Believers, eat of the wholesome things with which We have provided you and give thanks to Allah, if it is He whom you worship.

He has forbidden you carrion, blood, and the flesh of 2:173 swine; also any flesh that is consecrated other than in the name of Allah. But whoever is constrained to eat any of these, not intending to sin or transgress, incurs no guilt. Allah is forgiving and merciful.

2:174   Those that suppress any part of the Scriptures which Allah has revealed in order to gain some paltry end shall swallow nothing but fire into their bellies. On the Day of Resurrection Allah will neither speak to them nor purify them. Theirs shall be a woeful punishment.

Such are those that barter guidance for error and forgiveness for punishment. How steadfastly they seek the fire of Hell! That is because Allah has revealed the Book with the truth; those that disagree about it are in schism.

2:177   Righteousness does not consist in whether you face towards the east or the west. The righteous man is he who believes in Allah and the Last Day, in the angels and the Scriptures and the prophets; who for the love of Allah gives his wealth to his kinsfolk, to the orphans, to the needy, to the wayfarers and to the beggars, and for the redemption of captives; who attends to his prayers and pays the alms-tax; who is true to his promises and steadfast in trial and adversity and in times of war. Such are the true believers; such are the God-fearing.

2:178   Believers, retaliation is decreed for you in bloodshed: a free man for a free man, a slave for a slave, and a female for a female. He who is pardoned by his aggrieved brother shall be prosecuted according to usage and shall pay him a liberal fine. This is a merciful dispensation from your Lord. He that transgresses thereafter shall be sternly punished.

Men of understanding! In retaliation you have a safeguard for your lives; perchance you will guard yourselves against evil.

It is decreed that when death approaches, those of you that leave property shall bequeath it equitably to parents and kindred. This is a duty incumbent on the righteous. He that alters a will after hearing it shall be accountable for his crime. Allah hears all and knows all.

He that suspects an error or an injustice on the part of a testator and brings about a settlement among the parties incurs no guilt. Allah is forgiving and merciful.

2:183   Believers, fasting is decreed for you as it was decreed for those before you; perchance you will guard yourselves

against evil. Fast a certain number of days, but if any one of 2:184
you is ill or on a journey let him fast a similar number of
days later on; and for those that can afford it there is a
ransom: the feeding of a poor man. He that does good of
his own account shall be well rewarded; but to fast is better
for you, if you but knew it.

In the month of Ramadhan the Koran was revealed, a
book of guidance with proofs of guidance distinguishing
right from wrong. Therefore whoever of you is present in
that month let him fast. But he who is ill or on a journey
shall fast a similar number of days later on.

Allah desires your well-being, not your discomfort. He
desires you to fast the whole month so that you may magnify Him and render thanks to Him for giving you His
guidance.

When My servants question you about Me, tell them that 2:186
I am near. I answer the prayer of the suppliant when he calls
to Me; therefore let them answer My call and put their trust
in Me, that they may be rightly guided.

It is now lawful for you to lie with your wives on the
night of the fast; they are a comfort to you as you are to
them. Allah knew that you were deceiving yourselves. He
has relented towards you and pardoned you. Therefore you
may now lie with them and seek what Allah has ordained
for you. Eat and drink until you can tell a white thread
from a black one in the light of the coming dawn. Then resume the fast till nightfall and do not approach them, but
stay at your prayers in the mosques.

These are the bounds set by Allah: do not come near
them. Thus He makes known His revelations to mankind
that they may guard themselves against evil.

Do not usurp one another's property by unjust means,
nor bribe with it the judges in order that you may knowingly and wrongfully deprive others of their possessions.

They question you about the phases of the moon. Say: 2:189
'They are seasons fixed for mankind and for the pilgrimage.'

Righteousness does not consist in entering your

dwellings from the back.[1] The righteous man is he that fears Allah. Enter your dwellings by their doors and fear Allah, so that you may prosper.

2:190   Fight for the sake of Allah those that fight against you, but do not attack them first. Allah does not love the aggressors.

Kill them wherever you find them. Drive them out of the places from which they drove you. Idolatry is worse than carnage. But do not fight them within the precincts of the Holy Mosque unless they attack you there; if they attack you put them to the sword. Thus shall the unbelievers be rewarded: but if they mend their ways, know that Allah is forgiving and merciful.

Fight against them until idolatry is no more and Allah's religion reigns supreme. But if they mend their ways, fight none except the evil-doers.

2:194   A sacred month for a sacred month: sacred things too are subject to retaliation. If any one attacks you, attack him as he attacked you. Have fear of Allah, and know that Allah is with the righteous.

Give generously for the cause of Allah and do not with your own hands cast yourselves into destruction. Be charitable; Allah loves the charitable.

2:196   Make the pilgrimage and visit the Sacred House for His sake. If you cannot, send such offerings as you can afford and do not shave your heads until the offerings have reached their destination. But if any of you is ill or suffers from an ailment of the head, he must pay a ransom either by fasting or by alms-giving or by offering a sacrifice.

If in peacetime anyone of you combines the visit with the pilgrimage, he must offer such gifts as he can afford; but if he lacks the means let him fast three days during the pilgrimage and seven when he has returned; that is, ten days in all. That is incumbent on him whose family are not present at the Holy Mosque. Have fear of Allah: know that He is stern in retribution.

1. It was the custom of pagan Arabs, on returning from pilgrimage, to enter their homes from the back.

Make the pilgrimage in the appointed months. He that 2:197
intends to perform it in those months must abstain from
sexual intercourse, obscene language, and acrimonious disputes while on pilgrimage. Allah is aware of whatever good
you do. Provide yourselves well: the best provision is
piety. Fear Me, then, you that are endowed with understanding.

It shall be no offence for you to seek the bounty of your
Lord by trading. When you come running from Arafat[1]
remember Allah as you approach the sacred monument.
Remember Him that gave you guidance when you were in
error. Then go out from the place whence the pilgrims
will go out and implore the forgiveness of Allah. He is
forgiving and merciful. And when you have fulfilled your
sacred duties, remember Allah as you remember your forefathers or with deeper reverence.

There are some who say: 'Lord, give us abundance in
this world.' These shall have no share in the world to come.
But there are others who say: 'Lord, give us what is good 2:201
both in this world and in the next and keep us from the fire
of Hell.' These shall have a share of the reward. Swift is the
reckoning of Allah.

Give glory to Allah on the appointed days. He that de-
parts on the second day incurs no sin, nor does he who
stays longer, if he truly fears Allah. Have fear of Allah,
then, and know that you shall all be gathered before
Him.

There are some men whose views on this life please you:
they even call on Allah to vouch for that which is in their
hearts; whereas in fact they are the deadliest of your opponents. No sooner do they leave you than they hasten to
commit evil in the land, destroying crops and cattle. Allah
does not love evil.

When it is said to them: 'Have fear of Allah,' vanity
carries them off to sin. Hell shall be enough for them, a
dismal resting-place.

But there are others who would give away their lives in 2:207

1. Near Mecca.

order to find favour with Allah. Allah is compassionate to His servants.

2:208   Believers, submit all of you to Allah and do not walk in Satan's footsteps; he is your sworn enemy. If you lapse back after the veritable signs that have been shown to you, know that Allah is mighty and wise.

Are they waiting for Allah to come down to them in the shadow of a cloud, with all the angels? Their fate will have been settled then. To Allah shall all things return.

Ask the Israelites how many veritable signs We have given them. He that tampers with the boon of Allah after it has been bestowed on him shall be severely punished. Allah is stern in retribution.

For the unbelievers the life of this world is decked with all manner of temptations. They scoff at the faithful, but those that fear Allah shall be above them on the Day of Resurrection. Allah gives without measure to whom He will.

2:213   Mankind were once one nation. Then Allah sent forth prophets to give them good news and to warn them, and with these He sent down the Book with the truth, that it might judge the disputes of men. (None disputed it save those to whom it was given, and that was through envy of one another, after veritable signs had been vouchsafed them.) So Allah guided by His will those who believed in the truth which had been disputed. Allah guides whom He will to the right path.

2:214   Did you suppose that you would go to Paradise untouched by the suffering which was endured by those before you? Affliction and adversity befell them; and so battered were they that each apostle, and those who shared his faith, cried out: 'When will the help of Allah come?' His help is ever near.

They will ask you about alms-giving. Say: 'Whatever you bestow in charity must go to your parents and to your kinsfolk, to the orphan and to the poor man and to the stranger. Allah is aware of whatever good you do.'

2:216   Fighting is obligatory for you, much as you dislike it.

But you may hate a thing although it is good for you, and love a thing although it is bad for you. Allah knows, but you do not.

They ask you about the sacred month. Say: 'To fight in 2:217 this month is a grave offence; but to debar others from the path of Allah, to deny Him, and to expel His worshippers from the Holy Mosque, is far more grave in His sight. Idolatry is worse than carnage.'

They will not cease to fight against you until they force you to renounce your faith – if they are able. But whoever of you recants and dies an unbeliever, his works shall come to nothing in this world and in the world to come. Such men shall be the tenants of Hell, and there they shall abide for ever.

Those that have embraced the faith and those that have fled their land and fought for the cause of Allah, may hope for Allah's mercy. Allah is forgiving and merciful.

They ask you about drinking and gambling. Say: 'There 2:219 is great harm in both, although they have some benefit for men; but their harm is far greater than their benefit.'

They ask you what they should give in alms. Say: 'What you can spare.' Thus Allah makes plain to you His revelations, so that you may reflect upon this world and the hereafter.

They question you concerning orphans. Say: 'To deal justly with them is best. If you mix their affairs with yours, remember they are your brothers. Allah knows the just from the unjust. If Allah pleased, He could afflict you. He is mighty and wise.'

You shall not wed pagan women, unless they embrace the 2:221 faith. A believing slave-girl is better than an idolatress, although she may please you. Nor shall you wed idolaters, unless they embrace the faith. A believing slave is better than an idolater, although he may please you. These call you to Hell-fire; but Allah calls you, by His will, to Paradise and to forgiveness. He makes plain His revelations to mankind, so that they may take heed.

They ask you about menstruation. Say: 'It is an 2:222

indisposition. Keep aloof from women during their menstrual periods and do not touch them until they are clean again. Then have intercourse with them as Allah enjoined you. Allah loves those that turn to Him in repentance and strive to keep themselves clean.'

2:223 Women are your fields: go, then, into your fields as you please. Do good works and fear Allah. Bear in mind that you shall meet Him. Give good news to the believers.

Do not make Allah the subject of your oaths when you swear that you will deal justly and keep from evil and make peace among men. Allah knows all and hears all. He will not call you to account for that which is inadvertent in your oaths. But He will take you to task for that which is intended in your hearts. Allah is forgiving and lenient.

Those that renounce their wives on oath must wait four months. If they change their mind, Allah is forgiving and merciful; but if they decide to divorce them, know that He hears all and knows all.

2:228 Divorced women must wait, keeping themselves from men, three menstrual courses. It is unlawful for them, if they believe in Allah and the Last Day, to hide what He has created in their wombs: in which case their husbands would do well to take them back, should they desire reconciliation.

Women shall with justice have rights similar to those exercised against them, although men have a status above women. Allah is mighty and wise.

2:229 Divorce[1] may be pronounced twice, and then a woman must be retained in honour or allowed to go with kindness. It is unlawful for husbands to take from them anything they have given them, unless both fear that they may not be able to keep within the bounds set by Allah; in which case it shall be no offence for either of them if the wife ransom herself.

These are the bounds set by Allah; do not transgress them. Those that transgress the bounds of Allah are wrongdoers.

1. Revocable divorce, or the renunciation of one's wife on oath.

If a man divorce[1] his wife, he cannot remarry her until 2:230 she has wedded another man and been divorced by him; in which case it shall be no offence for either of them to return to the other, if they think that they can keep within the limits set by Allah.

Such are the bounds of Allah. He makes them plain to men of understanding.

When you have renounced your wives and they have 2:231 reached the end of their waiting period, either retain them in honour or let them go with kindness. But you shall not retain them in order to harm them or to wrong them. Whoever does this wrongs his own soul.

Do not make game of Allah's revelations. Remember the favours He has bestowed upon you, and the Book and the wisdom which He has revealed for your instruction. Fear Allah and know that He has knowledge of all things.

If a man has renounced his wife and she has reached the end of her waiting period, do not prevent her from remarrying her husband if they have come to an honourable agreement. This is enjoined on every one of you who believes in Allah and the Last Day; it is more honourable for you and more chaste. Allah knows, but you do not.

Mothers shall give suck to their children for two whole 2:233 years if the father wishes the sucking to be completed. They must be maintained and clothed in a reasonable manner by the father of the child. None should be charged with more than one can bear. A mother should not be allowed to suffer on account of her child, nor should a father on account of his child. The same duties devolve upon the father's heir. But if, after consultation, they choose by mutual consent to wean the child, they shall incur no guilt. Nor shall it be any offence for you if you prefer to have a nurse for your children, provided that you pay her what you promise, according to usage. Have fear of Allah and know that He is cognizant of all your actions.

Widows shall wait, keeping themselves apart from men, 2:234 for four months and ten days after their husbands' death.

1. By pronouncing the formula 'I divorce you' for the third time.

When they have reached the end of their waiting period, it shall be no offence for you to let them do whatever they choose for themselves, provided that it is decent. Allah is cognizant of all your actions.

2:235 It shall be no offence for you openly to propose marriage to such women or to cherish them in your hearts. Allah knows that you will remember them. Do not arrange to meet them in secret, and if you do, speak to them honourably. But you shall not consummate the marriage before the end of their waiting period. Know that Allah has knowledge of all your thoughts. Therefore take heed and bear in mind that Allah is forgiving and lenient.

2:236 It shall be no offence for you to divorce your wives before the marriage is consummated or the dowry settled. Provide for them with fairness; the rich man according to his means and the poor man according to his. This is binding on righteous men. If you divorce them before the marriage is consummated, but after their dowry has been settled, give them the half of their dowry, unless they or the husband agree to forgo it. But it is more proper that the husband should forgo it. Do not forget to show kindness to each other. Allah observes your actions.

Attend regularly to your prayers, including the middle prayer, and stand up with all devotion before Allah. When you are exposed to danger pray while riding or on foot; and when you are restored to safety remember Allah, as He has taught you what you did not know.

2:240 You shall bequeath your widows a year's maintenance without causing them to leave their homes; but if they leave of their own accord, no blame shall be attached to you for any course they may deem fit to pursue. Allah is mighty and wise. Reasonable provision should also be made for divorced women. That is incumbent on righteous men.

Thus Allah makes known to you His revelations that you may grow in understanding.

2:243 Consider those that fled the country in their thousands for fear of death. Allah said to them: 'You shall perish,' and then He brought them back to life. Surely Allah is bountiful to mankind, but most men do not give thanks.

Fight for the cause of Allah and bear in mind that He 2:244 hears all and knows all.

Who will grant Allah a generous loan? He will repay him many times over. It is Allah who enriches and makes poor. To Him you shall all return.

Have you not heard of what the leaders of the Israelites demanded of one of their prophets after the death of Moses? 'Anoint for us a king,' they said, 'and we will fight for the cause of Allah.'

He replied: 'What if you refuse to fight, when ordered so to do?'

'Why should we refuse to fight for the cause of Allah,' they replied, 'when we and all our children have been driven from our dwellings?'

But when at last they were ordered to fight, they all refused, except a few of them. Allah knows the evil-doers.

Their prophet said to them: 'Allah has appointed Saul to 2:247 be your king.' But they replied: 'Should he be given the kingship, when we are more deserving of it than he? Besides, he is not rich at all.'

He said: 'Allah has chosen him to rule over you and made him grow in wisdom and in stature. Allah gives His sovereignty to whom He will. He is munificent and all-knowing.'

Their prophet also said to them: 'The advent of the Ark shall be the portent of his reign. Therein shall be tranquillity[1] from your Lord, and the relics which the House of Moses and the House of Aaron left behind. It will be borne by the angels. That will be a sign for you, if you are true believers.'

And when Saul marched out with his army, he said: 2:249 'Allah will put you to the proof at a certain river. He that drinks from it shall cease to be my soldier, but he that does

1. See Note 2, p. 275.

not drink from it, or contents himself with a taste of it in the hollow of his hand, shall fight by my side.'[1]

But they all drank from it, except a few of them. And when Saul had crossed the river with those who shared his faith, they said: 'We have no power this day against Goliath and his warriors.'

But those of them who believed that they would meet Allah on Judgement-day replied: 'Many a small band has, by Allah's grace, vanquished a mighty army. Allah is with those who endure with fortitude.'

2:250 When they met Goliath and his warriors they cried: 'Lord, fill our hearts with steadfastness. Make us firm of foot and help us against the unbelievers.'

By Allah's will they routed them. David slew Goliath, and Allah bestowed on him sovereignty and wisdom and taught him what He pleased. Had Allah not defeated some by the might of others, the earth would have been utterly corrupted. But Allah is bountiful to His creatures.

Such are the revelations of Allah. We recite them to you 2:253 in all truth, for you are one of Our messengers. Of these messengers We have exalted some above others. To some Allah spoke directly; others He raised to a lofty status. We gave Jesus the son of Mary veritable signs and strengthened him with the Holy Spirit. Had Allah pleased, those who succeeded them would not have fought against one another after the veritable signs had been given them. But they disagreed among themselves; some had faith and others had none. Yet had Allah pleased they would not have fought against one another. Allah does what He will.

Believers, bestow in alms a part of what We have given you before that day arrives when there shall be neither trading nor friendship nor intercession. Truly, it is the unbelievers who are the wrongdoers.

2:255 Allah: there is no god but Him, the Living, the Eternal One.[2] Neither slumber nor sleep overtakes Him. His is what the heavens and the earth contain. Who can intercede

---

1. Cf. Judges vii.
2. The phrase is similar to *Hai we Qayyam*, in the Old Testament.

with Him except by His permission? He knows what is before and behind men. They can grasp only that part of His knowledge which He wills. His throne is as vast as the heavens and the earth, and the preservation of both does not weary Him. He is the Exalted, the Immense One.

There shall be no compulsion in religion. True guidance 2:256 is now distinct from error. He that renounces idol-worship and puts his faith in Allah shall grasp a firm handle that will never break. Allah hears all and knows all.

Allah is the Patron of the faithful. He leads them from darkness to the light. As for the unbelievers, their patrons are false gods, who lead them from light to darkness. They are the heirs of Hell and shall abide in it for ever.

Have you not heard of him who argued with Abraham 2:258 about his Lord because He had bestowed on him the Kingdom? Abraham said: 'My Lord is He who has power to give life and to cause death.'

'I, too,' replied the other, 'have power to give life and to cause death.'

'Allah brings up the sun from the east,' said Abraham. 'Bring it up yourself from the west.'

The unbeliever was confounded. Allah does not guide the evil-doers.

Or of him, who, when passing by a ruined and desolate 2:259 city, remarked: 'How can Allah give life to this city, now that it is dead?' Thereupon Allah caused him to die, and after a hundred years brought him back to life.

'How long have you stayed away?' asked Allah.

'A day,' he replied, 'or a few hours.'

'Know, then,' said Allah, 'that you have stayed away a hundred years. Yet look at your food and drink: they have not rotted. And look at the bones of your ass. We will make you a sign to mankind: see how We will raise them and clothe them with flesh.'

And when it had all become manifest to him, he said: 'I know now that Allah has power over all things.'

When Abraham said: 'Show me, Lord, how You raise 2:260 the dead,' He replied: 'Have you no faith?'

'Yes,' said Abraham, 'but I wish to reassure my heart.'

'Take four birds,' said He, 'draw them to you, and cut their bodies to pieces. Scatter them over the mountain-tops, then call them. They will come swiftly to you. Know that Allah is mighty and wise.'

2:261   He that gives his wealth for the cause of Allah is like a grain of corn which brings forth seven ears, each bearing a hundred grains. Allah gives abundance to whom He will; He is munificent and all-knowing.

Those that give their wealth for the cause of Allah and do not follow their almsgiving with taunts and insults shall be rewarded by their Lord; they shall have nothing to fear or to regret.

2:263   A kind word with forgiveness is better than charity followed by insult. Allah is self-sufficient and indulgent.

Believers, do not mar your almsgiving with taunts and mischief-making, like those who spend their wealth for the sake of ostentation and believe neither in Allah nor in the Last Day. Such men are like a rock covered with earth: a shower falls upon it and leaves it hard and bare. They shall gain nothing from their works. Allah does not guide the unbelievers.

But those that give away their wealth from a desire to please Allah and to reassure their own souls are like a garden on a hill-side: if a shower falls upon it, it yields up twice its normal crop; and if no rain falls upon it, it is watered by the dew. Allah takes cognizance of all your actions.

2:266   Would any one of you, being a man well-advanced in age with helpless children to support, wish to have his garden – a garden planted with palm-trees, vines and all manner of fruits, and watered by running streams – blasted and consumed by a fiery whirlwind?

Thus Allah makes plain to you His revelations, so that you may give thought.

2:267   Believers, give in alms of the wealth you have lawfully earned and of that which We have brought out of the earth for you; not worthless things which you yourselves would only reluctantly accept. Know that Allah is self-sufficient and glorious.

Satan threatens you with poverty and orders you to *2:268* commit what is indecent. But Allah promises you His forgiveness and His bounty. Allah is munificent and all-knowing.

He gives wisdom to whom He will; and he that receives the gift of wisdom is rich indeed. Yet none except men of sense bear this in mind.

Whatever alms you give and whatever vows you make are known to Allah. The evil-doers shall have none to help them.

To be charitable in public is good, but to give alms to the poor in private is better and will atone for some of your sins. Allah has knowledge of all your actions.

It is not for you to guide them. Allah gives guidance to *2:272* whom He will.

Whatever alms you give shall rebound to your own advantage, provided that you give them for the love of Allah. And whatever alms you give shall be paid back to you in full: you shall not be wronged.

As for those needy men who, being wholly preoccupied with fighting for the cause of Allah, cannot travel in the land in quest of trading ventures: the ignorant take them for men of wealth on account of their modest behaviour. But you can recognize them by their look – they never importune men for alms. Whatever alms you give are known to Allah.

Those that give alms by day and by night, in private and in public, shall be rewarded by their Lord. They have nothing to fear or to regret.

Those that live on usury shall rise up before Allah like *2:275* men whom Satan has demented by his touch; for they claim that usury is like trading. But Allah has permitted trading and forbidden usury. He that receives an admonition from his Lord and mends his ways may keep what he has already earned; his fate is in the hands of Allah. But he that pays no heed shall be consigned to Hell-fire and shall remain in it for ever.

2:276   Allah has laid His curse on usury and blessed almsgiving with increase. He bears no love for the impious and the sinful.

Those that have faith and do good works, attend to their prayers and pay the alms-tax, will be rewarded by their Lord and will have nothing to fear or to regret.

Believers, have fear of Allah and waive what is still due to you from usury, if your faith be true; or war shall be declared against you by Allah and His apostle. If you repent, you may retain your principal, suffering no loss and causing loss to none.

If your debtor be in straits, grant him a delay until he can discharge his debt; but if you waive the sum as alms it will be better for you, if you but knew it.

Fear the day when you shall all return to Allah; when every soul shall be requited according to its deserts. None shall be wronged.

2:282   Believers, when you contract a debt for a fixed period, put it in writing. Let a scribe write it down for you with fairness; no scribe should refuse to write as Allah has taught him. Therefore let him write; and let the debtor dictate, fearing Allah his Lord and not diminishing the sum he owes. If the debtor be a feeble-minded or ignorant person, or one who cannot dictate, let his guardian dictate for him in fairness. Call in two male witnesses from among you, but if two men cannot be found, then one man and two women whom you judge fit to act as witnesses; so that if either of them commit an error, the other will remember. Witnesses must not refuse to give evidence if called upon to do so. So do not fail to put your debts in writing, be they small or big, together with the date of payment. This is more just in the sight of Allah; it ensures accuracy in testifying and is the best way to remove all doubt. But if the transaction in hand be a bargain concluded on the spot, it is no offence for you if you do not commit it to writing.

See that witnesses are present when you barter with one another, and let no harm be done to either scribe or witness. If you harm them you shall commit a transgression. Have fear of Allah, who teaches you; He has knowledge of all things.

If you are travelling the road and a scribe cannot be found, then let pledges be taken. If anyone of you entrusts another with a pledge, let the trustee restore the pledge to its owner; and let him fear Allah, his Lord. 2:283

You shall not withhold testimony. He that withholds it is a transgressor. Allah has knowledge of all your actions.

To Allah belongs all that the heavens and the earth contain. Whether you reveal your thoughts or hide them, Allah will bring you to account for them. He will forgive whom He will and punish whom He pleases; He has power over all things.

The Apostle believes in what has been revealed to him by his Lord, and so do the faithful. They all believe in Allah and His angels, His scriptures, and His apostles: We discriminate against none of His apostles. They say: 'We hear and obey. Grant us your forgiveness, Lord; to You we shall all return. Allah does not charge a soul with more than it 2:286 can bear. It shall be requited for whatever good and whatever evil it has done. Lord, do not be angry with us if we forget or lapse into error. Lord, do not lay on us the burden You laid on those before us. Lord, do not charge us with more than we can bear. Pardon us, forgive us our sins, and have mercy upon us. You alone are our Protector. Give us victory over the unbelievers.'

In the Name of Allah, the Compassionate, the Merciful

4:1 MEN, have fear of your Lord, who created you from a single soul. From that soul He created its mate, and through them He bestrewed the earth with countless men and women.

Fear Allah, in whose name you plead with one another, and honour the mothers who bore you. Allah is ever watching over you.

4:2 Give orphans the property which belongs to them. Do not exchange their valuables for worthless things or cheat them of their possessions; for this would surely be a great sin. If you fear that you cannot treat orphans[1] with fairness, then you may marry other women who seem good to you: two, three, or four of them. But if you fear that you cannot maintain equality among them, marry one only or any slave-girls you may own. This will make it easier for you to avoid injustice.

Give women their dowry as a free gift; but if they choose to make over to you a part of it, you may regard it as lawfully yours.

Do not give the feeble-minded the property with which Allah has entrusted you for their support; but maintain and clothe them with its proceeds, and give them good advice.

4:6 Put orphans to the test until they reach a marriageable age. If you find them capable of sound judgement, hand over to them their property, and do not deprive them of it by squandering it before they come of age.

Let the rich guardian not touch the property of his orphan ward; and let him who is poor use no more than a fair portion of it for his own advantage.

When you hand over to them their property, call in some witnesses; Allah takes sufficient account of all your actions.

1. Orphan girls.

Men shall have a share in what their parents and kinsmen 4:7
leave; and women shall have a share in what their parents
and kinsmen leave: whether it be little or much, they are
legally entitled to their share.

If relatives, orphans, or needy men are present at the
division of an inheritance, give them, too, a share of it, and
speak to them kind words.

Let those who are solicitous about the welfare of their
young children after their own death take care not to
wrong orphans. Let them fear Allah and speak for justice.

Those that devour the property of orphans unjustly, 4:10
swallow fire into their bellies; they shall burn in the flames
of Hell.

Allah has thus enjoined you concerning your children:

A male shall inherit twice as much as a female. If there be
more than two girls, they shall have two-thirds of the inheritance; but if there be one only, she shall inherit the half.
Parents shall inherit a sixth each, if the deceased have a
child; but if he leave no children and his parents be his heirs,
his mother shall have a third. If he have two brothers, his
mother shall have a sixth after payment of his debts and any
legacies he may have bequeathed.

You may wonder whether your parents or your children
are more beneficial to you. But this is the law of Allah; He
is wise and all-knowing.

You shall inherit the half of your wives' estate if they die 4:12
childless. If they leave children, a quarter of their estate
shall be yours after payment of their debts and any legacies
they may have bequeathed.

Your wives shall inherit one quarter of your estate if you
die childless. If you leave children, they shall inherit one-
eighth, after payment of your debts and any legacies you
may have bequeathed.

If a man or a woman leave neither children nor parents
and have a brother or a sister, they shall each inherit one-
sixth. If there be more, they shall equally share the third of
the estate, after payment of debts and any legacies that may
have been bequeathed, without prejudice to the rights of

the heirs. That is a commandment from Allah. He is gracious and all-knowing.

4:13 Such are the bounds set by Allah. He that obeys Allah and His apostle shall dwell for ever in gardens watered by running streams. That is the supreme triumph. But he that defies Allah and His apostle and transgresses His bounds, shall be cast into Hell-fire and shall abide in it for ever. A shameful punishment awaits him.

If any of your women commit fornication, call in four witnesses from among yourselves against them; if they testify to their guilt confine them to their houses till death overtakes them or till Allah finds another way for them.

If two men among you commit indecency punish them both. If they repent and mend their ways, let them be. Allah is forgiving and merciful.

4:17 Allah forgives those who commit evil in ignorance and then quickly turn to Him in repentance. He will pardon them. Allah is wise and all-knowing. But Allah will not forgive those who do evil all their lives and, when death comes to them, say: 'Now we repent!' Nor will He forgive those who die unbelievers. For these We have prepared a woeful scourge.

Believers, it is unlawful for you to inherit the women of your deceased kinsmen against their will, or to bar them from re-marrying, in order that you may force them to give up a part of what you have given them, unless they be guilty of a proven crime. Treat them with kindness; for even if you do not love them, it may well be that you may dislike a thing which Allah has meant for your own good.

If you wish to divorce a woman in order to wed another, do not take from her the dowry you have given her even if it be a talent of gold. That would be improper and grossly unjust; for how can you take it back when you have lain with each other and entered into a firm contract?

Henceforth you shall not marry the women who were married to your fathers. That was an evil practice, indecent and abominable.

4:23 You are forbidden to take in marriage your mothers,

your daughters, your sisters, your paternal and maternal aunts, the daughters of your brothers and sisters, your foster-mothers, your foster sisters, the mothers of your wives, your step-daughters who are in your charge, born of the wives with whom you have lain (it is no offence for you to marry your step-daughters if you have not consummated your marriage with their mothers), and the wives of your own begotten sons. Henceforth you are also forbidden to take in marriage two sisters at one and the same time. Allah is forgiving and merciful.

You are also forbidden to take in marriage married wo- 4:24 men, except captives whom you own as slaves. Such is the decree of Allah. All women other than these are lawful to you, provided you seek them with your wealth in modest conduct, not in fornication. Give them their dowry for the enjoyment you have had of them as a duty; but it shall be no offence for you to make any other agreement among yourselves after you have fulfilled your duty. Allah is wise and all-knowing.

If any one of you cannot afford to marry a free believing 4:25 woman, let him marry a slave-girl who is a believer (Allah best knows your faith: you are born one of another). Marry them with the permission of their masters and give them their dowry in all justice, provided they are honourable and chaste and have not entertained other men. If after marriage they commit adultery, they shall suffer half the penalty inflicted upon free adulteresss. Such is the law for those of you who fear to commit sin: but if you abstain, it will be better for you. Allah is forgiving and merciful.

Allah desires to make this known to you and to guide you along the paths of those who have gone before you, and to turn to you in mercy. He is wise and all-knowing.

Allah seeks to forgive you, but those who follow their own appetites wish to see you far astray. Allah would lighten your burdens, for man was created weak.

Believers, do not consume your wealth among yourselves 4:29 in vanity, but rather trade with it by mutual consent.

You shall not kill one another. Allah is merciful, but he

4:30 that does that through wickedness and injustice shall be burnt in Hell-fire. That is no difficult thing for Allah.

If you avoid the enormities you are forbidden, We shall pardon your evil deeds and admit you with all honour to Paradise. Do not covet the favours by which Allah has exalted some of you above others. Men as well as women shall be rewarded for their labours. Rather implore Allah to bestow on you His gifts. Allah has knowledge of all things.

To every parent and kinsman We have appointed heirs who will inherit from him. As for those with whom you have entered into agreements, let them, too, have their due bequests. Allah bears witness to all things.

4:34 Men have authority over women because Allah has made the one superior to the other, and because they spend their wealth to maintain them. Good women are obedient. They guard their unseen parts because Allah has guarded them. As for those from whom you fear disobedience, admonish them and send them to beds apart and beat them. Then if they obey you, take no further action against them. Allah is high, supreme.

4:35 If you fear a breach between a man and his wife, appoint an arbiter from his people and another from hers. If they wish to be reconciled Allah will bring them together again. Allah is wise and all-knowing.

Serve Allah and associate none with Him. Show kindness to your parents and your kindred, to the orphans and to the needy, to your near and distant neighbours, to your fellow-travellers, to the wayfarers, and to the slaves whom you own. Allah does not love arrogant and boastful men, who are themselves niggardly and enjoin others to be niggardly also; who conceal the riches which Allah of His bounty has bestowed upon them (We have prepared a shameful punishment for the unbelievers); and who spend their wealth for the sake of ostentation, believing neither in Allah nor in the Last Day. He that chooses Satan for his friend, an evil friend has he.

4:39 What harm could befall them if they believed in Allah

and the Last Day and gave in alms of that which He has bestowed on them? Allah knows them all.

Not by an atom's weight will Allah wrong any man. He 4:40 that does a good deed shall be repaid twofold. Allah will bestow on him a rich recompense.

How will it be when We produce a witness from every nation and call upon you to testify against them? On that day those who disbelieved and disobeyed the Apostle will wish that they were levelled into dust; they shall hide nothing from Allah.

Believers, do not approach your prayers when you are 4:43 drunk, but wait till you can grasp the meaning of your words; nor when you are polluted – unless you are travelling the road – until you have washed yourselves. If you are ill and cannot wash yourselves; or, if you have relieved yourselves or had intercourse with women while travelling and can find no water, take some clean sand and rub your faces and your hands with it. Allah is benignant and forgiving.

Consider those to whom a portion of the Scriptures was 4:44 given. They purchase error for themselves and wish to see you led astray. But Allah best knows your enemies. You need none else to protect or help you.

Some Jews take words out of their context and say to the Apostle: 'We hear, but disobey. May you be bereft of hearing! *Ra'ina*!' – thus distorting the phrase with their tongues and reviling the true faith. But if they said: 'We hear and obey: hear us and *undhurna*,'[1] it would be better and more proper for them. Allah has cursed them in their unbelief. They have no faith, except a few of them.

You to whom the Scriptures were given! Believe in that 4:47 which We have revealed, confirming your own scriptures, before We obliterate your faces and turn them backward, or lay Our curse on you as We laid it on the Sabbath-breakers. What Allah ordains shall be accomplished.

1. These words mean 'Listen to us' and 'Look upon us respectively; but in seventh-century Judaeo-Arabic the sound of the first conveyed the sense, 'Our evil one'. Jewish Arabs may have used the expression as a derisive pun.

4:48 Allah will not forgive those who serve other gods besides Him; but He will forgive whom He will for other sins. He that serves other gods besides Him is guilty of a heinous sin.

Have you seen those who think themselves pure? Allah purifies whom He will. They shall not be wronged the husk of a date-stone.

See how they invent falsehoods about Allah. This in itself is a most grievous sin.

Consider those to whom a portion of the Scriptures was given. They believe in idols and false gods and say of the infidels: 'These are better guided than the believers.' These are they on whom Allah has laid His curse. He who is cursed by Allah has none to help him.

Will they have a share in the Kingdom? If so, they will not give so much as the speck on a date-stone to other men.

4:54 Do they envy others what Allah has of His bounty given them? We gave Abraham's descendants scriptures and prophethood, and an illustrious kingdom. Some believe in him,[1] but others reject him. Sufficient scourge is the fire of Hell.

Those that deny Our revelations We will burn in Hell-fire. No sooner will their skins be consumed than We shall give them other skins, so that they may truly taste Our scourge. Allah is mighty and wise.

As for those that have faith and do good works, We shall admit them to gardens watered by running streams, where, wedded to chaste virgins, they shall abide for ever. We shall admit them to a cool shade.

Allah commands you to hand back your trusts to their rightful owners, and to pass judgement upon men with fairness. Noble is that to which Allah exhorts you. He hears all and observes all.

4:59 Believers, obey Allah and the Apostle and those in authority among you. Should you disagree about anything refer it to Allah and the Apostle, if you truly believe in

1. Mohammed.

Allah and the Last Day. This will in the end be better and more just.

Have you seen those who profess to believe in what has 4:60 been revealed to you and to other prophets before you? They seek the judgement of false gods, although they are bidden to deny them. Satan would lead them far astray.

When it is said to them: 'Come to be judged by that which Allah has revealed and by the Apostle,' the hypocrites turn to you a deaf ear. But how would it be if some disaster befell them on account of what their hands committed? They would come to you swearing in the name of Allah that they desired nothing but amity and conciliation. But Allah knows the secret thoughts of these men. Let them be. Admonish them and sternly rebuke them.

We sent forth Our apostles so that men should do their bidding by Our leave. If, when they wronged themselves, they had come to you imploring Allah's pardon, and if you had sought of Allah forgiveness for them, they would have found Him forgiving and merciful.

But they will not – I swear by your Lord – they will not be 4:6 true believers until they seek your arbitration in their disputes. Then they will not doubt the justice of your verdicts and will submit to you entirely.

Had We commanded them to lay down their lives or to flee their country, only a few would have obeyed Us. Yet, had they done Our bidding, it would have been better for them and their faith would have been strengthened. We would have bestowed on them a rich reward and guided them to a straight path.

He that obeys Allah and the Apostle shall dwell with the prophet and saints, the martyrs and righteous men whom Allah has favoured. He shall have gracious companions.

Such is the bounty of Allah. He well knows how to reward you.

Believers, be ever on your guard. March in detachments or in one body. There are some men among you who lag be- 4:72 hind, so that if a disaster befell you, they would say: 'Allah has been gracious to us; we were not present with them.'

4:73 But if, by Allah's grace, you were successful, they would say, as though there was no friendship between them and you: 'Would that we had been with them! We should have surely won a great victory.'

Let those who would exchange the life of this world for the hereafter, fight for the cause of Allah; whether they die or conquer, We shall richly reward them.

And how should you not fight for the cause of Allah, and for the helpless old men, women, and children[1] who say: 'Deliver us, Lord, from this city of wrongdoers; send forth to us a guardian from Your presence; send to us one that will help us'?

The true believers fight for the cause of Allah, but the infidels fight for idols. Fight then against the friends of Satan. Satan's cunning is weak indeed.

4:77 Mark those to whom it has been said: 'Lay down your arms; recite your prayers and pay the alms-tax.' When they were ordered to fight, some of them feared man as much as Allah or even more. 'Lord,' they said, 'why do You bid us fight? Could you not give us a brief respite?'

Say: 'Trifling are the pleasures of this life. The hereafter is better for those who would keep from evil. You shall not *4:78* be wronged the husk of a date-stone. Wherever you be, death will overtake you: though you put yourselves in lofty towers.'

When they are blessed with good fortune, they say: 'This is from Allah.' But when evil befalls them, they say 'The fault was yours.'[2]

Say to them: 'All is from Allah!'

What has come over these men that they should show such lack of understanding?

Whatever good befalls you, man, it is from Allah: and whatever ill from yourself.

We have sent you forth as an apostle to mankind. Allah is your all-sufficient witness.

4:80 He that obeys the Apostle obeys Allah Himself. As for

1. In Mecca.   2. Mohammed's.

374

those that pay no heed to you, know then that We have not sent you to be their keeper.

They promise to obey you: but as soon as they leave you 4:81 a number of them plot in secret to do otherwise than what you bade them. Allah takes note of all their plots. Therefore let them be, and put your trust in Allah. He is your all-sufficient guardian.

Will they not ponder on the Koran? If it had not come from Allah, they could have surely found in it many contradictions.

When they hear any news, good or bad, they at once make it known to all and sundry; whereas if they reported it to the Apostle and to their other leaders, those who sought news could learn it from them. But for Allah's grace and mercy, all but a few of you would have followed Satan.

Therefore fight for the cause of Allah. You are accountable for none but yourself. Rouse the faithful: perchance Allah will defeat the unbelievers. He is mightier and more truculent than they.

He that mediates in a good cause shall gain by his media- 4:85 tion; but he that mediates in a bad cause shall be held accountable for its evil. Allah controls all things.

If a man greets you, let your greeting be better than his – or at least return his greeting. Allah keeps count of all things.

Allah: there is no god but Him. He will gather you all together on the Day of Resurrection: that day is sure to come. And whose is a truer word than Allah's?

Why are you thus divided concerning the hypocrites, when Allah Himself has cast them off on account of their misdeeds? Would you guide those whom Allah has caused to err? He whom Allah has led astray cannot be guided.

They would have you disbelieve as they themselves have done, so that you may be all alike. Do not befriend them until they have fled their homes for the cause of Allah. If they desert you, seize them and put them to death wherever you find them. Look for neither friends nor helpers among them except those who seek refuge with your allies or come 4:90

over to you because their hearts forbid them to fight against you or against their own people. Had Allah pleased, He would have given them power over you, so that they would have taken arms against you. Therefore, if they keep away from you and cease their hostility and offer you peace, Allah bids you not to harm them.

4:91 Others you will find who seek security from you as well as from their own people. Whenever they are called back to idol-worship they plunge into it headlong. If these do not keep their distance from you, if they neither offer you peace nor cease their hostilities against you, lay hold of them and kill them wherever you find them. Over such men We give you absolute authority.

4:92 It is unlawful for a believer to kill another believer except by accident. He that accidentally kills a believer must free one Muslim slave and pay blood-money to the family of the victim, unless they choose to give it away in alms. If the victim be a Muslim from a hostile tribe, the penalty is the freeing of one Muslim slave. But if the victim be a member of an allied tribe, then blood-money must be paid to his family and a Muslim slave set free. If a man cannot afford to do this, he must fast two consecutive months. Such is the penance imposed by Allah: He is wise and all-knowing.

4:93 He that kills a believer by design shall burn in Hell for ever. He shall incur the wrath of Allah, who will lay His curse on him and prepare for him a woeful scourge.

Believers, show discernment when you go to fight for the cause of Allah, and do not say to those that offer you peace: 'You are not believers,' – seeking the chance booty of this world; for in the world to come there are abundant gains. Such was your custom in days gone by, but now Allah has bestowed on you His grace. Therefore show discernment; for Allah is cognizant of all your actions.

4:95 The believers who stay at home – apart from those that suffer from a grave impediment – are not equal to those who fight for the cause of Allah with their goods and their persons. Allah has given those that fight with their goods and their persons a higher rank than those who stay at home. He has promised all a good reward; but far richer is the recompense of those who fight for Him: rank of His 4:96 own bestowal, forgiveness, and mercy. Allah is forgiving and merciful.

The angels will ask the men whom they carry off while steeped in sin: 'What were you doing?' 'We were oppressed in our land,' they will reply. The angels will say: 'Was not the earth of Allah spacious enough for you to fly for refuge in it?' Hell shall be their home: an evil fate.

As for the helpless men, women, and children who have neither the strength nor the means to escape, Allah may pardon them: He is benignant and forgiving.

He that flies his homeland for the cause of Allah shall find numerous places of refuge in the land and great abundance. He that leaves his dwelling to fight for Allah and His apostle and is then overtaken by death, shall be rewarded by Allah. Allah is forgiving and merciful.

It is no offence for you to shorten your prayers when travelling the road if you fear that the unbelievers may attack you. The unbelievers are your sworn enemies.

When you (Prophet), are with the faithful, conducting 4:102 their prayers, let one party of them rise up to pray with you, armed with their weapons. After making their prostrations, let them withdraw to the rear and then let another party who have not prayed come forward and pray with you; and let these also be on their guard, armed with their weapons. It would much please the unbelievers if you neglected your arms and your baggage, so that they could swoop upon you with one assault. But it is no offence for you to lay aside your arms when overtaken by heavy rain or stricken with an illness, although you must be always on your guard. Allah has prepared a shameful punishment for the unbelievers.

When your prayers are ended, remember Allah standing, sitting, and lying down. Attend regularly to your prayers so long as you are safe: for prayer is a duty incumbent on the faithful, to be conducted at appointed hours.

Seek out your enemies relentlessly. If you have suffered, 4:104

they too have suffered: but you at least hope to receive from Allah what they cannot hope for. Allah is wise and all-knowing.

4:105 We have revealed to you the Book with the truth, so that you may arbitrate among men by that which Allah has shown you. You shall not plead for traitors. Implore Allah's forgiveness: He is forgiving and merciful. Nor shall you plead for those who betray their own souls; Allah does not love the treacherous or the sinful.

They seek to hide themselves from men, but they cannot hide themselves from Allah. He is with them when they utter in secret what does not please Him: He has knowledge of all their actions.

Yes, you may plead for them in this life, but who will plead for them with Allah on the Day of Resurrection? Who will be their defender?

He that does evil or wrongs his own soul and then seeks pardon of Allah, will find Allah forgiving and merciful.

He that commits sin commits it against his own soul. Allah is wise and all-knowing.

4:112 He that commits an offence or a crime and charges an innocent man with it, shall bear the guilt of calumny and gross injustice.

But for Allah's grace and mercy you would have been led astray by some of them. They deceive none but themselves, nor can they do you any harm.

Allah has revealed to you the Book and His wisdom and taught you what you did not know before. Allah's goodness to you has been great indeed.

There is no virtue in much of their counsels: only in his who enjoins charity, kindness, and peace among men. He that does this to please Allah shall be richly rewarded.

He that disobeys the Apostle after Our guidance has been revealed to him and follows a path other than that of the faithful, shall be given what he has chosen. We will cast him into Hell: a dismal end.

4:116 Allah will not forgive idolatry. He will forgive whom He will all other sins. He that serves other gods besides Allah has strayed far from the truth.

The pagans pray to females: they pray to a rebellious 4:117 Satan. But Allah has laid His curse on Satan, for he had said: 'I shall entice a number of Your servants and lead them astray. I shall arouse in them vain desires and order them to slit the ears of cattle. I shall order them to tamper with Allah's creation.' Indeed, he that chooses Satan rather than Allah for his protector ruins himself beyond redemption.

He makes promises and stirs up in them vain desires; he makes them promises only to deceive them. Hell shall be their home: from it they shall find no refuge.

But those that have faith and do good works shall be ad- 4:122 mitted to gardens watered by running streams, and there they shall abide for ever. Such is the true promise of Allah: and whose is a truer word than Allah's?

It shall not be in accordance with your wishes, nor shall it be as the People of the Book wish. He that does evil shall be requited with evil: there shall be none to protect or help him. But the believers who do good works, whether men or women, shall enter the gardens of Paradise. They shall not suffer the least injustice.

And who has a nobler religion than the man who sur- 4:125 renders himself to Allah, does what is right, and follows the faith of saintly Abraham, whom Allah Himself chose to be His friend?

To Allah belongs all that the heavens and the earth contain. He has knowledge of all things.

They consult you concerning women. Say: 'Allah has instructed you about them, and so has the Book, which has been proclaimed to you, concerning the orphan girls whom you deny their lawful rights and refuse to marry; also regarding helpless children. He has instructed you to deal justly with orphans. Allah has knowledge of all the good you do.'

If a woman fear ill-treatment or desertion on the part of 4:128

her husband, it shall be no offence for them to seek a mutual agreement, for agreement is best. Man is prone to avarice. But if you do what is right and guard yourselves against evil, know then that Allah is cognizant of all your actions.

4:129   Try as you may, you cannot treat all your wives impartially. Do not set yourself altogether against any of them, leaving her, as it were, in suspense. If you do what is right and guard yourselves against evil, you will find Allah forgiving and merciful. If you separate, Allah will compensate you both out of His own abundance: He is munificent and wise.

4:131   To Allah belongs all that the heavens and the earth contain. We exhort you, as We have exhorted those to whom the Book was given before you, to fear Allah. If you deny Him, know that to Allah belongs all that the heavens and the earth contain. He is self-sufficient and worthy of praise.

To Allah belongs all that is in heaven and earth. Allah is your all-sufficient guardian. If He pleased, He could destroy you all and replace you by other men. This He has power to do.

Let the man who seeks the reward of this life know that Allah holds the rewards of this life and of the next. He hears all and sees all.

4:135   Believers, conduct yourselves with justice and bear true witness before Allah, even though it be against yourselves, your parents, or your kinsfolk. Whether the man concerned be rich or poor, know that Allah is nearer to him than you are. Do not be led by passion, lest you should swerve from the truth. If you distort your testimony or decline to give it, know that Allah is cognizant of all your actions.

Believers, have faith in Allah and His apostle, in the Book He has revealed to His apostle, and in the Scriptures He formerly revealed. He that denies Allah, His angels, His Scriptures, His apostles, and the Last Day, has strayed far from the truth.

4:137   Those who accept the faith and then renounce it, who

again embrace it and again deny it and grow in unbelief –
Allah will neither forgive them nor rightly guide them.

Give warning to the hypocrites of a stern chastisement: 4:138
those who choose the unbelievers rather than the faithful
for their friends. Are they seeking glory at their hands?
Surely all glory belongs to Allah.

Allah has instructed you in the Book that when you hear
His revelations being denied or ridiculed you must not sit
and listen to them unless they engage in other talk, or else
you shall yourselves become like them. Allah will surely
gather in Hell the hypocrites and the unbelievers.

They watch your fortunes closely. If Allah grants you a 4:141
victory, they say: 'Did we not stand on your side?' And if
the unbelievers are victorious, they say to them: 'Were
we not mightier than you, and did we not protect you
from the faithful?'

Allah will judge between you on the Day of Resurrection. He will not let the unbelievers triumph over the
faithful.

The hypocrites seek to deceive Allah, but it is Allah who
deceives them. When they rise to pray, they stand up slug-
gishly: they pray for the sake of ostentation and remember
Allah but little, wavering between this and that and belonging neither to these nor those. You cannot guide the
man whom Allah has led astray.

Believers, do not choose the infidels rather than the faithful for your friends. Would you give Allah a clear proof
against yourselves?

The hypocrites shall be cast into the lowest depths of
Hell: there shall be none to help them. But those who re- 4:146
pent and mend their ways, who hold fast to Allah and worship no other god besides Him – they shall be numbered
with the faithful, and the faithful shall be richly rewarded
by Allah.

And why should Allah punish you if you render thanks
to Him and truly believe in Him? Allah will reward your
labours, for He knows them all.

Allah does not love harsh words, except when uttered 4:148

by a man who is truly wronged. He hears all and knows
4:149 all. Whether you do good openly or in private, whether
you forgive those that wrong you – Allah is forgiving
and all-powerful.

Those that deny Allah and His apostles, and those that
draw a line between Allah and His apostles, saying: 'We
believe in some, but deny others,' – thus seeking a middle
way – these indeed are the unbelievers. For the unbelievers
We have prepared a shameful punishment.

As for those that believe in Allah and His apostles and
discriminate against none of them, they shall be rewarded
by Allah. He is forgiving and merciful.

4:153 The People of the Book ask you to bring down for them
a book from heaven. Of Moses they demanded a harder
thing than that. They said to him: 'Show us Allah distinctly.'
And for their wickedness a thunderbolt smote them. They
worshipped the calf after We had revealed to them Our
signs; yet We forgave them that, and bestowed on Moses
clear authority.

4:154 When We made a covenant with them We raised the
Mount above them and said: 'Enter the gates in adoration.
Do not break the Sabbath.' We took from them a solemn
covenant. But they broke the covenant, denied the revelations of Allah, and killed their prophets unjustly. They
said: 'Our hearts are sealed.'

(It is Allah who has sealed their hearts, on account
of their unbelief. They have no faith, except a few of
them.)

They denied the truth and uttered a monstrous falsehood
against Mary. They declared: 'We have put to death the
Messiah Jesus the son of Mary, the apostle of Allah.' They
did not kill him, nor did they crucify him, but they thought
they did.[1]

Those that disagreed about him were in doubt concerning his death, for what they knew about it was sheer con-
4:158 jecture; they were not sure that they had slain him. Allah
lifted him up to His presence; He is mighty and wise. There

1. Or, literally, he was made to resemble another for them.

is none among the People of the Book but will believe in 4:159
him before his death; and on the Day of Resurrection he
will be a witness against them.

Because of their iniquity, We forbade the Jews good
things which were formerly allowed them; because time
after time they have debarred others from the path of
Allah; because they practise usury – although they were
forbidden it – and cheat others of their possessions. We
have prepared a stern chastisement for those of them that
disbelieve. But those of them that have deep learning and
those that truly believe in what has been revealed to you
and to other prophets before you; who attend to their
prayers and pay the alms-tax and have faith in Allah and
the Last Day – these shall be richly rewarded.

We have revealed Our will to you as We revealed it to
Noah and to the prophets who came after him; as We revealed it to Abraham, Ishmael, Isaac, Jacob, and the tribes;
to Jesus, Job, Jonah, Aaron, Solomon and David, to whom
We gave the Psalms. Of some apostles We have already
told you (how Allah spoke directly to Moses); but there
are others of whom We have not yet spoken: apostles who
brought good news to mankind and admonished them, so 4:165
that they might have no plea against Allah after their
coming. Allah is mighty and wise.

Allah Himself bears witness by that which He has revealed to you that it has been revealed with His knowledge; and so do the angels. There is no better witness
than Allah.

Those that disbelieve and debar others from the path of
Allah have strayed far from the truth. Allah will not forgive
those who disbelieve and act unjustly; nor will He guide
them to any path other than that of Hell; in it they shall remain for ever. That is no difficult thing for Allah.

Men, the Apostle has brought you the truth from your
Lord. Have faith and it shall be well with you. If you disbelieve, know that to Allah belongs all that the heavens
and the earth contain. He is wise and all-knowing.

People of the Book, do not transgress the bounds of 4:171

your religion. Speak nothing but the truth about Allah. The Messiah, Jesus the son of Mary, was no more than Allah's apostle and His Word which He conveyed[1] to Mary: a spirit from Him. So believe in Allah and His apostles and do not say: 'Three.' Forbear, and it shall be better for you. Allah is but one God. Allah forbid that He should have a son! His is all that the heavens and the earth contain. Allah is the

4:172 all-sufficient Protector. The Messiah does not disdain to be a servant of Allah, nor do the angels who are nearest to him. Those who through arrogance disdain His service shall all be brought before Him.

Allah will reward those that have faith and do good works; He will enrich them from His own abundance. As for those who are scornful and proud, He will sternly punish them, and they shall find none besides Allah to protect or help them.

4:174 Men, you have received clear evidence from your Lord. We have sent forth to you a glorious light. Those that believe in Allah and hold fast to Him shall be admitted to His mercy and His grace; He will guide them to Him along a straight path.

4:176 They consult you. Say: 'Thus Allah instructs you regarding those that die childless. If a man die childless and he have a sister, she shall inherit the half of his estate. If a woman die childless, her brother shall be her sole heir. If a childless man have two sisters, they shall inherit two-thirds of his estate; but if he have both brothers and sisters, the share of each male shall be that of two females.'

Thus Allah makes plain to you His precepts so that you may not err. Allah has knowledge of all things.

1. Lit., cast.

DIVORCE

In the Name of Allah, the Compassionate, the Merciful

PROPHET and believers, if you divorce your wives, 65:1
divorce them at the end of their waiting period. Compute their waiting period and have fear of Allah, your
Lord. Do not expel them from their homes or let them go
away unless they commit a proven crime. Such are the
bounds set by Allah; he that transgresses Allah's bounds
wrongs his own soul. You never know; after that Allah
may bring to pass some new event.

When their waiting term is ended, either keep them 65:2
honourably or part with them honourably. Call to witness
two honest men among you and give your testimony before
Allah. Whoever believes in Allah and the Last Day is exhorted to do this. He that fears Allah, Allah will give him a
means of salvation and provide for him whence he does
not reckon: Allah is all-sufficient for the man who puts his
trust in Him. He will surely bring about what He decrees.
He has set a measure for all things.

If you are in doubt concerning those of your wives who
have ceased menstruating, know that their waiting period is
three months. And let the same be the waiting period of
those who have not yet menstruated.[1] As for pregnant
women, their term shall end with their confinement. Allah
will ease the hardship of the man who fears Him.

Such is the commandment which Allah has revealed to
you. He that fears Allah shall be forgiven his sins and richly
rewarded.

Lodge them in your own homes, according to your 65:6
means. Do not harass them so as to make life intolerable
for them. If they are with child, maintain them until the end
of their confinement; and if, after that, they give suck to
their children, give them their pay and consult together in

1. On account of their young age. Child marriages were very
common.

all reasonableness. But if you cannot bear with each other, let other women suckle for you.

65:7 Let the rich man spend according to his wealth, and the poor man according to what Allah has given him. Allah does not charge a man with more than He has given him; He will bring ease after hardship.

How many nations have rebelled against the commandments of their Lord and His apostles! Stern was Our reckoning with them, and grievous Our punishment. They tasted the fruit of their misdeeds: and the fruit of their misdeeds **65:10** was ruin. Allah has prepared a woeful scourge for them. Have fear of Allah, you men of understanding.

Believers, Allah has now sent down to you a warning; an apostle proclaiming to you the revelations of Allah in all plainness, so that he may lead the faithful who do good works from darkness to the light. He that believes in Allah and does good works shall be admitted to gardens watered by running streams where he shall dwell for ever. Allah has made for him a generous provision.

65:12 It is Allah who has created seven heavens, and earths as many. His commandment descends through them, so that you may know that Allah has power over all things, and that He has knowledge of all things.

THE TABLE

In the Name of Allah, the Compassionate, the Merciful

5:1 BELIEVERS, be true to your obligations. It is lawful for you to eat the flesh of all beasts other than that which is hereby announced to you. Game is forbidden while you are on pilgrimage. Allah decrees what He will.

Believers, do not violate the rites of Allah, or the sacred month, or the offerings or their ornaments, or those that repair to the Sacred House seeking Allah's grace and pleasure. Once your pilgrimage is ended, you shall be free to go hunting.

Do not allow your hatred for those who would debar you

from the Holy Mosque to lead you into sin. Help one another in what is good and pious, not in what is wicked and sinful. Have fear of Allah, for He is stern in retribution.

You are forbidden carrion, blood, and the flesh of swine; 5:3 also any flesh dedicated to any other than Allah. You are forbidden the flesh of strangled animals and of those beaten or gored to death; of those killed by a fall or mangled by beasts of prey (unless you make it clean by giving the death-stroke yourselves); also of animals sacrificed to idols.

You are forbidden to settle disputes by consulting the Arrows. That is a vicious practice.

The unbelievers have this day abandoned all hope of vanquishing your religion. Have no fear of them: fear Me.

This day I have perfected your religion for you and completed My favour to you. I have chosen Islam to be your faith.

He that is constrained by hunger to eat of what is forbidden, not intending to commit sin, will find Allah forgiving and merciful.

They ask you what is lawful to them. Say: 'All good 5:4 things are lawful to you, as well as that which you have taught the birds and beasts of prey to catch, training them as Allah has taught you. Eat of what they catch for you, pronouncing upon it the name of Allah. And have fear of Allah: swift is Allah's reckoning.'

All good things have this day been made lawful to you. The food of those to whom the Book was given[1] is lawful to you, and yours to them.

Lawful to you are the believing women and the free women from among those who were given the Scriptures before you, provided that you give them their dowries and live in honour with them, neither committing fornication nor taking them as mistresses.

He that denies the faith shall gain nothing from his labours. In the world to come he shall have much to lose.

Believers, when you rise to pray wash your faces and 5:6

1. The Jews (but not the Christians).

your hands as far as the elbow, and wipe your heads and your feet to the ankle. If you are polluted cleanse yourselves. But if you are sick or travelling the road; or if, when you have just relieved yourselves or had intercourse with women, you can find no water, take some clean sand and rub your hands and faces with it. Allah does not wish to burden you; He seeks only to purify you and to perfect His favour to you, so that you may give thanks.

5:7   Remember the favours which Allah has bestowed upon you, and the covenant with which He bound you when you said: 'We hear and obey.' Have fear of Allah. He knows your inmost thoughts.

Believers, fulfil your duties to Allah and bear true witness. Do not allow your hatred for other men to turn you away from justice. Deal justly; justice is nearer to true piety. Have fear of Allah; He is cognizant of all your actions.

5:9   Allah has promised those that have faith and do good works forgiveness and a rich reward. As for those who disbelieve and deny Our revelations, they shall become the heirs of Hell.

Believers, remember the favour which Allah bestowed upon you when He restrained the hands of those who sought to harm you. Have fear of Allah. In Allah let the faithful put their trust.

Allah made a covenant with the Israelites and raised among them twelve chieftains. He said: 'I shall be with you. If you attend to your prayers and pay the alms-tax; if you believe in My apostles and assist them and give Allah a generous loan, I shall forgive you your sins and admit you to gardens watered by running streams. But he that hereafter denies Me shall stray from the right path.'

5:13   But because they broke their covenant We laid on them Our curse and hardened their hearts. They have perverted the words of the Scriptures and forgotten much of what they were enjoined. You will ever find them deceitful, except for a few of them. But pardon them and bear with them. Allah loves the righteous.

With those who said they were Christians We made a *5:14*
covenant also, but they too have forgotten much of what
they were enjoined. Therefore We stirred among them
enmity and hatred, which shall endure till the Day of Resurrection, when Allah will declare to them all that they have
done.

People of the Book! Our apostle has come to reveal to
you much of what you have hidden of the Scriptures, and
to forgive you much. A light has come to you from Allah
and a glorious Book, with which He will guide to the paths
of peace those that seek to please Him; He will lead them
by His will from darkness to the light; He will guide them
to a straight path.

Unbelievers are those who declare: 'Allah is the Messiah, *5:17*
the son of Mary.' Say: 'Who could prevent Allah from
destroying the Messiah, the son of Mary, together with his
mother and all the people of the earth? His is the kingdom
of the heavens and the earth and all that lies between
them. He creates what He will and has power over all
things.'

The Jews and the Christians say: 'We are the children of
Allah and His loved ones.' Say: 'Why then does He punish
you for your sins? Surely you are mortals of His own
creation. He forgives whom He will and punishes whom
He pleases. His is the kingdom of the heavens and the
earth and all that lies between them. All shall return to
Him.'

People of the Book! Our apostle has come to reveal to
you Our will after an interval during which there were no
apostles, lest you should say: 'No one has come to give us
good news or to warn us.' Now a prophet has come to give
you good news and to warn you. Allah has power over all
things.

Bear in mind the words of Moses to his people. He said:
'Remember, my people, the favours which Allah has bestowed upon you. He has raised up prophets among you,
made you kings, and given you that which He has given to
no other nation. Enter, my people, the holy land which *5:21*

Allah has assigned for you. Do not turn back, or you shall be ruined.'

5:22 'Moses,' they replied, 'a race of giants dwells in this land. We will not set foot in it till they are gone. Only then shall we enter.'

Thereupon two God-fearing men whom Allah had favoured said: 'Go in to them through the gates, and when you have entered you shall surely be victorious. In Allah put your trust, if you are true believers.'

But they replied: 'Moses, we will not go in so long as *they* are in it. Go, you and your Lord, and fight. We will stay here.'

'Lord,' cried Moses, 'I have none but myself and my brother. Do not confound us with these wicked people.'

5:26 He replied: 'They shall be forbidden this land for forty years, during which time they shall wander homeless on the earth. Do not grieve for these wicked people.'

Recount to them in all truth the story of Adam's two sons: how they each made an offering, and how the offering of the one was accepted while that of the other was not. Cain said: 'I will surely kill you.' His brother replied: 'Allah accepts offerings only from the righteous. If you stretch your hand to kill me, I shall not lift mine to slay you; for I fear Allah, the Lord of the Creation. I would rather you should add your sin against me to your other sins and thus incur the punishment of Hell. Such is the reward of the wicked.'

Cain's soul prompted him to slay his brother; he killed him and thus became one of the lost. Then Allah sent down a raven, which dug the earth to show him how to bury the naked corpse of his brother. 'Alas!' he cried. 'Have I not strength enough to do as this raven has done and so bury my brother's naked corpse?' And he repented.

5:32 That was why We laid it down for the Israelites that whoever killed a human being, except as a punishment for murder or other wicked crimes, should be looked upon as though he had killed all mankind; and that whoever saved a human life should be regarded as though he had saved all mankind.

Our apostles brought them veritable proofs: yet it was not long before many of them committed great evils in the land.

Those that make war against Allah and His apostle and 5:33 spread disorders in the land shall be put to death or crucified or have their hands and feet cut off on alternate sides, or be banished from the country. They shall be held to shame in this world and sternly punished in the next: except those that repent before you reduce them. For you must know that Allah is forgiving and merciful.

Believers, have fear of Allah and seek the right path to Him. Fight valiantly for His cause, so that you may triumph.

As for the unbelievers, if they offered all that the earth contains and as much besides to redeem themselves from the torment of the Day of Resurrection, it shall not be accepted from them. Theirs shall be a woeful punishment.

They will strive to get out of the Fire, but they shall not: 5:37 theirs shall be a lasting punishment.

As for the man or woman who is guilty of theft, cut off their hands to punish them for their crimes. That is the punishment enjoined by Allah. He is mighty and wise. But whoever repents and mends his ways after committing evil shall be pardoned by Allah. Allah is forgiving and merciful.

Do you not know that to Allah belongs the kingdom of the heavens and the earth? He punishes whom He will and forgives whom He pleases. Allah has power over all things.

Apostle, do not grieve for those who plunge headlong 5:41 into unbelief; the men who say with their tongues: 'We believe,' but have no faith in their hearts, and the Jews who listen to the lies of others and pay no heed to you. They tamper with the words of the Scriptures and say: 'If this be given you, accept it; if not, then beware!'

You cannot help a man if Allah seeks to mislead him. Those whose hearts He does not please to purify shall be rewarded with disgrace in this world and a grievous punishment in the next.

5:42   They listen to falsehoods and practise what is unlawful. If they come to you, give them your judgement or let them be. If you avoid them they cannot harm you; but if you act as their judge, judge them with fairness. Allah loves those that deal justly.

But how will they come to you for judgement, when they already have the Torah which enshrines Allah's own judgement? Soon after they are bound to ignore you: they are no true believers.

5:44   There is guidance, and there is light, in the Torah which We have revealed. By it the prophets who surrendered themselves to Allah judged the Jews, and so did the rabbis and the divines; they gave judgement according to Allah's scriptures which had been committed to their keeping and to which they themselves were witnesses.

Have no fear of man; fear Me, and do not sell My revelations for a paltry end. Unbelievers are those who do not judge in accordance with Allah's revelations.

5:45   In the Torah We decreed for them a life for a life, an eye for an eye, a nose for a nose, an ear for an ear, a tooth for a tooth, and a wound for a wound. But if a man charitably forbears from retaliation, his remission shall atone for him. Transgressors are those that do not judge in accordance with Allah's revelations.

After those prophets We sent forth Jesus, the son of Mary, confirming the Torah already revealed, and gave him the Gospel, in which there is guidance and light, corroborating that which was revealed before it in the Torah, a guide and an admonition to the righteous. Therefore let the followers of the Gospel judge in accordance with what Allah has revealed therein. Evil-doers are those that do not base their judgements on Allah's revelations.

5:48   And to you We have revealed the Book with the truth. It confirms the Scriptures which came before it and stands as a guardian over them. Therefore give judgement among men in accordance with Allah's revelations and do not yield to their fancies or swerve from the truth that has been made known to you.

We have ordained a law and assigned a path for each of you. Had Allah pleased, He could have made you one nation: but it is His wish to prove you by that which He has bestowed upon you. Vie with each other in good works, for to Allah you shall all return and He will declare to you what you have disagreed about.

Pronounce judgement among them in accordance with *5:49* Allah's revelations and do not be led by their desires. Take heed lest they should turn you away from a part of that which Allah has revealed to you. If they reject your judgement, know that it is Allah's wish to scourge them for their sins. Many of them are wrongdoers.

Is it pagan laws that they wish to be judged by? Who is a better judge than Allah for men whose faith is firm?

Believers, take neither Jews nor Christians for your friends. They are friends with one another. Whoever of you seeks their friendship shall become one of their number. Allah does not guide the wrongdoers.

You see the faint-hearted hastening to woo them. They *5:52* say: 'We fear lest a change of fortune should befall us.' But when Allah grants you victory or makes known His will, they shall regret their secret plans. Then will the faithful say: 'Are these the men who solemnly swore by Allah that they would stand with you?' Their works will come to nothing and they shall be ruined.

Believers, if any of you renounce the faith, Allah will replace them by others who love Him and are loved by Him, humble towards the faithful and stern towards the unbelievers, zealous for Allah's cause and fearless of man's censure. Such is the grace of Allah: He bestows it on whom He will. He is munificent and all-knowing.

Your only friends are Allah, His apostle, and the faithful: those who attend to their prayers, pay their alms-tax, and kneel down in worship. Those who seek the friendship of *5:56* Allah, His apostle, and the faithful must know that Allah's followers are sure to triumph.

5:57 Believers, do not seek the friendship of the infidels and those who were given the Book before you, who have made of your religion a jest and a pastime. Have fear of Allah, if you are true believers. When you call them to pray, they treat their prayers as a jest and a pastime. They do this because they are devoid of understanding.

Say: 'People of the Book, do you hate us for any reason other than that we believe in Allah and in what has been revealed to us and to others before us, and that most of you are evil-doers?'

Say: 'Shall I tell you who will receive the worse reward from Allah? Those on whom Allah has laid His curse and with whom He has been angry, transforming them into apes and swine, and those who worship false gods. Worse is the plight of these, and they have strayed farther from the right path.'

When they came to you they said: 'We are believers.' Indeed, infidels they came and infidels they departed. Allah knew their secret thoughts.

5:62 You see many of them vie with one another in sin and wickedness and eat the fruits of unlawful gain. Evil is what they do.

Why do their rabbis and divines not forbid them to blaspheme or to practise what is unlawful? Evil indeed are their doings.

The Jews say: 'Allah's hand is chained.' May their own hands be chained! May they be cursed for what they say! By no means. His hands are both outstretched: He bestows as He will.

That which Allah has revealed to you will surely increase the wickedness and unbelief of many of them. We have stirred among them enmity and hatred, which will endure till the Day of Resurrection. Whenever they kindle the fire of war, Allah puts it out. They spread evil in the land, but Allah does not love the evil-doers.

If the People of the Book accept the true faith and keep from evil, We will pardon them their sins and admit them 5:66 to the gardens of delight. If they observe the Torah and the

Gospel and what is revealed to them from Allah, they shall be given abundance from above and from beneath.

Some of them are righteous men; but many of them do nothing but evil.

Apostle, proclaim what is revealed to you from your *5:67* Lord; if you do not, you will surely fail to convey His message. Allah will protect you from all men. He does not guide the unbelievers.

Say: 'People of the Book, you shall not be guided until you observe the Torah and the Gospel and that which is revealed to you from your Lord.'

That which is revealed to you from your Lord will surely increase the wickedness and unbelief of many of them. But do not grieve for the unbelievers.

Believers, Jews, Sabaeans, or Christians – whoever believes in Allah and the Last Day and does what is right – shall have nothing to fear or to regret.

We made a covenant with the Israelites and sent forth *5:70* apostles among them. But whenever an apostle came to them with a message that did not suit their fancies they either rejected him or slew him. They thought no harm would come to them: they were blind and deaf. Allah turned to them in mercy, but many of them again became blind and deaf. Allah is ever watching over their actions.

Unbelievers are those that say: 'Allah is the Messiah, the son of Mary.' For the Messiah himself said: 'Children of Israel, serve Allah, my Lord and your Lord.' He that worships other gods besides Allah shall be forbidden Paradise and shall be cast into the fire of Hell. None shall help the evil-doers.

Unbelievers are those that say: 'Allah is one of three.' There is but one God. If they do not desist from so saying, those of them that disbelieve shall be sternly punished.

Will they not turn to Allah in repentance and seek forgiveness of Him? He is forgiving and merciful.

The Messiah, the son of Mary, was no more than an *5:75* apostle: other apostles passed away before him. His mother was a saintly woman. They both ate earthly food.

See how We make plain to them Our revelations. See how they ignore the truth.

5:76 Say: 'Will you serve instead of Allah that which can neither harm nor help you? Allah hears all and knows all.'

Say: 'People of the Book! Do not transgress the bounds of truth in your religion. Do not yield to the desires of those who have already erred; who have led many astray and have themselves strayed from the even path.'

Those of the Israelites who disbelieved were cursed by David and Jesus, the son of Mary: they cursed them because they rebelled and committed evil and never restrained one another from wrong-doing. Evil were their deeds.

You see many of them making friends with unbelievers. Evil is that to which their souls prompt them. They have incurred the wrath of Allah and shall endure eternal torment. Had they believed in Allah and the Prophet and that which is revealed to him they would not have befriended them. But many of them are evil-doers.

5:82 You will find that the most implacable of men in their enmity to the faithful are the Jews and the pagans, and that the nearest in affection to them are those who say: 'We are Christians.' That is because there are priests and monks among them; and because they are free from pride.

When they listen to that which was revealed to the Apostle, you will see their eyes fill with tears as they recognize its truth. They say: 'Lord, we believe. Count us among Your witnesses. Why should we not believe in Allah and in the truth that has come down to us? Why should we not hope for admission among the righteous?' And for their words Allah has rewarded them with gardens watered by running streams, where they shall dwell for ever. Such is the recompense of the righteous. But those that disbelieve and deny Our revelations shall be the heirs of Hell.

5:87 Believers, do not forbid the wholesome things which Allah has made lawful to you. Do not transgress; Allah

does not love the transgressors. Eat of the lawful and *5:88*
wholesome things which Allah has given you. Have fear of
Allah, in whom you believe.

Allah will not punish you for that which is inadvertent in
your oaths. But He will take you to task for the oaths which
you solemnly swear. The penalty for a broken oath is the
feeding of ten needy men with such food as you normally
offer to your own people; or the clothing of ten needy men;
or the freeing of one slave. He that cannot afford any of
these must fast three days. In this way you shall expiate
your broken oaths. Therefore be true to that which you
have sworn. Thus Allah makes plain to you His revelations, so that you may give thanks.

Believers, wine and games of chance, idols and divining
arrows, are abominations devised by Satan. Avoid them, so
that you may prosper. Satan seeks to stir up enmity and
hatred among you by means of wine and gambling, and to
keep you from the remembrance of Allah and from your
prayers. Will you not abstain from them?

Obey Allah, and obey the Apostle. Beware; if you give no *5:92*
heed, know that Our apostle's duty is only to give plain
warning.

No blame shall be attached to those that have embraced
the faith and done good works in regard to any food they
may have eaten, so long as they fear Allah and believe in
Him and do good works; so long as they fear Allah and
believe in Him; so long as they fear Allah and do good
works. Allah loves the charitable.

Believers, Allah will put you to the proof by means of
the game which you can catch with your hands or with
your spears, so that He may know those who truly fear
Him. He that transgresses hereafter shall be sternly punished.

Believers, kill no game whilst on pilgrimage. He that *5:95*
kills game by design, shall present, as an offering to the
Ka'ba, a domestic beast equivalent to that which he has
killed, to be determined by two honest men among you; or
he shall, in expiation, either feed the poor or fast, so that he

may know the evil consequences of his deed. Allah has forgiven what is past, but if any one returns to sin He will avenge Himself on him: He is mighty and capable of revenge.

5:96   It is lawful for you to hunt in the sea and to eat its fish, a good food for you and for the seafarer. But you are forbidden the game of the land whilst you are on pilgrimage. Have fear of Allah, before whom you shall all be assembled.

Allah has made the Sacred House of the Ka'ba, the sacred month, and the sacrificial offerings with their ornaments, eternal values for mankind; so that you may know that Allah has knowledge of all that the heavens and the earth contain; that He has knowledge of all things.

Know that Allah is stern in retribution, and that He is forgiving and merciful.

The duty of the Apostle is only to give warning. Allah knows all that you hide and all that you reveal.

Say: 'Good and evil are not alike, even though the abundance of evil tempts you. Have fear of Allah, you men of understanding, so that you may triumph.'

5:101   Believers, do not ask questions about things which, if made known to you, would only pain you; but if you ask them when the Koran is being revealed, they shall be made plain to you. Allah will pardon you for this; He is forgiving and gracious. Other men inquired about them before you, only to flout them afterwards.

Allah demands neither a *bahirah*, nor a *saibah*, nor a *wasilah*, nor a *hami*.[1] This is a falsehood invented by the unbelievers. Most of them are lacking in judgement.

When it is said to them: 'Come to that which Allah has revealed, and to the Apostle,' they reply: 'Sufficient for us is the faith we have inherited from our fathers,' even though their fathers knew nothing and were not rightly guided.

5:105   Believers, you are accountable for none but yourselves; he that goes astray cannot harm you if you are on the right

1. Names given by pagan Arabs to sacred animals offered at the Ka'ba.

path. You shall all return to Allah, and He will declare to you what you have done.

Believers, when death approaches you, let two honest *5:106* men from among you act as witnesses when you make your testaments; or two men from another tribe if the calamity of death overtakes you whilst you are travelling in the land. Detain them after prayers, and if you doubt their honesty ask them to swear by Allah: 'We will not sell our testimony for any price even to a kinsman. We will not hide the testimony of Allah; for we should then be evil-doers.' If *5:107* both prove dishonest, replace them by another pair from among those immediately concerned, and let them both swear by Allah, saying: 'Our testimony is truer than theirs. We have told no lies, for we should then be wrongdoers.' Thus they will be more likely to bear true witness or to fear that the oaths of others may contradict theirs. Have fear of Allah and be obedient. Allah does not guide the evil-doers.

One day Allah will gather all the apostles and ask them: 'How were you received?' They will reply: 'We do not know. You alone have knowledge of what is hidden.' Allah will say: 'Jesus, son of Mary, remember the favour *5:110* I have bestowed on you and on your mother: how I strengthened you with the Holy Spirit, so that you preached to men in your cradle and in the prime of manhood; how I instructed you in the Scriptures and in wisdom, in the Torah and in the Gospel; how by My leave you fashioned from clay the likeness of a bird and breathed into it so that, by My leave, it became a living bird; how, by My leave, you healed the blind man and the leper, and by My leave restored the dead to life; how I protected you from the Israelites when you brought them veritable signs: when the unbelievers among them said: "This is nothing but plain magic"; how when I enjoined the disciples to believe in Me and in My apostle they replied: "We believe; bear witness that we submit to You utterly."'

'Jesus, son of Mary,' said the disciples, 'can Allah send *5:112* down to us from heaven a table spread with food?'

He replied: 'Have fear of Allah, if you are true believers.'

5:113 'We wish to eat of it,' they said, 'so that we may reassure our hearts and know that what you said to us is true, and that we may be witnesses of it.'

'Lord,' said Jesus, the son of Mary, 'send to us from heaven a table spread with food, that it may mark a feast for us and for those that will come after us: a sign from You. Give us our sustenance; You are the best Giver.'

5:115 Allah replied: 'I am sending one to you. But whoever of you disbelieves hereafter shall be punished as no man has ever been punished.'

Then Allah will say: 'Jesus, son of Mary, did you ever say to mankind: "Worship me and my mother as gods beside Allah?"'

'Glory to You,' he will answer, 'how could I say that to which I have no right? If I had ever said so, You would have surely known it. You know what is in my mind, but I cannot tell what is in Yours. You alone know what is hidden. I spoke to them of nothing except what You bade me. I said: "Serve Allah, my Lord and your Lord." I watched over them whilst living in their midst, and ever since You took me to You, You Yourself have been watching over them. You are the witness of all things. They are your own bondsmen: it is for You to punish or to forgive them. You are the Mighty, the Wise One.'

Allah will say: 'This is the day when their truthfulness will benefit the truthful. They shall for ever dwell in gardens watered by running streams. Allah is pleased with them and they with Him. That is the supreme triumph.'

5:120 To Allah belongs the kingdom of the heavens and the earth and all that they contain. He has power over all things.

THE UNBELIEVERS

In the Name of Allah, the Compassionate, the Merciful

SAY: 'Unbelievers, I do not serve what you worship, *109:1* nor do you serve what I worship. I shall never serve what you worship, nor will you ever serve what I worship. You have your own religion, and I have mine.' *109:6*

HELP

In the Name of Allah, the Compassionate, the Merciful

WHEN Allah's help and victory come, and you see *110:1* men embrace His faith in multitudes, give glory *110:3* to your Lord and seek His pardon. He is ever disposed to mercy.

PILGRIMAGE

In the Name of Allah, the Compassionate, the Merciful

MEN, have fear of your Lord. The catastrophe of the *22:1* Hour of Doom shall be terrible indeed.

When that day comes, every suckling mother shall forsake her infant, every pregnant female shall cast her burden, and you shall see mankind reeling like drunkards although not drunk: such shall be the horror of Allah's vengeance.

Yet there are some who in their ignorance dispute about *22:4* Allah and serve rebellious devils, though these are doomed to seduce their followers and lead them to the scourge of the Fire.

Men, if you doubt the Resurrection remember that We *22:5* first created you from dust, then from a living germ, then from a clot of blood, and then from a half-formed lump of flesh, so that We might manifest to you Our power.

We cause to remain in the womb whatever We please for

an appointed term, and then We bring you forth as infants, that you may grow up and reach your prime. Some die young, and some live on to abject old age when all that they once knew they know no more.

You sometimes see the earth dry and barren: but no sooner do We send down rain upon it than it begins to stir 22:6 and swell, putting forth every kind of radiant bloom. That is because Allah is Truth: He gives life to the dead and has power over all things.

The Hour of Doom is sure to come – in this there is no doubt. Those who are in the grave Allah will raise to life.

Some wrangle about Allah, though they have neither knowledge nor guidance nor divine revelation. They turn their backs in scorn and lead others astray from Allah's path. Such men shall incur disgrace in this life and taste the torment of Hell on the Day of Resurrection. 'This,' We shall say, 'is the reward of your misdeeds. Allah is not unjust to His servants.'

22:11 Some profess to serve Allah and yet stand on the very fringe of the true faith. When blessed with good fortune they are content, but when an ordeal befalls them they turn upon their heels, forfeiting this life and the hereafter. That way perdition lies.

They call on that which can neither harm nor help them. That is the supreme folly.

They call on that which would sooner harm than help them: an evil master and an evil friend.

As for those that have faith and do good works, Allah will admit them to gardens watered by running streams. Allah's will is ever done.

If any one thinks that Allah will not give victory to His apostle in this world and in the world to come, let him tie a rope to the ceiling of his house and hang himself. Then let him see if his device has done away with that which has enraged him.

We have revealed the Koran in clear verses. Allah gives guidance to whom He will.

22:17 As for the true believers, the Jews, the Sabaeans, the

Christians, the Magians, and the pagans, Allah will judge them on the Day of Resurrection. He bears witness to all things.

Do you not see how all who dwell in heaven and earth do *22:18* homage to Allah? The·sun and the moon and the stars, the mountains and the trees, the beasts, and countless men – all prostrate themselves before Him. Yet many have deserved His scourge. He who is humbled by Allah has none to honour him. Allah's will is ever done.

The faithful and the unbelievers contend about their Lord. Garments of fire have been prepared for the unbelievers. Scalding water shall be poured upon their heads, melting their skins and that which is in their bellies. They shall be lashed with rods of iron.

Whenever, in their anguish, they try to escape from Hell, the angels will drag them back, saying: 'Taste the torment of Hell-fire!'

As for those that have faith and do good works, Allah *22:23* will admit them to gardens watered by running streams. They shall be decked with pearls and bracelets of gold, and arrayed in garments of silk. For they have been shown the noblest of words and guided to the path of the Glorious Lord.

The unbelievers who debar others from the path of Allah and from the Sacred Mosque which We gave to all mankind, natives and strangers alike, and those who commit evil within its walls, shall be sternly punished.

When We prepared for Abraham the site of the Sacred Mosque We said: 'Worship none besides Me. Keep My House clean for those who walk around it and those who stand upright or kneel in worship.'

Exhort all men to make the pilgrimage. They will come to you on foot and on the backs of swift camels from every distant quarter; they will come to avail themselves of many a benefit and to pronounce on the appointed days the name of Allah over the beasts which He has given them. Eat of their flesh yourselves, and feed the poor and the unfortunate.

Then let the pilgrims spruce themselves, make their vows, *22:29*

22:30 and circle the Ancient House. Such is Allah's commandment. He that reveres the sacred rites of Allah shall fare better in the sight of his Lord.

The flesh of cattle is lawful to you, except that which has already been mentioned. Guard yourselves against the filth of idols and avoid all falsehoods. Dedicate yourselves to Allah and serve none besides Him. The man who serves other gods besides Allah is like him who falls from heaven and is snatched away by the birds or carried by the wind to some far-off region. Such is Allah's commandment.

He that reveres the offerings made to Allah shows the piety of his heart. Your cattle are useful to you in many ways until the time of their slaughter. Then they are offered for sacrifice at the Ancient House.

For every nation We have ordained a ritual, that they may pronounce the name of Allah over the beasts which He has given them for food. Your God is one God; to Him surrender yourselves. Give good news to the humble, *22:35* whose hearts are filled with awe at the mention of their Lord; who endure their misfortunes with fortitude, attend to their prayers, and bestow in charity of that which We have given them.

We have made the camels a part of Allah's rites. They are of much use to you. Pronounce over them the name of Allah as you draw them up in line and slaughter them; and when they have fallen down eat of their flesh and feed with it the poor man and the beggar. Thus We have subjected them to your service, so that you may give thanks.

Their flesh and blood does not reach Allah; it is your piety that reaches Him. Thus He has subjected them to your service, so that you may give glory to Him for guiding you.

Give good news to the righteous. Allah will ward off evil from true believers. He does not love the treacherous and the thankless.

Permission to take up arms is hereby given to those who are attacked, because they have been wronged. Allah has *22:40* power to grant them victory: those who have been unjustly driven from their homes, only because they said: 'Our Lord is Allah.' Had Allah not defended some men by the might of others, the monasteries and churches, the synagogues and mosques in which His praise is daily celebrated, would have been utterly destroyed. But whoever helps Allah shall be helped by Him. Allah is powerful and mighty: He will assuredly help those who, once made masters in the land, *22:41* will attend to their prayers and pay the alms-tax, enjoin justice and forbid evil. Allah controls the destiny of all things.

If they deny you, remember that before them the peoples of Noah, Abraham and Lot, the tribes of Thamoud and Aad, and the dwellers of Midian had denied their apostles: Moses himself was charged with imposture. I bore long with the unbelievers and in the end My scourge overtook them. And how terrible was My vengeance!

How many sinful nations We have destroyed! Their cities lie in ruin; desolate are their lofty palaces, and abandoned their wells.

Have they never journeyed through the land? Have they *22:46* no hearts to reason with, or ears to hear with? It is their hearts, and not their eyes, that are blind.

They bid you hasten the punishment of Allah. He will not fail His promise. Each day of His is like a thousand years in your reckoning.

I bore long with many nations: then in their sinfulness My vengeance smote them. To me shall all things return.

Say to them: 'I have been sent to warn you plainly. Those that accept the true faith and do good works shall be forgiven and richly rewarded; but those that seek to confute Our revelations shall be the heirs of Hell.'

Never have We sent a single prophet or apostle before you with whose wishes Satan did not tamper. But Allah abrogates the interjections of Satan and confirms His own revelations. Allah is wise and all-knowing. He makes Satan's interjections a temptation for those whose hearts are diseased or hardened – this is why the wrongdoers are in open schism – so that those to whom knowledge has been *22:54* given may realize that this[1] is the truth from your Lord and

1. The Koran.

thus believe in it and humble their hearts towards Him. Allah will surely guide the faithful to a straight path.

22:55 Yet the unbelievers will never cease to doubt it until the Hour of Doom overtakes them unawares or the scourge of the Woeful Day descends upon them. On that day Allah will reign supreme. He will judge them all. Those that have embraced the true faith and done good works shall enter the gardens of delight, but the unbelievers who have denied Our revelations shall receive an ignominious punishment.

As for those that have fled their homes for the cause of Allah and afterwards died or were slain, Allah will make a generous provision for them. He is the most munificent Giver. He will receive them well: benignant is Allah and all-knowing.

Thus shall it be. He that repays an injury in kind and then is wronged again shall be helped by Allah. Allah is merciful and forgiving.

He causes the night to pass into the day, and the day into the night. He hears all and observes all.

22:62 Allah is Truth, and Falsehood all that they invoke besides Him. He is the Most High, the Supreme One.

Do you not see how Allah sends down water from the sky and covers the earth with vegetation? He is wise and all-knowing.

His is all that the heavens and the earth contain. He is the Self-sufficient, the Glorious One.

Do you not see how He has subdued to you all that is in the earth? He has given you ships which sail the sea at His bidding. He holds the sky from falling down: this it shall not do except by His own will. Compassionate is Allah, and merciful to men.

It is He who has given you life, and He who will cause you to die and make you live again. Surely man is ungrateful.

22:67 For every nation We have ordained a ritual which they observe. Let them not dispute with you concerning this. Call them to the path of your Lord: you are rightly guided.

If they argue with you, say: 'Allah knows best all that you 22:68
do. On the Day of Resurrection He will judge all your disputes.'

Are you not aware that Allah has knowledge of what
heaven and earth contain? All is recorded in His Book.
That is no difficult thing for Allah.

Yet they worship besides Allah that for which no sanction is revealed and of which they know nothing. Truly, the
wrongdoers shall have none to help them.

When Our clear revelations are recited to them, denial
can be seen in the faces of the unbelievers. They can barely
restrain themselves from assaulting those who recite Our
revelations.

Say: 'Shall I tell you what is worse than that? The fire
which Allah has promised those who deny Him. An evil
fate.'

Listen to this aphorism. Those whom you invoke be- 22:73
sides Allah could never create a single fly though they
combined to do this. And if a fly carried away a speck of
dust from them they could never retrieve it. Powerless is
the suppliant, and powerless he whom he supplicates.

They do not render to Allah the homage due to Him. Yet
Allah is powerful and mighty.

He chooses His messengers from the angels and from
men. He hears all and observes all. He knows what is before
them and behind them. To Him shall all things return.

You that are true believers, kneel and prostrate yourselves. Worship your Lord and do good works, so that you
may triumph.

Fight for the cause of Allah with the devotion due to 22:78
Him. He has chosen you and laid on you no burdens in the
observance of your faith, the faith of Abraham your father.
In this as in former scriptures He has given you the name of
Muslims, so that His apostle may testify against you, and
that you yourselves may testify against your fellow-men.

Therefore attend to your prayers and pay the alms-tax
and hold fast to Allah, for He is your Guardian. A gracious
guardian and a gracious helper!

THE IMRANS

In the Name of Allah, the Compassionate, the Merciful

3:1 ALIF *lam mim*. Allah! There is no god but Him, the Living, the Ever-existent One.

He has revealed to you the Book with the truth, confirming the scriptures which preceded it; for He has already revealed the Torah and the Gospel for the guidance of men, and the distinction between right and wrong.

Those that deny Allah's revelations shall be sternly punished; Allah is mighty and capable of revenge. Nothing on earth or in heaven is hidden from Him. It is He who shapes your bodies in your mothers' wombs as He pleases. There is no god but Him, the Mighty, the Wise One.

It is He who has revealed to you the Koran. Some of its verses are precise in meaning – they are the foundation of the Book – and others ambiguous. Those whose hearts are infected with disbelief follow the ambiguous part, so as to create dissension by seeking to explain it. But no one knows its meaning except Allah. Those who are well-grounded in knowledge say: 'We believe in it: it is all from our Lord.

3:8 But only the wise take heed. Lord, do not cause our hearts to go astray after You have guided us. Grant us Your own mercy; You are the munificent Giver. Lord, You will surely gather all mankind before You upon a day that will indubitably come. Allah will not break His promise.'

As for the unbelievers, neither their riches nor their children shall in the least save them from Allah's wrath. They shall become the fuel of Hell. Like them, Pharaoh's people and those before them denied Our revelations; therefore Allah smote them in their sinfulness. Allah is stern in retribution.

Say to the unbelievers: 'You shall be discomfited and driven into Hell – an evil resting-place!'

3:13 Indeed, there was a sign for you in the two armies which met on the battlefield.[1] One was fighting for the cause of Allah, the other a host of unbelievers. The faithful saw with their very eyes that they were twice their own number. But Allah strengthens with His aid whom He will. Surely in that there was a lesson for the discerning.

Men are tempted by the lure of women and offspring, of *3:14* hoarded treasures of gold and silver, of splendid horses, cattle, and plantations. These are the comforts of this life, but far better is the return to Allah.

Say: 'Shall I tell you of better things than these, with which the righteous shall be rewarded by their Lord? Theirs shall be gardens watered by running streams, where they shall dwell forever: wives of perfect chastity, and grace from Allah.'

Allah is watching over His servants, those who say: 'Lord, we believe in You: forgive us our sins and keep us from the torment of Hell-fire'; who are steadfast, sincere, obedient, and charitable; and who implore forgiveness at break of day.

Allah bears witness that there is no god but Him, and so do the angels and the sages. He is the Executor of Justice, the Only God, the Mighty, the Wise One.

The only true faith in Allah's sight is Islam. Those to *3:19* whom the Scriptures were given disagreed among themselves through jealousy only after knowledge had been given them. He that denies Allah's revelations should know that He is swift in reckoning.

If they argue with you, say: 'I have surrendered myself to Allah and so have those that follow me.'

To those who have received the Scriptures and to the Gentiles say: 'Will you surrender yourselves to Allah?' If they become Muslims they shall be rightly guided; if they give no heed, then your only duty is to warn them. Allah is watching over all His servants.

Those that deny Allah's revelations and slay the prophets *3:21* unjustly and kill the men who preach fair dealing – warn

1. In the battle of Badr. There were 319 Muslims and a thousand Meccans.

3:22 them of a woeful scourge. Their works shall come to nothing in this world and in the next, and there shall be none to help them.

Consider those who have received a portion of the Scriptures. When they are called on to accept the judgement of Allah's Book, some turn their backs and pay no heed. For 3:24 they declare: 'We shall endure the fire of Hell for a few days only.' In their religion they are deceived by their own lies.

What will they do when We gather them all together upon a day which is sure to come, when every soul will be given what it has earned with no injustice?

Say: 'Lord, Sovereign of all sovereignty, You bestow sovereignty on whom You will and take it away from whom You please; You exalt whomever You will and abase whomever You please. In Your hand lies all that is good; You have power over all things. You cause the night to pass into the day, and the day into the night; You bring forth the living from the dead and the dead from the living. You give without stint to whom You will.'

Let believers not make friends with infidels in preference to the faithful – he that does this has nothing to hope for from Allah – except in self-defence. Allah admonishes you to fear Him: for to Him you shall all return.

3:29 Say: 'Whether you hide what is in your hearts or reveal it, it is known to Allah. He knows all that the heavens and the earth contain and has power over all things.'

The day will surely come when each soul will be confronted with whatever good it has done. As for its evil deeds, it will wish they were a long way off. Allah admonishes you to fear Him. He is compassionate towards His servants.

Say: 'If you love Allah follow me. Allah will love you and forgive you your sins. Allah is forgiving and merciful.'

Say: 'Obey Allah and the Apostle.' If they give no heed, then, truly, Allah does not love the unbelievers.

3:33 Allah exalted Adam and Noah, Abraham's descendants and the descendants of Imran[1] above all His creatures. They

1. Or Amran, the father of Moses and Aaron, say the commentators.

were the offspring of one another. Allah hears all and knows 3:34 all.

Remember the words of Imran's[1] wife. 'Lord,' she said, 'I dedicate to your service that which is in my womb. Accept it from me. You alone hear all and know all.'

And when she was delivered of the child, she said: 'Lord, 3:36 I have given birth to a daughter' – Allah well knew of what she was delivered: the male is not like the female – 'and have called her Mary. Protect her and all her descendants from Satan, the Accursed One.'

Her Lord graciously accepted her. He made her grow a goodly child and entrusted her to the care of Zacharias.

Whenever Zacharias visited her in the Shrine he found that she had food with her. 'Mary,' he said, 'where is this food from?'

'It is from Allah,' she answered. 'Allah gives without stint to whom He will.'

Thereupon Zacharias prayed to his Lord, saying: 'Lord, grant me upright descendants. You hear all prayers.'

And as he stood praying in the Shrine, the angels called out to him, saying: 'Allah bids you rejoice in the birth of John, who shall confirm the Word of Allah. He shall be princely and chaste, a prophet and a righteous man.'

'Lord,' said Zacharias, 'how shall I have a son when I 3:40 am now overtaken by old age and my wife is barren?'

'Such is the will of Allah,' He replied. 'He does what He pleases.'

'Lord,' said he, 'vouchsafe me a sign.'

'For three days and three nights,' He replied, 'you shall not speak to any man except by signs. Remember your Lord always; give glory to Him morning and evening.'

And remember the angel's words to Mary. He said: 'Allah has chosen you. He has made you pure and exalted you above all women. Mary, be obedient to your Lord; bow down and worship with the worshippers.'

This is an account of what is hidden. We reveal it to you.[2] 3:44

1. Imran is the name given in the Koran to Mary's father.
2. Mohammed.

You were not present when they cast lots to see which of them should have charge of Mary; nor were you present when they argued about her.

3:45 The angels said to Mary: 'Allah bids you rejoice in a Word from Him. His name is the Messiah, Jesus the son of Mary. He shall be noble in this world and in the next, and shall be favoured by Allah. He shall preach to men in his cradle and in the prime of manhood, and shall lead a righteous life.'

'Lord,' she said, 'how can I bear a child when no man has touched me?'

He replied: 'Such is the will of Allah. He creates whom He will. When He decrees a thing He need only say: "Be," and it is. He will instruct him in the Scriptures and in wisdom, in the Torah and in the Gospel, and send him forth *3:49* as an apostle to the Israelites. He will say: "I bring you a sign from your Lord. From clay I will make for you the likeness of a bird. I shall breathe into it and, by Allah's leave, it shall become a living bird. By Allah's leave I shall give sight to the blind man, heal the leper, and raise the dead to life. I shall tell you what to eat and what to store up in your houses. Surely that will be a sign for you, if you are true believers. I come to confirm the Torah that has already been revealed and to make lawful to you some of the things you are forbidden. I bring you a sign from your Lord: therefore fear Him and obey Me. Allah is my God and your God: therefore serve Him. That is the straight path."'

When Jesus observed that they had no faith, he said: 'Who will help me in the cause of Allah?'

The disciples replied: 'We are the helpers of Allah. We believe in Him. Bear witness that we have surrendered ourselves to Him. Lord, we believe in Your revelations and follow your apostle. Count us among Your witnesses.'

They plotted, and Allah plotted. Allah is the supreme *3:55* Plotter. He said: 'Jesus, I am about to cause you to die and lift you up to Me. I shall take you away from the unbelievers and exalt your followers above them till the Day of Resurrection. Then to Me you shall all return and I shall

judge your disputes. The unbelievers shall be sternly pun- 3:56
ished in this world and in the world to come: there shall be
none to help them. As for those that have faith and do good
works, they shall be given their reward in full. Allah does
not love the evil-doers.'

This revelation, and this wise admonition, We recite to
you. Jesus is like Adam in the sight of Allah. He created
him of dust and then said to him: 'Be,' and he was.

This is the truth from your Lord: therefore do not doubt
it. To those that dispute with you concerning Jesus after
the knowledge you have received, say: 'Come, let us
gather our sons and your sons, our wives and your wives,
our people and your people. We will pray together and call
down the curse of Allah on every liar.'

This is the whole truth. There is no god but Allah. It is
Allah who is the Mighty, the Wise One!

If they give no heed to you, Allah knows the evil-doers.

Say: 'People of the Book, let us come to an agreement: 3:64
that we will worship none but Allah, that we will associate
none with Him, and that none of us shall set up mortals as
gods besides Him.'

If they refuse, say: 'Bear witness that we have surrendered ourselves to Allah.'

People of the Book, why do you argue about Abraham
when both the Torah and the Gospel were not revealed till
after him? Have you no sense?

Indeed, you have argued about things of which you have
some knowledge. Must you now argue about that of which
you know nothing at all? Allah knows but you do not.

Abraham was neither Jew nor Christian. He was an upright man, one who had surrendered himself to Allah. He
was no idolater. Surely the men who are nearest to Abraham
are those who follow him, this Prophet, and the true believers. Allah is the guardian of the faithful. Some of the
People of the Book wish to mislead you; but they mislead
none but themselves, though they may not perceive it.

People of the Book! Why do you deny Allah's revelations 3:70
when you know that they are true?

3:71 People of the Book! Why do you confound the true with the false, and knowingly hide the truth?

Some of the People of the Book say to one another: 'Believe in that which is revealed to the faithful in the morning and deny it in the evening, so that they may themselves abandon their faith. Believe in none except those that follow your own religion.' (Say: 'The only guidance is the guidance of Allah!') 'Do not believe that any one will be given the like of that which you have been given, or that they will ever dispute with you in your Lord's presence.'

Say: 'Grace is in the hands of Allah: He bestows it on 3:74 whom He will. He is munificent and all-knowing. He is merciful to whom He will. His grace is infinite.'

Among the People of the Book there are some who, if you trust them with a heap of gold, will return it to you intact; and there are others who, if you trust them with one dinar, will not hand it back unless you demand it with importunity. For they say: 'We are not bound to keep faith with Gentiles.' Thus they deliberately say of Allah what is untrue. Indeed, those that keep faith and guard themselves against evil know that Allah loves the righteous.

Those that sell the covenant of Allah and their own oaths for a paltry price shall have no share in the world to come. Allah will neither speak to them, nor look at them, nor purify them on the Day of Resurrection. Theirs shall be a woeful punishment.

3:78 And there are some among them who twist their tongues when quoting the Scriptures, so that you may think that what they say is from the Scriptures, whereas it is not. They say: 'This is from Allah,' whereas it is not. Thus they knowingly ascribe a falsehood to Allah.

No mortal to whom Allah has given the Scriptures and whom He has endowed with judgement and prophethood would say to men: 'Worship me instead of Allah.' But rather: 'Be devoted servants of Allah, for you have studied 3:80 and taught the Scriptures.' Nor would he enjoin you to serve the angels and the prophets as your gods; for would

he enjoin you to be unbelievers after you have surrendered
yourselves to Allah?

When Allah made His covenant with the Prophets, He 3:81
said: 'Here are the Scriptures and the wisdom which I have
given you. An apostle will come forth to confirm them.
Believe in him and help him. Will you affirm this and accept
the burden I have laid on you in these terms?'

They replied: 'We will affirm it.'

'Then bear witness,' He said, 'and I will bear witness
with you. He that hereafter rebels is a transgressor.'

Are they seeking a religion other than Allah's, when
every soul in heaven and earth has submitted to Him,
willingly or by compulsion? To Him they shall all return.

Say: 'We believe in Allah and what is revealed to us; in
that which was revealed to Abraham and Ishmael, to Isaac
and Jacob and the tribes; and in that which Allah gave
Moses and Jesus and the prophets. We discriminate against
none of them. To Him We have surrendered ourselves.'

He that chooses a religion other than Islam, it will not be 3:85
accepted from him and in the world to come he will be one
of the lost.

How will Allah guide those who lapse into unbelief after
embracing the faith and acknowledging the apostle as true,
and after receiving veritable proofs? Allah does not guide
the evil-doers. Their reward shall be the curse of Allah,
the angels, and all men; under it they shall abide for ever.
Their punishment shall not be lightened, nor shall they be
reprieved; except those who afterwards repent and mend
their ways, for Allah is forgiving and merciful.

But those that recant after accepting the true faith and
grow in unbelief, their repentance shall not be accepted.
These are the truly erring ones.

As for those that recant and die unbelievers, no ransom
shall be accepted from them: although it be as much gold as
would fill the entire earth. They shall be sternly punished
and none shall help them.

You shall never be truly righteous until you give in alms 3:92

what you dearly cherish. The alms you give are known to Allah.

3:93   All food was lawful to the Israelites except what Israel forbade himself when the Torah had not yet been revealed. Say: 'Bring the Torah and read it, if what you say be true.'

Those that after this invent falsehoods about Allah are great transgressors.

Say: 'Allah has declared the truth. Follow the faith of Abraham. He was an upright man, no idolater.'

The first temple ever to be built for men was that at Beccah,[1] a blessed place, a beacon for the nations. In it there are veritable signs and the spot where Abraham stood. Whoever enters it is safe. Pilgrimage to the House is a duty to Allah for all who can make the journey. As for the unbelievers, Allah can surely do without them.

Say: 'People of the Book, why do you deny the revelations of Allah? He bears witness to all your actions.'

3:99   Say: 'People of the Book, why do you debar believers from the path of Allah and seek to make it crooked when you know that it is straight? Allah is watching over all your actions.'

Believers, if you yield to some of those who were given the Scriptures, they will rob you of your faith and lead you back to unbelief. But how can you disbelieve when Allah's revelations are recited to you and His own apostle is in your midst! He that holds fast to Allah shall be guided to the right path.

Believers, fear Allah as you rightly should, and when death comes, die true Muslims. Cling one and all to the faith of Allah and let nothing divide you. Remember the favours He has bestowed upon you: how He united your hearts when you were enemies, so that you are now brothers through His grace; and how He delivered you from the abyss of fire when you were on the very brink of it. Thus Allah makes plain to you His revelations, so that you may be rightly guided.

3:104   Let there become of you a nation that shall speak for

1. Another name for Mecca.

righteousness, enjoin justice, and forbid evil. Such men shall surely triumph.

Do not follow the example of those who became divided *3:105* and opposed to one another after veritable proofs had been given them. These shall be sternly punished on the day when some faces will be bright with joy and others blackened. To the black-faced sinners Allah will say: 'Did you recant after embracing the true faith? Taste then Our scourge, for you were unbelievers!' As for those whose faces will be bright, they shall abide for ever in Allah's mercy.

Such are the revelations of Allah; We recite them to you in all truth. Allah desires no injustice to His creatures. His is all that the heavens and the earth contain. To Him shall all things return.

You are the noblest nation that has ever been raised up *3:110* for mankind. You enjoin justice and forbid evil. You believe in Allah.

Had the People of the Book accepted Islam, it would have surely been better for them. Few of them are true believers, and most of them are evil-doers.

If they harm you, they can cause you no serious harm; and if they fight against you they will turn their backs and run away. Then there shall be none to help them. Ignominy shall attend them wherever they are found, unless they make a covenant with Allah or with man. They have incurred the wrath of Allah and have been utterly humbled: because they disbelieved His revelations and slew His prophets unjustly; and because they were rebels and transgressors.

Yet they are not all alike. There are among the People of the Book some upright men who all night long recite the revelations of Allah and worship Him; who believe in Allah and the Last Day; who enjoin justice and forbid evil and vie with each other in good works. These are righteous men: whatever good they do, its reward shall not be denied them. Allah knows the righteous.

As for the unbelievers, neither their riches nor their *3:116*

children shall in the least protect them from His scourge. They are the heirs of Hell, and there they shall remain for
3:117 ever. The wealth they spend in this world is like a freezing wind that smites the cornfields of men who have wronged themselves, laying them waste. Allah is not unjust to them; they are unjust to their own souls.

Believers, do not make friends with any men other than your own people. They will spare no pains to corrupt you. They desire nothing but your ruin. Their hatred is clear from what they say, but more violent is the hatred which their breasts conceal.

We have made plain to you Our revelations. Strive to understand them.

See how you love them and they do not love you. You believe in the entire Scriptures.

When they meet you they say: 'We, too, are believers.' But when alone, they bite their finger-tips with rage. Say: 'May you perish in your rage! Allah has knowledge of your inmost thoughts.'

3:120 When you are blessed with good fortune they grieve: but when evil befalls you they rejoice. If you persevere and guard yourselves against evil, their machinations will never harm you. Allah has knowledge of all their actions.

Remember when you[1] left your people at an early hour to lead the faithful to their battle-posts.[2] Allah heard all and knew all. Two of your battalions became faint-hearted, but Allah was their protector. In Him let the faithful put their trust.

Allah had already given you victory at Badr when you were helpless. Therefore have fear of Allah. Perhaps you will give thanks to Him.

You said to the believers: 'Is it not enough that your Lord should send down three thousand angels to help you?'
3:125 Yes! If you have patience and guard yourselves against

1. Mohammed.
2. The allusion is to the Battle of Uhud, in which the Muslims were defeated by the Quraysh of Mecca.

evil, Allah will send to your aid five thousand angels splendidly accoutred, if they suddenly attack you.

Allah designed this to be but good news for you, so that 3:126 your hearts might be comforted (victory comes only from Allah, the Mighty, the Wise One) and that He might cut off the flank of the unbelievers or put them to flight, that they might withdraw utterly defeated.

It is no concern of yours whether He will forgive or punish them. They are wrongdoers. His is all that the heavens and the earth contain. He pardons whom He will and punishes whom He pleases. Allah is forgiving and merciful.

Believers, do not live on usury, doubling your wealth many times over. Have fear of Allah, and you shall prosper. Guard yourselves against the fire of Hell, prepared for unbelievers. Obey Allah and the Apostle that you may find mercy. Vie with each other to earn the forgiveness of your Lord and a Paradise as vast as heaven and earth, prepared for the righteous: those who give alms alike in prosperity 3:134 and in adversity; who curb their anger and forgive their fellow-men (Allah loves the charitable); who, if they commit evil or wrong their souls, remember Allah and seek forgiveness of Him (for who but Allah can forgive sin?) and do not knowingly persist in their misdeeds. These shall be rewarded with forgiveness from their Lord and gardens watered by running streams, where they shall dwell for ever. Blessed is the reward of those who do good works.

There have been many examples before you. Roam the world and see what was the fate of those who disbelieved their apostles.

This is a declaration to mankind: a guide and an admonition to the righteous. Take heart and do not despair. Have faith and you shall triumph.

If you have suffered a defeat, so did the enemy. We alternate these vicissitudes among mankind so that Allah may know the true believers and choose martyrs from among you (He does not love the evil-doers); and that He may test 3:141 the faithful and annihilate the infidels.

3:142   Did you suppose that you would enter Paradise before Allah has proved the men who fought for Him and endured with fortitude? You used to wish for death before you met it, and now you have seen what it is like. Mohammed is no more than an apostle: other apostles have passed away before him. If he die or be slain, will you recant? He that recants will do no harm to Allah. But Allah will reward the thankful.

No one dies unless Allah permits. The term of every life is fixed. He that desires the reward of this world shall have it; and he that desires the reward of the life to come shall have it also. We will surely reward the thankful.

Many large armies have fought by the side of their prophet. They were never daunted by what befell them on the path of Allah: they neither weakened nor cringed abjectly. Allah loves the steadfast. Their only words were: 'Lord, forgive us our sins and our excesses; make us firm of foot and give us victory over the unbelievers.' Therefore Allah gave them the reward of this life, and the glorious recompense of the life to come; Allah loves the righteous.

3:149   Believers, if you yield to the infidels they will drag you back to unbelief and you will return headlong to perdition. But Allah is your protector. He is the best of helpers.

We will put terror into the hearts of the unbelievers. They serve other gods for whom no sanction has been revealed. Hell shall be their home; dismal indeed is the dwelling-place of the evil-doers.

Allah fulfilled His pledge to you when, by His leave, you defeated them. But afterwards your courage failed you; discord reigned among you and you disobeyed the Apostle after he had brought you within view of what you wished for. Some chose the gain of this world and others the world to come. He allowed you to be defeated in order to test you. But now He has forgiven you, for He is gracious to the faithful.

3:153   Remember how you fled in panic whilst the Apostle in your rear was calling out to you. Therefore Allah rewarded you with sorrow after sorrow so that you might not grieve for what you missed or what befell you. Allah is cognizant of all your actions.

Then, after sorrow, He let peace fall upon you – a sleep *3:154* which overtook some, while others lay troubled by their own fancies, thinking unjust and foolish thoughts about Allah.

'Have we any say in the matter?' they ask.

Say to them: '*All* is in the hands of Allah.'

They conceal in their minds what they do not disclose to you.

They complain: 'Had we had any say in the matter, we should not have been slain here.'

Say to them: 'Had you stayed in your homes, those of you who were destined to be slain would have gone to their graves nevertheless; for it was Allah's will to test your faith and courage. He has knowledge of your inmost thoughts.'

Those of you who ran away on the day when the two armies[1] met must have been seduced by Satan on account of some evil they had done. But now Allah has pardoned them; He is forgiving and benignant.

Believers, do not follow the example of the infidels, who *3:156* say of their brothers when they meet death abroad or in battle: 'Had they stayed with us they would not have died, nor would they have been killed.' Allah will cause them to regret their words. It is Allah who ordains life and death. He has knowledge of all your actions.

If you should die or be slain in the cause of Allah, His forgiveness and His mercy would surely be better than all the riches they amass. If you should die or be slain, before Him you shall all be gathered.

It was thanks to Allah's mercy that you[2] dealt so leniently with them. Had you been cruel or hard-hearted, they would have surely deserted you. Therefore pardon them and implore Allah to forgive them. Take counsel with them in the conduct of affairs; and when you are resolved, put your trust in Allah. Allah loves those that trust Him.

If Allah helps you, none can overcome you. If He *3:160*

1. In the Battle of Uhud.   2. Mohammed.

abandons you, who then can help you? Therefore in Allah let the faithful put their trust.

3:161 No prophet would rob his followers; for anyone that steals shall on the Day of Resurrection bring with him that which he has stolen. Then shall every soul be paid what it has earned: none shall be wronged.

Can the man who seeks to please Allah be compared to him who has incurred His wrath? Hell shall be his home. Evil shall be his fate.

Varied are the rewards of Allah. Allah is cognizant of all their actions.

Allah has surely been gracious to the faithful in sending them an apostle of their own to declare to them His revelations, to purify them, and to instruct them in the Book and in wisdom; for before that they were in monstrous error.

When a disaster befell you after you had yourselves inflicted losses twice as heavy, you exclaimed: 'Whose fault was that?'

Say to them: 'It was your own fault. Allah has power 3:166 over all things. The defeat which you suffered when the two armies met was ordained by Allah, so that He might know the true believers and the hypocrites.'

When it was said to them: 'Come, fight for the cause of Allah and defend yourselves,' they replied: 'If only we could fight, we would surely come with you.'

On that day they were nearer unbelief than faith. Their words belied their feelings: but Allah knew their secret thoughts. Such were the men who, as they sat at home, said of their brothers: 'Had they paid heed to us, they would not have been slain.'

Say to them: 'Ward off death from yourselves, then, if what you say be true!'

You must not think that those who were slain in the cause of Allah are dead. They are alive, and well provided for by their Lord; pleased with His gifts and rejoicing that those whom they left behind and who have not yet joined them 3:171 have nothing to fear or to regret; rejoicing in Allah's grace and bounty. Allah will not deny the faithful their reward.

As for the men who after their defeat answered the call of 3:172
Allah and the Apostle, those of them that do what is right
and keep from evil shall be richly rewarded. They are those
who, on being told: 'Your enemy has mustered a great force
against you: fear them,' grew more tenacious in their faith
and replied: 'Allah's help is all-sufficient for us. He is the
best Protector.'

Thus they earned Allah's grace and bounty and no harm
befell them. For they had striven to please Allah, whose
bounty is infinite.

It is Satan that prompts men to fear his followers. But
have no fear of them. Fear Me, if you are true believers.
Do not grieve for those that quickly renounce their faith.
They will not harm Allah in the least. He seeks to give them
no share in the hereafter. Their punishment shall be terrible
indeed.

Those that barter away their faith for unbelief will do
Allah no harm. A woeful punishment awaits them.

Let the unbelievers not think that We prolong their days 3:178
for their own good. We do so only that they may grow in
wickedness. Theirs shall be a shameful punishment.

Allah was not to leave the faithful in their present plight,
but only to separate the evil from the good. Nor was He
to reveal to you what is hidden. But He chooses those of
His apostles whom He will. Therefore have faith in Allah
and His apostle; for if you have faith and guard yourselves
against evil, your reward shall be rich indeed.

Let no misers who hoard the gifts of Allah think that
their avarice is good for them: it is nothing but evil. The
riches they have piled up shall become their fetters on the
Day of Resurrection. It is Allah who will inherit the heavens
and the earth. He is cognizant of all your actions.

Allah has heard the words of those who said: 'Allah is
poor, but we are rich.' Their words We will record, and the
fact that they have slain their prophets unjustly. We shall
say: 'Taste now the torment of Hell-fire. Here is the reward
of your misdeeds. Allah is not unjust to His servants.'

To those that declare: 'Allah has commanded us to 3:183

believe in no apostle unless he brings down fire to consume an offering,' say: 'Other apostles before me have come to you with veritable signs and worked the miracle you asked for. Why did you slay them, if what you say be true?'

3:184 If they reject you, know that other apostles have been rejected before you, although they worked miracles and brought down psalms and the light-giving Scriptures.

Every soul shall taste death. You shall receive your rewards only on the Day of Resurrection. Whoever is spared the fire of Hell and is admitted to Paradise shall surely gain his end; for the life of this world is nothing but a fleeting vanity.

You shall be bereaved of your possessions and dear ones, and be subjected to the insults of the pagans and of those to whom the Scriptures were given before you. But if you endure with fortitude and guard yourselves against evil, you shall surely triumph.

3:187 When Allah made a covenant with those to whom the Scriptures were given He said: 'Proclaim these to mankind and do not suppress them.' But they cast the Scriptures behind their backs and sold them for a paltry price. Evil was their bargain.

Do not think that those who rejoice in their misdeeds and wish to be praised for what they have not done – do not think they will escape Our scourge. A woeful punishment awaits them.

To Allah belongs the kingdom of the heavens and the earth. He has power over all things.

In the creation of the heavens and the earth, and in the alternation of night and day, there are signs for men of sense; those that remember Allah when standing, sitting, and lying down, and reflect on the creation of the heavens and the earth, saying: 'Lord, You have not created these in vain. Glory be to You! Save us from the torment of Hell-fire, Lord. Those whom You will cast into Hell shall be put 3:193 to eternal shame: none will help the evil-doers. Lord, we have heard a preacher call men to the true faith, saying: "Believe in your Lord," and we believed. Lord, forgive us our sins and remove from us our evil deeds and make us die with the righteous. Lord grant us what You promised 3:194 through Your apostles, and do not cast shame upon us on the Day of Resurrection. You will never break Your promise.'

Their Lord answers them, saying: 'I will deny no man or woman among you the reward of their labours. You are the offspring of one another.'

Those that fled their homes or were expelled from them, and those that suffered persecution and fought and died for My cause, shall be forgiven their sins and admitted to gardens watered by running streams, as a reward from Allah; it is He who holds the richest recompense.

Do not be deceived by the activities of the unbelievers in 3:196 this land. Their prosperity is brief. Hell shall be their home, a dismal resting-place. As for those that fear Allah, theirs shall be gardens watered by running streams in which they shall abide for ever, and a goodly welcome from their Lord. Allah's reward is surely better for the righteous.

Some there are among the People of the Book who truly believe in Allah, and in what has been revealed to you and to them. They humble themselves before Him and do not sell His revelations for a trifling price. These shall be rewarded by their Lord. Swift is Allah's reckoning.

Believers, be patient and let your patience never be ex- 3:200 hausted. Stand firm in your faith and fear Allah, so that you may triumph.

CATTLE

In the Name of Allah, the Compassionate, the Merciful

PRAISE is due to none but Allah, who has created the 6:1 heavens and the earth and ordained darkness and light. Yet the unbelievers set up other gods as equals with their Lord.

It is He who has created you from clay. He has decreed a term for you in this world and another in the next. Yet you are still in doubt.

6:3   He is God in the heavens and on earth. He has knowledge of all that you hide and all that you reveal. He knows what you do.

Yet every time a revelation comes to them from their Lord, the unbelievers give no heed to it. Thus they deny the truth when it is declared to them: but they shall learn the consequences of their scorn.

6:6   Can they not see how many generations We have destroyed before them – men whom We had made more powerful in the land than you,¹ sending down for them abundant water from the sky and giving them rivers that rolled at their feet? Yet because they sinned We destroyed them all and raised up other generations after them.

If We sent down to you a Book inscribed on real parchment and the unbelievers touched it with their own hands, they would still say: 'This is nothing but plain magic.'

6:8 They ask: 'Why has no angel been sent down to him?' If We had sent down an angel, their fate would have been sealed and they would have never been reprieved. If We had made him an angel, We would have given him the semblance of a man, and would have thus confused them with that in which they are already confused.

6:10   Other apostles have been laughed to scorn before you. But those that scoffed at them were overtaken by the very scourge they had derided.

Say: 'Roam the earth and see what was the fate of those that disbelieved their apostles.'

Say: 'To whom belongs all that the heavens and the earth contain?' Say: 'To Allah. He has decreed mercy for Himself, and will gather you all on the Day of Resurrection: that day is sure to come. Those who have forfeited their own souls will never have faith.'

His is whatever takes its rest in the night or in the day. He
6:14 hears all and knows all. Say: 'Should I take any but Allah for my Defender? He is the Creator of the heavens and the earth. He gives nourishment to all and is nourished by none.'

1. The Meccans.

Say: 'I was commanded to be the first to submit to Him.'
You shall serve no other god besides Him.

Say: 'I will never disobey my Lord, for I fear the torment 6:15
of a fateful day.'

He who is delivered from the torment of that day shall
have received Allah's mercy. That is the glorious triumph.

If Allah afflicts you with evil, none can remove it but He;
and if He blesses you with good fortune, know that He has
power over all things.

He reigns supreme over His servants. He alone is wise
and all-knowing.

Say: 'What thing counts most in testimony?'

Say: 'Let Allah be our witness. This Koran has been revealed to me that I may thereby warn you and all whom it
may reach. Will you swear that there are other gods besides
Allah?'

Say: 'I will swear to no such thing!'

Say: 'He is but one God. I deny the gods you serve besides Him.'

Those to whom We have given the Scriptures[1] know him
as they know their own children. But those who have forfeited their own souls will never have faith.

Who is more wicked than the man who invents a false- 6:21
hood about Allah or denies His revelations? The wrongdoers shall never prosper.

On the day when We gather them all together We shall
say to the idolaters: 'Where are your idols now, those whom
you supposed to be your gods?' They will not argue, but
will say: 'By Allah, our Lord, we have never worshipped
idols.'

You shall see how they will lie against themselves and
how the deities of their own invention will fail them.

Some of them listen to you. But We have cast veils over 6:25
their hearts and made them hard of hearing lest they understand your words. They will not believe in any of Our signs
even if they see them.

When they come to argue with you the unbelievers say:

1. Christians and Jews.

6:26 'This is nothing but old fictitious tales.' They forbid it and depart from it. They ruin none but themselves, though they do not perceive it.

If you could see them when they are set before the fire of Hell! They will say: 'Would that we could return! Then we would not deny the revelations of our Lord and would be true believers.' Indeed, that which they concealed will manifest itself to them.

But if they were sent back, they would return to that which they have been forbidden. They are liars all.

They declare: 'There is no other life but this; nor shall we ever be raised to life again.'

If you could see them when they are set before their Lord! He will say: 'Is this not real?' 'Yes, by the Lord,' they will reply, and He will say: 'Taste then Our scourge, the reward of your unbelief!'

They are lost indeed, those who deny that they will ever meet Allah. When the Hour of Doom overtakes them unawares, they will exclaim: 'Alas, we have neglected much in our lifetime!' And they shall bear their burdens on their backs. Evil are the burdens they shall bear.

6:32 The life of this world is but a sport and a pastime. Surely better is the life to come for those that fear Allah. Will you not understand?

We know too well that what they say grieves you. It is not you that they are disbelieving; the evil-doers deny Allah's own revelations. Other apostles have been denied before you. But they patiently bore with disbelief and persecution until Our help came down to them: for none can change the decrees of Allah. You have already heard of those apostles.

If you find their aversion hard to bear, seek if you can a chasm in the earth or a ladder to the sky by which you may bring them a sign. Had Allah pleased He would have given them guidance, one and all. Do not be foolish, then.

6:36 Those that can hear will surely answer. As for the dead, Allah will bring them back to life. To Him they shall all return.

They ask: 'Why has no sign come down to him from his 6:37 Lord?'

Say: 'Allah is well able to send down a sign.' But most of them are ignorant men.

All the beasts that roam the earth and all the birds that wing their flight are communities like your own. We have left out nothing in Our Book. They shall all be gathered before their Lord.

Deaf and dumb are those that deny Our revelations: they blunder about in darkness. Allah misleads whom he will, and guides to the right path whom He pleases.

Say: 'When Allah's scourge smites you and the Hour of Doom suddenly overtakes you, will you call on any but Allah to help you? Answer me, if you are men of truth! No, on Him alone you will call; and if He please, He will relieve your affliction. Then you will forget your idols.'

We sent forth apostles before you to other nations, and 6:42 afflicted them with calamities and misfortunes so that they might humble themselves. If only they humbled themselves when Our scourge overtook them! But their hearts were hardened, and Satan made their foul acts seem fair to them.

And when they had clean forgotten Our admonition We granted them all that they desired; but just as they were rejoicing in what they were given, We suddenly smote them and they were plunged into utter despair. Thus were the evil-doers annihilated. Praise be to Allah Lord of the Creation!

Say: 'Tell me: If Allah took away your hearing and your sight and set a seal upon your hearts, could any but Allah restore them to you?'

See how We make plain to them Our revelations. And yet they turn away.

Say: 'Tell me: if the scourge of Allah overtook you unawares or openly, would any perish but the transgressors?'

We send forth Our apostles only to give good news to 6:48 mankind and to warn them. Those that believe in them and mend their ways shall have nothing to fear or to regret. But

6:49 those that deny Our revelations shall be punished for their misdeeds.

Say: 'I do not tell you that I possess the treasures of Allah or know what is hidden, nor do I claim to be an angel. I follow only that which is revealed to me.'

Say: 'Are the blind and the seeing alike? Can you not think?'

6:51 Tell those who dread the judgement of their Lord that they have no guardian or intercessor besides Allah, so that they may guard themselves against evil. Do not drive away those that call on their Lord morning and evening, seeking only to gain His favour. You are not by any means accountable for them, nor are they accountable for you. If you drive them away, you shall yourself become an evil-doer.

Thus We have made some of them a means for testing others, so that they should say: 'Are these the men whom Allah favours amongst us?' But does not Allah best know the thankful?

When those that believe in Our revelations come to you, say: 'Peace be upon you. Your Lord has decreed mercy for Himself. If any one of you commits evil through ignorance and then repents and mends his ways, he will find Allah forgiving and merciful.'

Thus We make plain Our revelations, so that the path of the wicked may be laid bare.

6:56 Say: 'I am forbidden to serve the gods whom you invoke besides Allah.'

Say: 'I will not yield to your wishes, for then I should have strayed from the right path.'

Say: 'I have received veritable proofs from my Lord, yet you deny Him. I have no power to hasten that which you challenge; judgement is for Allah only. He declares the truth and is the best of arbiters.'

Say: 'Had I the power to hasten that which you challenge, our dispute would be ended. But Allah best knows the evil-
6:59 doers. He has the keys of all that is hidden: none knows them but He. He has knowledge of all that land and sea contain: every leaf that falls is known to Him. There is no

grain of soil in the darkest bowels of the earth, nor anything green or sear, but is recorded in His glorious Book.

'It is He that makes you sleep like the dead by night, 6:60 knowing what you have done by day, and then rouses you up to fulfil your allotted span of life. To Him you shall all return, and He will declare to you all that you have done.

'He reigns supreme over His servants. He sends forth guardians who watch over you and carry away your souls without fail when death overtakes you. Then are all men restored to Allah, their true Lord. His is the Judgement, and most swift is His reckoning.'

Say: 'Who delivers you from the perils of land and sea, when you call out to Him humbly and in secret, saying: "Save us, and we will be truly thankful!"'

Say: 'Allah delivers you from them, and from all afflictions. Yet you worship idols.'

Say: 'He has power to let loose His scourge upon you 6:65 from above your heads and from beneath your feet, and to divide you into discordant factions, causing the one to suffer at the hands of the other.'

See how We make plain Our revelations, that they may understand them.

Your people have rejected this[1] although it is the very truth. Say: 'I am not your keeper. The time will come when every prophecy shall be fulfilled, and you shall know of it.'

When you meet those that scoff at Our revelations, withdraw from them till they engage in some other talk. If Satan causes you to forget this, leave the wrongdoers as soon as you remember. Those that fear Allah are not by any means accountable for them. We remind them only so that they may guard themselves against evil.

Avoid those that treat their faith as a sport and a pastime 6:70 and are seduced by the life of this world. Admonish them hereby lest their souls be damned by their own sins. They have no guardian or intercessor besides Allah: and though they offer every ransom, it shall not be accepted from them. Such are those that are damned by their sins. They shall

1. The Koran.

431

drink boiling water and be sternly punished for their unbelief.

6:71   Say: 'Are we to call on idols which can neither help nor harm us? Are we to turn upon our heels after Allah has guided us, like men who, being bewitched by devils, blunder aimlessly here and there, although their friends call them to the right path, shouting: "Come this way!"?'

Say: 'The guidance of Allah is the only guidance. We are commanded to surrender ourselves to the Lord of the Crea-
6:72   tion, to pray, and to fear Him. Before Him you shall all be assembled.'

It was He who created the heavens and the earth in all truth. On the day when He says: 'Be,' it shall be. His word is the truth. His shall be the kingdom on the day when the trumpet is sounded. He has knowledge of the visible and the unseen. He alone is wise and all-knowing.

Tell of Abraham, who said to Azar, his father: 'Will you worship idols as your gods? Surely you and all your people are in palpable error.'

Thus We showed Abraham the kingdom of the heavens and the earth, so that he might become a firm believer.

When night drew its shadow over him, he saw a star. 'That,' he said, 'is surely my God.'

But when it faded in the morning light, he said: 'I will not worship gods that fade.'

6:77   When he beheld the rising moon, he said: 'That is my God.' But when it set, he said: 'If Allah does not guide me, I shall surely go astray.'

Then, when he beheld the sun shining, he said: 'That must be my God: it is larger than the other two.'

But when it set, he said to his people: 'I am done with your idols. I will turn my face to Him who has created the heavens and the earth, and live a righteous life. I am no idolater.'

6:80   His people argued with him. He said: 'Will you argue with me about Allah, who has given me guidance? I do not fear your idols, for only by His will would they have any power to harm me. My Lord has knowledge of all

things. Will you not be warned? And how should I fear 6:81
your false gods when you yourselves are not afraid of
serving idols not sanctioned by Allah? Which of us is more
deserving of salvation? Tell me, if you know the truth.
Those that have faith and do not taint their faith with
wrongdoing shall surely earn salvation, for they follow the
right path.'

Such was the argument with which We furnished
Abraham against his people. We raise whom We will to an
exalted rank. Your Lord is wise and all-knowing.

We gave him Isaac and Jacob and guided them as We 6:84
guided Noah before them. Among his descendants were
David and Solomon, Job and Joseph and Moses and Aaron
(thus are the righteous rewarded); Zacharias, John, Jesus
and Elias (all were upright men); and Ishmael, Elisha,
Jonah and Lot. All these We exalted above Our creatures,
as We exalted some of their fathers, their children, and
their brothers. We chose them and guided them to a
straight path.

Such is Allah's guidance; he bestows it on whom He
pleases of His servants. Had they served other gods besides
Him, their labours would have been vain indeed.

On those men We bestowed the Scriptures, wisdom, and
prophethood. If this generation denies these, We will entrust them to others who truly believe in them.

Those were the men whom Allah guided. Follow then
their guidance and say: 'I demand of you no recompense
for this. It is an admonition to all mankind.'

They have no true notion of Allah's glory, those that say: 6:91
'Allah has never revealed anything to a mortal.'

Say: 'Who, then, revealed the Scriptures which Moses
brought down, a light and a guide for mankind? The
Scriptures which you have transcribed on scraps of paper,
declaring some of them and suppressing much, although
you have now been taught what neither you nor your
fathers knew before?'

Say: 'It was surely Allah who revealed them.' Then
leave them to amuse themselves with foolish chatter.

6:92   This is a blessed Book which We have revealed, confirming what came before it, that you may warn the mother city[1] and those that dwell around her. Those who have faith in the life to come will believe in it and be steadfast in their prayers.

Who is more wicked than the man who invents a falsehood about Allah, or says: 'This has been revealed to me,' when nothing has been revealed to him? Or the man who says: 'I can reveal the like of what Allah has revealed'?

Could you but see the wrongdoers when death overwhelms them! With hands outstretched, the angels will say: 'Yield up your souls. You shall be rewarded with a shameful punishment this day, for you have said of Allah what is untrue and scorned His revelations. And now you have returned to Us, alone, as We created you at first, leaving behind all that We have bestowed on you. Nor do We see with you your intercessors, those whom you claimed to be the equals of Allah. Broken are the ties which bound you, and that which you presumed has failed you.'

6:95   It is Allah who splits the seed and the fruit-stone. He brings forth the living from the dead, and the dead from the living. Such is Allah. How then can you turn away from Him?

He kindles the light of dawn. He has ordained the night for rest and the sun and the moon for reckoning. Such is the ordinance of Allah, the Mighty One, the All-knowing.

It is He that has created for you the stars, so that they may guide you in the darkness of land and sea We have made plain Our revelations to men of wisdom.

It was He that created you from one being and furnished you with a dwelling and a resting-place. We have made plain Our revelations to men of understanding.

6:99   He sends down water from the sky, and with it brings forth the buds of every plant. From these We bring forth green foliage and close-growing grain, palm-trees laden with clusters of dates, vineyards and olive groves and all

1. Mecca.

manner of pomegranates. Behold their fruits when they ripen. Surely in these there are signs for true believers.

Yet they regard the jinn as Allah's equals, though He 6:100 Himself created them, and in their ignorance ascribe to Him sons and daughters. Glory to Him! Exalted be He above their imputations!

He is the Creator of the heavens and the earth. How should He have a son when He had no consort? He created all things and has knowledge of all things.

Such is Allah, your Lord. There is no god but Him, the Creator of all things. Therefore serve Him. He is the Guardian of all things.

No mortal eyes can see Him, though He sees all eyes. He is benignant and all-knowing.

Momentous signs have come to you from your Lord. He 6:104 that sees them shall himself have much to gain, but he who is blind to them shall lose much indeed. I am not your keeper.

Thus We make plain Our revelations, so that they may say: 'You[1] have studied deep,' and that this may become clear to men of understanding. Therefore follow what has been revealed to you from your Lord. There is no god but Him. Avoid the pagans. Had Allah pleased, they would not have worshipped idols. We have not made you their keeper, nor are you their guardian.

Do not revile[2] the idols which they invoke besides Allah, lest in their ignorance they should spitefully revile Allah. We have planned the actions of all men. To their Lord they shall return, and He will declare to them all that they have done.

They solemnly swear by Allah that if a sign be given them they would believe in it. Say: 'Signs are vouchsafed by Allah.' And how can you tell that if a sign be given them they will indeed believe in it?

We will turn away their hearts and eyes from the truth 6:110 since they refused to believe in it at first. We will leave them to blunder about in their wrongdoing.

1. Mohammed.　2. These words are addressed to the believers.

6:111 If We sent down the angels to them and caused the dead to speak with them, and ranged all things before them, they would still not believe, unless Allah willed it. But most of them are ignorant men.

Thus We have assigned for every prophet an enemy: the devils among men and jinn, who inspire one another with vain and varnished falsehoods. But had your Lord pleased, they would not have done so. Therefore leave them to their own inventions, so that the hearts of those who have no faith in the life to come may be inclined to what they say and, being pleased, persist in their sinful ways.

Should I[1] seek a judge other than Allah when it is He who has revealed the Koran for you with all its precepts? Those to whom We have given the Scriptures know that it is the truth revealed by your Lord. Therefore have no doubts.

6:115 Perfected are the words of your Lord in truth and justice. None can change them. He hears and knows all.

If you obeyed the greater part of mankind, they would lead you away from Allah's path. They follow nothing but idle fancies and preach nothing but falsehoods. Allah best knows the men who stray from His path and those that are rightly guided.

Eat only of such flesh as has been consecrated in His name, if you truly believe in His revelations. And why should you not eat of such flesh when He has already made plain to you what is forbidden, except when you are constrained?

Many are those that are misled through ignorance by their appetites: but your Lord best knows the transgressors.

Sin neither openly nor in secret. Those that commit sin shall be punished for their sins.

Do not eat of any flesh that has not been consecrated in the name of Allah; for that is sinful.

The devils will teach their votaries to argue with you. If you obey them you shall yourselves become idolaters.

6:122 Can the dead man whom We have raised to life, and given

1. Mohammed.

436

a light with which he may be guided among men, be compared to him who blunders about in darkness from which he will never emerge? Thus their foul acts seem fair to the unbelievers.

We have placed in every city arch-transgressors who *6:123* scheme within its walls. But they scheme only to bring about their own ruin, though they may not perceive it. When a sign is revealed to them they say: 'We will not believe in it unless we are given that which Allah's apostles have been given.' But Allah knows best whom to entrust with His message.

Allah will humiliate the transgressors and mete out to them a grievous punishment for their scheming. If Allah wills to guide a man, He opens his bosom to Islam. But if He pleases to mislead him, He makes his bosom small and narrow as though he were climbing up to heaven. Thus Allah lays His scourge on the unbelievers.

Such is the path of your Lord, a straight path. We have made plain Our revelations to thinking men. They shall dwell in peace with Allah. He will give them His protection in reward for their good works.

On the day when He assembles them all together, He will *6:128* say: 'Jinn, you have seduced mankind in great numbers.' And their votaries among men will say: 'Lord, we have enjoyed each other's company. But now we have reached the end of the appointed term which You decreed for us.'

Allah will say: 'The Fire shall be your home, and there you shall remain for ever unless Allah ordains otherwise.' Your Lord is wise and all-knowing.

Thus We give the wicked sway over each other as a punishment for their misdeeds.

Then He will say: 'Jinn and men! Did there not come to you apostles of your own who proclaimed to you My revelations and warned you of this day?'

They will reply: 'We bear witness against our own souls.' Indeed, the life of this world seduced them. They will testify to their own faithlessness.

Your Lord will not destroy a nation without just cause *6:131*

6:132 and due warning. They shall be rewarded according to their deeds. Your Lord is watching over all their actions.

Your Lord is self-sufficient and merciful. He can destroy you if He wills and replace you by whom He pleases, just as He raised you from the offspring of other nations.

That with which you are threatened is sure to come. You shall not escape it.

Say: 'Do all that is in your power, my people, and I will do what is in mine. You shall before long know who is to gain the reward of Paradise. The wrongdoers shall not triumph.'

They set aside for Allah a share of their produce and of their cattle, saying: 'This is for Allah' – so they pretend – 'and this for our idols.' Their idols' share never reaches Allah, but the share of Allah is wholly given to their idols. How ill they judge!

Their idols have induced many pagans to kill their children so that they may ruin them and confuse them in their faith. But had Allah pleased they would not have done so. Therefore leave them to their false inventions.

6:138 They say: 'These animals and these crops are forbidden. None may eat of them save those whom we permit.' So they assert. And there are other beasts which they prohibit men from riding, and others over which they do not pronounce the name of Allah, thus committing a sin against Him. Allah will punish them for their invented lies.

They also say: 'The offspring of these beasts is lawful to our males but not to our females.' But if it is still-born, they all partake of it! Allah will punish them for that which they impute to Him. He is wise and all-knowing.

Lost are those that in their ignorance have wantonly slain their own children and made unlawful what Allah has given them, inventing falsehoods about Allah. They have gone astray and are not guided.

6:141 It is He who brings forth all manner of plants: creepers and upright trees, the palm and the olive, and pomegranates of every kind. Eat of these fruits when they ripen and give away what is due of them upon the harvest day. But do not be prodigal; Allah does not love the prodigal.

He has given you beasts, some for carrying burdens and 6:142 others for slaughter. Eat of that which Allah has given you and do not walk in Satan's footsteps; he is your sworn enemy.

He has given you eight kinds of livestock. Take first a pair of sheep and a pair of goats. Say: 'Of these, has He forbidden you the males, the females, or their offspring? Answer me, if you are men of truth.' Then a pair of camels and a pair of cattle. Say: 'Of these, has He forbidden you the males, the females, or their offspring? Were you present when Allah gave you these commandments?'

Who is more wicked than the man who in his ignorance invents a lie about Allah to mislead others? Allah does not guide the wrongdoers.

Say: 'I find nothing in what has been revealed to me that 6:145 forbids men to eat of any food except carrion, running blood, and the flesh of swine – for these are unclean – and any flesh that has been profanely consecrated to gods other than Allah. But whoever is constrained to eat of any of these, not intending to sin or transgress, will find Allah forgiving and merciful.'

We forbade the Jews all animals with undivided hoofs and the fat of sheep and oxen, except what is on their backs and intestines and what is mixed with their bones. Such is the penalty with which We rewarded them for their misdeeds.

What We say is true. If they disbelieve in you, say: 'Your Lord is merciful and munificent: but His punishment cannot be warded off from the evil-doers.'

The idolaters will say: 'Had Allah pleased, neither we nor 6:148 our fathers would have served other gods besides Him; nor would we have forbidden anything.' In the same way those who have gone before them denied the truth until they felt Our scourge.

Say: 'Have you any proofs you can show us? You

believe in nothing but conjecture and preach nothing but falsehoods.'

6:149   Say: 'Allah alone has the conclusive proof. Had He pleased He would have guided you all.'

Say: 'Bring me those witnesses of yours who can testify that Allah has forbidden this.' If they swear to it, do not swear with them, nor yield to the wishes of those that deny Our revelations, disbelieve in the life to come, and set up other gods as equals with their Lord.

Say: 'Come, I will tell you what your Lord has made binding on you: that you shall serve no other gods besides Him; that you shall show kindness to your parents; that you shall not kill your children because you cannot support them (We provide for you and for them); that you shall not commit foul sins, whether openly or in secret; and that you shall not kill – for that is forbidden by Allah – except for a just cause. Thus Allah exhorts you, that you may grow in wisdom.'

6:152   Do not tamper with the property of orphans, but strive to improve their lot until they reach maturity. Give just weight and full measure; We never charge a soul with more than it can bear. Speak for justice, even if it affects your own kinsmen. Be true to the covenant of Allah. Thus Allah exhorts you, so that you may take heed.

This path of Mine is straight. Follow it and do not follow other paths, for they will lead you away from Him. Thus Allah exhorts you, so that you may guard yourselves against evil.

To Moses We gave the Scriptures, a perfect code for the righteous, with precepts about all things, and a guide and a blessing, so that his people might believe in the ultimate meeting with their Lord. And now We have revealed this Book with Our blessings. Observe it and keep from evil, so that you may find mercy and not say: 'The Scriptures were revealed only to two sects[1] before us; we have no know-
6:157 ledge of what they read'; or: 'Had the Scriptures been revealed to us we would have been better guided than they.'

A veritable sign has now come to you from your Lord:

1. Jews and Christians.

440

a guide and a blessing. And who is more wicked than the man who denies the revelations of Allah and turns away from them? Those that turn away from Our revelations shall be sternly punished for their indifference.

Are they waiting for the angels or Allah Himself to come 6:158 down to them, or for a sign of His to be given them? On the day when such a sign is given them, faith shall not avail the soul which had no faith before or did not put its faith to good uses.

Say: 'Wait if you will; we too are waiting.'

Have nothing to do with those who have split up their religion into sects. Allah will call them to account and declare to them what they have done.

He that does a good deed shall be repaid tenfold; but he that does evil shall be rewarded with evil. None shall be wronged.

Say: 'My Lord has guided me to a straight path, to an 6:161 upright religion, to the faith of saintly Abraham, who was no idolater.'

Say: 'My prayers and my devotions, my life and my death, are all for Allah, Lord of the Creation: He has no peer. Thus I am commanded, being the first of the Muslims.'

Say: 'Should I seek any but Allah for my God, when He is the Lord of all things? Each man shall reap the fruits of his own deeds: no soul shall bear another's burden. In the end you shall all return to your Lord, and He will resolve for you your disputes.'

He has given you the earth for your heritage and exalted 6:165 some of you in rank above others, so that He might prove you with His gifts. Swift is your Lord in retribution; yet He is forgiving and merciful.

In the Name of Allah, the Compassionate, the Merciful

66:1 PROPHET, why do you prohibit that which Allah has made lawful to you, in seeking to please your wives?[1] Allah is forgiving and merciful.

Allah has given you absolution from such oaths. Allah is your master. He is the Wise One, the All-knowing.

When the Prophet confided a secret to one of his wives; and when she disclosed it and Allah informed him of this, he made known to her one part of it and said nothing about the other. And when he had acquainted her with it she said: 'Who told you this?' He replied: 'The Wise One, the All-knowing, told me.'

66:4 If you two[2] turn to Allah in repentance (for your hearts have sinned) you shall be pardoned; but if you conspire against him, know that Allah is his protector, and Gabriel, and the righteous among the faithful. The angels too are his helpers.

It may well be that, if he divorce you, his Lord will give him in your place better wives than yourselves, submissive to Allah and full of faith, devout, penitent, obedient, and given to fasting; both widows and virgins.

Believers, guard yourselves and guard your kindred against the Fire which has fuel of men and stones, whose keepers are fierce and mighty angels who never disobey Allah's command and promptly do His bidding. They will say to the unbelievers: 'Make no excuses for yourselves this day. You shall be rewarded according to your deeds.'

66:8 Believers, turn to Allah in true repentance. Your Lord may forgive you your sins and admit you to gardens

1. Mohammed, we are told, was once found by his wife Hafsa with a Coptic slave from whom he had promised her to separate. Of this Hafsa secretly informed A'isha, another wife of his. To free Mohammed from his promise to Hafsa was the object of this chapter. Some of the references are obscure.
2. Hafsa and A'isha.

442

watered by running streams, on a day when the Prophet and those who believe with him will suffer no disgrace at the hands of Allah. Their light will shine in front of them and on their right, and they will say: 'Lord, perfect our light for us and forgive us. You have power over all things.'

Prophet, make war on the unbelievers and the hypocrites *66:9* and deal sternly with them. Hell shall be their home, evil their fate.

Allah has set an example to the unbelievers in the wife of Noah and the wife of Lot. They were married to two of Our righteous servants and deceived them. Their husbands could not protect them from Allah. The angels said to them: 'Enter the Fire, together with those that shall enter it.'

But to the faithful Allah has set an example in Pharaoh's wife, who said: 'Lord, build me a house with You in Paradise and deliver me from Pharaoh and his misdeeds. Deliver me from a wicked nation.'

And in Mary, Imran's daughter, who preserved her *66:12* chastity and into whose womb We breathed of Our spirit; who put her trust in the words of her Lord and His scriptures and was truly devout.

TRADITIONAL SEQUENCE OF CHAPTERS (SURAS)

A PENGUIN CLASSIC

TALES FROM THE THOUSAND AND ONE NIGHTS

Translated by N. J. Dawood

Originating from India, Persia and Arabia, the *Tales from the Thousand and One Nights* represent the lively expression of a lay and secular imagination in revolt against religious austerity and zeal in Oriental literature. They depict a fabulous and fanciful world of jinn and sorcerers, but their bawdiness, realism and variety of subject matter also firmly anchor them to everyday life. In this volume the translator has caught the freshness and spontaneity of the stories – which, although imaginative and extravagant, are a faithful mirror of medieval Islam.